Praise for Ronald J. Rychlak
and
Hitler, the War, and, the Pope

"Rychlak's *Hitler, the War, and the Pope* [is] the best and most careful of the recent works [on Pius xii], an elegant tome of serious, critical scholarship."

Rabbi David Dalin, *Weekly Standard*

—

"Rychlak has buried the myth [of Pius xii] under an avalanche of facts. . . . Rychlak has done more than anyone else to set the record straight."

Robert P. George
McCormick Professor of Jurisprudence
Princeton University

—

"A systematic response to Pius's critics, [with a] devastating, point-by-point refutation of Cornwell's *Hitler's Pope*. . . . For now, the magisterial volume on the subject."

J. Bottum, *Crisis*

—

"A brave man and careful scholar. . . . Rychlak's careful book, as complete as a lawyer's brief, will prompt readers to re-examine the charges worked into the grain of culture against Pius xii."

Eugene Kennedy, *Dallas Morning News*

Rychlak ... approaches his topic with the intensity of a defense attorney and the balance of a legal scholar. . . . In closely reasoned arguments, he effectively refutes the charges that Pius was anti-Semitic, that he was influenced by Hitler, that any statement by him would have lessened the suffering of the Jews, that he was fearful of his own safety and therefore restrained in his comments and that he should have excommunicated Hitler. . . . Rychlak accomplishes what he sets out to do—put Pius XII in a more balanced perspective.

George F. Giacomini Jr., *America*

RIGHTEOUS GENTILES

RIGHTEOUS
GENTILES

How Pius XII and the Catholic Church
Saved Half a Million Jews from the Nazis

RONALD J. RYCHLAK

foreword by Michael Novak

SPENCE PUBLISHING COMPANY · DALLAS
2005

Published in the United States by
Spence Publishing Company
111 Cole Street
Dallas, Texas 75207

Library of Congress Control Number: 2005931671
ISBN 1-890626-60-0
978-1-890626-60-0

Printed in the United States of America

To Joseph, Lindsey, Susanna,
Mary Helen, Sally, and Olivia

with a father's hope that you always have
the drive to seek the truth, the tenacity to find it,
and the courage to defend it.

Contents

Foreword   xi

Preface   xv

1   Due Process   3

2   Achille Ratti: Pope Pius XI   21

3   The German Clergy   44

4   Eugenio Pacelli: Pope Pius XII   69

5   "Charity That Fears No Death"   100

6   "The Jews Are Our Brothers"   150

7   The Hidden Pius XII   182

8   Illogical Arguments
and Manufactured Evidence   193

9   A Righteous Gentile   252

Notes   261

Bibliography   349

Index   367

Foreword

Michael Novak

R ONALD RYCHLAK's *Hitler, the War, and the Pope* blew me away by
its lawyerly orderliness. It was just the book I had needed
for many years and had not had. I had not even imagined that
a book that good could be written.

What had happened, I later learned, is that a colleague of his got
him thinking about the accusations against Pius XII at a time when
Rychlak actually knew little about the facts. As a well-known attorney
who had studied civil rights cases in Mississippi, and as a teacher of
courses in evidence, criminal law, and trial practice at the University
of Mississippi, Rychlak determined to get the best possible statements
he could concerning the charges against Pius XII. Then he would research the facts on which they were based, and then the wider circle
of facts that actually constituted the full picture. Finally, he would lay
out the prosecutors' case and then the case for the defense, against the
backdrop of the wider history.

This was exactly what I had been looking for. I remember my own
studies in Rome during the last two years of the papacy of Pius XII,
October of 1956 to October of 1958. Pius XII was at that time honored
on all sides for his courage in World War II, his resistance to Musso-

lini and the Nazis, the wisdom with which he had conducted Vatican policy, and his protection of the Jews and other unforgettably abused minorities.

Still, in all the fires of youthful zeal, I was prepared to admit, when the great controversy was aroused by Rolf Hochhuth's *The Deputy* in 1963, that perhaps Pius XII might have cut his difficult decisions too close to the lines laid down by prudence, and not far enough over toward the edge of courage and self-sacrificing witness. Having a clear idea of just how small the territory of the Vatican is, and how totally dependent it is for electricity, water, sanitation, and workforce on the surrounding city of Rome (and thus on the Government of Italy), I sympathized with the dilemma that faced Pius XII. Yet I also could see how much glory would now attach to the Catholic Church if, somehow, the pope had been able to make some dramatically courageous, confrontational act. I wasn't very clear on what that act could or should have been, or on its probable consequences. (Would the whole Vatican have been firebombed? Or rudely thrown open for vandalization?) In my judgment I was torn, and I longed to know more.

The early books I read, by Guenter Lewy and Saul Friedländer, seemed to me insufficiently sensitive to the range of considerations Pius XII was responsible for thinking about. They made their own harsh judgment too easily. They had too low an opinion of the moral quality of Pius XII the man, and perhaps of the Catholic Church as an institution, to deserve full credence. But were their facts right? And what were they overlooking?

Professor Rychlak's lawyerly tome, read in this context, was a breath of fresh air. I had meanwhile read Owen Chadwick's presentation of the autobiographical account of the British ambassador to the Vatican during the War years, who was virtually forced by events to take an apartment inside the Vatican. Now with Professor Rychlak's volume also at hand, I felt I was getting a rounded view of what it was like inside the Vatican at that time, and of the great network of actions that radiated outwards from there.

But then, after Rychlak came a whole deluge of books—mostly, but not entirely, by "progressive" Catholics opposed to Pope John Paul II —attacking Pius XII on this or that ground. Most took no account of Rychlak, motivated by their own passions as they were. They were in some ways diversions, and yet each assault had to be answered on its own ground. With the full picture that Rychlak possessed, and with new documents and sources being turned up almost every month, virtually all of them favorable to Pius XII, an examination of those attacks by Rychlak, dealing with them one by one, would only serve to fill in the general picture with more material and in more vivid detail. Indeed, the attacks would in some ways flush elements of the situation into fuller light than they had before been bathed in.

Over dinner, therefore, or perhaps later over the phone, I suggested to Professor Rychlak that he put together the rebuttals to each of these attacks that he had already been asked to prepare, and to make a whole new work to go alongside his earlier one. In that way, persons like myself, trying to reach a decision on the whole situation, would have at hand not only the general picture, but also specific answers, in great detail, to specific new accusations.

As it happens, one of those heavily criticized earlier by Rychlak, John Cornwell, has in the meantime significantly recanted some of the extreme charges he had earlier made, and Rychlak had unmasked. In general, it appears that the argument seems to be swinging back into Pius XII's favor. The memoirs of many ambassadors to the Vatican, American chaplains (especially rabbis) who went into Italy during the war, and survivors of those events in various walks of life are still becoming available month by month. The admiration for and gratitude to Pius XII extended at that time keeps growing in its dimensions.

Some witnesses in a position to know say that if Oskar Schindler is honored for saving almost two thousand Jews, and Raoul Wallenberg for saving tens of thousands, then all the more should Pius XII be honored for saving hundreds of thousands. No one during that whole era did more than he, and few at higher risk and with greater stakes. But I should allow Professor Rychlak, who knows far more about these historical matters than I, to sort them out and recount them in his own voice.

It remains only for me to thank him for picking up the challenge that a colleague long ago laid down at his feet, for investing enormous labor in it, and for delivering himself so cheerfully of so much good work. We are all in your debt, Ronald Rychlak. You have made an enormous contribution to the healing of relations among Catholics and Jews, and to the possibility of discussing important parts of our mutual past in a factual and discriminating way.

Preface

WHEN I FIRST BEGAN MY WORK on Pope Pius XII and the Holocaust, the subject was rarely in the news. Two books had been written on the topic in 1980, but little new work had been published between that time and 1999, when I submitted the manuscript that became *Hitler, the War, and the Pope*. Then, with my book already at the publisher, John Cornwell's *Hitler's Pope* was released and brought the issue to the forefront.

I added an epilogue to *Hitler, the War, and the Pope*, responding to Cornwell's charges, but the success of his book inspired far too many imitators. Over the next several years I was frequently asked to review or respond to new books critical of Pope Pius XII, Pope Pius XI, the Germany clergy, or some other aspect of Catholic history. It seemed that I was constantly writing or speaking on this broad topic.

In November 2002, my wife and I traveled together to the Washington, D.C., area so that I could make a presentation on Pope Pius XII. While we were in town, we stopped by to say hello to Michael Novak.

Michael had followed my writings on Pope Pius XII, and he said that in light of all of the new books critical of the Catholic Church during World War II, it would be helpful to have a book that responded to all of the falsehoods and misunderstandings. With his encouragement and some good advice from Mitchell Muncy at Spence Publishing, I eventually put this new book together.

In these pages I respond to arguments made by critics of Pope Pius XII and other leaders of the Catholic Church during the Nazi era. I tried to avoid doing that in *Hitler, the War, and the Pope* (except in the epilogue), because I wanted to lay out the facts of what had actually happened. As Michael Novak noted, however, it has become necessary to address the numerous and often inconsistent arguments against the Catholic Church that have been asserted by various critics. This book therefore does not replace my first book; it stands along side of it.

In writing this book, I was able to draw upon some documents that I saw for the first time in March 2003, when I traveled to Rome to examine materials from newly-opened Vatican archives. I returned to Rome in April 2004, at which time I was given extraordinary access to the still confidential internal Vatican report (the "*Positio*") prepared by historians for the Congregation for the Causes of Saints on the life and heroic virtue of Pope Pius XII. I was gratified to learn that not only had the Congregation reached conclusions very similar to my own, but that there were several citations to and quotations from my articles and my book, *Hitler, the War, and the Pope*. I would like to thank the historians for their review of this manuscript, which was independently prepared but reflects findings completely consistent with those of the Congregation.

I would also like to thank several people who regularly read and comment on early drafts of my work or who share helpful analysis and new information. Often they are my harshest critics. This group includes: Bill Doino, Dimitri Cavalli, Fr. John Jay Hughes, Kevin Doyle, Fr. Peter Gumpel, Fr. Paul Molinari, and Fr. Vincent Lapomarda. The secretaries at the University of Mississippi School of Law, particularly Niler Franklin, also have my appreciation and gratitude. Just as this book was going to press I was saddened to learn of the premature death of Scott Robey, who was inspired to write a screenplay based on *Hitler, the War, and the Pope*. He will be missed.

Renato Cardinal Martino and Archbishop Celestino Migliore, the former and current papal nuncios to the United Nations, provided me with the opportunity to serve as an advisor to the Holy See's mission to the UN and as a delegate at various international meetings. That experience opened many doors, and I am deeply in their debt. The support of my friends and colleagues John Czarnetzky, Jack Nowlin, Kyle Duncan, and George Cochran is also most appreciated. As always, my wife, Claire, makes the greatest sacrifices for my work.

RIGHTEOUS GENTILES

— 1 —

Due Process

Do you want peace? Do justice, and you will have peace.
Pope Pius XII

FROM THE END OF WORLD WAR II until long after his death, Pope
Pius XII was well respected for his leadership during the war and
for Catholic efforts to protect those who suffered at the hands of
the Nazis. At the liberation of Rome, at the end of the war, and again
at Pius XII's death, tributes poured in from all around the globe. Jewish
leaders in particular offered thanks for what the Church had done to
help during this horrific era. The achievement was all the more amazing because it was well understood that Catholics themselves were, as
Reader's Digest described it: "Nazi Scapegoat Number 2."[1]

This perception began to change in 1963 when German playwright
Rolf Hochhuth wrote a play entitled *The Deputy* (*Der Stellvertreter*).[2]
It was a scathing indictment of Pius XII's alleged indifference to Jewish suffering in the Holocaust. Not only did this pope lack Christian
charity, but as depicted by Hochhuth he lacked even simple human
decency. Although the play was fictional, Hochhuth appended a text

3

to the play in which he argued that his depiction was justified by the historical record.[3]

The Deputy spawned a great deal of writing about the role of the Church and the papacy during World War II.[4] Pope Paul VI, who strongly defended Pius XII,[5] in 1964 asked a team of three Jesuit historians, Pierre Blet, SJ, Burkhart Schneider, SJ, and Angelo Martini, SJ, to conduct research in closed Vatican archives and publish relevant documents from the war years.[6] A few years later, the three Jesuits were joined by a fourth, Robert A. Graham, SJ. The project was completed in 1981 with the publication of the eleventh and final volume of the *Actes et Documents du Saint Siège relatifs à la seconde guerre mondiale* (ADSS).[7]

Publication of these documents seemed to quell the controversy. They clearly showed that the Vatican and the Catholic Church in general were involved in efforts to rescue Jewish and other victims from the Nazis. They also showed that Pope Pius XII was strongly anti-Nazi and that he was concerned about all of the victims. As one early commentator noted, the importance of the ADSS collection "is fully evident only when one compares it with the facile hypotheses on which some journalist-historians have feverishly constructed certain publications. Fr. Blet and his confreres have allowed the discussion to begin again on sure foundations; they have done their work in such a way that what was only a pastime for journalists may now become the object of serious historical research."[8] It was called "a model of meticulous editorship."[9] Very little was written about this controversy from 1981 until the release of John Cornwell's book, *Hitler's Pope*, in 1999.

Cornwell's Pius was not anti-Semitic, nor was he attracted to Hitler's ideology. The theme of *Hitler's Pope* was that Pius XII, from the earliest days of his priesthood, wanted to establish a strong papacy. This caused him to pull authority away from the German Catholics who might have blocked Hitler from coming to power. It also, according to Cornwell, caused him not to be as concerned as he should have been about Nazi efforts to exterminate the Jews.

Since 1999, there have been numerous books and articles critical of Pope Pius XII and the Catholic Church. Authors including Garry Wills,[10] James Carroll,[11] Susan Zuccotti,[12] Michael Phayer,[13] Daniel Goldhagen,[14] David Kertzer,[15] and Robert Wistrich[16] have written highly critical books. Cornwell even came back with a second book touching on the topic.[17] Robert Katz, author of two books critical of Pius XII back in the 1960s, has authored a new book that largely combines his earlier complaints.[18] At least two older books critical of the pope have reportedly been scheduled for re-release,[19] and Rolf Hochhuth's play, *The Deputy*, was filmed and released as a motion picture entitled *Amen*.[20] There have also been some more nuanced books[21] and several that support Catholic efforts during that era.[22] Articles, of course, have been written on both sides of the debate.

This flurry of attention has resulted in several new allegations, many of which are inconsistent with the charges raised by other critics. One book charges that Pius helped Nazis escape to South America. Another book dismisses that, but raises the charge that he was too concerned about centralization of papal power. The next book rejects those charges, but raises new claims. Along the way, Pope Pius XI—traditionally presented by the critics as a strong opponent of the Nazis as opposed to the more complacent Pius XII—has come under heavy (though inconsistent) criticism. The German Catholic hierarchy has also been strongly criticized. The argument eventually reached beyond the Catholic Church and challenged the very foundation of Christianity—the New Testament itself.[23] As Rabbi David Dalin has noted, many of the critics are not honestly seeking the truth; they are instead distorting the truth in order to influence the future of the Catholic Church.[24]

LEGAL ANALYSIS AND HISTORY

Some papal critics have bemoaned the role that non-historians play in this debate,[25] though one has the impression that they are not that upset with the role played by playwright Rolf Hochhuth or journalist John Cornwell. It is completely appropriate, however, for attorneys to be involved in historical debates like this. As Oliver Wendell Holmes wrote, the path of law is experience.[26] In a way, lawyers are professional historians.

A good lawyer must discover all verifiable facts, analyze the credibility of witnesses, develop a theory of the case that accounts for all of the evidence, and then determine how best to proceed. In many cases, the attorney will end up making a presentation to an impartial judge or jury. In other cases, the lawyer will advise the client to settle or plea bargain. Part of being a good lawyer is knowing when to fight and when to settle. That is why a lawyer must know the weaknesses of his own case better than anyone else. He also knows when he has a strong case.

When a lawyer presents a case in court, there are set procedures designed to test the evidence and assure a fair result. Evidence must be established as authentic; exhibits must be more probative than prejudicial; witnesses are subjected to cross-examination; hearsay evidence is usually excluded; and the credibility of anyone who testifies is subject to question. The procedures are fixed, and everything is designed to help the court reach a just result. This is a very logical way to analyze history as well: lay out the evidence; subject it to cross examination; and then (but only then) argue a theory that accounts for the facts. In fact, that is the only way to get to the truth of a matter.

One recent book critical of Pope Pius XII, contains several presumptions—"it can be assumed," "it is logical to conclude," "in all likelihood"—at several crucial points early in the manuscript.[27] Any author permitted to introduce assumptions and suppositions into a basic accounting of the facts can take an argument anywhere and prove almost anything. That is why courts do not permit argument until all of the evidence has been introduced.

In American courts, criminal defendants are presumed innocent until they are proven guilty. Even in civil trials, the plaintiff has the burden of proof to show that the defendant more likely than not is responsible. In other words, the defendant is presumed to be not liable or not responsible.

Related to the presumption of innocence is the Fifth Amendment right of criminal defendants to remain silent at trial. They need not introduce any evidence at all. The burden of proof on all issues is on the prosecution. Moreover, in a criminal case, the prosecution must prove the charges *beyond a reasonable doubt.*

Unfortunately, too many critics make assumptions regarding papal motivations and actions, without granting any benefit of the doubt to the accused. Too often, once charges are made, they are taken as having been established unless they are rebutted. In other words, the burden of proof is put on the defense.[28] Of course, this can be a very difficult situation, especially when the defense is asked to disprove a negative or to address ever-changing charges.[29]

As a lawyer prepares for a trial, he or she knows precisely what the charges are, what the standards are, and what the rules regarding evidence will be. A last minute change that would force the defendant to address different issues is prohibited as an unconstitutional "variance."[30] When it comes to Pope Pius xii, however, the goal posts are always shifting.

The difficult thing about answering every shifting charge is that it unfairly puts one in a consistently defensive position. Every lawyer knows that if enough charges are made ("a shotgun approach"), eventually the defendant will begin to look defensive. If he is seen as defensive, the jury tends to believe there is something to the charges, even if there is no evidence to support them. Thus, a prosecutor may raise many charges with the ultimate hope of forcing the defendant into a bad light in front of the jury. Unfortunately, this regularly happens with Pope Pius xii, and it taints the analysis. It is not the way to get to the truth.

In law, there are rules designed to assure the reliability of evidence. There are, of course, some sources upon which everyone can agree. These are called almanac-type facts. A newspaper can be cited for historical matters. It is a secondary source, but there is no obvious reason to doubt it. It is usually admissible because it is normally considered reliable.[31] Other evidence and witnesses are tested through the practice of cross-examination.

A witness's testimony is reliable (or not) depending primarily upon his or her basis of knowledge and veracity.[32] By "basis of knowledge," we mean how the witness knows what he has testified about. Historians give citations of their sources in order to establish the basis of their knowledge. Later scholars can then come along and check on the earlier work. When the citation is of a secondary source, it may be necessary to work back through several earlier sources to determine whether the claim is valid.

Too many stories about Pius XII have not been properly traced back to the original source to test the basis of knowledge. For instance, in his book *Constantine's Sword*, James Carroll shows an unreasonable eagerness to accept and readily advance a supposed death-bed condemnation of Pius XII by Pope John XXIII.[33] No eyewitness has ever come forward to support that story. "The Postulator of John XXIII's Cause for Canonization, Fr. Luca De Rosa, OFM, states that the story is 'absolutely untrue.' He adds that Pope John was, in fact, 'full of admiration and devotion' for Pius XII."[34] Archbishop Loris Capovilla, formerly private secretary to Pope John, also categorically denies that Pope John ever said any such thing, calling it "a lie."[35]

Throughout his life, John praised Pius. Before he was made pope, John was offered thanks for his wartime efforts to save Jewish refugees. He replied: "In all these painful matters I have referred to the Holy See and simply carried out [Pius XII's] orders: first and foremost to save human lives."[36] When Pius died, the future John XXIII said that he had been like a "public fountain" pouring forth good waters at which all the world, great and lowly, could profitably drink.[37] John's staff had a photograph of Pius published with a prayer on the back asking for his canonization as a saint. The prayer called Pius "a fearless defender of the Faith, a courageous struggler for justice and peace . . . a shining model of charity and of every virtue."[38] A million of these prayer cards were soon in circulation, and John xxiii (who prayed monthly before the tomb of Pius xii) said in an audience that surely one day Pius would be raised to the catholic altars.[39]

John even considered taking the name "Pius xiii," and one of the first things that he did upon becoming Pope was to have a photo of Pius xii put on his desk.[40] In his first Christmas broadcast to the world after his election, John paid the high honor of saying that Pius xii's doctrinal and pastoral teaching "assure a place in posterity for the name of Pius xii. Even apart from any official declaration, which would be premature, the triple title of 'Most excellent Doctor, Light of Holy Church, Lover of the divine law' evokes the sacred memory of this pontiff in whom our times were blessed indeed."[41] Yet *Constantine's Sword* is at least the third publication in which Carroll has advanced the fabricated death-bed story, and he did so twice in the book.

Similarly, the claim that Pius was worried about putting Germans into a conflict of conscience if he were to condemn Nazism traces back to a highly suspect source.[43] Also, many critics are all too quick to accept Robert Katz's claim that Pius knew of the March 1944 massacre before it took place. But the "evidence" for this is really nothing more than pure speculation.[44]

Unlike witnesses at trial, historians do not usually put their credibility at issue. They do not "testify" the way a witness does at trial. Thus, the second prong of the reliability test—veracity—is not usually a concern. Where Pius xii is concerned, however, perhaps because it is so serious and so personal, some writers have crossed the line and become witnesses. At such a time, the author's credibility becomes a legitimate matter of concern.

John Cornwell interjected himself into this story by reporting that when he started his work on *Hitler's Pope* he was convinced of Pius xii's holiness. He went on to claim that due to previous writings that caused the Vatican to look favorably upon him, he was given special access to secret archives. He further reported that he was left in a state of moral shock by what he found in those archives. Having thereby made himself not just a reporter, but an actual witness to this story, he put his credibility at issue.

Evidence that would otherwise be inadmissible or even irrelevant can become admissible for the limited purpose of seeing how it reflects on the witness's credibility.[45] For instance, Cornwell's twenty years as a lapsed Catholic, during which time he wrote very hostile books against the Catholic faith, were never mentioned in the promotional literature for *Hitler's Pope*. In *Breaking Faith*, however, he admitted that he was aware of the relevance of this information: "there is a world of difference between an authentic believing Catholic, writing critically from within, and a 'Catholic bashing' apostate who lies about being a Catholic in order to solicit an unwarranted hearing from the faithful." Of course, in *Hitler's Pope*, he played up his status as an "authentic believing Catholic, writing critically from within," and that is why it was fair to question his credibility on this issue, as I did in *Hitler, the War, and the Pope*.

One might contrast this valid examination of an author's credibility with the way some critics have dismissed certain Jewish witnesses who praised Pius XII. Rabbi Zolli, the chief rabbi of Rome, who held Pius XII in great esteem, is impeached simply because he became a Catholic. Golda Meir, Nahum Goldmann, and A.L. Eastman, each of whom lavished praise on Pius, are said to have lied in order to garner international good will for Israel. This is pure speculation.[46] It is reminiscent of the unfair cross examination tactics that defense attorneys used to use against victims of sexual assault.[47] Laws now prohibit that practice in rape trials. It is just as unfair in this case.

One final comment on cross examination is that we obviously cannot cross examine people who are no longer with us. In such cases, courts have special rules that sometimes admit testimony even though it would otherwise constitute inadmissible hearsay. One important factor is the consistency of the evidence. Can it be corroborated? In the Pius xii controversy, the following witnesses have given evidence to the effect that Pope Pius xii asked Catholics to come to the aid of Jews: Righteous Gentiles Cardinal Pietro Palazzini and Tibor Baranski; rescuers John Patrick Carroll-Abbing and Fr. Marie-Benoît; Americans Cardinal Francis Spellman and Archbishop Fulton Sheen; Deputy Chief Prosecutor at Nuremberg, Robert Kempner; Popes John xxiii and Paul vi; Rabbi Isaac Herzog of Jerusalem; Elio Toaff, who would later become Chief Rabbi of Rome; Joseph Hertz, the Grand Rabbi of the British Empire; Miroslav Freiberger, the Grand Rabbi of Zagreb; Israel Zolli, the Chief Rabbi of Rome during the war; and Chief Rabbi Alexander Safran of Bucharest. There are also numerous other named and unnamed bishops, priests, nuns, rabbis, laypersons, victims, and rescuers. No defendant in history has had such an impressive array of witnesses.

With only a few exceptions, a defendant in a criminal case cannot be convicted of a crime unless he has committed a specific bad act (*actus reus*) while exhibiting a certain degree of mental culpability (*mens rea*). If Mary accidentally harms Susanna, Mary might owe reparations to Susanna, but it is probably not going to be a crime. Similarly, if Mary tries to do something bad but fails, she is not guilty of the crime that she tried to commit (though she may be guilty of a lesser crime such as attempt). In other words, we do not find people guilty easily, and we do not normally convict people who have good intentions.

When it comes to Pope Pius xii, things get all turned around. He is usually accused of inaction, not of a bad act. (We have some crimes like this—failing to pay income taxes or to care for a child—but they are rare and only apply when there is a legal duty to act.) More troubling is the issue of the *mens rea* (intent).

The evidence that we already have, from the *Actes et Documents* collection,[48] shows that the pope did not have a guilty mind. He tried to intervene frequently, he encouraged others who took action, and he supported rescue efforts. Was he right in the course he selected? Could he have done more? Would a different approach have worked better with the Nazis? These are fair questions for historians to ask. Too often, however, critics do more than ask whether the pope made the correct decision. They suggest that he did not care about the victims, that he was anti-Semitic, or that he was "Hitler's Pope." Without evidence, they attribute to him evil intentions. In doing this, they violate the norms of historical analysis; they cease writing history and instead engage in character assassination.[49] These ad hominem attacks against the pope simply turn up the heat and not the light.

When the Catholic-Jewish study group went to Rome in October 2000, they met with Fr. Peter Gumpel, SJ, the relator (independent, investigating judge) of Pius XII's cause for canonization. When he reviewed their preliminary report, he said: "Didn't you people, I mean if I may ask you, feel that the Vatican had tried to do what it can? This is a completely different question, whether they succeeded in doing everything. But, I miss a little bit the question here of appreciation of what the Vatican did." Fr. Gumpel was correct.

Pope Pius XII and the Vatican might not have been totally successful. Maybe they should have tried different things, but the evidence that we already have from the archives shows that no prosecutor could prove a guilty mind regarding the Vatican's efforts for the victims. If this were a court of law, there would be enough evidence already, regardless of whatever might exist in the sealed archives, to have the charges dismissed. That is what Fr. Gumpel meant when he told the Catholic-Jewish study group that he did not think that it was necessary to open these archives in order to reach a judgment about Pope Pius XII.

Similarly, at trial the defendant has the right to assert legal claims like self-defense, necessity, defense of others, and choice of evils.[50] If he were on trial, Pius would certainly be able to avail himself of doctrines like this. He had reason to be concerned that if he provoked Hitler to a greater degree it might cause others to suffer Nazi retaliation.

The common refrain here is that retaliation would have been less than the harm that was suffered, or that some Catholics would have suffered, but things would have improved for many more Jews. Of course there is no way of knowing what would have happened, but in a utilitarian sense, these rejoinders might make a point. The problem is that Catholic teaching—regardless of any other factor—does not permit decisions like this to be made on utilitarian grounds.

Many know that the Catholic Church prohibits abortion. Few may be aware of the hypothetical situation of a mother who finds her life threatened if she carries the baby to term. Abortion is still prohibited in this situation. One life is not to be sacrificed, even to save another.[51] Failure to understand this aspect of Catholic doctrine has caused some confusion about the Vatican's position in World War II.[52]

The point here is simply that had Pius taken a more openly confrontational approach to the Nazis, he probably would have caused the death of different innocents. That would have been in violation of Catholic doctrine. Pius once stated that martyrdom cannot be imposed on a person, but must be freely accepted. His decision not to impose it on others is quite in keeping with Catholic teaching.

History does not demand the finality that is necessary in law. As such, things are never solved "once and for all" when it comes to historical analysis. One must ask, however, whether it is fair to refuse, in Pius xii's case, to apply the rules that we would apply in the case of any living person who was accused of similarly serious crimes.

THE NEW EVIDENCE

No allegation brought forth in recent years changes the true picture of Pope Pius xii. In fact, the new information brought to my attention since the publication of *Hitler, the War, and the Pope* (2000) includes the following:

1. Giovanni Palatucci, named by Yad Vashem as a "Righteous Gentile" is credited with having saved five thousand Jewish lives. He did this in close collaboration with his uncle, Giuseppe Maria Palatucci,

bishop of Campagna, a small town near Salerno, where the largest internment camp in southern Italy was located. In 1940, Bishop Palatucci received two letters from the Vatican. The first one, sent to the bishop on October 2, 1940, said that Pope Pius XII agreed to grant to him the sum of 3,000 lire. This letter was signed by Cardinal Maglione, Pius XII's secretary of state, and it stated: "This sum is preferably to be used to help those who suffer for reason of race" (*questo denaro è preferibilmente destinato a chi soffre per ragioni di razza*). In the second letter, the future Pope Paul VI, Giovanni Battista Montini, then an official in the Vatican's Secretariat of State, notified Bishop Palatucci that Pope Pius XII had granted him the sum of 10,000 lire "to distribute in support of the interned Jews" (*da distribuirsi in sussidi agli ebrei internati*).[53]

2. On April 4, 1933, the Holy See sent a letter, signed by Secretary of State Pacelli, the future Pope Pius XII, informing Monsignor Cesare Orsenigo, the nuncio in Germany, that requests had come to the pope for his "intervention against the danger of anti-Semitic excesses in Germany."[54] The letter continues: "Given that it is part of the traditions of the Holy See to carry out its mission of universal peace and charity toward all men, regardless of the social or religious condition to which they belong, by offering, if necessary, its charitable offices, the Holy Father asks your Excellency to see if and how it is possible to be involved in the desired way."[55]

3. In 1923, Nuncio Pacelli wrote to the Holy See to report that a militant group ("followers of Hitler and Ludendorff") were persecuting Catholics and Jews.[56] He referred to this group (not yet known as Nazis) as "right-wing radicals." He also praised the "learned and zealous" Cardinal Archbishop Michael Faulhaber of Munich who was attacked because he "had denounced the persecutions against the Jews."[57]

4. Sir Martin Gilbert, one of the world's renowned historians, in his book, *The Righteous: The Unsung Heroes of the Holocaust*, offered praise to Pope Pius XII and the Catholic Church. In a subsequent

interview he said: "I hope that my book can restore, in a way, on the foundation of historical fact, the true and wonderful achievements of Catholics in helping Jews during the war." He also suggested that thanks are due to Pius for the hundreds of thousands of Jewish lives saved by the Catholic Church under his leadership.[58]

5. The German resistance was in regular contact with the Vatican.[59] In 1945, Fabian von Schlabrendorff, a Protestant member of the German resistance, wrote a memorandum to U.S. General William ("Wild Bill") Donovan, in which Schlabrendorff reported that resistance member Joseph Müller, a Catholic lawyer who coordinated efforts between the German resistance and the Vatican, "had orders from the Catholic Church to negotiate with representatives of the Protestant Church in order to harmonize their measures in the struggle against Hitler."[60] In fact, on February 15, 1944, Dietrich Bonhoeffer's close friend and co-resister Eberhard Bethge wrote to him of having had an audience with the pope. He reported that the pope looked "older than I expected from the pictures," and added that he (Bethge) "wasn't able to make any more visits."[61] In a collection of letters, Bethge explained that this oblique reference related to meetings with Pope Pius XII's close assistant Monsignor Robert Leiber and Monsignor Johannes Schönhöffer "who had been let in on the conspiracy."[62]

6. Adolf Eichmann's memoirs confirm that following the notorious roundup of October 16, 1943, the Vatican "vigorously protested the arrest of Jews, requesting the interruption of such action."[63]

7. Catholic nuns who immigrated to the U.S. in 1942 on a boat with seven hundred Jewish people report that a letter in the pope's own hand allowed them and the Jews safe passage.[64]

8. Edith Stein's 1933 letter to Pope Pius XI has been released, and the deep respect that she had for his 1937 encyclical, *Mit brennender Sorge* (*With Burning Anxiety*) has been discovered.[65]

9. A collection of letters from Rabbi Steven Wise, America's leading spokesman for the Jewish cause during World War II, reveals that

he was critical of numerous organizations and individuals who did not seem sufficiently concerned about the plight of the Jews in Germany. He was, however, generally positive toward the Catholic Church, was very impressed with Pius XI, and wrote in 1942 that it seems that Pius XII "follows the high example set by his saintly predecessor."[66]

10. Righteous Gentile Tibor Baranski not only credits Pius XII for support and direct instruction, but reports that Swedish diplomat and rescuer Raoul Wallenberg (also a Righteous Gentile) knew of Pius XII's support and that Catholic officials, at the direction of Pius, worked closely with Wallenberg.[67] In fact, a memo from U.S. representative Harrold Tittmann, dated June 4, 1945, reports on a meeting he had with Joseph Müller, the Vatican's main contact with the resistance in Germany: "Dr. Müller said that during the war his anti-Nazi organization in Germany had always been very insistent that the pope should refrain from making any public statement singling out the Nazis and specifically condemning them and had recommended that the pope's remarks should be confined to generalities only."[68]

11. At their annual meeting in November 1942, the U.S. Bishops released a statement which said: "We feel a deep sense of revulsion against the cruel indignities heaped upon Jews in conquered countries and upon defenseless peoples not of our faith. . . . Deeply moved by the arrest and maltreatment of the Jews, we cannot stifle the cry of conscience. In the name of humanity and Christian principles, our voice is raised."[69]

In 2002, I was granted access to the archives that house the papers of Francis Cardinal Spellman, one of the signatories of the statement. Based upon information contained therein, it seems certain that the statement was made in cooperation with Pope Pius XII, whom the bishops cited three times. In a letter to the bishops and archbishops, written at this very time, Pius expressed his satisfaction with their "constant and understanding collaboration."[70]

12. During a 1937 meeting with Alfred W. Klieforth, then U.S. consul general in Cologne, Germany, Pacelli "opposed unilaterally every compromise with National Socialism. He regarded Hitler not only as an untrustworthy scoundrel but as a fundamentally wicked person. He did not believe Hitler capable of moderation, in spite of appearances, and he fully supported the German bishops in their anti-Nazi stand."[71]

13. In April 1938, Cardinal Pacelli gave to Ambassador Joseph P. Kennedy, then U.S. ambassador to Britain, a report to be forwarded to President Roosevelt. In that report, Pacelli made clear that the Nazi program struck at the "fundamental principle of the freedom of the practice of religion," and indicated the emergence of a new Nazi Kulturkampf against the Catholic Church. He told Kennedy that any political compromise with the Nazi regime was "out of the question."[72]

14. In 1939, on the day after his coronation, Pius held a series of meetings with Ambassador Kennedy. Afterwards, Kennedy wrote to his superiors at the U.S. Department of State indicating that the new Pope held a "subconscious prejudice that has arisen from his belief that Nazism and Fascism are pro-pagan, and as pro-pagan, they strike at the roots of religion." Pius was greatly disturbed by the "trend of the times." Nevertheless, Kennedy deemed it prudent to keep these opinions private, and he urged the pope to enter into negotiations with the Reich. The Pope's final remark was: "The Church can only do so much, but what it can do, it will."[73]

15. During the war years, Pope Pius XII frequently confided in the Jesuit Father Giacomo Martegani, director of *La Civilta Cattolica*, who kept a diary of their conversations. The diary shows that the pope was aware of and approved of the Church's efforts to help Jews threatened with deportation from Rome.[74] In the fall of 1943, when the Nazis were expelling Roman Jews to death camps, Father Martegani recorded that Pius told him that "he has looked into the well-being of the Jews."[75] Some weeks later, after a number of Nazi

raids on church properties that harbored Jews, Father Martegani noted that the pope "no longer trusted in the safety of the ecclesiastical refugees." The Pope told him that it was important not to push the Nazis to the point where they undertook a generalized shakedown of religious houses in the city.

16. In March 2004, St. Bonaventure University awarded a medal to Don Aldo Brunacci, an Italian Catholic priest from Assisi. The award was presented at the Holocaust Memorial Museum in Washington D.C. and was given in recognition of Fr. Brunacci's having helped to save more than two hundred Jews during World War II. On March 31, 2004, National Public Radio broadcast an interview with him. Through a translator, Fr. Brunacci said: "In September 1943, the bishop of Assisi received a very classified letter from the secretary of state of the Vatican asking the bishop to organize help to take care of all the refugees, especially the Jews." Fr. Brunacci added that Pope Pius XII "did unbelievable things to save Jews. And as a matter of fact, there recently was published a list of church organizations, religious communities, who saved Jews during those years. Just only in Rome there were thousands."[76]

17. In 2004, the posthumous memoirs of Harold H. Tittmann Jr. were published.[77] These memoirs from the assistant to Myron C. Taylor (President Roosevelt's personal representative to the Holy See) reveal the high esteem that both Taylor and Tittmann had for Pius XII and the pope's wartime record. Tittmann affirms that Pius XII "detested the Nazi ideology and everything it stood for," and he praises the papal diplomacy: "The Holy Father chose the better path... and thereby saved many lives."[78] Tittmann also wrote: "There were no signs that the pope was pro-Fascist or pro-Nazi. In fact, the opposite seemed more the case."[79]

18. In his 2004 book, *The Pontiff in Winter*, John Cornwell admits that *Hitler's Pope* lacked balance. He now reports that "in the light of the debates and evidence following *Hitler's Pope*," Pope Pius XII "had so little scope of action" that it is impossible to judge his motives

"while Rome was under the heel of Mussolini and later occupied by the Germans."[80] The *Economist* reported that he was "chastened" by the experience.

All of this only serves to confirm the positive evaluation of Pope Pius XII that was set forth in *Hitler, the War, and the Pope.*[81]

REPORT FROM THE CONGREGATION FOR THE CAUSES OF SAINTS

Perhaps the most important recent development in understanding Pope Pius XII is the completion of the thirty-nine-year study into his life that was undertaken by historians for the Vatican's Congregation for the Causes of Saints.[82] This report, which fills six volumes,[83] includes 1,420 pages on his life (*Vita Documentata*); almost one thousand pages of sworn testimony transcripts given by ninety-eight witnesses (*Summarium*);[84] a three-hundred-page synthetic exposition of his virtues of faith, hope, charity, and prudence (*Informatio*); and a three-hundred-page appendix addressing specific issues in the life of Pius XII, including his work vis-a-vis the Jewish victims of the Holocaust [85] Cumulatively, these documents are known as the *Positio.*[86]

The importance of the *Positio* comes not from the evidence that it reviews, but from the analysis of that evidence. It sets forth a compelling case that Pius XII lived a life of heroic virtue.[87] As for the charges raised by a slew of papal critics, the *Positio* concludes that they are part of a campaign to denigrate his personality and his work.[88]

The evidence that it reviews is essentially the same evidence that has been available to all researchers in this area. The difference is that with papal critics, Pius XII is asked to stand in judgment before a tribunal with no judge, no clearly defined rules of evidence, no universally accepted precedents, no process for assuring a fair jury, no presumption of innocence, and numerous prosecutors—each charging him with different and often inconsistent acts of malfeasance. There is no way that an accused can obtain a fair hearing under such circumstances.

In contrast to the various papal critics, the Congregation for the Causes of Saints has a history of looking into the lives of important people. It uses reasonable standards of general applicability and tries to apply them fairly. All charges and claims on both sides of the issue are explored,[89] and true scholars take as much time as is necessary to reach the right conclusion. In a forum such as that, the charges against Pope Pius xii are easily refuted.

The procedures that are used in courtroom hearings cannot be made fully applicable to academic history. They can and should, however, inform the approach taken in analyzing the character of historical figures. This is especially true when one makes serious allegations about the intention, purpose, and desire of people who are no longer around to defend themselves. When that is done in this case, Pope Pius xii acquits himself quite well.

Achille Ratti: Pope Pius XI

Where there is a question of saving souls,
We feel the courage to treat with the Devil in person.
Pope Pius XI (1933)

NE OF THE MORE REMARKABLE DEVELOPMENTS in the debate
about the Catholic Church and the Holocaust is the shift in
the perception of Pope Pius XI. Until recent years, Pius XI
was presented as the "good, outspoken" leader, in contrast to the "silent" Pope Pius XII.[1] Close examination revealed, however, that Pius
XII took an approach very similar to that of his predecessor. The result
should have been to acknowledge that Pius XII, like his predecessor,
was a staunch opponent of the Nazis and a champion of their victims.
Instead, many critics turned on Pius XI.[2] In doing this, they made the
most preposterous of arguments.

Pope Pius XI, the Church's 261st Pope, was born Ambrose Damian
Achille Ratti in Desio, Italy, on May 31, 1857. He first showed his desire
for the priesthood by entering a preparatory seminary when he was ten
years old. He went to seminary in Milan and took a three-year course

in the College of San Carlo in Milan. He then entered the Lombard College at Rome. He went on to earn degrees in canon law, theology, and philosophy from the new Academy of St. Thomas Aquinas. On December 20, 1879, Ratti was ordained a priest. He soon thereafter began teaching sacred eloquence and dogmatic theology at the seminary in Milan.

In 1888, Ratti was appointed as a doctor of the great Ambrosian Library in Milan. In 1912, Pope Pius x named him assistant librarian at the Vatican, and he eventually became head of the Vatican Library. For thirty years, Ratti was a respected librarian and prolific scholar. He prepared over fifty monographs and papers during these years. Those who worked at the library said that he was kind, courteous, and willing to set aside his own research to help others.

In 1918, Poland was freed from Russian domination for the first time in more than a century. The Polish bishops urged the Holy See to send them an apostolic visitor. In a rather surprising move, Pope Benedict xv asked Fr. Ratti to fill that role. In 1919, Benedict made him an archbishop and formally named him papal nuncio to Poland.[3]

Archbishop Ratti did a good job under difficult circumstances in Poland, so when the opportunity arose in 1921, Benedict named him Archbishop of Milan and elevated him to the cardinalate. Only five months later, he was elected pope. Ratti chose the name Pius xi and stepped into a very difficult situation.[4]

Popes at this time considered themselves "prisoners" in the Vatican. The problem extended back to the time when Italy seized the remnants of the once-powerful Papal States. With the capture of Rome on September 20, 1870, the papacy was left without a home. Italy made certain concessions to the Holy See, but since they were imposed and not part of a negotiated agreement, the popes refused to recognize them. This difficulty between Italy and the Holy See was known as the "Roman Question."

Benito Mussolini came to power in Italy only a few months after Pius xi's election. "Il Duce" had previously expressed a very hostile attitude toward the Catholic Church, but now it was to his political advantage to reach an agreement with the Holy See.[5] Negotiations began early in the fall of 1926 and continued over the next few years. An agreement, known as the Lateran Treaty, was signed on February 11, 1929.[6] Under its terms, the Church got her independent state (although it only amounted to about one hundred acres); Italy recognized Catholicism as its official state religion; anti-clerical laws which had been in effect since 1870 were declared null and void; and the Holy See received a cash settlement for the lands that had been confiscated.

Despite this new relationship, Mussolini's government did not treat the Church well. Pius XI, who did not favor Catholic political parties, strove to energize the laity through the organization, Catholic Action, which he described as "the participation of the laity in the work of the hierarchy."[7] That organization did not, however, please the Fascists. Pius and Mussolini "crossed swords" often.[8]

In the spring of 1931, Mussolini's "black shirts" harassed and beat up members of Catholic Action. By the early summer, the pope issued an encyclical entitled *Non Abbiamo Bisogno* (*On Catholic Action in Italy*), in which Pius XI stated that although the Church was grateful to the state for spreading the "welfare of religion," the recent attacks on Catholic youth groups led the Holy Father to wonder whether the earlier treatment was an honest reflection of respect for religion or a "pure calculation and to an ultimate goal of domination." An uneasy truce developed later that year, but an even more ominous threat was forming north of Italy.[9]

THE 1933 CONCORDAT WITH GERMANY

One of the most controversial matters during the pontificate of Pope Pius XI involves the document signed by Germany and the Holy See in 1933. Critics have long argued that this concordat (treaty or agreement) signified some type of alignment between the two. At the very least, many have argued, this agreement prevented Popes Pius XI and

Pius XII from taking a stronger stand against Hitler and the Nazis. These arguments are wrong.

Hitler was appointed chancellor, the head of the German government, on January 30, 1933. Six months later, on July 20, Germany and the Holy See signed the concordat. It has been incorrectly reported that this was "Nazi Germany's first international treaty."[10] In fact, the Four Powers Pact between Germany, France, Italy, and Great Britain was signed in Rome on June 7, 1933 (more than a month before the concordat was signed).[11] The Soviet Union, on May 5, 1933, (more than two months before the concordat was signed) renewed a trade and friendship agreement with Germany,[12] and on that same day the British Parliament voted to accept an Anglo-German trade agreement.[13] Moreover, Hitler's representatives were fully accredited and recognized by the League of Nations and took part in the disarmament discussions in Geneva, which also came before the signing of the concordat.[14] In other words, Italy, France, the United Kingdom, the Soviet Union, and the whole League of Nations recognized the new German government before the concordat was signed.

Some critics argue that the concordat was a Vatican initiative, designed to garner good will with the new German government. Pius XI did believe in establishing diplomatic agreements with nations. Concordats helped assure the Church's ability to hold services and carry out its functions:[15] "Their primary end has always been to safeguard and defend the freedom of worship of the faithful."[16] Under Pius XI's leadership, the Church reached agreement with twenty-one countries, including Czechoslovakia, Austria, Italy, Germany, Poland, Yugoslavia, Latvia, and Lithuania. As nuncio in Germany, Cardinal Pacelli had been largely responsible for negotiating the agreements with Bavaria (1924), Prussia (1929), and Baden (1932). He also attempted to secure an agreement with the Soviet Union.[17] Pius XI was, in fact, known as "the pope of the concordats."[18]

Because Pius XI favored this approach, the Church had been working toward agreement with Germany long before Hitler rose to power.

In fact, through Pacelli, Pius xi tried to secure such an agreement with Germany for the better part of the 1920s. Officials from the Weimar Republic, however, refused to meet the Vatican's demands.

When Hitler rose to power, things changed. He never intended to keep his promises, so he was happy to agree to all of the Church's long-standing demands. Moreover, Hitler made it quite clear that if the Church were to reject his offer, he would simply publish his own terms and blame the pope for having rejected a favorable treaty that the Holy See itself had proposed.[19]

In a private conversation with Ivone Kirkpatrick, British chargé d'affaires to the Vatican, Pacelli emphasized that the concordat was not to be seen as an approval of Nazism. In fact, he expressed "disgust and abhorrence" of Hitler's reign of terror.[20] "The Cardinal Secretary of State was reluctant to accept the early offer of the New Hitler Government for a Reich Concordat, although he had worked hard for such an agreement during the days of the Weimar Republic. In the spring of 1933, the cardinal knew that perhaps ninety per cent of the German Catholics were protected at least temporarily by concordats he had negotiated with Bavaria, Prussia, and Baden since 1924."[21]

Kirkpatrick reported to the British Foreign Office on August 19, 1933, that

> these reflections on the iniquity of Germany led the Cardinal to explain apologetically how it was that he had signed a Concordat with such people. A pistol, he said, had been pointed at his head and he had no alternative. The German government had offered him concessions, concessions, it must be admitted, wider than any previous German Government would have agreed to, and he had to choose between an agreement on their lines and the virtual elimination of the Catholic Church in the Reich. Not only that, but he was given no more than one week to make up his mind. . . . If the German Government violated the Concordat–and they were certain to do that–the Vatican would have at least a treaty on which to base a protest.[22]

Mussolini, who had signed a similar agreement with the Church four years earlier, supported the treaty.[23] Not all Nazis, however, agreed. Joseph Goebbels, Reinhart Heydrich, and others in the party objected and may even have tried to sabotage the agreement by creating violent incidents involving the clergy and Catholic organizations.[24]

The Church had been making agreements with foreign governments for centuries. It did not view them as endorsements of the existing government. Pope Pius XI explained his thinking in 1937, in his encyclical *Mit brennender Sorge* (*With Burning Anxiety*):

> When, in 1933, We consented . . . to open negotiations for a concordat, We were prompted by the desire . . . to secure for Germany the freedom of the Church's beneficent mission and the salvation of the souls in her care, as well as by the sincere wish to render the German people a service essential for its peaceful development and prosperity. Hence, despite many and grave misgivings, We then decided not to withhold Our consent for We wished to spare the Faithful of Germany . . . the trials and difficulties they would have had to face . . . had the negotiations fallen through. It was by acts that We wished to make it plain, that the pacific and maternal hand of the Church would be extended to anyone who did not actually refuse it.[25]

As Pius XI told a meeting of bishops in Rome in May 1933: "If it is a matter of saving a few souls, of averting even graver damage, we have the courage to negotiate even with the devil."[26]

In June 1933, after negotiations for the concordat were well underway, the Archbishop of Munich, Cardinal Michael von Faulhaber, cautioned that Hitler wanted an agreement with the Vatican for propaganda purposes. He said that Hitler "sees what a halo his government will have in the eyes of the world if the Pope makes a treaty with him." He argued that Catholic people would not understand the Holy See making a treaty with the Third Reich when "a whole row of Catholic officials are sitting in prison or have been illegally ejected."[27] Critics often cite this language. Later, however, Faulhaber learned all of the reasons why the Church had agreed to the concordat, he said: "With the concordat we are hanged, without the concordat we are hanged, drawn and quartered."[28] Faulhaber became an outspoken opponent of Hitler, and support from Pius was one a reason for his outspokenness.

From the Vatican's perspective, at least on paper, the German concordat was very favorable—one of the best that it had ever signed.[29] The State essentially met all of the demands that the Church had long made of the Weimar Republic, including independence of Catholic organizations, freedom of the Church, freedom for Catholic schools, free communication with Rome, Church control over religious orders and ecclesiastical property, and religious education in public schools (taught by teachers approved by the bishop).[30] Only minimal restrictions were placed on ecclesiastical appointments: bishops were to be appointed by Rome, subject to political objections by the Reich Government; clergy were to be appointed by bishops, the only requirement being that they be German nationals. The Vatican also received the long-sought right to maintain theological faculties at state institutions and to establish seminaries. In short, "the Catholic religion in Germany was placed on an even footing with the Protestant faith and was guaranteed the same rights and privileges as the latter."[31]

The signing of a concordat is sometimes mistakenly assumed to signify a close relationship between the government and the Holy See. That, however, is not the case. As one commentator noted: "This is the precise opposite of the fact; a country which was on ideally good terms with Rome would not need to have a Concordat at all; and the existence of such a document implies that the two signatory parties are, in a more or less degree, distrustful of each other's intentions. It is an attempt to regularize a difficult situation by tying down either party, on paper, to a minimum of good behavior. . . . *Nothing could be more absurd than to represent* [the Concordat of July 1933] *as if it meant that the New Germany and the Vatican were working hand in hand*."[32] Peter Godman, who reviewed archival documents that concern the relations between the Holy See and German from 1923 to 1939 concluded: "The notion that [Pius XI or Pacelli] harbored sympathies for National Socialism, because they continued to negotiate with its leaders, must be rejected."[33]

On July 25, just five days after Germany ratified the concordat, the Reich government announced a sterilization law designed to achieve "perfection of the Aryan race."[34] Germans who were less than perfect were to be sterilized for the glory of Reich. Sterilization was, of course, in direct conflict with Catholic teaching about the sanctity of human life, including Pius XI's 1930 encyclical, *Casti Connubii* (*On Chastity in Marriage*). Prominent Catholic clergy immediately denounced the program.[35] On July 26 and 27, the Vatican newspaper *L'Osservatore Romano* carried a two-part article by Pacelli in which he vehemently denied any assertion that the concordat indicated approval of National Socialism and instead explained that it was intended to protect the Church's interests in Germany.[36]

The concordat was ignored from the beginning by Hitler. Between 1933 and 1937, the Holy See filed more than fifty formal written protests with the German government, charging that it had violated the concordat. The Nazis never replied, but the Holy See circulated the protests to the bishops in Germany, so that they would know what the Vatican was doing.[37] The flow of protests eventually slowed. "[I]n the war years there were no longer the steady protests with regard to the Catholic Schools or associations, for these had virtually ceased to exist."[38]

Before long, the concordat was being used by the Holy See as a weapon in its battle against the Nazis. As Protestant Rev. Martin Niemoeller, who spent seven years in prison for his opposition to Hitler and the Nazis, said: "In the struggle that has ensued, the Catholic Church, because of its stronger international position, has done heroic work. And by means of the concordat between the Pope and the Hitler government the Catholic Church was put in position to counteract the Nazis' vicious propaganda against Catholic history and Catholic dogma."[39] Hitler would later vow to "put a swift end" to the concordat.[40]

The Vatican issued so many complaints regarding violations of the concordat that by 1938, the Nazis were trying to disavow it.[41] On February 17, 1938, *Das Schwarze Korps,* the official paper of the ss, contained an article protesting that the concordat presupposed the old Germany resting upon a federation of states, a party system, and a liberal outlook. The argument continued that since this agreement was based largely on the Weimar Constitution of 1918, not the Third Reich of Adolf Hitler, a number of clauses were obsolete. As such, the concordat was out of date, and should be abandoned.[42] The article argued that in 1933 Hitler had expected the moral support of the Church in his work of national reconstruction, but he had not received this support. Instead, pastoral letters, sermons, pamphlets, and encyclicals had insulted the government. Later, Hitler promised to end the concordat following the war, saying "it will give me the greatest personal pleasure to point out to the Church all those occasions on which it has broken the terms of it."[43]

Reporting from Berlin in 1940, William Shirer wrote of the concordat in the past tense and noted that German Foreign Minister Joachim von Ribbentrop went to Rome in March of that year to obtain a new concordat.[44] (He also noted that "Germany didn't observe the last concordat, persecuting the church whenever it pleased.") As later accounts established, Ribbentrop, dressed in his full Nazi uniform, marched into the pope's office intending to present a lecture on German might and the folly of the Vatican having sided with the democracies. Pius xii, however, pulled out a ledger and recited a long list of outrageous abuses by the Nazis in Poland, giving the precise date, time, and details of each. The *New York Times* reported that "the Pontiff, in the burning words he spoke to Herr Ribbentrop . . . came to the defense of the Jews in Germany and Poland."[45] Pius then terminated the audience. Ribbentrop reportedly felt faint as he left.[46]

The concordat, which may on the surface seem to indicate friendly relations between the Holy See and Nazi Germany, was in fact an indication of precisely the opposite, as the historical record now plainly reveals.[47] It was not a recognition of Hitler's Third Reich. It did not indicate the Holy See's support for Nazism, and in no way did it suggests that Pope Pius XII or the Holy See supported the German cause in World War II. It was, instead, Hitler's attempt to take advantage of the Vatican. He accepted long-standing demands, forced the Holy See to agree to them, and then ignored his commitments. Ultimately, however, this proved to be but one more serious miscalculation made by the most notorious madman of the twentieth century. The concordat came back to haunt the Nazis, as Pope Pius XII and the Catholic Church used it to shield Jewish victims and resist Nazi advances.[48]

THE ITALIAN INVASION OF ETHIOPIA

In 1896, Italy had unsuccessfully tried to conquer Ethiopia. In 1935, Mussolini decided to avenge that defeat. He believed that a victory there would strengthen Italy's position in the Middle East. It would also reveal him as a true military leader.

Ethiopia, also called Abyssinia, lay in Africa adjacent to Italian Somaliland. A dispute arose, perhaps manufactured by Mussolini, regarding the border between these two areas. In October 1935, Mussolini made his move. With mechanized troops facing poorly armed Ethiopians, Mussolini's forces did not take long to finish the job. In spite of appeals for help issued by the Ethiopian Emperor, Italian forces captured the capital in May 1936 and Mussolini claimed victory. Over half a million Ethiopians were killed. Mussolini was then able to unite Ethiopia with the Italian colonies of Eritrea and Italian Somaliland into one large colony which he named Italian East Africa.

During the Ethiopian war, Mussolini controlled the press and invoked the provisions of the Lateran Treaty that provided for Catholic neutrality, thereby silencing any opposition. After the war, the reaction of other countries was a clear example of appeasement. Although the League of Nations briefly imposed an embargo against Italy, it was of little consequence. "Italy at last has her Empire," Mussolini announced. "It is a Fascist empire because it bears the indestructible sign of the will and power of Rome."[49] Ethiopia was formally annexed, and King Victor Emmanuel III of Italy assumed the title of Emperor. Mussolini announced that Italy was now satisfied and ready for peace.

Some critics have said that Pope Pius XI supported the Italian aggression, suggesting that he favored it because it could expand the Church's influence. Actually, Pius XI had a special interest in the Ethiopians,[50] and he strongly opposed this war.

Prior to the invasion, Pius XI "spoke out strongly on at least three occasions, condemning unprovoked aggression as a crime against the moral law."[51] He called it a "crime so enormous, a manifestation of such folly, that We hold it to be absolutely impossible that nations could again take up arms against each other. . . . But if anyone should dare to commit this heinous crime, which God forbids, then We could not but turn to Him with bitterness in Our hearts, praying Scatter the peoples who want war."[52] In September, when receiving Catholic hospital workers, the Pontiff spoke of his "unutterable grief" at this "war that is simply one of conquest."[53] Additionally, when Mussolini ordered Rome illuminated to celebrate Italian victories, Pius kept Vatican City dark, drawing criticism from the Fascist press.[54]

Writing from Rome in October 1935, *New York Times* reporter Anne O'Hare McCormick noted Pius XI's efforts against Italy's aggression:

> Three times since the Papal Secretary of State [Pacelli] inaugurated the three-day prayer for peace in the Catholic world at Lourdes last July, the Pope had prayed for peace with direct references to the Italio-Ethiopian conflict.
>
> Late in August, while addressing an international congress of nurses, he expounded the doctrine of the church in regard to aggressive war. A month later he denounced the crime of war, particularly war of conquest, to 15,000 war veterans gathered in Rome. The third time, it is learned on good authority, he spoke to Mussolini himself.[55]

In December of that year, McCormick noted that the pope rejected the Italian justification for the war as being necessary for population expansion and as a defense of the nation's frontier.[56] Surely, neither Mussolini nor any other reasonably well-informed world leader of that era thought that Pope Pius xi supported Italy's invasion of Ethiopia.

MIT BRENNENDER SORGE

The Vatican under Pope Pius xi issued several strong condemnations of anti-Semitism. On March 25, 1928, an official decree of the Holy Office proclaimed: "Moved by the spirit of charity, the Apostolic See has protected the people [of Israel] against unjust persecutions, and since it condemns all jealousy and strife among peoples, it accordingly condemns with all its might the hatred directed against a people which was chosen by God; that particular hatred, in fact, which today commonly goes by the name anti-Semitism."[57]

In the spring of 1933, as the Nazis were just beginning to exercise their newfound power, Pope Pius xi met with several prominent Jewish leaders to address the way Jews were being treated in Germany. The *Jewish Chronicle of London*—the leading English-language Jewish newspaper in Europe—reported: "The Pope received in audience a delegation [of Jewish leaders]. . . and had a long private talk with them about the situation of the Jews in Germany. It is understood that the Pope was extremely concerned about the sufferings imposed on the Jews, and expressed his sympathy with them and his desire to be of help. Rabbi da Fano, who is eighty-six years of age, is a personal friend of the Pope and was his teacher of Hebrew when the Pope was Director of the Catholic Ambrosian Library in Milan."[58]

The Church's opposition to anti-Semitism and racism was well recognized by the Jewish community. In September of 1933, the *Jewish Chronicle of London* again reported: "The Pope, having received reports of the persistence of anti-Semitic persecution in Germany, has publicly expressed his disapproval of the movement. He stated that these persecutions are a poor testimony to the civilisation of a great people. He recalled the fact that Jesus Christ, the Madonna, the apostles, the prophets and many saints were all of Hebrew race, and that the Bible is a Hebrew creation. The Aryan races, he declared, had no claim to superiority over the Semites."[59]

Vatican opposition to anti-Semitism and racism continued to be reflected in directives from the Holy See, speeches by Pius XI and Cardinal Pacelli, and statements on Vatican Radio and written in *L'Osservatore Romano*.

By 1937, it was clear that the long list of informal condemnations of anti-Semitism and Nazism would not suffice. In that year, Pius XI released the encyclical *Mit brennender Sorge* (*With Burning Anxiety*).[60] While critics have tried to minimize the importance of that document, it was the strongest condemnation of Hitler and the Nazis to be issued by any national leader prior to World War II. It strongly condemned racism, and it was directed right at Nazi Germany.

A shortened version of this encyclical was translated into English and published during the war in a popular anthology of Catholic literature.[61]

TO THE GERMAN PEOPLE

Whoever exalts race, or the people, or the State, or a particular form of State, or the depositories of power, or any other fundamental value of the human community—however necessary and honorable be their function in worldly things—whoever raises these notions above their standard value and divinizes them to an idolatrous level, distorts and perverts an order of the world planned and created by God; he is far from the true faith in God and from the concept of life which that faith upholds.

Beware, Venerable Brethren, of that growing abuse, in speech as in writing, of the name of God as though it were a meaningless label, to be affixed to any creation, more or less arbitrary, of human speculation. Use your influence on the Faithful, that they refuse to yield to this aberration. Our God is the Personal God, supernatural, omnipotent, infinitely perfect, one in the Trinity of

Persons, tri-personal in the unity of divine essence, the Creator of all existence, Lord, King and ultimate Consummator of the History of the world, who will not, and cannot, tolerate a rival god by His side.

This God, this Sovereign Master, has issued commandments whose value is independent of time and space, country and race. As God's sun shines on every human face, so His law knows neither privilege nor exception. Rulers and subjects, crowned and uncrowned, rich and poor are equally subject to his word. From the fullness of the Creators' right there naturally arises the fullness of His right to be obeyed by individuals and communities, whoever they are. This obedience permeates all branches of activity in which moral values claim harmony with the law of God, and pervades all integration of the ever-changing laws of man into the immutable laws of God.

None but superficial minds could stumble into concepts of a national God, of a national religion; or attempt to lock within the frontiers of a single people, within the narrow limits of a single race, God, the Creator of the universe, King and Legislator of all nations before whose immensity they are "as a drop of a bucket" (Isaiah xi, 15).

POPE PIUS XI

The full version of the encyclical went on to praise leaders in the Church who stood firm and provided a good example to others. It concluded that "enemies of the Church, who think that their time has come, will see that their joy was premature."[62]

Unlike most encyclicals, which are written in Latin, *Mit brennender Sorge* was written in German. It was signed by Pius xi on March 14, 1937, and was smuggled into Germany, distributed to all parishes, and read from the pulpits on Palm Sunday, March 21, 1937.[63] German rescuers heard it and were encouraged in their work.[64]

The pope's message was also well understood in the United States. *Newsweek* magazine reported:

On Palm Sunday, priests read their 21,000,000 German Catholics a papal encyclical which had been smuggled across the border. It bluntly charged that the Nazis had violated their 1933 Concordat with the Vatican, that civil officials were trying to undermine the Catholic religion; it condemned the ideology of race, blood, and soil as articles of faith.

—

Pius' proclamation echoed the bitterness of four years of Church-State strife. Catholicism, like Protestantism, has paid a high price for its resistance to "coordination." Arrests of 3,500 priests and religious for all the offences in the Nazi lexicon pointed in only one direction: a frantic effort to tear away the clergy's cloak of piety and nobility. More than anything else the Reich wanted to break the church's grip on the minds of 2,000,000 German children. Patriotism must replace Catholicism as the religion of the youth; Germany's totalitarian future depended on it.[65]

The reading of the encyclical was like a bomb going off in Germany.[66] Naturally, the Nazis did not take the papal rebuke lightly. As *Newsweek* reported, *Mit brennender Sorge* soon led to a "fight to the finish."[67]

The day following the release of *Mit brennender Sorge*, the *Völkischer Beobachter* carried a strong counterattack on the "Jew-God and His deputy in Rome."[68] *Das Schwarze Korps* called it "the most incredible of Pius XI's pastoral letters; every sentence in it was an insult to the new Germany."[69] The German ambassador to the Holy See was instructed not to take part in the solemn Easter ceremonies, and German missions throughout Europe were told that the encyclical "calls upon Catholic citizens to rebel against the authority of the Reich."[70]

An internal German memorandum dated March 23, 1937 said that the papal statement was "almost a call to do battle against the Reich government."[71] The prosecution report for the Nuremberg trials stated that all available copies of *Mit brennender Sorge* were confiscated,

twelve printing offices were closed, people convicted of distributing
the encyclical were arrested, and the Church-affiliated publications
that ran the encyclical were banned. Later on, the mere mention of
the encyclical was made a crime in Nazi Germany.[72]

This retaliation led to a notable statement made by Cardinal Mundelein of the United States at a quarterly diocesan conference with five
hundred priests and prelates in attendance:

> Perhaps you will ask how it is that a nation of 60,000,000 people,
> intelligent people, will submit in fear and servitude to an alien,
> an Austrian paperhanger, and a poor one at that, I am told, and
> a few associates like Goebbels and Goering, who dictate every
> move of the people's lives, and who can, in this age of rising
> prices and necessary high cost of living, say to an entire nation:
> "Wages cannot be raised."
>
> Perhaps because it is a country where every second person
> is a government spy, where armed forces come and seize private
> books and papers without court procedures, where the father can
> no longer discipline his son for fear that the latter will inform on
> him and land him in prison.[73]

As the press reported, this statement "provoked the Hitlerites to fury."[74]

The Nazis protested to the Vatican about Cardinal Mundelein's
statement, but "Cardinal Pacelli refused to accept the Reich's demand
for an apology."[75] The Vatican's reply was that the statement was made
on the cardinal's own initiative, but this "does not mean that the Vatican disapproves . . . because what the Holy See thinks of the German
religious situation has been so clearly expressed [in *Mit brennender
Sorge*]"[76] *Newsweek* interpreted the Vatican's response as follows: "Cardinal Mundelein spoke for himself, but his opinion of Nazism is higher
than ours."[77] It went on to explain that over the years Pius XI's "disapproval" of the Nazis had grown to "outright enmity."[78] The Germans
broke off normal relations with the Holy See.[79]

Critics of Pope Pius xii often suggest that had he only been more outspoken in his condemnations of Nazis and their anti-Semitism, he could have lessened the harshness of (if not prevented) the Holocaust. The lesson from *Mit brennender Sorge*, however, suggests otherwise. Not only did the Nazis retaliate against the Church, the persecution of Jews also got worse after this encyclical was released.

CONDEMNATIONS OF ANTI-SEMITIC LAWS

Accusations that Pope Pius xi was anti-Semitic are somewhat infrequent, and rightly so.[80] Pius xi was long known to be on good terms with Jews. As a young man he learned Hebrew from a rabbi, and he enjoyed warm relations with Italian Jewish leaders in the early years of his priesthood. Instructed by Pope Benedict to direct the distribution of Catholic relief in postwar Poland, he provided funds to impoverished Jews who had lost their homes and businesses.

Papal critics sometimes, however, suggest that Pius xi's Vatican went along with anti-Semitic legislation. They question *L'Osservatore Romano*'s campaign against Italian anti-Semitic laws.[81] Daniel Goldhagen even argues that the Vatican "endorsed" Italy's anti-Semitic laws. The written record proves otherwise.

Mussolini issued his "Aryan Manifesto" on July 14, 1938. This pseudo-scientific document had been commissioned by Mussolini, but it was signed by a group of "racial experts." It announced the discovery of an Italian race and set forth the following racial precepts:

1.   Human races exist.
2.   There are great and small races.
3.   The concept of race is purely biological.
4.   The population of modern Italy is of Aryan origin and its civilization is Aryan.
5.   It is a myth that other peoples have mingled with the Italian population during the modern era.

6. There now exists an Italian race.
7. The time has come for Italians frankly to proclaim themselves racists.
8. It is necessary to distinguish between European Mediterranean people and Africans and Orientals.
9. Jews do not belong to the Italian race.
10. The European physical and psychological traits of Italians must not be altered in any way.[82]

The very next day, July 15, Pius XI branded the Manifesto "a true form of apostasy. It is no longer merely one or another erroneous idea; it is the entire spirit of the doctrine that is contrary to the Faith of Christ."[83] On July 21, Pius XI openly declared: "Catholic means universal, not racist, nationalistic, separatist. . . . The spirit of Faith must fight against the spirit of separatism and exaggerated nationalism, which are detestable, and which, just because they are not Christian, end up by not even being human"[84] Two weeks later to the day, Pius XI made a public speech in which he said: "The entire human race is but a single and universal race of men. There is no room for special races. We may therefore ask ourselves why Italy should have felt a disgraceful need to imitate Germany." This was reprinted in full on the front page of the Vatican newspaper on July 30, under a four-column headline. The sub-headline mentioned both "universal concepts" and the "great human family."[85]

Other articles condemning National Socialism, racism, or anti-Semitism appeared in 1938 issues of *L'Osservatore Romano* on April 2,[86] July 17,[87] July 21,[88] July 23,[89] August 13[90], August 22-23,[91] October 17-18,[92] October 20,[93] October 23,[94] October 25,[95] October 26,[96] October 27,[97] November 3,[98] November 13,[99] November 14-15,[100] November 16,[101] November 17,[102] November 19,[103] November 20,[104] November 21-22,[105] November 23,[106] November 24,[107] November 26,[108] December 25,[109] and January 19, 1939.[110] As one contemporary commentator explained:

The Vatican newspaper, *Osservatore Romano*, had been forthright
and downright in its denunciation of Hitler for his excesses against
the Jews, his sterilization law, his restrictions upon the freedom of
speech and assembly and freedom of religious worship. This little
newspaper, published within the Vatican state, was one of the few
remaining in Europe that dared to criticize Hitler or Mussolini.
Even the French press had become respectful toward Hitler, and
in Poland, Norway, Sweden, Denmark, the Netherlands, Finland,
Hungary, Rumania, Jugoslavia and Czechoslovakia, newspapers
were silent on Hitler. His name did not appear in Lithuania. But
the Vatican newspaper fulminated and poured its criticism upon
his head, even while he was in Italy. The newspaper had been just
as persistent in its attacks upon Mussolini.[111]

Secretary of State Pacelli oversaw *L'Osservatore Romano* and Vatican Radio. "Without exaggerating the international impact of these
labours, they provide more than enough evidence that the future
Pope had no tenderness towards National Socialism."[112] A.C. Jemolo,
a noted opponent of Italian Fascism during the war years, wrote: "It
may be recognized without qualification that there was no heretical
principle, no proposition against dogma, against orthodox history or
against morals which was even tentatively advanced by Fascist men
or journals of any authority, which was not immediately refuted by
pontifical acts, by very authoritative ecclesiastical reviews or by the
Osservatore Romano.[113]

Similarly, in March 1949, Piero Calamandrei, a left-leaning political activist, who was no friend of the Church, stated to the Italian
Constituent Assembly that: "At a certain moment, during the years of
greatest oppression, we were aware that the sole newspaper in which it
was still possible to find some accent of liberty, of our own liberty and
of the common liberty of all free men, was the *Osservatore Romano*."[114]
Upon the liberation of Rome from German occupation (July 1944),
the chief rabbi of Rome, "made a solemn declaration in the Roman

synagogue, paying tribute to the Holy See for having condemned the anti-Semitic laws and diminished their effects."[115]

On October 21, 1938, in one of his last public appearances, Pope Pius XI personally attacked Hitler, likening him to Julian the Apostate (Roman Emperor Flavius Claudius Julianus), who attempted to "saddle the Christians with responsibility for the persecution he had unleashed against them."[116] Shortly thereafter, Hitler's Nazis undertook the infamous *Kristallnacht* pogrom of November 1938 during which Jews were beaten and their buildings were vandalized.

For three days following *Kristallnacht*, *L'Osservatore Romano*, ran a series of articles reporting on the atrocities. On November 13, under the headline *"Dopo le manifestazioni antisemite in Germania"* ("After the manifestations of anti-Semitism in Germany"), the Vatican newspaper noted the moral outrage expressed in many countries around the world over the pogrom. It even quoted the critical dispatches of the Jewish-owned *Havas News Agency.*[117]

Pius also instructed three prominent cardinals, Ildefonso Schuster of Milan, Pierre Verdier of Paris, and Joseph-Ernest Van Roey of Belgium, to publicly condemn Nazi racial theories. "Very close to us, in the name of racial rights, thousands and thousands of people were tracked down like wild beasts, stripped of their possessions . . . [when all they were doing was] seeking in vain in the heart of civilization for shelter and a piece of bread," said Cardinal Verdier. "There you have the result of the racial theory." *L'Osservatore Romano* published all three statements along with a strong attack on totalitarianism delivered by Michael Cardinal Faulhaber of Munich.[118]

The same month that *Kristallnacht* took place in Germany, racial laws in Italy were tightened with passage of the "law for the defense of the Italian race."[119] That law prohibited interracial marriages involving Italian Aryans, and declared that such marriages would not be recognized. Civil recognition of Church marriages had been one of the most important aspects of the 1929 Lateran Treaty between the Holy See and Italy, and this was a clear breach, despite Mussolini's attempts to argue otherwise.

Pope Pius XI was the first official to file a protest regarding the racial laws.[120] He had no influence with the Fascists or the Nazis, but his example may have been part of the reason why Italians were never very willing to enforce racial laws. Additionally, the American bishops used their annual national radio broadcast that year to condemn the attacks on Jewish synagogues and businesses in no uncertain terms. The bishops of New York, Richmond, and Albany all blasted the Nazis.

In 1938, Pius ordered that in all Catholic universities, the sciences—from biology to philosophy, including the juridical sciences—refute Nazi racist theories. The letter from the Sacred Congregation for Seminaries and Universities (now the Congregation for Catholic Education), whose prefect at the time was the pope himself, was sent on April 13, 1938, to the rectors and presidents of Catholic universities worldwide. It was signed by Monsignor Ernesto Ruffini, secretary of the congregation (and a future cardinal). It began by recalling the pope's address on Christmas Eve, 1937 in which he denounced the persecution that the Church was suffering in Germany. It went on to say that "the Holy Father's principal affliction" was that pernicious doctrines were being promoted, falsely called scientific, "for the purpose of perverting spirits and uprooting authentic religion."[121]

In announcing the appointment of several Jewish scholars to positions of importance in the Vatican, Pius XI said: "All human beings are admitted equally, without distinction of race, to participate, to share, to study and to explore truth and science."[122] As a commentator noted, "this was the spirit that guided Pius XI in gathering to the bosom of the Vatican the great Jewish scholars cast out by fascist Italy."[123] That spirit again made itself known to the world just months before the pontiff passed away.[124]

SPIRITUALLY WE ARE ALL SEMITES

On September 6, 1938, in a statement which—though barred from the Fascist press—quickly made its way around the world, Pope Pius XI said: "Mark well that in the Catholic Mass, Abraham is our Patriarch and forefather. Anti-Semitism is incompatible with the lofty thought which that fact expresses. It is a movement with which we Christians can have nothing to do. No, no, I say to you it is impossible for a Christian to take part in anti-Semitism. It is inadmissible. Through Christ and in Christ we are the spiritual progeny of Abraham. Spiritually, we are all Semites.[125]

As some critics have noted, the Pope's speech was not reprinted in nations where the press was intimidated by Fascists or Nazis, but the critics are wrong to suggest that these words were not well known or to minimize their effect.[126]

The *Tablet* of London, the Church's semi-official newspaper to English-speaking nations, ran the remarks on September 24, 1938, under the headline: "Italy: The Holy Father on the Jews." Secretary of State Eugenio Pacelli (the future Pope Pius XII) repeated the statement in a public speech he gave shortly thereafter in Rome;[127] the *New York Times* carried a front page story on the statement;[128] and Jacques Maritain, perhaps the leading Catholic philosopher of the era wrote an important and beautiful essay which was translated into English and published in the United States by the spring of 1939. He wrote: "Spiritually we are Semites—no stronger word has been uttered by a Christian against anti-Semitism, and this Christian was the successor to the Apostle Peter."[129]

The victims of the Nazis certainly took note of the Pope's commitment. In January 1939, The *National Jewish Monthly* reported that "the only bright spot in Italy has been the Vatican, where fine humanitarian statements by the Pope have been issuing regularly."[130] The February 1939 issue of The *National Monthly*, published by B'nai B'rith, put Pope Pius XI on its cover, along with the headline: "Pope Pius XI attacks Fascism." Inside the journal, on page 207, under the title "Pope Assails Fascism," it stated: "Regardless of their personal religious beliefs, men and women everywhere who believe in democracy and the rights of man have hailed the firm and uncompromising stand of Pope Pius XI against Fascist brutality, paganism and racial theories." Even the

United States Congress passed a joint resolution acknowledging Pius XI as a symbol for "the re-establishment of the rule of moral law in human society."[131]

The Axis leaders also took note of Pius XI's words. They called him the "Chief rabbi of the Western World."[132] On February 16, 1939, just days before he passed away, the official publication of the Nazi ss labeled him as "the sworn enemy of National Socialism."[133] When he died, Mussolini remarked: "At last that stiff-necked old man is dead."[134]

3 —

The German Clergy

*Once only in my life have I been stupid enough to try to
unite some twenty different sects under one head; and
God, to whom be thanks, endowed my twenty Protestant
Bishops with such stupidity, that I was saved from my
own folly. If I had succeeded, I should now have two
Popes on my back! And two blackmailers!*
Adolf Hitler (1942)[1]

SOME CRITICS HAVE EXTENDED THE CRITICISM of the Catholic
leadership to include Catholic priests and bishops in Germany.
Daniel Goldhagen, for instance, makes the sweeping and in-
defensible claim that "the great majority" of Catholic military chaplains
"weighed in on the side of the perpetrators, condoning and blessing
their crimes. . . . This virtually unknown and unmentioned chapter of
the Catholic clergy's role in the Holocaust has barely been investigated."
In fact, this subject has been extensively analyzed, but the findings do
not support Goldhagen's conclusion.

Catholic clergy were among the first people in Germany to recognize the threat posed by the Nazis.[2] As early as 1923, papal representa-

tive and future pope Eugenio Pacelli wrote from Germany to the Holy See reporting that "followers of Hitler and Ludendorff"[3] were persecuting Catholics because Catholic leaders had denounced the persecution of the Jews. He referred to this group as "right-wing radicals."[4] He also praised the "learned and zealous" Cardinal Archbishop Michael Faulhaber of Munich who was attacked because he "had denounced the persecutions against the Jews."[5]

In 1930, the bishops of Berlin and Westphalia condemned the Nazis in pastoral letters.[6] In that same year, the Bishop of Mainz affirmed that "every Catholic is forbidden to be a member of the Nazi Party."[7] In the spring of 1931, the Bavarian bishops also condemned National Socialism and described it as heretical and incompatible with Catholic teaching.[8] Similar statements were made by bishops in Cologne, Paderborn, and the upper Rhine.[9] "In 1931 the bishops of Bavaria, the upper Rhine, Köln, and Paderborn all issued statements proclaiming the incompatibility of National Socialism and Catholicism," and by the end of that year "the entire German episcopacy had declared itself against the movement."[10]

The 1932 common pastoral letter contained an "all-inclusive" prohibition on Nazi party membership.[11] The bishops "emphasized the Nazi threat to religious liberty, and they attacked Nazi racist policy."[12] They also forbade uniformed groups of National Socialists to attend Mass.[13] The 1933 common pastoral letter attacked the pagan emphasis on blood and race.[14] Quoting from the Gospel of Matthew, the letter said that "the messengers of Christianity are to be the 'salt of the earth,' and 'the light of the world,' and 'should let their light shine before the people.' The Church should be as 'a city on the hill,' visible from afar in the life of the people."[15]

Hitler responded on September 11 that he was not against Christianity itself, "but we will fight for the sake of keeping our public life free from those priests who have failed their calling and who should have become politicians rather than clergymen."[16] Four days later, proving that words had no effect on the Nazis, they passed the Nuremberg

Laws, which defined German citizenship and paved the way for later anti-Semitic laws.[17]

The 1934 and 1935 joint episcopal letters both reminded Catholics that the Ten Commandments and the moral law bound all races. All people were subject to sin, and the Nordic race was no exception.[18] A number of bishops, including Clemens Count von Galen, stressed the universality of the moral law for all races in their 1934 individual letters.[19] In their 1935 joint memorandum to Hitler, the bishops bluntly accused the government of attempted race-breeding.[20]

Between April 1933 and June 1936, the Vatican filed more than fifty protests against the Nazis.[21] Even before the concordat was ratified, the Vatican had made many objections to German officials regarding treatment of the Church.[22] German foreign secretary Joachim von Ribbentrop testified at Nuremberg that he had a "whole deskfull of protests" from Rome.[23] Of course, since the Nazis controlled the press, few of these protests were published during the Nazi era.[24]

Fabian von Schlabrendorff, a Protestant member of the German resistance, wrote a memorandum to U.S. General William ("Wild Bill") Donovan, in which Schlabrendorff reported:

> Immediately after Hitler had seized the power, National Socialism showed itself as an ideology plainly opposed to Christianism. Only a minority among the princes of the Catholic Church like for example Bishop Berning from Osnabrück and later Cardinal Innitzer from Vienna tried to show a friendly attitude towards Hitler. The majority of the princes of the Catholic Church left no doubt in their declarations and pastoral letters that there was no bridge between Naziism and the Catholic Church. As the years went by, the attitude of the Catholic Church became ever clearer. The rejection of Hitler became more and more obvious.[25]

He went on to explain that "Because of the hierarchic organizations of the Church, the denunciation of Hitler was propagated by the majority of Catholic clergy in the land. The result of this was that the enmity towards Hitler was promulgated not only by the high clerics but was also carried to the masses by the low clerics."[26]

Donovan, in his own report for the oss War Crimes Staff, which was approved by the Nuremberg Prosecution Review Board, examined the relationship between the German Catholic leadership and the Nazis as they came to power: "During this period the relations between the Nazi Party and the Catholic Church were extremely bitter. . . . On their part, the German bishops, stigmatizing the Nazi movement as anti-Christian, forbade the clergy to participate in any ceremonies, such as funerals, in which the Nazi Party was officially represented, and refused the sacraments to party officials. In several pastorals, they expressly warned the faithful against the danger created to German Catholicism by the party."[27] Donovan explained that the bishops' endorsement of the 1933 concordat between the Holy See and Germany did not indicate any sympathy with the Nazis. Rather, they thought that such an agreement might moderate the Nazis as had happened in Italy following the Lateran Treaty.[28]

Even after the war began, German clergy were noted for their opposition to the regime.[29] In 1940, most of the bishops mounted a "full-scale assault" against the Nazi euthanasia plan.[30] In December 1942, the bishops of West Germany and Berlin issued a joint pastoral letter that said: "The ultimate principles of right are not conditioned by time nor the result of national character so can the claim to . . . such rights not be a prerogative of a single people. Whoever bears a human countenance has rights, which no earthly power may take. . . . All the original rights of man . . . can and must not be denied to one who is not of our blood or does not speak our language."[31] That same month, the German bishops in a joint letter to the government complained about the treatment of the people of Poland.[32] The following year, the bishops urged respect for the right to life of all people, including the old and sick, hostages, prisoners of war, and members of a foreign race.[33]

A fairly constant theme of reports from the nuncio in Berlin was concern that this resistance was driving Germans away from the Church.[34] On April 13, 1940 he wrote: "I consider it my duty to point out that a part of the clergy has adopted an almost openly hostile attitude towards a Germany at war. This attitude of the clergy which goes as far as a desire for complete defeat. This attitude of the clergy, which unfortunately remains no secret, arouses not only the displeasure of the government, but gradually also that of the entire people, as the people are almost all of them enthusiastic for their leader; and therefore I fear a painful reaction will follow one day which will isolate the clergy and even the church from the people."[35] While Nuncio Orsenigo's attitude has been subject to question,[36] "his assessment was certainly closer to the truth than the assumption that Germany's Roman Catholics— about one third of the total population—were like so many divisions that the Pope could throw into battle against Hitler."[37]

Critic Daniel Goldhagen cites the notorious pro-Nazi Bishop Franz-Justus Rarkowski, but he was the exception that proved the rule. As an intitial point, he was virtually forced upon the Church by the Nazis (under the threat of having no military ordinary or military chaplains), and the Church banned Rarkowski from participation in the German episcopacy. When he made a statement favoring the German cause early in the war, Vatican Radio responded: "The German episcopate has so far avoided taking a position on this war that would transcend their pastoral duty towards the faithful. If the army bishop [Rarkowski] has read or heard what the Head of this Church has repeatedly and unequivocally said about the injustice done to Poland, he must be aware of the discrepancy between his position and that of the Holy See."[38] Vatican Radio went on to declare that: "Hitler's war is not a just war and God's blessing cannot be upon it"[39] and "It almost looks as if the army bishop sometimes finds it easier to align himself with the Nazis than with his church."[40]

Even at the height of German military power, the German bishops were outspoken against Nazi barbarism.[41] In 1942, the *New York*

Times reported: "The lesson is by now so clear that in all the occupied countries the most open and defiant opposition to Nazi tyranny comes from the religious leaders. This is strikingly true in Germany itself."[42] In 1943 the German bishops issued a statement proclaiming: "The extermination of human beings is per se wrong, even if it is purportedly done in the interests of society; but it is particularly evil if it is carried out against the innocent and defenseless people of alien races or alien descent."[43] The pastoral letters of the German bishops have been published in full.[44] They vindicate Albert Einstein's 1940 statement in that the only organization in Nazi Germany that stood up against Nazi evil was the Church.[45]

In a recent, detailed study of Nazi attitudes towards Christianity, Richard Steigmann-Gall evaluated the attitude of the German clergy towards National Socialism.[46] He wrote that "the Catholic Church opposed the Nazi Party" not only because of its attacks against the Church, "but also for the Nazis' racialist dogma and extreme nationalism."[47] Steigmann-Gall noted that "in several parts of Germany, Catholics were explicitly forbidden to become members of the Nazi Party, and Nazi members were forbidden to take part in church ceremonies and funerals."[48] Perhaps of greatest importance was Steigmann-Gall's ultimate conclusion that: "Those isolated Catholic churchmen who publically supported Nazism . . . were the exceptions that proved the rule. . . . [A]lmost none in the ideological or political leadership of the party were active participants in Catholic Church life. Concomitantly, the Catholic Church hierarchy refused all formal contact with the party before 1933."[49]

A report from the Nuremberg prosecutor's office outlines dozens of cases where Catholic priests were persecuted due to their opposition to the Nazis.[50] It also shows that the Nazis took steps to silence the Church: "On 28 October 1935 the Propaganda Ministry imposed censorship before publication on all Church periodicals, and on 30 November 1935 this was extended to all writings and picture material multigraphed for distribution."[51] After 1937, the German Catholic bishops gave up attempts to print their pastorals, and had them merely read from the pulpit.[52] Of course, sometimes it was impossible even to read statements from the pulpit. The Bavarian bishops' pastoral letter of September 4, 1938, was confiscated and forbidden, as was the pastoral letter of the Bishops Conference of Fulda, dated August 19, 1938.[53]

Hitler certainly did not see the Catholic clergy in Germany as his allies. In 1941, he complained bitterly about the Catholic clergy turning against the State.[54] He claimed that many priests were leaving the Church (for the State) but added that he would be unable to convert the pope.[55] In 1942, Hitler said: "The evil that's gnawing our vitals is our priests, of both creeds. . . . It's all written down in my big book. The time will come when I'll settle my accounts with them."[56] On August 11, 1942, he expressed his frustration:

> I'll make these damned parsons feel the power of the State in a way they never would have dreamed possible! For the moment I am just keeping my eye on them; if I ever have the slightest suspicion that they are getting dangerous, I will shoot the lot of them. This filthy reptile raises its head wherever there is a sign of weakness in the State, and therefore it must be stamped on whenever it does so. We have no sort of use for a fairy story invented by the Jews. . . . The foulest of the carrion are those who come clothed in the cloak of humility, and the foulest of the foul is Count Preysing! What a beast! . . . The uselessness of the parson is nowhere better illustrated than here at the front. Here we have enemies who are dying by the million—and without a single one of these liars. The Catholic Church has but one desire, and that is to see us destroyed.[57]

Hitler also called Christianity one of the two great scourges (along with the pox) in history, and complained bitterly that: "the priests continue to incite the faithful against the State."[58]

Hitler verbally attacked the German bishops at a mass rally in the Berlin *Lustgarten*.[59] He later said: "Now, the priests' chief activity consists in undermining National-Socialist policy."[60] In 1934, ss Chief Heinrich Himmler circulated a fifty-page memorandum complaining about hostile clergy.[61] His plan was to let "each petty little district" have its own pope.[62]

One particular charge set forth against German clergy is that they collaborated by turning over to the Nazis documents that could be used to identify who was or was not Jewish. Actually, much of this information was already available to the Nazis by virtue of the German census. To the extent that information was uniquely in the hands of the clergy, and was demanded by the Nazis (with severe threats), the collaboration of the German Catholic clergy was far from wholesale. As early as 1946, Monsignor Johann B. Neuhäusler, who himself was imprisoned in Dachau, published a massive series of primary documents demonstrating extensive Church resistance to Nazi anti-Semitism, including refusal to hand over genealogical records.[63]

MICHAEL CARDINAL FAULHABER

Daniel Goldhagen singled out a number of German clergy members as having been too accommodating to the National Socialists. His targets were very poorly chosen. Declassified documents from the oss show that American intelligence during the war knew well that two of the German Catholic leaders Goldhagen focused upon (Cardinal Faulhaber of Munich and Bishop von Galen of Münster) were particularly strong in their opposition to the Nazis.[64]

When Nuncio Pacelli wrote to Rome in 1923 complaining about the Nazi persecution of Catholics, he noted that the attacks "were especially focused" on the "learned and zealous " Michael Cardinal Faulhaber, who "had denounced the persecutions against the Jews."[65] In the 1930s, Cardinal Faulhaber wrote Secretary of State Pacelli, describing the persecution of the Jews as "unjust and painful."[66] In 1935, at an open meeting, Nazis called for him to be killed.[67] In February 1936, Nazi police confiscated and destroyed one of his sermons. This happened twice again the following year.[68] On October 25, 1936, members of the Hitler Youth hurled insults at him as he was entering his car.[69] In August 1938, the Nazis ransacked his office.[70] In late November 1938, after he had given a speech, a uniformed detachment arrived in front of his residence and threw stones at the windows. They shouted "Take the traitor to Dachau" and shattered window frames and shutters.[71] In May 1939, demonstrations against Faulhaber took place throughout Bavaria, and posters were hung which read: "Away with Faulhaber, the friend of the Jews and the agent of Moscow."[72] After the war began, Cardinal Faulhaber relied upon Pius XII's encyclical *Summi Pontificatus* (*Darkness over the Earth*)[73] in an address condemning Nazis, resulting in a headline reading "Cardinal Faulhaber Indicts Hitlerism" in the London *Tablet*.[74]

On page 178 of his book, Goldhagen has a photograph of a prelate who seems to be at a ceremony alongside some Nazis. The caption beneath the photo reads: "Cardinal Michael Faulhaber marches between rows of SA men at a Nazi rally in Munich."[75] In fact, the photo shows papal nuncio Cesare Orsenigo, not Bavarian bishop Faulhaber, and the city is not Munich, but Berlin. Moreover, it is not a Nazi rally but a May Day labor parade. As nuncio and ex-officio dean of the diplomatic corps, Orsenigo was expected to attend such functions.[76] A spokesman for the archdiocese of Munich reported that Faulhaber "never attended a Nazi demonstration."[77] The archdiocese of Munich obtained a court order blocking the distribution of Goldhagen's book in Germany because of the falsely captioned picture.[78] Surely someone could have verified this photograph, had the author, editors, and publisher not been so anxious to distort the truth.[79]

Rev. Martin Niemoeller, a noted German Protestant leader who spent seven years in concentration camps for his opposition to Hitler and the Nazis, said that Faulhaber's sermons showed him "to be a great and courageous man."[80] Niemoeller went on to say that Faulhaber's "sermons are monuments to the Christian faith, and they will be remembered forever."[81]

In his 1945 memorandum to General Donovan, Fabian von Schlabrendorff praised Faulhaber for stating his opposition to the Nazis and
influencing other Catholics to do the same. Schlabrendorff reported
that "decisive credit" for the Catholic opposition to Nazism "ought to
be given to Cardinal von Faulhaber from Munich and whose personal
sermons branded Nazism as the enemy of Christendom."[82]

After the war, Rabbi Stephen S. Wise, one of the leading American
voices for the Jewish cause, called Faulhaber "a true Christian prelate"
who "had lifted his fearless voice" in defense of the Jews.[83] In fact, Wise
said that Faulhaber had been a much better friend to the Jews of Europe
than even the widely heralded Martin Niemoeller.[84]

BISHOP CLEMENS AUGUST GRAF VON GALEN

Bishop (later Cardinal) Clemens August Graf von Galen also took a
leading role in opposing Nazi racial laws from the very beginning.[85]
On February 9, 1936, he made a public anti-Nazi speech at Xanten
Cathedral. In response, the Nazis charged that Galen was trying to
shelter "the corrupters of our race."[86] Galen (like Secretary of State
Pacelli) helped Pius XI draft the anti-Nazi encyclical *Mit brennender
Sorge*.[87] During the war, it was written of him that "Without the slightest
regard for his personal safety, he has not hesitated to write or telegraph
Hitler direct whenever he has violated the Concordat. The Bishop
has gone in person to the highest authorities in the land in order to
lodge a long series of vigorous protests against the persecution of the
Catholic Church, and, risking his very life, he has publicly stigmatized
the Gestapo and its chief, Himmler, as murderers and despots."[88] His
reputation for standing against the Nazis became international when
news of three "amazingly bold" sermons denouncing Nazi principles
filtered to the international press in 1941.[89] Later, Pius XII sent Galen a
letter praising his "open and courageous pronouncements" and telling
him that letters he had mailed to the Holy See laid the groundwork
for Pius XII's 1942 Christmas message.[90]

Upon his death, the regional association of the Jewish communities wrote to the Capitular Vicar in Münster, saying: "Cardinal von Galen was one of the few upright and conscientious men who fought against racialism in a most difficult time. We shall always honor the memory of the deceased Bishop."[91]

Most critics make some mention of Galen's protests against the Nazi euthanasia program,[92] but they draw the wrong conclusions. Some criticize him for being outspoken against the persecution of other groups, but not against the persecution of Jews. According to the Congregation for the Causes of Saints, however, when "he wanted to speak against the persecution of the Jews in Germany, the Jewish elders of his diocese begged him not to because it would only damage them."[93]

Daniel Goldhagen argues that the Nazis did not retaliate against Galen, and he asks why the German bishops and the Vatican did not "rally behind Bishop Galen." Actually, however, on December 2, 1940—well before Galen's famous sermons against euthanasia—Pius XII published an official Vatican statement in the Catholic press that unequivocally condemned the killing of "life unworthy of life."[94] This decree went into every diocese in Germany, and was favorably and publicly commented on by the German bishops.[95] On March 9, 1941, in a public sermon, then-Bishop Konrad von Preysing (whom Goldhagen wrongly portrays as a critic of Pius XII) made reference to Pius XII, "whom we all know—I should say from personal experience—as a man of global horizons and broadmindedness [who] has reaffirmed the doctrine of the Church, according to which there is no justification and no excuse for the killing of the sick or of the abnormal on any economic or eugenic grounds."[96] Other German bishops followed suit,[97] culminating in (not beginning with) Galen's famous sermons of July and August of 1941.

To compound his errors, Goldhagen (like some other critics) charges that Galen's protests were successful in ending the euthanasia program and that the Nazis did not retaliate. In fact, the euthanasia campaign was not ended, but continued under greater secrecy until the end of the war.[98] Moreover, there was retaliation. As one of Galen's successors, Reinhard Lettmann, the Bishop of Münster, explained: "After having preached these sermons the Bishop was prepared to be arrested by the Gestapo. . . . The Bishop was deeply dejected when in his place twenty-four secular priests and thirteen members of the regular clergy were deported into concentration camps, of whom ten lost their lives."[99]

In 1942, Hitler expressed his plans for Galen: "I am quite sure that a man like the Bishop von Galen knows full well that after the war I shall extract retribution to the last farthing. And, if he does not succeed in getting himself transferred in the meanwhile to the Collegium Germanicum in Rome, he may rest assured that in the balancing of our accounts, no 'T' will remain uncrossed, no 'I' undotted."[100] Hitler vowed that "The Bishop of Münster will one day face a firing squad."[101] The Nuremberg prosecution report shows that Galen was at times forbidden to speak to the public or to give blessings.[102] In fact, as a result of his outspokenness, Galen's diocese suffered a far higher death rate than most others.[103] None of these crucial facts are recited by the critics who claim that the Nazis did not retaliate against Galen.

The Catholic Church is considering Galen for sainthood, and it has already recognized his "heroic virtue."[104] Perhaps the final assessment, however, should be left to the Jewish Anti-Defamation League, the world's leading organization fighting anti-Semitism. In a press release dated December 28, 2004, the ADL commended the Vatican for clearing the way for the beatification of Galen. The release said: "'Cardinal von Galen, ignoring great personal risks, refused to remain silent in the face of Nazi atrocities,' said Abraham H. Foxman, ADL National Director, and Rabbi Gary Bretton-Granatoor, ADL Director of Interfaith Affairs. 'He is credited with stopping advancement of Nazi euthanasia programs and was a passionate advocate speaking out against the persecution of European Jewry.'"[105]

ADOLPH CARDINAL BERTRAM

Cardinal Adolph Bertram of Breslau, also singled out by the critics for being too friendly towards the Nazis, first expressed his opposition to National Socialism in 1930, when he refused a religious funeral for a well-known Nazi official.[106] In a widely publicized statement, he criticized as grave error the one-sided glorification of the Nordic race and the contempt for divine revelation that was increasingly taught throughout Germany. He warned against the ambiguity of the concept of "positive Christianity," a highly nationalistic religion that the Nazis were encouraging. Such a religion, he said, "for us Catholics cannot have a satisfactory meaning since everyone interprets it in the way he pleases."[107]

In his New Year's message for 1931, Bertram reiterated his warning against false prophets, declaring that by glorifying race, extreme nationalism could only lead to rejection of the commandments of God.[108] "Away therefore with the vain imaginings of a national religious society, which is to be torn away from the Rock of Peter, and only guided by the racial theories of an Aryan-heathen teaching about salvation. This is no more than the foolish imaginings of false prophets."[109] On nationalism, he said: "There is a nationalism that justifies itself, and its characteristics are love of the mother tongue, devotion to one's own people and the customs of the country, and recognition to God for all hereditary advantages. All this is justified so long as truth and charity are not offended. It is justified only so long as one keeps an eye open to the value of other races and nations and recognizes God as the Creator of the soul, as the distributor of all the gifts of nature and sees in the progress of races and nations the evolution of the handiwork of God."[110]

In response to Bertram, the Nazi press cited some of Pope Leo XIII's pronouncements about the relations of practicing Catholics to political parties to bolster the argument that Catholics could be National Socialists. Secretary of State Pacelli then ordered a lengthy article to be published in the Vatican newspaper correcting the Nazis' distortions of Leo's pronouncements, and saying that a Christian should not belong to any political party which works against Christian ideals.[111]

In 1933, Bertam wrote a pastoral letter concerning his "grievous and gnawing anxiety" concerning the safety of Catholic organizations (particularly Catholic Action), the freedom of Catholic charitable efforts, Catholic youth groups, freedom of the press, and political prisoners.[112] His circular letter to the bishops voiced concern over Nazi control over the government.[113]

It is true that Bertram originally disagreed with other German bishops about how best to counter Hitler, but this does not imply any sympathy for Hitler. He, at first, hoped to reduce the government's hostility by avoiding unnecessary criticism of the state.[114] "Unlike von Galen, Faulhaber, or Preysing, Bertram opposed mobilizing public opinion to any extent against the regime. His main weapon was the petition and the memo addressed to the bureaucratic apparatus of the state."[115] As he explained in a letter to the other bishops, dated March 25, 1933, Bertram was concerned that by keeping National Socialists out of the Church until Hitler proved that he would keep his promises, the salvation of many individuals was being put at risk.[116]

The bishops took Bertram's advice, and on March 28 issued a joint episcopal letter indicating a desire to cooperate with the new government.[117] The experiment was short-lived. On April 6, the bishops sent their first letter of protest to the new government.[118] (Two days before that, the pope instructed the papal nuncio to intervene with the new government on behalf of the Jews.)[119] Hitler's comments on Bertram suggest that while the bishop was willing to work with him shortly after he came to power, the relationship quickly soured.[120]

Rev. Martin Niemoeller, while serving time in a Nazi concentration camp, spoke of Bertram to a Jewish friend. "He mentioned the example of the Cardinal of Breslau, who, when the Nazis threatened him with internment in a concentration camp, replied, 'Nothing would give me greater happiness than to suffer and die for the Holy Church.'"[121]

Critics have also claimed that Bertram scheduled a requiem Mass upon Hitler's death.[122] In point of fact, this is what is known: Bertram was elderly and ill when the war ended. When he died (just weeks later), his papers included a handwritten order scheduling a requiem Mass for all Germans who died in the war, including Hitler (who was originally reported to have died while fighting), and for the protection of the Catholic Church in Germany. This order was never issued, and the Mass was never held. Bertam's personal secretary later reported being unaware of this paper or any such proposed order. In fact, the order itself was crossed through with two broad strokes. In other words, the evidence suggests that someone (perhaps Bertram, but perhaps someone else) considered scheduling a requiem Mass but that Bertram canceled it. Particularly deceptive in this matter is Klaus Scholder's book *A Requiem for Hitler and Other New Perspectives on the German Church Struggle*.[123] The cover of that book shows part of the order, but omits the portion showing that it was crossed through.

NAZI PERSECUTION OF CATHOLIC LEADERS

The lead article in the February 1939 issue of *Reader's Digest* explained the situation in Germany for the Catholic Church on the verge of World War II. Entitled "Nazi Scapegoat Number 2," it painted an ugly picture that too many modern commentators have forgotten:

> Nuns in Nazi prisons, priests in concentration camps, Catholic leaders shot, Cardinals' homes wrecked—Americans read such news and, shocked at the barbarism of the Reich, are puzzled besides. . . .
>
> As Hilaire Belloc, the eminent Catholic writer, admitted, the conflict between Catholicism and Nazism is "beyond all reconciliation." One or the other must destroy its opponent.

The *Völkischer Beobachter*, principal Nazi party organ, in its Vienna edition of October 15, 1938, says flatly, "We are armed to continue the battle against Catholicism until the point of total annihilation."

German Catholics are facing the same fate as the Jews. They are Nazi Scapegoat No. 2.[124]

In 1940, Pope Pius XII helped smuggle to London the documents that were published in *The Persecution of the Catholic Church in the Third Reich*. This book is a collection of protests, reports, and accounts that demonstrate the abuse suffered by the Church at the hands of the National Socialists throughout the 1930s. To review these reports is to wonder how German Catholic leaders were able to stand as firmly against the National Socialists as they did.

In May and June 1934, SS chief Heinrich Himmler circulated a fifty-page memorandum on the religious bodies in the Reich. Under the heading "Hostile Clergy," it reported:

The most dangerous activity of countless Catholic clergy is the way in which they 'mope about,' spreading despondency. Favorite topics are the 'dangers of a new time,' 'the present emergency,' 'the gloomy future.' Prophecies are made about the speedy downfall of National Socialism or at the very least mention is made of the transience of all political phenomena, compared with the Catholic Church which will outlive them all. National Socialist achievements and successes are passed over in silence.

There is thus a deliberated undermining of the very basis of the National Socialist programme of reconstruction, the people's trust in the leadership of the state.[125]

Before long Hitler had anti-Nazi Catholic priests imprisoned on immorality charges. Erich Klausener, leader of Catholic Action, was murdered in a June 1934 purge. Hundreds of priests and Catholic officials were arrested or driven into exile, while others were accused of violating currency regulations or morality rules.[126] The campaign was "intended to destroy the loyalty felt by Catholics for their clergy and especially for members of religious orders."[127]

In 1940, the Germans decided to put all priests from the concentration camps into one location where they could be tightly controlled. They were kept together in Dachau Barracks 26, 28, and 30 (later they were squeezed into barracks 26 and 28 which had room and beds for 360, even though there were rarely fewer than 1,500 priests interned there). These barracks were ringed with a barbed-wire fence, which restricted the ability of priests to minister to other prisoners during their few free hours.[128]

These Dachau priests worked in the enormous ss industrial complex immediately to the west of the camp, but the Nazis had other uses for them as well. Some were injected with pus so that the Nazi doctors could study gangrene; others had their body temperature lowered to study resuscitation of German fliers downed in the North Atlantic; one priest was crowned with barbed wire and a group of Jewish prisoners was forced to spit on him.[129] Fr. Stanislaus Bednarski, a Pole, was hanged on a cross. In November 1944, three priests were executed "not because they were criminals," as one judge stated, "but because it was their tragedy that they were Catholic priests."[130]

As the tide of the war began to turn, and the Germans needed to get all the labor possible out of the prisoners, the ss decided to use these generally well-educated prisoner-priests as secretaries and managers. With priests in the offices where they could manipulate labor schedules, they were able to engage in forms of sabotage. Thus, a planned gas oven at Dachau never became functional due, at least in part, to the efforts of these imprisoned Catholic priests.[131]

On March 2, 1943, Cardinal Maglione sent a long letter to German Foreign Minister Joachim von Ribbentrop protesting the Nazi persecution of the Catholic Church in Poland. The letter cited atrocity after atrocity. "No less painful was the fate reserved for the regular clergy," the cardinal wrote. "Many religious were shot or otherwise killed; the great majority of the others were imprisoned, deported or expelled."[132]

In an allocution to the Sacred College on June 2, 1945, which was also broadcast on Vatican Radio, Pius noted the death of about two thousand Catholic priests at Dachau and described National Socialism as "the arrogant apostasy from Jesus Christ, the denial of His doctrine and of His work of redemption, the cult of violence, the idolatry of race and blood, the overthrow of human liberty and dignity."[133] With "the satanic apparition of National Socialism" out of the way, Pius expressed his confidence that Germany would "rise to a new dignity and a new life." He went on to point out that Nazi persecution of the Catholic Church both in Germany and occupied nations had been continuous, and that he had been aware of Nazism's ultimate goal: "its adherents boasted that once they had gained the military victory, they would put an end to the Church forever. Authorities and incontrovertible witnesses kept Us informed of this intention."[134]

The Vatican's efforts to win freedom for its bishops and priests imprisoned in Dachau were all frustrated, but no one really doubts the Holy See's desire to win their freedom. Pope Pius XII used no different technique in his efforts to help Catholic priests than he did when trying to help Jewish peasants.[135] In each case, his words and actions were calculated so as to achieve the best results for the victims. As one bishop who was imprisoned at Dachau reported: "The detained priests trembled every time news reached us of some protest by religious authority, but particularly by the Vatican. We all had the impression that our wardens made us atone heavily for the fury these protests evoked . . . whenever the way we were treated became more brutal, the Protestant pastors among the prisoners used to vent their indignation on the Catholic priests: 'Again your big naive Pope and those simpletons, your bishops, are shooting their mouths off . . . why don't they get the idea once and for all, and shut up. They play the heroes and we have to pay the bill.'"[136]

THE CATHOLIC CHURCH AND FORCED LABOR

During World War II, Nazi victims faced one of two fates. They were killed, or they were conscripted into forced labor. These slave laborers came primarily from Poland and other occupied nations in eastern Europe. Most workers were poorly housed, badly fed, and made to work long hours at backbreaking work.

In recent years there has been an effort to identify those firms that benefitted from these prisoner-workers and to force them to pay reparations. Germany even established a $4.6 billion fund from which surviving laborers will be compensated. All organizations that might have used slave or forced labor, including the churches, were called on to contribute.

It turns out that in the wartime German economy, when most able-bodied men were off fighting for the Fatherland, almost every operating entity benefitted in some way from forced labor. In the year 2000, the German Evangelical Church admitted that it had used such labor and agreed to pay 10 million marks ($5,660,000) into the fund. Attention then focused on the Catholic Church.

Since almost all Catholic records from that era were destroyed during the Nazi persecutions, there was no evidence in the central archives that the Church had used forced laborers. Accordingly, the German bishops checked ss records and the archives of other churches. They determined that, indeed, some parishes had used prisoners.[137]

Rudolf Hammerschmidt, a spokesman for the Episcopal Conference, said a special working group discovered forced labor had indeed been used in fields, vineyards, and hospitals of the Catholic dioceses. "We think we can put together records that establish 30 to 40 cases of forced labor," he said.[138] Some other estimates are higher, but Karl Lehmann, chairman of the German Catholic Bishops Conference, said the Catholic Church did not use slave labor "in a significant way."[139]

German bishops agreed to match the amount of money that the Evangelical Church promised to pay—10 million marks.[140] This was in line with similar contributions (totaling at least 27 million marks) that the German Catholic Church has donated to Nazi victims in the recent past. The bishops, however, denied that the forced laborers who worked for the Church were badly treated.

Most of the laborers used by the Catholic Church worked as household servants and in agriculture. No cases have come to light of workers for the Catholic Church being forced to do hard labor. "Sources uncovered so far show that the conditions of slave laborers in Catholic-run facilities were not comparable with those of slave laborers in industry and the munitions factories," said Georg Konen, chairman of a federation which represents Catholics in industry and administration.[141]

The German bishops agreed to a 10 million mark donation, but they opted not to pay it into the official government fund. Instead, 5 million marks were paid by the Church's Caritas social agency, and an additional 5 million marks were set aside for use by Catholic social organizations such as Pax Christi to further reconciliation in society as a whole.[142]

Chairman Lehmann explained that the Church had no part in the "collective guilt" of the other entities that profited from the slave labor.[143] The abuses noted above only begin to scratch the surface of the ways in which the Church was victimized by the Nazis. The agreement of the German bishops to continue donating money to other victims should not be used to rewrite history and turn the Catholic Church into a perpetrator. It should be seen for what it is—a praiseworthy act of Christian charity.

EDITH STEIN

Edith Stein was canonized in 1998 by the Catholic Church as St. Teresa Benedicta of the Cross. Though born to a Jewish family, she quit practicing her faith by her teenage years. She joined the Catholic Church in 1922 and eventually became a leading voice in the Catholic Woman's movement in Germany.[144] In 1934 she relinquished her life as an author and lecturer and became a cloistered nun in the Carmelite order, taking the name Teresa Benedicta of the Cross. After *Kristallnacht*, when Nazis in Germany terrorized so many Jews, Edith and her sister moved to a convent in Holland.

Recounting what happened next, most papal critics fail to provide important details. Dutch bishops had warned their followers about the dangers of Nazism as early as 1934,[145] and in 1936 they ordered Catholics not to support Fascist organizations or they would risk excommunication.[146] They forbade Catholic policemen from hunting down Jews, even if it meant losing their jobs.[147]

At first, Jewish converts to Christianity were exempted from deportation. Nevertheless, the leaders of the Protestant and Catholic churches in Holland agreed to read a public protest against the deportations. The Nazis replied that the holy men should keep quiet or things would get worse. The Catholic Archbishop of Utrecht ignored this warning and had the following letter read in all of the Catholic churches on July 26, 1942:

> Ours is a time of great tribulations of which two are foremost: the sad destiny of the Jews and the plight of those departed for forced labor . . . all of us must be aware of the terrible sufferings which both of them have to undergo, due to no guilt of their own. . . . we have learned with deep pain of the new dispositions which impose upon innocent Jewish men, women and children, the deportation into foreign lands. . . . the incredible suffering which these measures cause to more than 10,000 people is in absolute opposition to the Divine Precepts of Justice and Charity. . . . let us pray to God and for the intercession of Mary . . . that He may lend His Strength to the people of Israel, so sorely tried in anguish and persecution.[148]

Far from making things better, this statement led to Nazi retaliation.[149]

On July 30, 1942, a memorandum from the ss declared: "Since the Catholic bishops—without being involved—have interfered in these affairs, the entire population of Catholic Jews will now be sent off this week yet. No intervention will be considered."[150] Up until this time, a Dutch Jew holding a Catholic baptismal certificate was exempt from deportation. As part of the Church's rescue efforts, such certificates were distributed freely during the war.[151] Now, however, they no longer protected the holder.

The official announcement from the General-Kommissar stated: "If the Catholic clergy can thus ignore negotiations, then we in turn are forced to consider the Catholic full-blooded Jews as our worst opponents and to take measures to ship them off to the East as quickly as possible."[152] Since Protestant leaders had refrained from making statements that outraged the Germans, Jews holding Protestant baptismal certificates were not deported. Jewish converts to Catholicism (including Edith Stein and her sister—neither of whom survived the war) and Jews with false Catholic baptismal certificates, however, were deported.[153]

Of particular importance to the papal critics is a letter written by Stein in 1933. The letter was only recently made public (though it had been known about for some time). It makes the case for a papal statement regarding Nazi persecution of Jews and Catholics, as such it has been used to argue that Stein was angry about the papal approach to the war (the letter was written to Pius xi, though critics also use it against Pius xii). It turns out, however, critics were wrong in thinking that Stein wanted a papal encyclical on the matter. As the Vatican analyst for cnn explained when the letter was finally made public: "She wrote this letter in April of 1933, complaining about Nazi persecution of the Jews to Pius xi. Now a lot of people have long believed that in that letter she asked the Pope to write an encyclical letter. That's a major papal document condemning the Nazis. And the fact that Pius didn't do it has been used as part of the campaign against him. What we now know, as of yesterday morning, once that letter is on the record, is that the she did not make any such request. So at least in that way, it resolves a historical debate in favor of the Vatican's position."[154]

It was long known that the Holy See replied by sending a papal blessing to Stein. It was not known until recently, however, that the Pope had already sent a message to the papal nuncio in Berlin on April 4, 1933, instructing him to intervene with the new government on behalf of the Jews.[155] In other words, the Pope had anticipated Stein's concern and acted on it before he got her letter. Because it was a delicate diplomatic matter, the reply did not explain all of this to Stein, who was a layperson, not yet a nun, at the time of her letter.[156]

Contrary to what the critics would have their readers believe, Stein was not upset with the Vatican. She did, after all, become a nun after this letter was sent. Additionally, later in 1933 she sent a gift to the Holy See—her new two volume translation of St. Thomas Aquinas's writings. Later, when Pacelli became Pope Pius XII, Stein grew even closer to the papacy.

Stein first met Pacelli in the 1920s, when he gave a speech in Speyer, Germany, at St. Magdalen's Convent, where Stein was teaching. She warmly saluted Pacelli in the welcoming speech, and she kept those warm feelings over the years. In her collected letters there is one dated November 17, 1940, in which Stein wrote: "Next Sunday we will be united with the Holy Father in the prayer campaign."[157] In another letter dated July 10, 1940, she writes of the tremendous Church struggle and "fight" against Nazism and her prediction of the ultimate "victory" of the Church over Nazism.[158]

It has even been suggested that Pope Pius XI's 1937 encyclical, *Mit brennender Sorge*, one of the strongest condemnations of any national regime that the Holy See ever published, was written in answer to her letter.[159] In her July 10, 1940 letter, Stein wrote favorably about a pastoral letter written by Bishop Lemmens (her bishop). That pastoral letter was dated February 11, 1939, right after Pius XI's death, and it repeatedly quoted from *Mit brennender Sorge*. In her letter, Stein mentioned that Bishop Lemmens was interrogated by the Nazis, who had just overrun Holland, and she praised him for giving this pastoral letter to the Nazis who interrogated him. Stein marveled at his courage, and said how right he was to give this pastoral, so that the Nazis might learn from this letter which repeatedly invoked *Mit brennender Sorge*.[160]

On a related note, in an article entitled "The Saint and the Holocaust," in the June 7, 1999 edition of the *New Yorker*, critic and excommunicated former priest James Carroll argued that by declaring Edith Stein a saint, the Catholic Church elevated her death above that of six million Jews and in the process may have "subverted" the value of Edith Stein's life. Carroll argued that Stein was killed because she was Jewish. This is true. Had she not been Jewish the Nazis would not have deported her at that time. However, if Carroll had quoted the Nazi statements mentioned above, he would have had to acknowledge that Stein was deported due to her Catholicism as well.

To make his point, Carroll reported that on her way to Auschwitz, Stein was supposedly offered the opportunity to use her baptism as a shield from deportation. She declined the offer, according to Carroll, saying: "Why should there be an exception made in the case of a particular group? Wasn't it fair that baptism not be allowed to become an advantage?"

This decision to decline an offer of freedom (and, indeed, life itself) seems particularly noble, even saintly. Carroll, however, gives this act of selflessness an unusual interpretation, arguing that in declining this offer, Edith was not being selfless and noble. Rather, Carroll would have us believe that Stein was rejecting her baptism and the Catholicism that she had adopted twenty years earlier and had fully devoted her life to for the previous nine years. This is a very strained interpretation of her reported words. Perhaps more telling is Carroll's willingness to use this statement at all, much less to build a central argument around it.

Carroll acknowledges that the story came out years after Stein had been deported and killed and that it came from a Dutch official who claimed to have met Stein in a transit camp on her way to Auschwitz.

It is reasonable to be suspect of any unconfirmed, self-serving memory that is asserted years after the fact, but there is an even greater reason to be suspicious in this case.

The focus of Nazi deportation at this time was on Jews who had been baptized into the Catholic Church. Therefore, it is very unlikely that someone would have asked whether one of the numerous Catholic Jews would want to use her baptism in order to avoid deportation. Far more likely is the account given by other sources, that Stein was offered the opportunity to use her status as a nun to avoid the concentration camp. That story, however, would not have fit with Carroll's premise that Stein was rejecting her religion.

Relating a story about his study of Edith Stein when he was a young seminarian, Carroll says "it never occurred to us then that there could be something offensive to Jews in our honoring her as a young woman in search of the truth." He now suggests that there is something wrong with honoring this young woman who went in search of the truth. The only real reason he has given for that is that she was born Jewish. That seems to be a most inappropriate reason.

4

Eugenio Pacelli: Pope Pius XII

During the ten years of Nazi terror, when our
people went through the horrors of martyrdom, the
Pope raised his voice to condemn the persecutors
and to commiserate with their victims.
Golda Meir (From the United Nations, 1958)[1]

POPE PIUS XII, the Church's 260th Pope, was born in Rome on March 2, 1876, as Eugenio Maria Giuseppe Giovanni Pacelli. His family had a long history of service to the Holy See. Eugenio's grandfather, Marcantonio Pacelli, entered the service of the Holy See in 1819, where he ultimately became Under Secretary of the Interior and helped to establish the Vatican's newspaper, *L'Osservatore Romano.* Eugenio's father, Filippo Pacelli, served as a counselor to the Holy See and head of the Bank of Rome. He also belonged to the so-called "Black Nobility." Members of this group stood by the Church during the "Roman Question," when the Vatican was in conflict with Italy (1870-1929). Eugenio's brother, Francesco Pacelli, was right-hand man to the Vatican secretary of state, Cardinal Pietro Gasparri, during the negotiations with Benito Mussolini that led to the historic Lateran Treaty and the end of the Roman Question.

Young Eugenio was an exceptional student, and he was accepted into a prestigious seminary in Rome, the Capranica. He excelled in all of his studies, particularly languages. He became fluent in Latin, Greek, English, French, German, Spanish, Portuguese, Hebrew, and Aramaic. He also took classes at another great seminary, the Gregoriana. His demanding schedule caused him to develop a hacking cough, and the family doctor warned that he was on the brink of tuberculosis. That nearly ended Eugenio's study, but he had been noticed by Pope Leo XIII who permitted young Pacelli to live at home while completing his courses. He was ordained on Easter Sunday, April 2, 1899.

Pope Leo XIII had a program for training exceptional young clerics to serve in the Vatican diplomatic service, and two years after Pacelli was ordained, Cardinal Gasparri invited him into this program. Leo died in 1903, but the next year, the new pope, Pius X, named Pacelli a monsignor and assigned him to a team that was charged with codifying Church canon law. For the next fifteen years, Pacelli served as a research aide in the office of the Congregation of Ecclesiastical Affairs. He also served as the pope's *Minutante*, editing and correcting the pope's speeches and minutes, and as a personal envoy from the pope to the Austrian Emperor.

In 1914, Pius X named Cardinal Gasparri Vatican secretary of state, and Pacelli was promoted to the post Gasparri vacated, secretary of the Congregation of Ecclesiastical Affairs. Pope Pius X died later this same year and was replaced by Pope Benedict XV. When World War I broke out, Pacelli and Gasparri were charged with maintaining liaison with the hierarchies on both sides of the conflict, answering appeals for aid from all over Europe, and organizing a war relief program.

In the summer of 1917, the papal representative to Bavaria, Archbishop Giuseppe Aversa, passed away. With Germany at the center of a war that affected most of Europe, the pope needed to send a replacement immediately. Benedict consecrated Pacelli as bishop in a special ceremony in the Sistine Chapel and at the same time elevated him to the rank of Archbishop. Pacelli was then sent off to Munich.

Pacelli soon became a common sight in the streets of Munich, distributing food and clothing to those who were impoverished. He has been credited with helping sixty-five thousand prisoners of war return home. In 1920 he was also appointed first apostolic nuncio to Germany, and he eventually established two nunciatures, one in Munich and one in Berlin.

In 1929, Pacelli was recalled to Rome and elevated to the cardinalate. Early the next year he was made secretary of state. Working with Pope Pius XI, Pacelli opposed the expansion of nationalistic politics, particularly in Italy and Germany. In 1933 he negotiated on behalf of the Vatican for an agreement that was instrumental in protecting Catholics and the Church from the Nazis. He also made trips on behalf of the Pope to France, the United States, Buenos Aires, and Hungary.

On March 2, 1939, Pacelli became the first secretary of state to be elected pope since Clement IX in 1667.[2] He crusaded for peace before and throughout World War II, and he forcefully denounced the extermination of peoples on account of race.[3] Through the Pontifical Aid Commission, he operated a vast program of relief for all victims of the war. When Hitler occupied Rome in September 1943, Pius opened Vatican City to refugees of all backgrounds.

It is commonly estimated that the Church under Pius aided more than half a million Jewish refugees during the war.[4] With his encouragement, a vast underground of priests, religious, and laity throughout Italy and the rest of Europe served as a covert organization dedicated to protecting Jewish and non-Jewish refugees from the Nazis.

The end of the war saw Pius XII hailed as "the inspired moral prophet of victory," and he enjoyed near-universal acclaim for aiding European Jews through diplomatic initiatives, thinly veiled public pronouncements, and the unprecedented continent-wide network of sanctuary.[5] With the end of hostilities, the Pope concentrated on try-ing to help people recover from the ravages of war. Papal money was sent to every war-torn nation and distributed without regard to race, creed, or nationality.

Throughout the war, Pius had feared that a Soviet victory would mean that eastern Europe would fall to Communism, and after the Al-lies' victory much of it did. The Soviets established several satellite state governments that were beholden to (if not dominated by) Moscow. In light of the Church's history with Communism, Pius was afraid that the spread of Soviet influence would bring persecution to the Church, and in many places that is what happened. He actively worked to limit the Communist influence in Western Europe, especially in Italy.

Until failing health forced him to restrict his activities, Pius XII was extraordinarily accessible. He celebrated more public masses and held more private audiences than any of his recent predecessors had, and each week he held a special audience just for newlyweds. He also used television and radio to reach out directly to the people.

In December 1954, Pius fell seriously ill, and his physicians feared for his life, but he recovered his strength and returned to work. Dur-ing this illness, Pius reported an apparition of the Lord. After this, the crowds drawn to him grew even larger.

In July 1958, Pius XII summoned his last ounce of energy for the necessary paperwork that included nominations for six new auxiliary bishops in Poland. One of the openings was in the Kraków archdiocese. He signed the nomination of Karol Wojtyla (who would go on to be Pope John Paul II), to be the titular Bishop of Ombia and auxiliary bishop in Kraków. It was Pius XII's final great historic act. He died on October 9, 1958, at Castel Gandolfo.

During his pontificate, Pius expanded and internationalized the Church by creating fifty-seven new bishoprics, forty-five of them in America and Asia. He also caused the percentage of non-Italians in the College of Cardinals to rise above 50 percent, paving the way for the eventual election of a non-Italian Pope. He replaced colonial bishops with native hierarchies, approved the "Dialogue Mass," and relaxed communion fasting rules.

An ardent devotee of the Immaculate Heart of Mary, Pius consecrated the world to the Immaculate Heart in 1942 and established a Feast of the Immaculate Heart of Mary in 1945. In 1950, he issued an *ex cathedra* proclamation defining the dogma of the Assumption of Mary. Pius saw more positive elements in the ecumenical movement than did his recent predecessors.

In December 1949, shortly after the formation of the World Council of Churches, Pius formally recognized the ecumenical movement and permitted Catholic scholars to dialogue with non-Catholics on matters of faith. That same year the Holy Office issued a decree, with papal approval, stating that actual incorporation into the Catholic Church was not necessary for salvation. He also encouraged Catholic nuns to study theology, scripture, and psychology. Pius even considered calling a council which might have completely changed the face of the Church, but he ultimately decided against it due to the complexities and expense involved. His work, however, encouraged his successor, Pope John XXIII, to convene Vatican II. As others have concluded, without Pacelli, Vatican II would have been unthinkable.[6]

In 1963, Pope John XXIII passed away and was succeeded by Pope Paul VI (Cardinal Giovanni Battista Montini). In 1965, Paul proposed that "his great model," Pius XII, be considered for sainthood.[7] He has been declared "Servant of God," and the cause of his beatification is still underway.

PACELLI'S CHILDHOOD

Some critics, notably John Cornwell, begin their analysis of Pacelli's life by looking at his childhood. Because they are trying to build a case for calling Pacelli anti-Semitic, they do not mention Eugenio's boyhood friendship with a Jewish schoolmate.[8] Instead, they tell an incorrect story about the young boy's teacher.

According to Cornwell, the headmaster of Eugenio's school "was in the habit of making speeches from his high desk about the 'hard-heartedness of the Jews.'" Cornwell cites for this proposition the English translation of Nazareno Padellaro, *Portrait of Pius XII*.[9] That edition did indeed support this thesis. The original Italian version of Padellaro's work, however, provides the true quotation about young Pacelli's headmaster: he scolded "not against hard-hearted Jews, but against block-headed pupils."[10] An error in translation completely changed the meaning of the whole incident.

Another mistake about young Pacelli's schooling relates to an essay he wrote while enrolled in a secular school. According to Cornwell, "For an essay assignment on a 'favorite' historical figure, Pacelli is said to have chosen Augustine of Hippo, prompting sneers from his classmates. When he attempted to expand a little on the history of Christian civilization, a theme absent in the curriculum, his teacher chided him." Cornwell offers no citation for this incident with the authoritarian teacher, but German scholars have written on this matter. The teacher involved is Professor Della Giovanna. Cornwell, however, got the story wrong. The professor, Della Giovanna, did not chide young Eugenio; rather, Della Giovanna praised the young boy for his willingness to stand up for his beliefs.[11] The event was precisely the opposite of what Cornwell would have his readers believe.

These errors relating to Pacelli's schooling are rather trivial, but Cornwell builds them up significantly. He argues that as a young boy, Pacelli saw anti-Semitism and authoritarianism in the men he respected and goes on to argue that "the impressions gained by small children are never lost." In a similar vein, Cornwell argues that Pacelli might have read certain anti-Semitic articles and been influenced by them. Of course, "on such evidence of association, no one would escape conviction."[12] As it turns out, however, Pacelli had good teachers, and he grew to be a good man.

To support their case, some papal critics have cited a project that Pacelli worked on shortly after his ordination. In 1903, Pope Pius x assigned the young Pacelli to a team charged with codifying Church canon law. For the next decade and a half, he served as a research aide in the office of the Congregation of Ecclesiastical Affairs helping to organize Church law, which had been built up over a thousand years, into a single code that could easily be referenced. This was much more manageable than the edicts, papal encyclicals, instructions, decrees, regulations, and precedents which were confused and perhaps even contradictory. In fact, "most theologians view centralization as a vast improvement over what went before."[13] Critic John Cornwell, however, argues in *Hitler's Pope* that this code was part of Pacelli's life-long effort to centralize authority in the papacy and that is what eventually led to the rise of Hitler.

As an initial matter, codification projects reduce various pronouncements into a single code, but they do not create fundamentally different rules.[14] Certainly a junior prelate like Pacelli had no authority to write new law. Not only did the codification team have to agree that the new code reflected existing Church law, the code also had to be approved by the Pope. Pope Pius x commissioned the process, and Pope Benedict xv received and approved what became known as the 1917 Code of Canon Law. The project was carried out with a very large group of bishops and canonists all working on various portions, with a review committee of cardinals. It was then approved by the Pope and his closest advisors. If the 1917 Code reflects any personality, it is that of the Pope in office at the time of promulgation, Benedict xv. To assert that Pacelli, who was nothing more than a promising young diplomat at the time, rewrote Church law in this process is to credit him with far more authority than he (or any other individual) actually had. In fact, it is a preposterous suggestion.[15]

The first concordat about which critics complain was signed by the Vatican and Serbia in 1914. John Cornwell, in *Hitler's Pope*, argues that Pacelli was the driving force behind this concordat, and he further suggests that it helped bring about World War I.

Cornwell argues that the Serbian concordat "implied the abrogation of the ancient protectorate rights of the Austro-Hungarian Empire over the Catholic enclaves in Serbia's territories." Under this agreement, Serbia granted control over the Catholic regions in the new areas of the Balkans directly to the Vatican, rather than granting Austria extraterritorial control over Catholic property within Serbia.[16] Cornwell argues that this threatened the influence of Emperor Franz Josef. He goes on to report that "Vienna reacted to news of the concordat with outrage." He quotes opposition newspapers *Die Zeit* and *Arbeiterzeitung* expressing the anger that, according to Cornwell, led to the First World War. In manufacturing this history, Cornwell leaves out some important details.

Cornwell ominously suggests that all of the various materials were "once in the keeping of Eugenio Pacelli." Of course they were. Pacelli was a junior member of the Vatican team, and his primary obligation was to take minutes at the negotiations. This does not suggest that he was an important participant in setting terms of the agreement. In fact, it suggests precisely the opposite. As one noted historian wrote, blaming Pacelli for what took place is tantamount to blaming the "minute taker for the minutes."[17] More importantly, as others have noted, the Serbian concordat was absolutely irrelevant to the outbreak of war.[18]

For his authority that Pacelli had been warned by the papal nuncio in Vienna of the risk posed by the concordat, Cornwell cites a secondary source.[19] Vatican archives, however (in a fascicle that was signed out to John Cornwell while he was researching his book), revealed a handwritten letter from the nuncio in Vienna to the Vatican secretary of state in Rome. That letter, dated June 24, 1914, reported that Vienna had no displeasure with the negotiations for the concordat. According to that dispatch, the *opposition* press (these are the newspapers

Cornwell cites) argued that this concordat was a defeat for Austro-Hungarian diplomacy, but the serious press agreed that this was the only solution to the difficult problems regarding religious interests in Serbia.[20]

The nuncio's letter went on to explain that the Austro-Hungarian government had from the very beginning been informed about the negotiations in Rome and had followed them with "benevolent interest." A signed concordat is what Austria-Hungary had wanted for Catholics and was in accord with the government's wishes.[21] In fact, the government issued a publication noting the praiseworthiness of the proposed concordat.[22] The thesis that a power-driven Pacelli forced this concordat despite the risk of war is a wild accusation that is completely contradicted by the evidence.[23] Moreover, even if the concordat did lead to some unrest, neither Pacelli nor anyone else in the Vatican had grounds to think other than what the nuncio reported.

NUNCIO PACELLI IN GERMANY

In 1917, Pope Benedict xv sent Pacelli to Munich as papal representative. He first presented the Pope's peace plan to German leaders, then concentrated on alleviating the pain of victims, prisoners of war, and dislocated people.[24]

John Cornwell writes of Pacelli's 1917 departure from Rome to become nuncio in Munich that: "not only had Pacelli commandeered his own private compartment, but an additional sealed carriage had been added to the train to transport sixty cases of groceries to ensure that his troublesome stomach would not be affected by the food of wartime Germany." For his authority, Cornwell cites the diary of Carlo Monti, which was published by the Vatican in 1997.[25]

Monti reported the facts, as outlined above, to Pope Benedict shortly after Pacelli's departure. Monti wrote that the Pope was scandalized. However, the introduction to Monti's diary explains that Pacelli had angered Monti sometime prior to the 1917 departure by refusing to meet with him. At that time, Monti complained to Pope Benedict, hoping that he would rebuke Pacelli. The Pope, however, sided with Pacelli. Now, as Pacelli was leaving Rome, Monti again sought to have the Pontiff rebuke Pacelli. Had Benedict truly been scandalized, he certainly would have rebuked the new nuncio. He did not do so, however, because he well knew that Pacelli—who would later go on a war-rations diet and live without heat or coffee even though he had food and coal—was actually taking the food to provide for the war-torn city, prisoners of war, and others.[26] This was explained in the very text that Cornwell cited. The Pope ignored the claim by Monti with good reason. The food was destined for the the nunciatures of Munich and Vienna. Anyone who was really interested in finding the truth should have seen through this absurd charge.

Critics claim to have found two pieces of evidence from this era to support the conclusion that Pacelli was an anti-Semite. The first is a letter the nuncio wrote in 1917. A rabbi had requested Pacelli's assistance in obtaining palm fronds from Italy to be used in a synagogue festival. Pacelli welcomed the rabbi, but—in the middle of a nation torn by World War—it was not easy to comply with his request, especially since the Vatican did not have diplomatic relations with Italy at that time. In fact, with Italy and Germany at war, such assistance would have been in direct violation of Italian law. In his report back to Rome, Pacelli said that he declined to offer help because the assistance sought was not in a matter pertaining to "civil or natural rights common to all human beings," but rather in a matter pertaining to the ceremony of a "Jewish cult." Pacelli noted that the rabbi understood the difficulty and thanked him for his efforts.

The critics completely overlook the importance of Pacelli's qualification. In the report to Rome, Pacelli clearly indicated his belief that if this matter had pertained to civil or natural rights (that is, "human rights"), he would have offered help. He did not, however, see any similar duty to help another religion conduct a ceremony. To grant the request at that time would have been a violation of both trade embargos and canon law.

Another difficulty with this letter is the pejorative meaning that is today associated with the word "cult." The critics suggest that the use of this word indicates Pacelli's contempt for Judaism. The actual Italian word used by Pacelli was "culto." The first three meanings for this word in *Webster's 3rd International Dictionary* all deal with religious rites and worship. The *American Heritage Dictionary*'s first definition of cult is: "A system or community of religious worship or ritual." The word itself is derived from the Latin *cultus*, which means "worship."

The Vatican still uses the word to refer to the Church's own rites and worship, such as "the cult of the saints" and "the cult of the Virgin Mary." Thus, the word does not carry any derogatory connotation.[27] Critic John Cornwell, who first raised this issue, is well aware of this non-pejorative meaning, as he uses the term several times himself.[28] To stretch the word to include an anti-Semitic sentiment reveals the ill-disguised motive. In fact, the rabbi's willingness to approach Pacelli for help like this confirms Pacelli's well-deserved reputation for being friendly to Jews.[29]

The other controversial letter was written in 1919. That year, Bolshevik revolutionaries temporarily took power in Bavaria. Many foreign dignitaries left Munich, but Pacelli stayed at his post and became a target of Bolshevik hostility. On one occasion, a car sprayed Pacelli's residence with machine-gun fire.[30] When he called in a protest, he was told to leave the city that night or he would die.[31] (He stayed.) Another time, a small group of Bolsheviks broke into the nunciature, threatened Pacelli at gunpoint, and tried to rob him.[32] Yet another time, an angry mob descended on Pacelli's car, screaming insults and threatening to turn the car over.[33]

With the Bolsheviks in power, there was valid reason for concern. Their leaders occupied the royal palace and began operating what might best be described as a rogue government. Of particular concern to all diplomats in Munich was that the Bolsheviks violated the sovereign immunity of foreign missions and representatives. Two legations were invaded, and a car was requisitioned from another.[34] The Austro-Hungarian Consul General was arrested without cause and held for several hours.[35]

Alarmed by this behavior and concerned for the safety of people under his charge, Nuncio Pacelli sent his assistant, Monsignor Lorenzo Schioppa, to meet with the leaders of the new government. Schioppa, accompanied by a representative from the Prussian legation, met with the head of the Republic of the Councils of Munich, Eugen Levine. Their purpose was to force Levine (incorrectly identified as Levien in the later report), "to declare unequivocally if and how the actual Communist Government intends to recognize and oversee the immunities of the Diplomatic Representatives."[36]

The meeting did not go well. The only "commitment" that the representatives could get from Levine was that the Republic of Councils would recognize the extra-territoriality of the foreign legations "if, and as long as the representatives of these Powers . . . do nothing against the Republic of the Councils." Schioppa was warned that if the nuncio did anything against the new government, he would be "kicked out."[37] Levine made it clear that "they had no need of the Nunciature."[38]

Pacelli wrote a letter to Rome, reporting on this meeting. Cornwell translated a few sentences from that letter and set them forth as "proof" that Pacelli was an anti-Semite. Other critics, including Daniel Goldhagen blindly followed that translation and compounded the error. The key passage, as translated by the critics, described the palace as follows: ". . . a gang of young women, of dubious appearance, Jews like all the rest of them, hanging around in all the offices with lecherous demeanor and suggestive smiles. The boss of this female rabble was Levien's mistress, a young Russian woman, a Jew and a divorcee, who was in charge. . . . This Levien is a young man, of about thirty or thirty-five, also Russian and a Jew. Pale, dirty, with drugged eyes, hoarse voice, vulgar, repulsive, with a face that is both intelligent and sly.[39] To the critics, these words (taken from Schioppa's report to his superior, Pacelli) prove that Pacelli was an anti-Semite.

In truth, this translation is grossly distorted. It uses pejorative words, instead of neutral ones that are more faithful to the original Italian. For instance, the most damning phrase in the translation, "Jews like all the rest of them," turns out to be an inaccurate translation of the Italian phrase *i primi*. The literal translation would be "the first ones" or "the ones just mentioned."[40] In context, "also Jewish" seems most appropriate. Similarly, the Italian word *schiera* is translated by Cornwell as "gang" instead of "group," which would be more appropriate. Additionally, the Italian *gruppo femminile* should be translated as "female group" or "group of women," not "female rabble."[41]

This letter was published in its original Italian in 1992.[42] Church historian John Conway—an Anglican and a distinguished scholar—reviewed the book in which it was included for the *Catholic Historical Review*. Neither he, nor anyone else at that time, suggested that the letter was anti-Semitic. Considering the centrality of this letter to *Hitler's Pope*, one might have expected (and editors should have demanded) that Cornwell publish it in full.[43] That did not happen, however, perhaps because when the entire letter is read in an accurate translation it is not anti-Semitic. The tone of anti-Semitism is introduced only by the critics' calculated mis-translation.

Any disrespect reflected in the language that was actually used (as opposed to the mis-translation) would not stem from racial or even religious differences, but from the Bolshevik activity in Munich. There was clear animosity between the Church and the revolutionaries, and those revolutionaries are the focus of the comment, not all Jewish people.[44] In fact, this letter was describing the leaders of a rogue government. It was written fourteen years before Hitler came to power and the Jewish persecution began. The language used to describe a similar event in 1943 might well have been very different.

Rather than using unfair translations and fabricating an argument, the critics could have looked to direct, relevant evidence from that same period. During World War I, the American Jewish Committee of New York petitioned the Vatican for a statement on the "ill-treatment" suffered by Jewish people in Poland. The response came on February 9, 1916, from the office of the secretary of state, where Eugenio Pacelli was—by absolutely every account—working hand-in-hand with Cardinal Secretary of State Gasparri.[45] It said:

> The Supreme Pontiff . . . as Head of the Catholic Church, which, faithful to its divine doctrine and to its most glorious traditions, considers all men as brothers and teaches them to love one another, he never ceases to inculcate among individuals, as well as among peoples, the observance of the principles of natural law and to condemn everything which violates them. This law must be observed and respected in the case of the children of Israel, as well as of all others, because it would not be conformable to justice or to religion itself to derogate from it solely on account of religious confessions. The Supreme Pontiff at this moment feels in his fatherly heart . . . the necessity for all men of remembering that they are brothers and that their salvation lies in the return to the law of love which is the law of the gospel.[46]

This pronouncement was published in the *New York Times* on April 17, 1916, under the headline "Papal Bull Urges Equality for Jews." It also appeared in *La Civiltà Cattolica* on April 28 of that year and in the *London Tablet* on April 29. In 1936, when he was visiting the United States as Cardinal Secretary of State, Pacelli met with two officials of the American Jewish Committee, Lewis Strauss and Joseph Proskauer, and he reaffirmed this teaching, promising to make it better known.[47] The critics fail even to mention it.

CARDINAL SECRETARY OF STATE

John Cornwell and those who follow him argue that Pacelli, as cardinal secretary of state, withdrew support from the Catholic Center Party in Germany, transferring power to the Holy See. In particular, these critics fault Pacelli for having negotiated the 1933 concordat with Germany. This agreement, according to the critics, silenced the one entity that could have stopped the National Socialists from coming to power.[48]

Since the concordat came during Pope Pius XI's reign, most discussion of that document is in chapter two of this book. Cornwell, however, presents an interesting twist on this matter. He argues that Secretary of State Pacelli pursued the concordat because he was motivated by the desire to strengthen the papacy. In so doing, Cornwell argues that Pacelli (not Pius XI) eliminated the only force that could have stopped Hitler's rise to total power, the Catholic Center Party. The concordat, according to Cornwell, silenced political priests and bishops who might have held Hitler in check.[49]

The Catholic Center Party advanced the Church's interests in Germany until Hitler's rise. By early 1933, however, Hitler largely stripped it of power. Cornwell himself reports that the party considered forming a coalition with the Nazis in 1932, just for survival.[50] The party was almost eliminated by the Nazis in March 1933.[51] For the next three months, Nazis brutalized the remaining members of the Center Party as well as other Catholics. On July 5, 1933, two weeks before the concordat was signed, the party membership decided to dissolve voluntarily in the hope that his would stop the persecution.[52] When Pacelli heard the news he said: "Too bad that it happened at this moment. Of course the party couldn't have held out much longer. But if it only had put off its dissolution at least until after the conclusion of the concordat, the simple fact of its existence would have still been useful in the negotiations."[53] As reflected by this statement, the party was not negotiated away with the concordat.[54] There was, however, a concession regarding political activity.

Pius XI, like all popes since at least Pius X (1903-1914), agreed with removing clergy from direct political involvement.[55] Pius thought that the Church could be more effectively defended by the terms of the concordat than by parliamentary action.[56] Moreover, the pope was concerned about the legitimacy of direct political activity by the clergy, and he looked with more favor on the lay organization, Catholic Action.[57] Therefore, he agreed to a term barring German priests and bishops from involvement in party politics.

The relevant provision, paragraph 32 of the concordat, said: "the Holy See will prescribe regulations which will prohibit *clergymen and members of religious institutes* from membership in political parties and from working on their behalf."[58] The supplemental protocol relating to this paragraph said: "The conduct enjoined upon the pastors and members of religious institutes in Germany does not entail any limitation of the prescribed preaching and interpretation of the dogmatic and moral teachings and principles of the Church."

Cornwell argues that direct political involvement by Catholic clergy could have held Hitler in check, but that Pacelli, the 1917 Code, and the concordat all served to restrict this possibility in order to centralize the Vatican's authority. This criticism is based upon four assumptions: 1) that Pacelli made the decision, not Pius XI; 2) that the party would have remained viable; 3) that the party would have opposed Hitler; and 4) that the concordat effectively silenced the German bishops. Three of these four assumptions are demonstrably false, and the fourth is far from certain.

As for the assumption that Pacelli was the driving force behind the concordat, Cornwell and critics who follow him credit (or blame) Pacelli for decisions that were far beyond his control. They suggest that Pacelli was the instigator of all the international moves that took place while he was secretary of state. That is not, however, the way that diplomats saw it at the time. Reporting back to London on the prospects of the 1939 papal election, the British Minister to the Holy See, Francis D'Arcy Osborne, wrote that "it was always [Pacelli's] task to execute the policy of the late Pope rather than to initiate his own."[59] In fact, Osborne reported that Pacelli had not garnered the ill will typically found between the secretary of state and other cardinals precisely because he only carried out Pius XI's objectives.[60] Pacelli took pride in executing the will of Pius XI. The Pontiff himself said, "Cardinal

Pacelli speaks with my voice."[61] Either young Pacelli dominated the Church's international policies years before he had any true authority (as the critics assert) or he carried out the will of his superiors (as Pope Pius XI and others who actually knew what Pacelli said). All relevant evidence points to the latter scenario.[62]

Regarding the claim that the Catholic Center Party would have remained viable but for the concordat, that too must fail. Hitler's power was sufficiently secure, and his means sufficiently brutal, that by March 1933 no religious institution—in fact, no political party—could stand up to him.[63] The Catholic Center Party was seriously weakened and almost eliminated by the Nazis in March 1933.[64] An editorial written by the editors of the American Catholic magazine *Commonweal* and published on April 5, 1933, reported that "nothing other than the overthrow of Hitlerism by the German people itself will bring justice to the Jews, and to other oppressed minorities, including the Catholics. The German Catholic bishops have condemned the ultra-nationalism of the Nazi party, and that condemnation still stands, even although the Center party has been forced to vote for its own suppression."[65]

For the next two months, the Nazis brutalized the remaining members of the Center Party as well as other Catholics. On July 5, 1933, two weeks before the concordat was signed, the party membership decided to dissolve voluntarily in the hope that this would stop the persecution.[66]

Neither the concordat nor Church doctrine prohibited Catholic laypersons from being involved in politics,[67] but even had the Catholic Center Party survived, it is not certain that is would have opposed Hitler.[68] "The party was split and many Roman Catholics were attracted by the early achievements of the Nazis, as were most Germans."[69] Today one wonders how this could have been possible. At the time, however, Hitler promised to provide economic prosperity, free Germany from the Treaty of Versailles, end daily street fighting, clean up the vice, and promote social justice.[70] Add to these matters that Hitler's socialistic programs were purportedly designed to help people in need, and it becomes easier to see how some Christian people might have been attracted to his policies.

The assumption that German bishops would have been outspoken against the Nazi regime but were silenced by the concordat is wrong. The German bishops voted to ask the Vatican to ratify the concordat without delay.[71] They understood that because of the supplemental protocol they would not be silenced by this concordat.[72] The concordat, in fact, did no more than assert traditional Church teaching (predating the 1917 Code of Canon Law and surviving Vatican II) when it limited the participation of clergy in party politics.[73]

Despite the removal of Catholic clergy from direct participation in the political process, they were not restricted from making statements that went to basic human rights, and many did make such statements about the Nazi government.[74] Moreover, Catholic laypersons were in no way restricted from political activity by the terms of the concordat. The political restrictions, set forth in paragraph 32 of the concordat, apply only to "clergymen and members of conventual orders."

The agreement with Germany was very similar in this respect to the Lateran Treaty signed with Italy in 1929 and to instructions given to the French clergy in the mid-1920s.[75] The Church did not in any way agree to restrictions on its right to involve itself in politics whenever "the fundamental rights of man or the salvation of souls requires it."[76] As such, the Catholic clergy was not silenced.[77]

Perhaps most importantly, by the time that the concordat was signed, there was only one party left in Germany—the Nazi party. Because of the concordat, Catholic clergy had a clear basis to resist when pressured to join the Nazis. Many protestant ministers, unprotected by such an agreement, were coerced into joining the party.

Regardless of Nazi doctrine to the contrary, the Church would not accept the view that a person who had been duly converted to Catholicism was still a Jew. To the Church, the issue was one of faith, not race. Accordingly, as part of the concordat, German officials agreed to regard baptized Jews as Christians. This ended up being one of the most important agreements between the Vatican and the Third Reich—one that saved the lives of thousands of Jews, baptized or not.

Because of this provision, when National Socialists argued that someone baptized into the Catholic faith remained a Jew, it was not just an assault on the Church's authority, it was a breach of the concordat. As such, the Church had a legal basis for its argument to the contrary. Tens of thousands of false baptismal certificates were handed out by Church authorities and used by Jewish people to avoid deportation.[78]

Pope Pius XI spent much of the 1930s grooming Secretary of State Pacelli to one day succeed him as pope. In 1935, Pius XI organized a huge peace pilgrimage to Lourdes, just before the outbreak of the Ethiopian war.[79] On April 28, he had Pacelli address 250,000 pilgrims. The cardinal spoke of the National Socialists and said that they were "in reality only miserable plagiarists who dress up old errors with new tinsel. It does not make any difference whether they flock to the banners of the social revolution, whether they are guided by a false conception of the world and of life, or whether they are possessed by the superstition of a race and blood cult."[80] The *New York Times* called the address an "attack on both Hitlerism and communism."[81]

Two years later, France's Popular Front government, supported by the Communist Party, extended an invitation to the pontiff to visit France. The pope's health prevented him from making the voyage, so he asked Pacelli to go in his place. Pacelli had already made a strong impression from his 1935 trip to France by protesting against the "superstitions of race and blood," that underlie Nazi theology. This time, in a speech at Notre Dame Cathedral in Paris, he again denounced the Nazi cult of race and spoke of "that noble and powerful nation whom bad shepherds would lead astray into an idolatry of race."[82] He struck out against the "iniquitous violence" and the "vile criminal actions" being perpetrated by German leaders, and he denounced the "pagan cult of race."[83]

The Nazis knew what he meant. The Reich and Prussian Minister for Ecclesiastical Affairs wrote to the German Foreign Ministry that

Pacelli's "unmistakable allusion to Germany . . . was very well understood in the France Popular Front and the anti-German world."[84] Other German leaders also complained about the political nature of Pacelli's statement, and he was mocked in political comics published in Nazi journals.[85]

Pacelli's appearance was lauded in the French press, and French leaders sought to normalize relations between the Holy See and the French government.[86] His words, however, did not change the political landscape of the day. In August 1937, the Soviets put thirty churchmen on trial for a fascist plot, and teachers in Berlin were instructed on the need to teach anti-Semitism.

In 1938, Pius XI sent Pacelli to the International Eucharistic Congress in Budapest. Pacelli, speaking for the pope, said: "Face to face with us is drawn up the lugubrious array of the military godless shaking the clenched fist of the Anti-Christ against everything we hold most sacred. Face to face with us spreads the army of those who would like to make all peoples of the earth and every individual human believe that they can find prosperity only by receding from the Gospel of Christ."[87]

Critic Michael Phayer preposterously tried to turn Pacelli's comments all around. He reported that Pacelli was condemning not the Nazis but the Jews.[88] Nowhere in the speech did Pacelli mention "Jews." He spoke of the "military godless," and said that their "lips cursed Christ" and their "hearts reject him even today." No one at the time thought that he was speaking of the Jews. Jenö Levai, the esteemed Jewish author of *Hungarian Jewry and the Papacy: Pius XII Was Not Silent* (1968), personally witnessed the speech. As the title of his book implies, he was a great supporter of Pacelli. He also noted the pope's early intervention following the occupation of Hungary. The anti-Jewish interpretation is pure post-Holocaust reconstruction.

The Germans refused to send a delegation to the International Eucharistic Congress when they learned that Pacelli would be there. He had, after all, berated them the year before when he went to France for the pope. In fact, the Germans permitted no news of the Congress to be transmitted in Germany, even though Pacelli gave one of his two addresses in German (as Pius xi had released his anti-Nazi encyclical, *Mit brennender Sorge*, in German for wider distribution in that nation.)[89] Certainly, had they been able to link the Pope to their anti-Semitic views, the Nazis would not have missed the chance.

The Eucharistic Congress came in the same month (May 1938) that Pacelli and Pius xi left Rome for the summer (one month earlier than normal) to avoid being there when Hitler came. They also closed all the Vatican museums so that Hitler could not be photographed touring them. The idea of leaving and closing the museums was apparently Pacelli's.[90] "The air here makes me feel sick," Pius xi said to those seeing him off.[91] From his summer retreat, Castel Gandolfo, Pius held a public audience at which he listed among his sorrows that on the feast of the Holy Cross, people in Rome were hosting "the symbol of another cross which is not that of Christ."[92] Later that same year Pope Pius xi gave his famous "Spiritually, we are all Semites" talk.[93] Critics who claim that Pacelli was speaking against the Jews are simply fabricating arguments.

THE HIDDEN ENCYCLICAL

The so-called "hidden encyclical" of Pius xi is a story told by many papal critics.[94] The typical version is that Pius xi was prepared to make a strong anti-Nazi statement. He commissioned a draft but died before releasing it. His successor, Pius xii, decided not to issue it. Critics then argue that had Pius xii not "hidden" this encyclical, much suffering would have been avoided.

The true story of the "hidden encyclical" is that there never was an encyclical or even a draft encyclical. Pope Pius xi asked for a paper from Fr. John LaFarge, sj. The thought was that this might one day be used as the basis for an encyclical. LaFarge was not an expert theologian or historian, so he sought help from two other priests, Fr. Gustav Grundlach from Germany and Fr. Gustave Desbuqouis from France.[95] This resulted in three different papers, one written in French, one in English, and one in German.[96]

The source upon which most critics rely, Georges Passelecq and Bernard Suchecky's *The Hidden Encyclical of Pius XI*, deals with the French and the English papers, but not the German one. That book also makes clear that Pius XI was not the author of any of the documents. In fact, as that book further makes clear, there is no evidence that either he or Pius XII even saw these documents. A copy of the paper was sent to Pius XI, but by that time the Pope was already gravely ill. When it was found after his death, there were no notations suggesting that he ever reviewed it. The book also explains that the paper disappeared immediately after Pius XI's death, and the men who were working on the project believed (indeed were certain) that Pius XII had not seen it.[97] He therefore could not have hidden it.

The primary author of the German draft, Professor Gustav Grundlach, SJ, helped Pius XII with his first encyclical, *Summi Pontificatus* (*Darkness over the Earth*),[98] which was released on October 20, 1939, just after the outbreak of war. Not surprisingly, *Summi Pontificatus* (which urges solidarity with all who profess a belief in God and—contrary to the claims of some critics—expressly mentions Jews) contains language that is similar to the paper on which Gundlach had worked. In fact, Fr. LaFarge wrote in *America* magazine that it was obvious that *Summi Pontificatus* applied to the Jews of Europe. He was only concerned that Americans might not realize that it also applied to racial injustice in the United States.[99]

One of the problems that critics have had with the traditional story of the hidden encyclical is that the so-called "original draft" contained some anti-Semitic statements. Critics of Pius XII are sometimes reluctant to attribute such sentiments to Pius XI. John Cornwell resolved this problem in his book *Hitler's Pope* by accusing Pacelli of having written the draft when he was secretary of state, then of having buried it when he became Pope. (In fact, Cornwell even suggests that he suppressed the encyclical while he was still secretary of state, during Pius XI's illness.) Thus, Cornwell criticizes Pius XII twice—first for writing it, then for suppressing it. It is really too great a stretch of logic to be considered legitimate. There is absolutely no evidence that Pacelli had anything to do with the drafting of this text.

POPE PIUS XII'S FIRST ENCYCLICAL

Some critics have charged that Pius changed his allegiance to favor the Allies during the war as he saw them begin to have more success. This, of course, runs counter to the critics who charge that his main concern was in opposing the Soviets (in which case he would have favored the Allies early but then shifted to the Axis powers later). Actually, in his first encyclical, *Summi Pontificatus*, released in October 1939, Pius set forth his position on Hitler, the war, and the role that he would play. He stayed true to that position throughout the war.

After the Nazi invasion of Poland on September 1, Pius XII, far from remaining passive, addressed the war in three separate speeches during that same month. On September 14, addressing the new Belgian ambassador, Pius described the Nazi invasion as "an immeasurable catastrophe" and declared that "this new war, which already shakes the soil of Europe, and particularly that of a Catholic nation, no human prevision can calculate the frightful carnage which it bears within itself, nor what its extension and its successive complications will be."[100] He also condemned "the use of asphyxiating and poison gasses," which had been used during World War I, and which the Nazis, in a radically different manner, would later employ for the gas chambers.[101]

On September 26, addressing a group of German pilgrims, Pius called the war "a terrible scourge of God" and directly warned the German clergy not to celebrate German militarism but to repent: "The priest must now, more than ever before, be above all political and national feelings. He must console, comfort, help, exhort to prayer and penance, and must himself do penance."[102]

On September 30, while addressing Cardinal Hlond and a group of Polish pilgrims, Pius made an unmistakable reference to the Nazis as "the enemies of God," and spoke directly to the suffering Poles, whose country was under attack: "Before our eyes pass as a vision frightened crowds and, in black desperation, a multitude of refugees and wanderers—all those who no longer have a country or a home. There rise toward Us the agonized sobs of mothers and wives. . . ."[103]

Pius followed these three strong statements with a profound encyclical, *Summi Pontificatus*. This papal statement made reference to "the ever-increasing host of Christ's enemies" (paragraph 7), and noted that these enemies of Christ "deny or in practice neglect the vivifying truths and the values inherent in belief in God and in Christ" and want to "break the Tables of God's Commandments to substitute other tables and other standards stripped of the ethical content of [Christianity]." In the next paragraph, Pius charged that Christians who fell in with the enemies of Christ suffered from cowardice, weakness, or uncertainty.

In paragraph 13, Pius wrote of the outbreak of war: "Our paternal heart is torn by anguish as We look ahead to all that will yet come forth from the baneful seed of violence and of hatred for which the sword today ploughs the blood drenched furrow." In the next paragraph, he wrote of the enemies of Christ, an obvious reference to Hitler's National Socialists, becoming bolder.

Paragraphs 24 through 31 laid out the pope's belief that prayer, not public condemnation, was the most appropriate response for the Bishop of Rome. Obviously, Pius viewed this as an important act of faith. Moreover, it was the lack of Christianity that he identified as the cause of the "crop of such poignant disasters." Faith and prayer were the things he could contribute to the world at that time, not political or military strength.

Discussing *Summi Pontificatus*, critic Susan Zuccotti writes: "The encyclical never mentioned Jews. Indeed, despite references to the unity of the human race, it seemed to single out Christians, or perhaps Catholics, for special consideration." One cannot help but wonder whether she read the encyclical.

Paragraphs 45 to 50 of the encyclical dealt with racial matters and expressed the pope's belief that the Church could not discriminate against any given race of people. Pius firmly stated that all races and nationalities were welcome in the Church and had equal rights as children in the house of the Lord. In paragraph 48, he put meaning to those anti-racist statements by naming new bishops of different races and nationalities. Moreover, he expressly said that the Church must always be open to all: "The spirit, the teaching and the work of the Church can never be other than that which the Apostle of the Gentiles preached: 'putting on the new (man) him who is renewed unto knowledge, according to the image of him that created him. Where there is neither Gentile nor Jew, circumcision nor uncircumcision, barbarian nor Scythian, bond nor free. But Christ is all and in all' (Colossians iii. 10, 11)." The equating of Gentiles and Jews was a clear rejection of Hitler's fundamental ideology and stands as a clear refutation of the false charges made by too many critics.

Paragraphs 51 to 66 seem to be Pius XII's view of a just society. Here he asserts that the first reason for the outbreak of war is that people have forgotten the law of universal charity. The second reason is the failure to put God above civil authority. He argues that when civil authority is placed above the Lord, the government fills that void and problems develop. This is exactly what Hitler had done. This analysis would likely also apply to Pius XII's view of the Soviet Union, which at that time had an agreement with Hitler.

Pius said that nations must have a religious basis. He wrote that the goal of society must be development of the individual, not the power of the state. Again, this was a slap at Hitler's dismantling of religious institutions and development of the state in Germany. In fact, paragraph 60 was a direct answer to Hitler's view of the state as set forth in *Mein Kampf:* "To consider the State as something ultimate to which everything else should be subordinated and directed, cannot fail to harm the true and lasting prosperity of nations. This can happen either when unrestricted dominion comes to be conferred on the State as having a mandate from the nation, people, or even a social order, or when the State arrogates such dominion to itself as absolute master, despotically, without any mandate whatsoever." Similarly, Pius presented an answer to Hitler's views of the family and of education in this section of the encyclical.

Pius made note of how "powers of disorder and destruction" stand ready to take advantage of sorrow, bitterness, and suffering in order to make use of them "for their dark designs." This was a description of how Fascists in Italy and Nazis in Germany took advantage of the chaos following the First World War to rise to power. Pius also responded to the demands of Hitler and Mussolini (and, for that matter, Stalin) for stronger central governments. While acknowledging that there may be difficulties that would justify greater powers being concentrated in the State, the pope also said that the moral law requires that the need for this be scrutinized with greatest rigor. The State can demand goods and blood, but not the immortal soul.

Paragraphs 73 to 77 dealt with the Pope's ideas on international relations: "Absolute autonomy for the State stands in open opposition to this natural way that is inherent in man . . . and therefore leaves the stability of international relations at the mercy of the will of rulers, while it destroys the possibility of true union and fruitful collaboration directed to the general good." Pius stressed the importance of treaties and wrote of an international natural law which requires that treaties be honored. With Hitler having recently breached several treaties and the concordat, this must be seen as another swipe at the Nazi leader.

Interestingly, in paragraph 85, Pius accurately described the challenges he would face, and he set forth the code of conduct that he followed throughout the rest of the war:

And if belonging to (the Kingdom of God), living according to its spirit, laboring for its increase and placing its benefits at the disposition of that portion of mankind also which as yet has no part in them, means in our days having to face obstacles and oppositions as vast and deep and minutely organized as never before, that does not dispense a man from the frank, bold profession of our Faith. Rather, it spurs one to stand fast in the conflict even at the price of the greatest sacrifices. Whoever lives by the spirit of Christ refuses to let himself be beaten down by the difficulties which oppose him, but on the contrary feels himself impelled to work with all his strength and with the fullest confidence in God.

In paragraphs 93 to 95, Pius expressed the importance that he attached to the spirit as opposed to the physical world. Here he made clear that the most important thing would be to open people to Christ. He said that the Church must be protected so that it can fulfill its role as an educator by teaching the truth, by inculcating justice, and by inflaming hearts with the divine love of Christ. Indeed, throughout the war, he would protect the Church so that it could carry out its life and soul-saving functions.

Paragraphs 101 to 106 drew distinctions between the Holy See and other secular nations and explained the Church's special role in the world. The Church "does not claim to take the place of other legitimate authorities in their proper spheres." Instead, Pius wrote, the Church should be a good example and do good works. The Church "spreads its maternal arms towards this world not to dominate but to serve. She does not claim to take the place of other legitimate authorities in their proper spheres, but offers them her help after the example and in the spirit of her Divine Founder Who 'went about doing good' (Acts x. 38)." This same thought was expanded upon when Pius wrote "render therefore to Caesar the things that are Caesar's." In other words, the Church plays an important, but limited role in resolving disputes in the secular world. His obligation was to pray for peace and offer comfort to the afflicted.

Pius expressed his confidence that the Church would always prevail in the long run. Any structure that is not founded on the teaching of Christ, he wrote, is destined to perish. Read in context, this was a promise of the ultimate failure of Nazism. In fact, he expressly foresaw that Poland would be resurrected:

> This . . . is in many respects a real 'Hour of Darkness,'... in which the spirit of violence and of discord brings indescribable suffering on mankind. . . . The nations swept into the tragic whirlpool of war are perhaps as yet only at the 'beginnings of sorrows,' . . . but even now there reigns in thousands of families death and desolation, lamentation and misery. The blood of countless human beings, even noncombatants, raises a piteous dirge over a nation such as Our dear Poland, which, for its fidelity to the Church, for its services in the defense of Christian civilization. . . has a right to the generous and brotherly sympathy of the whole world, while it awaits, relying on the powerful intercession of Mary, Help of Christians, the hour of a resurrection in harmony with the principles of justice and true peace.

The reference to Poland should resolve any doubts about to whom Pius was referring.

In paragraphs 107 to 112, Pius wrote that it was his duty to try for peace, and that duty had to be fulfilled even if it meant that the Church was misunderstood in the effort: "While still some hope was left, We left nothing undone in the form suggested to us by Our Apostolic office and by the means at Our disposal, to prevent recourse to arms and to keep open the way to an understanding honorable to both parties. Convinced that the use of force on one side would be answered by recourse to arms on the other, We considered it a duty inseparable from Our Apostolic office and of Christian Charity to try every means to spare mankind and Christianity the horrors of a world conflagration, even at the risk of having Our intentions and Our aims misunderstood." He encouraged people to keep faith that good will prevail, and he once again expressed his faith in the ultimate triumph of God's will.

World leaders well understood Pius XII's message in *Summi Pontificatus*. François Charles-Roux, the French ambassador to the Vatican during the 1930s, lavished praise on the encyclical, because in it Pius XII took a stand "against exacerbated nationalism, the idolatry of the state, totalitarianism, racism, the cult of brutal force, contempt of international agreements, against all the characteristics of Hitler's political system; he laid the responsibility for the scourge of the war on these aberrations."[104]

Papal critics ignore this encyclical. Daniel Goldhagen, for instance, quotes from the encyclical once (page 158), without mentioning it by name. He refers to it as "Pius XII's inaugural encyclical" and mocks Pius for claiming that the papacy's role is "to testify to the truth with Apostolic Firmness." Goldhagen refers to *Summi Pontificatus* by name only in a footnote (note 95, p.321).

This encyclical, which had a significant impact in Germany,[105] shows that Pius did not waver in his approach to Hitler and the Nazis. In 1939 he laid out his vision, which he followed for the rest of the war. Thus, it was not a matter of fear, nor did Pius change his behavior based upon his perception of who was winning the war. All along he thought that the best way to assure peace was through prayer. He charted his course and stayed with it. Importantly, people at that time recognized the importance of this encyclical.

In January 2002, documents from the personal archive of General William Donovan, who served as special assistant to the U.S. chief counsel during the International Military Tribunal at Nuremberg, were made public and posted on the Internet by the *Rutgers Journal of Law & Religion*.[106] In a confidential report documenting Nazi persecution of the Church, prepared for the Nuremberg prosecution, the situation surrounding *Summi Pontificatus* is discussed as providing grounds for a separate count against the Nazis. The report notes that priests who read that document were reported to the authorities and that Nazi officials stopped its reproduction and distribution.[107]

"This Encyclical," wrote Heinrich Mueller, head of the Gestapo in Berlin, "is directed exclusively against Germany, both in ideology and in regard to the German-Polish dispute; how dangerous it is for our foreign relations as well as our domestic affairs is beyond dispute."[108] Reinhard Heydrich, leader of the ss Security Office in Warsaw, wrote: "This declaration of the Pope makes an unequivocal accusation against Germany."[109] A headline in the London *Daily Telegraph* read "Pope condemns Nazi theory."[110] It even earned a three-column, above-the-fold headline in the *New York Times*: "Pope Condemns Dictators, Treaty Violators, Racism; Urges Restoring of Poland."[111] Allied forces later dropped 88,000 copies of it behind enemy lines for propaganda purposes.[112]

Pius followed his first encyclical with a Christmas address that also condemned Nazi aggression. He spoke of "a series of deeds, irreconcilable either with natural law or with the most elementary human feelings. . . . In this category falls the premeditated aggression against a small, hardworking and peaceful people, under the pretext of a 'threat' nonexistent, not thought of, not even possible."[113] The pontiff cried out against "atrocities . . . and the unlawful use of destructive weapons against non-combatants and refugees, against old men and women and children; a disregard for the dignity, liberty, and life of man, showing itself in actions which cry to heaven for vengeance: 'The voice of thy brother's blood crieth to me from the earth.'"[114]

By March of 1940, *Look* magazine was able to proclaim that "the most important axis of the world is no longer the Rome-Berlin, but the Rome-Washington. This is the peace axis."[115] President Roosevelt praised the Vatican, urging other churches to "synchronize their peace efforts . . . to the outline of Pope Pius xii of his conception of a just peace"[116] Nazi propagandist Joseph Goebbels, on the other hand, complained in his diary: "The Pope has made a Christmas speech. Full of bitter, covert attacks against us, against the Reich and National Social-ism. All the forces of internationalism are against us. We must break them."[117]

The Nazis did not break the Church under Pius XII. Strong state-ments were issued by various leaders throughout the war. During Christmastime 1941, the *New York Times* wrote: "The voice of Pius XII is a lonely voice in the silence and darkness enveloping Europe this Christmas. . . . the Pope put himself squarely against Hitlerism."[118] That same paper, one year later wrote: "This Christmas more than ever he is a lonely voice crying out of the silence of a continent."[119]

In August of 1943, *Time* magazine wrote: "it is scarcely deniable that the Church Apostolic, through the encyclicals and other Papal pronouncements, has been fighting totalitarianism more knowingly, devoutly, and authoritatively, and for a longer time, than any other organized power."[120] Following the liberation of Rome, in October 1944, the *New York Times* wrote: "under the Pope's direction the Holy See did an exemplary job of sheltering and championing the victims of the Nazi-Fascist regime."[121]

This perception of Pope Pius XII as a staunch opponent of the Nazis and a protector of victims, Christian or not, was widely shared from the time of the war until several years after his death. The Nazis despised him, the victims praised him, and the rescuers cited him as their inspiration. When it comes to something as serious as the Holo-caust, these eyewitnesses are too important to be ignored.

— 5 —

"Charity that Fears No Death"

The delegates of the Congress of the Italian Jewish Communities. . . feel that it is imperative to extend reverent homage to Your Holiness, and to express the most profound gratitude that animates all Jews for your fraternal humanity toward them during the years of persecution when their lives were endangered by Nazi-Fascist barbarism.
Message to Pius XII
from the Italian Jewish Community (April 5, 1946)

FOLLOWING MONTHS OF RESEARCH in the Yad Vashem archives, Israeli diplomat Pinchas Lapide estimated that the Catholic Church saved 700,000 to 860,000 Jewish lives during the Holocaust.[1] Other commentators have come to similar or higher tallies.[2] Lapide made clear that this number was attributable to "The Holy See, the nuncios, and the entire Catholic Church."[3] As historian Sir Martin Gilbert has noted: "the test for Pacelli [Pope Pius XII] was when the Gestapo came to Rome to round up Jews. And the Catholic

Church, on his direct authority, immediately dispersed as many Jews as they could."[4] Because of the example that Pius XII set in Rome, it is not surprising that Lapide's figures have become so widely accepted, despite protests from papal critics.

The relief effort undertaken by the Vatican when Hitler moved troops into Italy has been called "probably the greatest Christian program in the history of Catholicism."[5] At the direction of the pope, convents and monasteries throughout Italy were made available as safe refuges for victims of Nazi terror.[6] A nun in Rome recorded in the convent diary: "New demands come in to increase the number of families already welcomed, and there is beginning to be a lack of space, but how can we refuse any of the distressed?"[7]

All available Church buildings—including those in Vatican City—were put to use. One hundred and fifty such sanctuaries were opened in Rome alone. As the Nazis intensified their persecution, the Church also placed Jews in monasteries, parish houses, and private homes.[8] As the *New York Times* reported: "Jews received first priority—Italian Jews and Jews who escaped here from Germany and other countries—but all the hunted found sanctuary in the Vatican and its hundreds of convents and monasteries in the Rome region."[9] Almost five thousand Jews, a third of the Jewish population of Rome, were hidden in buildings that belonged to the Catholic Church.[10] The Vatican provided food and clothes.[11] Deserting German soldiers were also given sanctuary, as were Allied soldiers who were trapped behind enemy lines.[12]

Catholic hospitals were ordered to admit Jewish patients, even if their ailments were fictitious.[13] The chief rabbi of Rome reported: "No hero in history has commanded such an army; an army of priests works in cities and small towns to provide bread for the persecuted and passports for the fugitives. Nuns go into canteens to give hospitality to women refugees. Superiors of convents go out into the night to meet German soldiers who look for victims. . . . Pius XII is followed by all with the fervor of that charity that fears no death."[14] Pius XII's actions accomplished much more than empty words ever could have done.

Convents were normally closed to outsiders. These rules were very strict and could not have been violated without instructions from high Church authorities. At first, refugees were kept in common areas, out of the cloistered rooms, but as more and more people sought protection from the Germans, all rooms were opened.[15] Still, however, everyone in the convents and monasteries had to abide with strict separation of the sexes rules. As a result, most Jewish families were split up. Priests sometimes had to play "postmen," carrying messages between husband and wife. On rare occasions, Church officials would bend the rules to accommodate married couples.[16] Catholic authorities also made provisions for Kosher food and tried to provide decent burials when Jewish people were killed in the war.[17]

Having received assurances that its properties in Rome would be regarded as extraterritorial, not part of German occupied Italy, the Holy See posted signs on the buildings to warn German soldiers that they should not search them. Susan Zuccotti complains that the Vatican put protection notices on all of its buildings, instead of just the 160 or so where refugees are known to have been hiding. From this she concludes that the Church was protecting its property, not the refugees. She suggests that the warnings should have been put on only those churches, monasteries, and schools that contained Jews or other refugees. That, however, would have been nothing but a clear indication to the Nazis that refugees were hidden therein. If the Nazis had been provided with such information and they had used it to deport more Jews, the Vatican would indeed have been responsible. Besides, by putting signs on every building, refugees were informed that these buildings were safe, and they could be entered on a moment's notice.

Castel Gandolfo, the papal summer home, is worth particular note. This facility was used to shelter thousands of refugees during the war. In *Hitler, the War, and the Pope* I used the (apparently low) number of five hundred. In fact, photos from Castel Gandolfo show people not only sleeping in the halls, but even up and down the staircases,[18] and some accounts place the number of people sheltered there as high as twelve thousand. Many critics, however, neglect even to mention it.

Zuccotti speculated that perhaps none of the people sheltered there were Jewish. The director of the papal villa at Castel Gandolfo during the Second World War, Emilio Bonomelli, wrote a book in 1953 in which he discussed caring for Jews and other refugees during the war.[19] According to another account, about three thousand Jews were sheltered there at one time.[20] The papal apartments were opened up to shelter pregnant women nearing the days of childbirth, and some forty children were born there.[21] Today in Castel Gandolfo there is on display a beautifully decorated, enormous wooden cross, which was given to Pius XII at the end of the war by the Jews who lived there during those terrifying days.[22]

A wartime U.S. intelligence document reported that the "bombardment of Castel Gandolfo resulted in the injury of about 1,000 people and the death of about 300 more. The highness of the figures is due to the fact that the area was crammed with refugees."[23] No one but Pope Pius XII had authority to open these buildings to outsiders. As at least one witness testified under oath, the orders came from the pope.[24]

Blank and forged documents were freely handed out by Church authorities. Many Jews used these to show that they had been baptized into the Catholic faith, and—because of the provisions of the 1933 concordat—Germans would usually leave them alone. Pius also assisted Jewish people as they emigrated to safe nations.[25] Many Jewish people with these documents were transported to safety in Spain or Switzerland, but as the border became better secured by the Germans, relocation became more dangerous. Many Jews were dressed in clerical garb and taught to chant the liturgy.[26] (Some survivors recall switching in mid-prayer from the Hebrew Shema to the Latin *Ave Maria* when a stranger approached.)[27] Catholic priests then began personally escorting these "monks and nuns" across the Allied lines.[28] Even later, some were sent in trucks disguised as food delivery vehicles.

The Catholic Church provided papers indicating Latin American citizenship to many Jews in occupied France. When the papers were discovered to be fraudulent, the Latin American countries withdrew recognition of them. This made the Jews subject to deportation to the concentration camps. Pursuant to a request from the Union of Orthodox Rabbis of the United States and Canada, and working in conjunction with the International Red Cross, the Vatican contacted the countries involved and urged them to recognize the documents, "no matter how illegally obtained."[29]

During the Nazi occupation, a white line on the ground separated occupied Rome from neutral Vatican City. On September 10, 1943 at 4:00 PM, Nazi troopers in full battle dress took up "protective patrol" around the Vatican.[30] On one side of that line, German soldiers carried their machine guns. On the other side, the Vatican's Swiss Guards stood at attention with their largely decorative pikes.[31] These Vatican soldiers represented the remnants of an era when the pope actually commanded a military force. These young men, of course, were employees of the Holy See and as such were permitted to enter Vatican City and were largely exempt from Nazi persecution. Prior to the occupation, there were three hundred such men in service to the Holy See. Once the Germans arrived, however, the Vatican issued four thousand identity cards to men who were able to use the cards to avoid Nazi brutality.[32]

As the pope placed himself in danger and sacrificed much to save others, the world Jewish community took note. A note from the Israelite Central Committee of Uruguay to the papal nuncio reported:

> We deem it a high honor to make known to Your Excellency our fondness and support of His Holiness, Pius xii, who already directly suffers the consequences of the actual conflict that strikes the world.
>
> [T]he Community that we represent has always followed the news ... of the situation of the Vatican and the August person of His Holiness ... And from the depths of their hearts the Israelites of Uruguay pray [for]... news that assures the cessation of the

danger that threatens His Holiness, Pius xii, ardent defender of the cause of those who are unjustly persecuted.[33]

The Germans had a list of priests who had given shelter to Jews, and they tried to capture these priests and send them to concentration camps. As the Nazis moved into Italy, many "listed" priests moved into the Vatican, and they did not re-emerge until the Allies had liberated the city. In Northern Italy, where the priests had more difficulty hiding out, the Nazis executed many of them.

CONVERSIONS AND FALSE IDENTIFICATION

Many Jews were quickly converted for the purpose of avoiding Nazi persecution. Undoubtedly Church leaders would have been glad to welcome converts to Christianity. However, in a great many more cases, false baptismal documents were provided so that Jewish people could avoid persecution, even though they had not actually converted.

Sometimes Church officials were embarrassed about how quickly they would convert Jews to Catholicism for the purpose of avoiding persecution. One small church in Budapest averaged about four or five conversions a year before the occupation. In 1944, those numbers shot up dramatically. Six were converted in January, 23 in May, 101 in June, over 700 in September, and over 1,000 in October. According to the records, three thousand Jews became Catholics at this one small church in 1944.[34] The Nazi occupying forces soon recognized that these conversions were being done only to avoid deportation, so they started persecuting the "converts." Since it no longer assured protection, the flood of conversions dried up.[35]

Archives of the Jesuit magazine *La Civiltà Cattolica* contain a letter from an Italian officer, addressed to the Vatican's Secretariat of State, criticizing Italian Msgr. Alfredo Ottaviani, who later became a cardinal and head of the Vatican's doctrinal congregation, for pro-Jewish activities, in particular the practice of giving Jews baptismal certificates in order to support false identities. "How is it that Msgr. Ottaviani hands out baptismal certificates and certificates of Aryan lineage? Is it so easy to become a Christian, even without renouncing the Jewish religion?" The officer also accused Msgr. Ottaviani of hiding Jews in the buildings of the Lateran Palace, which housed Rome's diocesan offices.[36]

The Catholic Church was so open to Jewish converts that some have suggested that the Church pushed them too hard to convert. In a papal allocution of October 6, 1946, Pope Pius addressed the issue of "forced conversions." He found the best evidence to be a memorandum, dated January 25, 1942, from the Vatican Secretariat of State to the Legation of Yugoslavia to the Holy See. The pope read from that document: "According to the principles of Catholic doctrine, conversion must be the result, not of external constraint, but of an interior adherence of the soul to the truths taught by the Catholic Church. It is for this reason that the Catholic Church does not admit to her communion adults who request either to be received or to be readmitted, except on condition that they be fully aware of the meaning and consequences of the step that they wish to take."[37] Canon 750 of the 1917 *Code of Canon Law*, which was supplemented during World War II by orders from the Holy See and the local bishops, prohibited forced conversions.

A related claim concerns Jewish children who were entrusted to Catholic institutions during the war. Both canon law and the Holy See made clear that hidden Jewish children were not to be baptized without parental consent.[38] Even when parents requested the baptism, it was recognized that this was often a matter of duress and was sometimes prohibited.[39] In fact, some Catholic institutions established classes to let the sheltered Jewish children study their own religion.[40] Nevertheless, some Catholics did indeed baptize the children—perhaps out of their own faith conviction, or as an effort to further deceive the Nazis.

On December 28, 2004 an Italian professor from Bologna named Alberto Melloni published an article in the Italian newspaper *Il Corriere della Sera* entitled "Pius XII to Nuncio Roncalli: Do Not Return the

Jewish Children." The article cited a document that Melloni claimed to have received from an unidentified archive in France. This document, dated October 23, 1946, was said to be "a disposition of the Holy Office" (the Congregation for the Doctrine of the Faith's former name), and it purportedly contained Pope Pius XII's directives to his representative in France—Archbishop Angelo Roncalli, the future Pope John XXIII—on how to handle the Jewish children, especially any who had been baptized by their Catholic rescuers.

According to Melloni, the letter said: "Children who have been baptized must not be entrusted to institutions that cannot ensure their Christian education." Also according to Melloni, the letter said that children whose families survived the Holocaust should be returned, "as long as they had not been baptized." The clear implication was that baptized Jewish children should not be returned to their families. Melloni quoted the letter as saying: "It should be noted that this decision taken by the Holy Congregation of the Holy Office has been approved by the Holy Father."

The *New York Times* reported that the letter was made available to it "on the condition that the source would not be disclosed."[41] This, in and of itself, should have set off alarms. Moreover, the letter was not signed, not on Vatican letterhead, and Vatican officials immediately noted that the words used were not typical for directives from the Vatican. Importantly, the letter was in French, not in Italian as it would have been had this actually been an instruction from the pope to his nuncio.[42] Moreover, Archbishop Roncalli certainly never acted in a way that this report said he was instructed to act. In fact, he has been repeatedly praised for all he did to assist Jewish refugees, and he gave all credit to Pius XII (whom, according to his private papers, he "venerated and loved").[43] Nevertheless, and despite all of these warning signs, critics like Daniel Goldhagen and Rabbi Shmuley Boteach were quickly in the press explaining how this document proved that Pius was indeed an evil man.[44]

Melloni did not identify the archive from which the French memo came, but Italian journalist Andrea Tornielli and historian Matteo Luigi Napolitano were able to find the original memo in the Centre National des Archives de l'Eglise de France. They made an amazing discovery: the French letter that Melloni was promoting as a startling find, was not, in fact, a papal directive, but a summary of an earlier, completely seperate document, written in Italian—a letter, dated September 28, 1946, by Monsignor Domenico Tardini to nuncio Roncalli.[45]

The instructions from Tardini, approved by Pius XII, said that if institutions (not families) wanted to take those children who had been entrusted to the Church, each case had to be examined individually. There was indeed special concern about baptized children. In some cases, their parents (or appointed relatives) had requested baptism, perhaps because they thought that would best protect the children. In those cases, the Church would breach its obligation to the parents if it turned the children over to the wrong organization. When Catholic rescuers had baptized Jewish children without the consent of their Jewish parents, the Church was still concerned about turning them over to organizations that were not associated with the children's family.

As for the rest of the children, the instructions provided: "also those children who were not baptized and who no longer have living relatives, having been entrusted to the Church, which has taken them under its care, as long as they are not able to decide for themselves, they cannot be abandoned by the Church or delivered to parties who have no right to them." There were very few facilities fit for children in Palestine or wartorn Europe.

The Tardini document made clear that these instructions related solely to institutions wanting to relocate orphaned children after the war: "Things would be different if the children were requested by their relatives." This qualification of the directive changes the entire meaning of the instructions. They did not relate to children being sought by their parents or other relatives. This is completely different from what the initial news reports led people to believe.

Archbishop Loris Capovilla, secretary to Nuncio Roncalli during and after the war, explained the need for close scrutiny of organizations: "It was then natural to screen the situations case by case, paying the highest attention to those who knocked on the door to reclaim the children: What should those [Catholic] families have done? Give the children raised together with their own to those who first presented themselves? The Church did nothing other than to counsel a rule of prudence, and to watch over the protection of the little ones."[46] Archbishop Capovilla said that he was not aware of any case in which a Jewish child was impeded from reentering his or her natural family.

These Vatican instructions on the return of Jewish children were prompted by a meeting between the pope and Chief Rabbi Isaac Herzog of Palestine in March 1946. In a surviving letter sent at that time, the rabbi expressed his profound thanks for the "thousands of children who were hidden in Catholic institutions." Herzog noted that Pius XII "has worked to banish anti-Semitism in many countries" and concluded with an invocation: "God willing, may history remember that when everything was dark for our people, His Holiness lit a light of hope for them."[47]

The *Palestine Post* (March 31, 1946) reported that Rabbi Herzog "told of his audience with the Pope, who had received him on a Sunday early in March. Their conversation . . . was mainly on the subject of the 8,000 Jewish children in Poland, France, Belgium and Holland who were [being] brought up in monasteries and by Christian families. He had the Vatican's promise of help to bring those children back into the Jewish fold." The pope must have come through on that promise. As Dr. Leon Kubowitzky, of the World Jewish Congress, said in 1964: "I can state now that I hardly know of a single case where Catholic institutions refused to return Jewish children."[48]

There are very few cases in which a petition from a Catholic parent who did not want to return Jewish children to their natural par-

ents made its way to the pope. On of them was the case of the Polish
Catholic woman Leokadia Jaromirska, who was later honored as a
Righteous Gentile. She sought the pope's permission to keep the little
girl whom she was raising as a Catholic even though the Jewish father had returned. Jaromirska "was instructed by the Pope to return
the child to its father." The Pope explained that it "was her duty as a
Catholic not only to give back the child, but do it with good will and
in friendship."[49]

The critics often cite the Finaly affair from France, but they omit
the details. In that case, on February 14, 1944, Gestapo agents entered
the village of Tronche, France. They arrested two Jewish refugees from
Austria, Fritz and Annie Finaly (also sometimes spelled Finely). The
Finalys were never seen again. Their children (Robert, aged three, and
Gerald, aged two) were left behind. A Catholic woman named An-
toinette Brun took the two young boys into the Grenoble foundling
home, which she ran. Eventually she came to love them, and in 1945
she began the process to formally adopt the boys. In 1948, she had
them baptized into the Catholic Church.

The boys parents were gone, but an aunt from New Zealand wrote
a letter asking that they be sent to her. Brun resisted that overture, but
in 1949 the Finaly family filed suit asking that the boys be sent to live
with a different aunt in Israel. The lawsuit went on for almost four
years, and the evidence was conflicting. The boys' late father had told
friends that he wanted to have his sons brought up in France, but there
was no clear evidence as to his (or their mother's) religious wishes. For
their part, the boys wanted to stay in France with Brun.

The French court ultimately sided with the Finaly relatives, but
when the authorities went to pick up the boys, they were missing.
Friends and supporters of Ms. Brun, including several Catholic priests
and nuns, had spirited the boys off to Spain.

Several arrests were made, and according to *Time* (March 16, 1953),
French socialists used this as an opportunity to bash the Catholic
Church. These Catholics, however, were not acting on behalf of the

Church. *Time* also reported that Bishop Alexandre Calliot of Grenoble made a radio broadcast in which he demanded that anyone with information about the boys get in touch with the authorities. One of the first to comply was a priest in Spain who reported on the boys' whereabouts.

Forty-eight hours after the final appeal was decided in favor of the Finaly family, a representative of Pierre Cardinal Gerlier, Archbishop of Lyon, made the final of several trips into Spain to find the boys. They were waiting in the home of a Spanish provincial governor, and the Church official helped bring them back to France. As the November 7, 1955, issue of *Time* explained, "the Roman Catholic hierarchy had helped in getting the Finely brothers back" to their Jewish relatives.[50]

Critics often claim that the Holy See's rescue efforts were directed towards Catholics who converted from Judaism, as opposed to Jews who were not Catholics.[51] Joseph Lichten, director of the Inter-cultural Affairs Department of the Anti-Defamation League of B'nai B'rith, recognized this argument as a red herring as early as 1963. "There is an element of naiveté" on the part of those who make such allegations, he wrote, because the Catholic Church issued tens of thousands of blank and forged baptismal certificates during the war.[52] With these documents, any Jewish person could avoid deportation by the Nazis as long as converted Jews were protected.[53]

Vatican officials had legal standing to object to persecution of Catholics. Unfortunately, they did not have similar standing when it came to non-Catholics—be they Protestants, Jews, or unbelievers. As it turns out, the Nazis rarely responded positively when protests were made on behalf even of Catholics. (At Nuremberg, German Foreign Minister Ribbentrop stated that there was a whole desk full of protests from the Vatican. Most went unanswered; many were not even read.)[54] A regime that would not heed Church protests on behalf of its own members would certainly never have listened to Vatican protests on behalf of non-Catholics. The best the Church could do was to try to pass off non-Catholic victims as Catholics and try to intervene to save them on that basis. That is what the Church did by, for example, distributing tens of thousands of false baptismal certificates.[55]

Documents discovered only since the Vatican opened archives in 2003 show that Pope Pius XI and Secretary of State Pacelli were very concerned about Jewish victims, regardless of whether they were baptized. Peter Godman, who reviewed these documents explained: "both Pius XI and his second-in-command [Pacelli] recognized the Church's duty to intervene in order to alleviate the suffering of German Jews. Not only Jews converted to Catholicism but all people—irrespective of race, rank, or religion—in need of Christian charity."[56] Godman further explained that by 1936 (well before *Kristallnacht*) the Vatican understood that Nazi treatment of the Jews violated "the law of justice toward all races" which the Supreme Tribunal of the Roman Church regarded as a binding principle.[57]

More evidence that Pope Pius XII was concerned about Jewish victims, regardless of whether they were baptized, appeared in the book, *The Heresy of National Socialism*. Released in 1941 by the "Publishers to the Holy See" (Burns, Oates, & Washburn), and carrying both an *imprimatur* and a *nihil obstat*, this book laid out a strong condemnation of Nazism, focusing on both Nazi persecution of the Catholic Church and on Hitler's extreme hatred of the Jews.[58] Catholics who read this book had no doubt about where the Holy See stood.

VATICAN RADIO

Critics usually overlook Vatican Radio, but it was a significant part of Pope Pius XII's war against the Nazis. A 1941 profile of Pius XII reported that "Rumors of accord with the Reich have repeatedly been smashed by new outbursts against Nazi persecutions from the Vatican radio or the semi-official Vatican newspaper, *Osservatore Romano*."[59] The Allies appreciated the way Vatican Radio "withstood every pressure brought against it by the Italian Fascists and their German masters."[60] In fact,

Vatican Radio was the first media outlet "to inform the world of the depths of Nazi atrocities."[61]

One reason why Vatican Radio is often overlooked is that its records are hard to uncover. Susan Zuccotti, for instance, suggests that the only versions available to researchers today are the re-broadcasts of the BBC, which she says are unreliable. In this she is clearly wrong. Accounts exist in many languages and from many sources, and they are fully consistent with the BBC transcripts.[62] The late Fr. Robert Graham, one of the people assigned to go through the Vatican's wartime records, described Vatican Radio's role in detail: "Research into the broadcasts during the crucial period 1940-1941 reveals a massive denunciation of persecutions and oppressions in Germany and in the German occupied territories. . . . Some of the most important of them were due to the initiative of Pius XII. A note from Msgr. Montini, substitute in the Secretariat of State, refers to the start of this campaign. Under a January 19, 1940 date he notes a directive from the Pope [on the appalling situation in Poland]: 'Provide information to Vatican Radio for German broadcast.'"[63]

As Pius XII knew, these broadcasts had concrete results because they inspired the resistance to stand in support of the victims, regardless of their nationality or background.[64] (Later, however, the Polish bishops would complain that papal statements sometimes created problems for them by infuriating the Nazis.)

Vatican Radio broadcasts regularly prompted vigorous protests from Mussolini and the Germans.[65] Goebbels vowed to silence Vatican Radio, and it was a capital crime to listen to it in Nazi Germany.[66] The Nazis called it the "Voice of the Pope."[67] Vatican officials responded that Vatican Radio was run by the Jesuits as an independent concern. Researchers, however, have discovered that Pius XII personally authored many of the intensely anti-German statements beamed around the world.[68] In other cases, directives were found from the pope regarding the content of the broadcasts. Fr. Robert Graham said: "I was stupefied at what I was reading. How could one explain actions so contrary to the principle of neutrality?"[69]

In January 1940, Pope Pius XII told Msgr. Montini that Vatican Radio must broadcast a report on the conditions of the Catholic Church in German-occupied Poland.[70] The first report, broadcast in German, took place on January 21. Two days later, in England, the *Manchester Guardian* reported: "Tortured Poland has found a powerful advocate in Rome." The paper went on to note that Vatican Radio's campaign had exposed Nazi abuse and the threat to all of Europe. The story was also reported in the January 23 edition of the *New York Times* under the headline "Vatican Denounces Atrocities in Poland; Germans Called Even Worse than Russians." The Vatican report confirmed that "the horror and inexcusable excesses committed on a helpless and a homeless people have been established by the unimpeachable testimony of eyewitnesses."[71] In March, the *American Israelite* reported that Pius XII was "taking actions that were obviously a rebuke to Jewish anti-Semitism."[72]

These broadcasts created a great deal of controversy. In the West, newspapers editorialized that Vatican Radio had set forth "a warning to all who value our civilization that Europe is under a mortal danger."[73] The Germans, on the other hand, warned the Vatican that such broadcasts could lead to "disagreeable repercussions."[74] Even John Cornwell admitted that Vatican Radio "attracted a flow of protests implying that the Holy See was continuously breaking the terms of the Reich Concordat" by its reporting on events in Poland.[75]

U.S. Representative to the Pope Harrold Tittmann explained why these broadcasts had to be eventually toned down: "In October 1939, the Jesuit-operated Vatican Radio started to broadcast first-hand accounts of atrocities perpetrated by the Nazis in Poland. . . . However, the Polish bishops hastened to notify the Vatican that after each broadcast had come over the air, various local populations suffered 'terrible' reprisals. The thought that there were those paying with their lives for the information publicized by the Vatican Radio made the continuation

of these broadcasts impossible."[76] Eventually, the Superior General of
the Jesuits gave the order to desist: "How I hated to give the order to
stop these broadcasts, especially since I am a Pole myself. But what
else could I do? They [the Nazis] have the power, and they use it as
they please."[77]

It was clear by now that the Church was strongly opposed to Hitler's
National Socialism. On January 26, under the headline "Vatican Radio Denounces Nazi Acts in Poland," an American Jewish newspaper
reported: "The Vatican radio this week broadcast an outspoken denunciation of German atrocities in Nazi [occupied] Poland, declaring
they affronted the moral conscience of mankind."[78] This same month,
the United Jewish Appeal for Refugees and Overseas Needs donated
$125,000 to help with the Vatican's efforts on behalf of victims of racial
persecution. The *Jewish Ledger* of Hartford, Connecticut, called the
donation in support of the papal efforts an "eloquent gesture" which
"should prove an important step in the direction of cementing bonds
of sympathy and understanding" between Jews and Catholics.[79]

Daniel Goldhagen quotes a Vatican Radio broadcast of January
1940, trying to make the point that the Vatican was concerned only
about Polish Catholics and could not spare a good word for Jews. He
then asks, rhetorically: "Why, as a moral and practical matter, did [Pius
XII] speak out publicly on behalf of the suffering of Poles, but not of
Jews? No good answer."[80] In doing this, Goldhagen badly misrepresents
the truth.

As an initial matter, the radio broadcast quoted by Goldhagen did
not limit itself to Christian Poles. It merely refered to "Poles." Writings of that time sometimes distinguished "Poles" and "Jews," using
the former designation to refer only to Polish Christians, but this was
far from always the case. Moreover, Goldhagen implies that Jews were
never mentioned on Vatican Radio. This is simply false.

Goldhagen seems to have taken his Vatican Radio quotation from
Pierre Blet's *Pius XII and the Second World War*. That book presents
itself as a synopsis of the *Actes et Documents* collection. Had Goldhagen

actually researched the Vatican Radio transcripts from January 1940 (the month upon which he focuses) he would have found that Jews were indeed expressly and clearly identified. A widely-reported upon broadcast stated the following: "A system of interior deportation and zoning is being organized, in the depth of one of Europe's severest winters, on principles and by methods that can be described only as brutal; and stark hunger stares 70 percent of Poland's population in the face, as its reserves of food-stuffs and tools are shipped to Germany to replenish the granaries of the metropolis. Jews and Poles are being herded into separate 'ghettos,' hermetically sealed and pitifully inadequate for the economic subsistence of the millions destined to live there."[81]

On July 30, 1940, in response to a speech given at the National Socialist Congress at Nuremberg, Vatican Radio instructed listeners to look to the teachings of St. Paul that were repeated by Popes Pius XI and Pius XII in *Mit Brennender Sorge* and *Summi Pontificatus*. The doctrine of human equality, said the broadcast, was the very heart of Christian Revelation. That destiny was common to all men, Germans, Poles, Jews, and Christians alike.

On October 15, 1940, Vatican Radio denounced "the immoral principles of Nazism,"[82] and it returned to this topic on November 19, 1940. The Spanish newspaper *Alcazar* had published an editorial denying that National Socialism was opposed to religion. In rebuttal, Vatican Radio not only set forth the facts of what was taking place in occupied areas, it also broadcast a reading of Nazi Party literature.[83] On March 30, 1941, Vatican Radio explicitly condemned "the wickedness of Hitler."[84] These broadcasts were among the first to break the news of the Nazi persecutions, but they were not the only such stories on Vatican Radio.

As suggested earlier, most Vatican Radio broadcasts are not easily accessible to researchers. There are, however several ways to learn about them. The broadcasts of Pius himself have been published in a twenty-volume set extending over his entire pontificate; many transcripts (translated from original broadcast transcripts provided by the Jesuits who ran Vatican Radio) were published in the *Tablet* of London; and—of greatest interest—a small, underground newsletter from Vichy France published several transcripts.

The Vichy publication was known as *La Voix du Vatican* (The Voice of the Vatican).[85] The broadcasts were directed to French listeners, and the "voice" of most of these broadcasts was Fr. Emmanuel Mistiaen.[86] In addition to reassuring the French that they would eventually emerge from the horror of Nazi occupation, Fr. Mistiaen continually reminded his listeners that mankind was indivisible and there were no superior or inferior races. His broadcasts resulted in several protests and threats from the German government (which also regularly jammed the broadcasts).[87]

In the summer of 1941, when foreign Jews were rounded up and deported from Vichy, the highest dignitaries of the Church immediately denounced the deportations and the treatment of Jews. Pope Pius XII "spoke with exceptional decisiveness against the over-valuation of blood and race."[88] On August 1, 1941, the Vatican Radio broadcast did the same: "A great scandal is presently taking place and this scandal is the treatment suffered by the Jews; it is why I desire that a free voice, the voice of a priest, should be raised in protest. In Germany the Jews are killed, brutalized, tortured because they are victims bereft of defense. How can a Christian accept such deeds . . . these men are the sons of those who 2,000 years ago gave Christianity to the world."[89] Continuing with this theme the following spring, a broadcast quoted Cardinal Van Roey, the primate of Belgium, condemning Nazi race theory.[90]

On July 16, 1942, French police officers spread out through Paris, rounded up thirteen thousand Jews, and locked them up for deportation. The French bishops issued a joint protest which stated: "The mass arrest of the Jews last week and the ill-treatment to which they were subjected . . . has deeply shocked us. There were scenes of unspeakable horror when the deported parents were separated from their children. Our Christian conscience cries out in horror. In the name of humanity and Christian principles we demand the inalienable rights of all individuals. From the depths of our hearts we pray Catholics to express their sympathy for the immense injury to so many Jewish mothers."[91]

At Pius XII's direction, the bishops' protests were broadcast and discussed for several days on Vatican Radio.[92] One of those broadcasts explained: "We must do everything to support these unhappy, persecuted people. There are no grounds—without committing grave sin—for us participating in this horror, participating in the degradation of human beings for whom our Savior gave his life."[93]

On September 14, 1942, Fr. Mistiaen's theme was "Let us not betray our brothers." There was no doubt about who was to be considered a brother: "Our Lord, Jesus-Christ, has always showed immense respect for each individual and for all human beings in general. . . . He first turns his attention to the flock of his own beloved Jewish people, to all those of his race who helped to save the world, among them his mother, his friends, his disciples. He gazed at the Jewish people with an everlasting love. . . . Those who refuse in their heart to recognize the dignity of all of God's children are committing a sacrilege."[94]

When Lord Bishop Bruno de Solages from Montauban spoke up against the deportation of Jews, he made clear that he considered Vatican Radio to be the authentic voice of the pope.[95] That helps account for all of the rescuers who have cited Vatican Radio as one of their inspirations. It also would account for the persecution of listeners by the Nazis.[96]

Of course, *La Voix du Vatican* did not reprint the broadcasts that were beamed into nations other than France. The July 3, 1943 issue of the *Tablet* published part of a transcript of a Vatican Radio broadcast into Germany from the bishops of Slovakia in which they expressly defended the rights of Jews under natural law. Similar broadcasts were made in other nations,[97] but the impact did not always reach into Nazi-controlled areas. For instance, on June 2, 1943, Pius delivered a speech to the College of Cardinals. Vatican Radio broadcast it in to Germany, including the statement: "He who makes a distinction between Jews and other men is unfaithful to God and is in conflict with God's commands."[98] When this was reprinted in occupied areas, Axis leaders deleted that section of the allocution.[99]

On January 29, 1944, Vatican Radio broadcast a strong condemnation of anti-Semitic legislation.[100] Less than two weeks later, the *New York Times* reported: "Vatican Radio, commenting on the Fascist raid on St. Paul's Basilica last Thursday in which sixty-four Italian officers and Jews who had received sanctuary there were arrested, said tonight that the Church would not yield in offering charity to everyone . . . Charity is above human constitutions. On this point, the priest can never yield. It is the demarcation line between good and evil."[101]

When the Catholic faithful were permitted to hear these broadcasts, they reacted accordingly. French priest-rescuer (and later Cardinal) Henri de Lubac paid tribute to the pope's radio station, describing the profound impact it had upon the French resistance.[102] Similarly, Michel Riquet, sj, an ex-inmate of Dachau who was recognized for saving Jewish lives, stated: "Pius xii spoke; Pius xii condemned; Pius xii acted. . . . Throughout those years of horror, when we listened to Radio Vatican and to the Pope's messages, we felt in communion with the Pope in helping persecuted Jews and in fighting against Nazi violence."[103] Riquet repeated these sentiments in 1965, when he led a pilgrimage of French Catholics to Israel.[104]

1942 AND THE CHRISTMAS STATEMENT

In September 1942, President Roosevelt sent a message to the Pope detailing reports from the Warsaw ghetto and asking whether the Vatican had any information that would tend to confirm or deny the reports of Nazi crimes.[105] In mid-October, the Holy See replied, stating that it, too, had reports of "severe measures" taken against the Jews, but that it had been impossible to verify the accuracy of the reports. The statement went on, however, to note that "the Holy See is taking advantage of every opportunity offered in order to mitigate the suffering of non-Aryans."[106]

The following month, at their annual meeting in Washington, D.C., the U.S. Bishops released a statement indicating that the Vatican had come to believe the horrible news coming from Germany and occupied nations: "Since the murderous assault on Poland, utterly devoid of every semblance of humanity, there has been a premeditated and systematic extermination of the people of this nation. The same satanic technique is being applied to many other peoples. We feel a deep sense of revulsion against the cruel indignities heaped upon Jews in conquered countries and upon defenseless peoples not of our faith. . . . Deeply moved by the arrest and maltreatment of the Jews, we cannot stifle the cry of conscience. In the name of humanity and Christian principles, our voice is raised."[107]

Daniel Goldhagen attempted to portray this statement as a slap at Pius XII and an "all but explicit rebuke of the Vatican." Actually, the American bishops repeatedly invoked Pius XII's name and teachings with favor ("We recall the words of Pope Pius XII"; "We urge the serious study of peace plans of Pope Pius XII"; "In response to the many appeals of our Holy Father"). Moreover, in a letter written at this very time, Pius expressed thanks for the "constant and understanding collaboration" of the American bishops and archbishops.[108]

Parts of the pope's letter of thanks were published in the very same issue of a Catholic newspaper that contained the bishops' statement.[109] It should be noted that there was a general thanks given to the "hierarchy, clergy, and faithful" for their efforts, but the thanks for collaboration was separate and directed to the bishops and archbishops. The bishops replied with a letter pledging "anew to the Holy Father our best efforts in the fulfillment of his mission of apostolic charity to war victims." They also offered a prayer for his collaborators.

The very idea that the bishops were trying to insult the Holy Father is preposterous. Archbishop (later Cardinal) Francis Spellman said: "Our President and our Holy Father have combined the forces of our country and the forces of religion in a battle for peace."[110]

For his part, in late 1942, Pius sent three letters of support to bishops in Poland. The letters were intended to be read and distributed by the bishops to the faithful. The bishops all thanked the Pontiff, but responded that they could not publish his words or read them aloud, because that would lead to more persecution of Jews and of Catholics.[111]

With the Vatican having recognized Nazi atrocities earlier than many other nations and having assisted western powers early during the hostilities, Allied leaders sought to have the pope join in a formal declaration concerning the atrocities taking place in Germany and in German-occupied areas. In a message dated September 14, 1942, the Brazilian ambassador, Ildebrando Accioly, wrote: "It is necessary that the authorized and respected voice of the Vicar of Christ be heard against these atrocities."[112] On that same day, British Minister D'Arcy Osborne and American representative Harold H. Tittmann requested a "public and specific denunciation of Nazi treatment of the populations of the counties under German occupation."[113] Interestingly, neither Tittmann nor Accioly mentioned the treatment of Jews by the Nazis. Osborne, who did mention the treatment of Jewish people in his request to the pope, reported back to London that the coordinated requests to the pontiff looked like an effort to involve the pope in political and partisan action.[114]

Pius was non-committal in response to these requests, and a few weeks later President Roosevelt's representative, Myron Taylor, renewed the request on behalf of the Allies. American representatives ultimately reported back that the Holy See was convinced that an open condemnation would "result in the violent deaths of many more people."[115] A secret British telegram from this same time period reported on an audience with the pope: "His Holiness undertook to do whatever was possible on behalf of the Jews, but His Majesty's Minister doubted whether there would be any public statement."[116]

Critics have sometimes used this episode to argue that the Allies were upset with Pope Pius XII's stance in the war. Recently however, the Franklin D. Roosevelt Library posted several wartime documents on the Internet, including an official summary prepared by Myron Taylor of the conversations that he had with the Pope on September 19, 22, and 26, 1942. Taylor made it clear that the Holy See and the Allies saw eye-to-eye: "We have seen how the Vatican and America were not self-seeking, were and are free from materialistic or ambitious motives; how the parallel efforts of His Holiness and President Roosevelt for the maintenance of peace were energized by their very spiritual qualities. We have seen the Encyclical of Pope Pius XI and the allocutions of Pope Pius XII. . . . All have harmonized in upholding the moral code which aims to protect mankind in freedom and justice under the moral law."[117]

Taylor read to the pope from a statement that had been approved by President Roosevelt:

Before the war became general, President Roosevelt, in parallel effort with the Holy See, explored every possible avenue for the preservation of the peace. The experience of those days of fruitful cooperation, when the high moral prestige of the Holy See was buttressed by the civil power of the United States of America, is a precious memory. Although totalitarian aggression defeated those first efforts to prevent world war, the United States looks forward to further collaboration of this kind when the anti-Christian philosophies which have taken the sword shall have perished by the sword, and it will again be possible to organize world peace.

In the just war which they are now waging, the people of the United States of America derive great spiritual strength and moral encouragement from a review of the utterances of His Holiness Pope Pius XII and of his venerated Predecessor. Americans, Catholic and non-Catholic, have been profoundly impressed by the searing condemnation of Nazi religious persecution pronounced by Pope Pius xi in his "Mit Brennender Sorge;" by the elevated teaching on law and human dignity contained in the "Summi Pontificatus" of Pope Pius xii; by the famous Five Points laid down in 1939 by the same Pope as the essential postulates of a just peace; and by the forthright and heroic expressions of indignation made by Pope Pius xii when Germany invaded the Low Countries. Now that we are fighting against the very things which the Popes condemned, our conviction of complete victory is one with our confidence in the unwavering tenacity with which the Holy See will continue its magnificent moral leading.[118]

Reporting on the pope's reaction to this statement, Taylor wrote: "The prompt reaction of His Holiness to the positive statements of American attitude was one of surprising satisfaction, of immediate and happy response and the repetition, several times, by His Holiness of words to the effect that America would not compromise but would continue the war until victory was achieved."[119]

Reporting on his second meeting with the pope (September 22, 1942), Taylor gave more details about Pius xii's attitude:

Despite all propaganda, His Holiness "would never propose or approve of peace by compromise at any cost;" "there can be no compromise of moral principles," and "it is gratifying to know that the peace aims of the United States uphold this approach to the ultimate conclusion of the war."

He emphatically asserted that "we need have no fear that any pressure from outside the Vatican will ever make it change its course."[120]

The pope did not join in this condemnation, perhaps because as a *New York Times* editorial concluded, the joint Allied statement was "an official indictment."[121] Pius did not want to breach the Church's official neutrality by joining in a declaration made by either side, and he was concerned that the Allies' statement would be used as part of the war effort (as happened with some of his earlier radio broadcasts).[122] He did, however, make his own statement.[123]

In his 1942 Christmas statement, broadcast over Vatican Radio, Pope Pius XII said that the world was "plunged into the gloom of tragic error," and that "the Church would be untrue to herself, she would have ceased to be a mother, if she were deaf to the cries of suffering children which reach her ears from every class of the human family."[124] He spoke of the need for mankind to make "a solemn vow never to rest until valiant souls of every people and every nation of the earth arise in their legions, resolved to bring society and to devote themselves to the services of the human person and of a divinely ennobled human society." He said that mankind owed this vow to all victims of the war, including "the hundreds of thousands who, through no fault of their own, and solely because of their nation or race, have been condemned to death or progressive extinction."[125]

Pius also condemned totalitarian regimes and acknowledged some culpability on the part of the Church: "A great part of the human race, and not a few—We do not hesitate to say it—not a few even of those who call themselves Christians, bear some share in the collective responsibility for the aberrations, the disasters, and the low moral state of modern society." He urged all Catholics to give shelter wherever they could.

The Polish ambassador thanked the pontiff, who "in his last Christmas address implicitly condemned all the injustices and cruelties suffered by the Polish people at the hands of the Germans. Poland acclaims this condemnation; it thanks the Holy Father for his words."[126] British records reflect the opinion that "the Pope's condemnation of the treatment of the Jews & the Poles is quite unmistakable, and the message is perhaps more forceful in tone than any of his recent statements. The Pope informed the United States Minister to the Vatican that he considered his recent broadcast to be clear and comprehensive in its condemnation of the heartrending treatment of Poles, Jews, hostages, etc. And to have satisfied all recent demands that he should speak out."[127]

The Dutch bishops issued a pastoral letter in defense of Jewish people on February 21, 1943, making express reference to the Pope's statement.[128] Moreover, a well-known Christmas Day editorial in the *New York Times* praised Pius XII for his moral leadership in opposing the Nazis:

> No Christmas sermon reaches a larger congregation than the message Pope Pius XII addresses to a war-torn world at this season. This Christmas more than ever he is a lonely voice crying out of the silence of a continent. . . .
>
> When a leader bound impartially to nations on both sides condemns as heresy the new form of national state which subordinates everything to itself; when he declares that whoever wants peace must protect against "arbitrary attacks" the "juridical safety of individuals"; when he assails violent occupation of territory, the exile and persecution of human beings for no reason other than race or political opinion; when he says that people must fight for a just and decent peace, a "total peace"—the "impartial judgment" is like a verdict in a high court of justice.[129]

A similar editorial from the *Times* of London, commenting on the Pope's statements in general, said: "A study of the words which Pope Pius XII has addressed since his accession in encyclicals and allocutions to the Catholics of various nations leaves no room for doubt. He condemns the worship of force and its concrete manifestation in the suppression of national liberties and in the persecution of the Jewish race."[130] Obviously, in contrast to what the critics would have us believe, everyone knew to whom the Pope was referring, including the Axis powers.

According to an official Nazi report by Heinrich Himmler's Superior Security Office (the Reichssicherheitshauptamt—the main security department of the Nazi government) to Foreign Minister Joachim von Ribbentrop's office: "In a manner never known before, the Pope has repudiated the National Socialist New European Order.... It is true, the Pope does not refer to the National Socialists in Germany by name, but his speech is one long attack on everything we stand for.... God, he says, regards all people and races as worthy of the same consideration. Here he is clearly speaking on behalf of the Jews.... [H]e is virtually accusing the German people of injustice toward the Jews, and makes himself the mouthpiece of the Jewish war criminals.[131]

An American report noted that the Germans were "conspicuous by their absence" at a midnight Mass conducted by the pope for diplomats on Christmas Eve following the papal statement.[132] German Ambassador Diego von Bergen, on the instruction of Ribbentrop, warned the pope that the Nazis would seek retaliation if the Vatican abandoned its neutral position. But the German ambassador reported to his superiors that "Pacelli is no more sensible to threats than we are."[133]

Popes of this era did not speak as directly as a modern American politician might speak. Yet, when Pope Pius xii spoke of "the hundreds of thousands" condemned to death because of their "nation or race" [or descent, or *stirpe*],[134] the press, rescuers, and even the Jewish victims knew what he meant. As he explained after the war: "We know in fact that Our broadcasts ... were in spite of every prohibition and obstacle studied by diocesan conferences and expounded to the people."[135]

That people understood papal messages is reflected in the anger that Pius xii's protests provoked in Nazi ranks. Radio operator François de Beaulieu (later a Protestant minister) was arrested and imprisoned for carrying a translation of the broadcast and thereby spreading a "subversive and demoralizing document." He was also accused of having a critical view of the war and of being "spiritually attracted to Jewish environments and sympathetic toward Jews." De Beaulieu later explained: "The Pope could not do much more. He would have had to set himself on fire in front of the Vatican to awaken consciences worldwide. Many political leaders knew that there were extermination camps in Hitler's time. Of what used would it have been for the Pope to set himself on fire in front of the Vatican?"[136]

Karl Otto Wolff, ss chief in Italy toward the end of the war, testi-fied to having received the orders to invade the Vatican from Hitler himself.[137] The German Ambassador to Italy and an aide to the Ger-man Ambassador to the Holy See both confirmed that Hitler had such plans.[138] Fortunately, he was dissuaded from them, but the reaction from Hitler and other Nazi leaders is strong evidence about how they viewed the pope and the Vatican leadership. In fact, in 1944, before the Allies liberated Rome, Wolff approached Pius xii to discuss a possible peace treaty. At that time Wolff provided Pius with documents regard-ing Hitler's plans to invade the Vatican.[139]

MYSTICI CORPORIS CHRISTI

Pope Pius xii's 1943 encyclical, *Mystici Corporis Christi* (*On the Mystical Body*) was primarily a letter on theology, so it contained no express references to Hitler or the Nazis. Still, it was an obvious attack on the theoretical basis of National Socialism.[140] Critics seem to miss the im-portance of this document, but as Israeli diplomat Pinchas E. Lapide said: "Pius chose mystical theology as a cloak for a message which no cleric or educated Christian could possibly misunderstand."[141] "Clerics and educated Christians" would, of course, include priests and bishops who would "translate" messages for other Christians.

Historians like to rely upon documentary evidence in original lan-guages. This places a premium on linguistic abilities. Translation issues, however, show that the ability to read a given language is not in and of itself sufficient to come to a full understanding of papal statements.[142] The ability to understand "Vatican-talk" is equally important. Those who look at papal statements without that ability are like someone looking at a language that they do not understand. Unfortunately, crit-ics seem completely lost when it comes to understanding how Vatican leaders spoke in the early twentieth century.

In *Mystici Corporis Christi*, Pius wrote: "The Church of God. . . is despised and hated maliciously by those who shut their eyes to the light of Christian wisdom and miserably return to the teachings, customs, and practices of ancient paganism." He wrote of the "passing things of earth," and the "massive ruins" of war. He offered prayers that world leaders be granted the love of wisdom and expressed no doubt that "a most severe judgment" would await those leaders who did not follow God's will.

Pius appealed to "Catholics the world over" to "look to the Vicar of Jesus Christ as the loving Father of them all, who . . . takes upon himself with all his strength the defense of truth, justice, and charity." He explained, "Our paternal love embraces all peoples, whatever their nationality or race."

Despite claims by the critics that Pius never mentioned Jews in his wartime pronouncements, in this document he made a statement that was quite remarkable for its time: "Christ, by his blood, made the Jews and Gentiles one, 'breaking down the middle wall of partition . . . in his flesh' by which the two peoples were divided." He noted that Jews were among the first people to adore Jesus. Pius then made an appeal for all to "follow our peaceful King who taught us to love not only those who are of a different nation or race, but even our enemies."[143]

The impact of the encyclical was expanded as it was repeated. In June, Vatican Radio followed up with a broadcast that expressly stated: "He who makes a distinction between Jews and other men is unfaithful to God and in conflict with God's commands."[144] On July 28, 1943, a Vatican Radio broadcast further reported on the Pope's denunciation of totalitarian forms of government and support for democratic ideals: "The life and activities of all must be protected against arbitrary human action. This means that no man has any right on the life and freedom of other men. Authority . . . cannot be at the service of any arbitrary power. Herein lies the essential differences between tyranny and true usefulness. . . . The Pope condemns those who dare to place the fortunes of whole nations in the hands of one man alone, a man who as such, is the prey of passions, error and dreams."[145] Adolf Hitler's name was not used, but there was no doubt to whom the pope was referring. Critics who today say otherwise are either very poorly informed or they are acting in bad faith.

THE ROUNDUP OF ROMAN JEWS ON OCTOBER 16, 1943

When the Germans occupied Rome, they sought a ransom from Jewish leaders in exchange for the promise not to deport Jews. When the Jewish community had trouble raising the necessary amount of gold, they appealed to the pope, who offered to loan as much gold as necessary for as long it was needed.[146] Ultimately, it seems that the community raised the money itself, without needing the loan. Unfortunately, the ransom merely bought a bit of time. Shortly thereafter, Colonel Kappler, SS commander in Rome, received an order to arrest the eight thousand Jews who were living in the Roman ghetto and send them to northern Italy where they would face eventual extermination. On October 16, 1,269 Jews were captured.[147] The next day, German Ambassador Ernst Von Weizsäcker wired to Berlin that "The Curia is particularly shocked that the action took place, so to speak, under the pope's windows. This reaction would be perhaps softened if the Jews could be used for military work in Italy."[148]

In the 1960s, critic Robert Katz set forth the hypothesis that Pope Pius XII knew of the October 16, 1943, roundup before it took place, but he did nothing to prevent it.[149] Katz's account has many holes in it.[150] He says that he talked to a German diplomat (Eitel Möllhausen) who claimed to have told the German ambassador to the Holy See, Baron Ernst von Weizsäcker, about the roundup in advance. Katz then suggests that Weizsäcker told Vatican officials and they must have told the pope. Weizsäcker, however, never mentioned this matter in his memoirs.[151] No wonder that the Congregation for the Causes of Saints ended up quoting the *New York Times* review that called Katz's book "hostile," "uninformed," and "downright offensive."[152]

The only recorded witness to the pope's reaction upon learning of the roundup is Italian Princess Enza Pignatelli. She went to the Pope to seek help as soon as she learned of the roundup. She reported that Pius was "furious" when he learned of it.[153] "Let's go make a few phone calls," he said.[154]

Pius immediately filed a protest through Cardinal Secretary of State Maglione with German Ambassador Weizsäcker, demanding that the Germans "stop these arrests at once."[155] The British representative to the Holy See sent a secret telegram to the Foreign Office in which he reported: "As soon as he heard of the arrests of Jews in Rome Cardinal Secretary of State sent for the German Ambassador and formulated some [sort] of protest."[156] The result, according to British records, was that "large numbers" of the Jews were released.[157]

The recently-released memoirs of Adolf Eichmann confirm that Vatican protests played a crucial part in obstructing Nazi plans for Roman Jews following the roundup on October 16, 1943.[158] Eichmann wrote that the Vatican "vigorously protested the arrest of Jews, requesting the interruption of such action."[159] He explained that "the objections given [by the Church] and the excessive delay . . . resulted in a great part of Italian Jews being able to hide and escape capture."[160] At the trial, Israeli Attorney General Gideon Hausner, in his opening statement, said "the Pope himself intervened personally in support of the Jews of Rome."[161] A Protestant minister, Heinrich Grober, testified at the trial that Pius helped him save Jews.[162] Documents introduced in the trial also show Vatican efforts for a halt to the arrests of Roman Jews.[163] In rejecting Eichmann's appeals following his conviction, the Israeli Supreme court noted the pope's protest regarding the deportation of Hungarian Jews.[164] Such evidence overwhelms conflicting arguments from the critics.

The raid on Roman Jews ended abruptly at 2:00 PM on October 16, after the Nazis had seized about twelve hundred of the originally-intended eight thousand Jews. Critics, however, refuse to acknowledge that the Vatican played any part in this decision. Susan Zuccotti, for instance, emphatically declares that there is "no evidence for this position. On the contrary, the chronology refutes it. [ss Chief] Himmler could not have learned of the possibility of a papal protest until . . . the evening of October 16. . . . Sometime that same evening, Kappler, the chief of the security police in Rome who had organized and conducted the roundup on Himmler's orders, informed ss Lieutenant General Karl Wolff, commander of the ss in Italy, that arrests had ceased that afternoon. . . . Clearly there were no plans for continuing the action."[165]

According, however, to sworn testimony given by German diplomat Gerhard Gumpert (for the 1948 trial of Baron Ernst von Weizsäcker), Pius XII's personal emissary, Fr. Pancratius Pfeiffer, delivered a letter of protest to General Rainer Stahel, the German army commander in Rome, "toward noon" on October 16th.[166] The general telephoned Himmler shortly after receiving this message.[167] Thus, there was plenty of time—two full hours—for Stahel to contact Himmler and for Himmler to order Kappler to end the raids. Indeed, Bishop Alois Hudal reported that on October 17th, he received a phone call from General Stahel who assured him that he had "referred the matter at once to the local Gestapo and to Himmler, Himmler ordered that in view of the special character of Rome these arrests were to be halted at once."[168]

On November 7, 2000, the German Catholic news agency KNA, released a remarkable interview with Nikolaus Kunkel, a German officer stationed in Rome during the round-up. Kunkel, a lieutenant on the staff of General Stahel revealed that the pope forcefully intervened behind the scenes to rescue Rome's Jews and that as a result of the pope's actions, General Stahel, persuaded the Nazi authorities to stop the anti-Jewish raids at once. Kunkel went on to note that if Pius had publicized these efforts, it would have backfired and caused immense harm.[169]

Susan Zuccotti argued that "clearly, there were no plans for continuing the [roundup] action" by the Nazis. That claim, however, is made without any supporting documentation and is flatly contradicted by Jewish historian Michael Tagliacozzo (himself a survivor of the Roman raid). Commenting on Pius XII's actions during the raid, he explained:

> The documents clearly prove that, in the early hours of the morning, Pius XII was informed of what was happening and he immediately had German Ambassador von Weizsäcker called and ordered State Secretary Luigi Maglione to energetically protest the Jews' arrest, asking that similar actions be stopped. . . . In addition, by his initiative he had a letter of protest sent through Bishop Alois Hudal [delivered by Fr. Pfeiffer] to the military commander in Rome, General Rainer Stahel, requesting that the persecution of Jews cease immediately. As a result of these protests, the operation providing for two days of arrests and deportations was interrupted at 2 PM the same day. Instead of the 8,000 Jews Hitler requested, 1,259 were arrested. After meticulous examination of identity documents and other papers of identification, the following day an additional 259 people were released. Moreover, after the manhunt in Rome on Oct. 16, the Germans did not capture a single Jew. Those who were arrested were handed over by collaborators.[170]

Shortly after the roundup, Pius XII published an article in *L'Osservatore Romano* that made clear the pope's view.[171] The *Jewish Chronicle* of London ran a headline proclaiming: "Jewish Hostages in Rome: Vatican Protests."[172] Commenting on this episode, others have noted that "those Romans reading between the lines understood that Pius XII wanted Catholics to 'do all they possibly can, to hide and save Jews.'"[173]

In other words, all of our best evidence suggests that the pope was not warned about this roundup. Nevertheless, Katz's theory has been embraced by critics like Susan Zuccotti, even though she claims to base her analysis on archival evidence.[174] In fact, in her 1986 book Zuccotti acknowledged that the story about Weizsäcker alerting the pope might be "untrue."[175] In a footnote, she even noted that Weizsäcker's secretary,

Albert von Kessel, did not know whether the pope had been informed and that Weizsäcker never mentioned the incident in his memoirs.[176] In her 2001 book, however, she dropped all qualifications and cautionary notes and presented Pius XII's foreknowledge as fact.[177]

In *Hitler's Pope*, John Cornwell suggested that the October 16, 1943, deportation did not sufficiently concern Pius XII. Part of the "evidence" cited by Cornwell was a message sent from U.S. official Harold Tittmann to the State Department regarding a meeting he had with Pius.[178] The message was dated October 19, and reported not the Pope's outrage at the Nazis roundup a few days earlier, but his concern that "Communist bands" might "commit violence in the city." If things were actually as Cornwell reported them, Pius would indeed appear indifferent to this Nazi abuse of Jewish people. Such, however, is not the case.

The Vatican keeps precise records of audiences given by the pope. The transcribed message to Washington from Harold Tittmann is dated October 19th, but this is a mistake. Vatican records show that the meeting between Pius and Tittmann took place on October 14th.[179] In fact, *L'Osservatore Romano* of October 15, 1943 reported on page one (top of the first column) that Tittmann was received by the pope in a private audience on October 14, 1943.[180] Apparently a handwritten "4" was misread as a "9" when the documents were typed. The pope did not mention the roundup of Jews because it had not yet happened. His concern was that a group of Communists would commit a violent act and this would lead to serious repercussions. Of course, he proved to be exactly correct the following spring.[181]

THE PLOT TO KIDNAP THE POPE

Critics often dismiss it, but the possibility of a German invasion of Vatican City was very real.[182] Napoleon had done this in 1809, capturing Pope Pius VII at bayonet point and taking him away.[183] Rolf Hochhuth rejected the notion that Pius XII feared "violence against himself or, say, against St. Peters,"[184] but even he admitted that Hitler considered invading the Vatican. In fact, minutes of a Berlin high command meeting show that Hitler spoke of wanting to enter the Vatican and "pack up that whole whoring rabble."[185]

Ernst von Weizsäcker, the German Ambasador to the Vatican, wrote that he heard of Hitler's plan to kidnap Pius XII.[186] Weizsäcker regularly cautioned Vatican officials not to provoke Berlin.[187] Written statements by the German Ambassador to Italy, Rudolf Rahn, also describe the plot and attempts by himself and other Nazi officials to head it off.[188] "The fact of [the plan's] existence and its target is solidly anchored in my memory," reported Rahn.[189] Albrecht von Kessel, Weizsäcker's closest aide, explained, "All we could do . . . was to warn the Vatican, the church, and the Pope himself against rash utterances and actions."[190] (Pius told Cardinal Nasalli Rocca, "If the Nazis decide to kidnap me, then they're going to have to drag me away by force. Because I'm staying here.")[191]

Karl Wolff, SS chief in Italy toward the end of the war, reported the following conversation from 1943:

> HITLER: Now, Wolff, I have a special mission for you, with significance for the whole world, and it is a personal matter between you and me. You are never to speak of it with anyone without my permission, with the exception of the Supreme Commandant of the SS [Himmler], who is aware of everything. Do you understand?
>
> WOLFF: Understood, *Führer*!
>
> HITLER: I want you and your troops, while there is still a strong reaction in Germany to the Badoglio treachery, to occupy as soon as possible the Vatican and Vatican City, secure the archives and the art treasures, which have a unique value, and transfer the Pope, together with the Curia, for their protection, so that they cannot fall into the hands of the Allies and exert a political influence. According to military and political developments it will be determined whether to bring him to Germany or place him in neutral Liechtenstein. How quickly could you prepare this operation?[192]

Wolff said that it would take four to six weeks in order to come up with a plan. Hitler replied: "That's far too long. It's crucial that you let me know every two weeks how you are getting on. I should prefer to take the Vatican immediately."[193]

When someone suggested to Hitler that such an attack would create a public relations problem for the party, he dismissed the concern: "That doesn't matter, I'll go right into the Vatican. Do you think I worry about the Vatican? We'll take that right off. All the diplomatic corps will be hiding in there. I don't give a damn; if the entire crew's in there, we'll get the whole lot of swine out. Afterward, we can say we're sorry. We can easily do that. We've got a war on."[194]

Embarrassment was one thing, but when Wolff reported his plan back to Hitler in early December 1943, he expressed his opinion that the Italian people would defend their Church at all costs and any action against the Church would make occupation all the more difficult. Reportedly, Foreign Minister Joachim Von Ribbentrop gave similar advice about an attack on the Vatican: "If you send aircraft over to bomb the Vatican, it will be the last move we will make. Our own people can overlook much, even our attacks on priests of other countries; but if we attack the Vatican, we will most assuredly have a civil war in Germany within the hour the first bomb falls."[195] In light of this advice, Hitler dropped the kidnaping plan.[196]

The existence of a plan to kill or kidnap the pope was documented on July 5, 1998, when an article in the Milan newspaper *Il Giornale* reported on the discovery of a letter dated September 26, 1944, from Paolo Porta, the Fascist leader in Como, to Vincenzo Costa, the Fascist leader in Milan. In that letter, Porta cited a high ss official to the effect that in December 1943, Hitler personally delegated Himmler and Gestapo head Heinrich Müller to study and execute a plan to eliminate the pope. The plan called for Germans dressed as Italian partisans to attack the Vatican. German troops would then come to the "rescue," with the hope that Pius would be killed in the foray. If he were not killed, he would be sent to Germany for "protection." After the attack, "the persecution of the Catholic Church would begin with mass deportations to Germany of all ecclesiastics in Italy and throughout the world. They are to be considered the cause of ignorance, of domination, of conspiracies. . . ." The reason for the attack was identified as "the papal protest in favor of the Jews."[197]

Hochhuth tried to diminish the threat of an invasion by saying that Hitler made this comment "among his intimates" and suggesting that it was not serious. Hochhuth then went on to discuss "feverish diplomatic activity" on behalf of the Vatican.[198] This would be natural, especially since thousands of Jewish people were being hidden from the Nazis in the Vatican. It would also indicate that the Vatican took the threat very seriously.

THE LIBERATION OF ROME

On June 2, 1944 (the feast day of St. Eugenio), the pope spoke about his war-related efforts: "To one sole goal our thoughts are turned, night and day: how it may be possible to abolish such acute suffering, coming to the relief of all, without distinction of nationality or race."[199] On June 4, the Allies finally made their way to Rome. Fortunately, despite Hitler's earlier warnings (and Mussolini's call for street-fighting),[200] as the Allies entered on one side of Rome, the Germans left quietly from the other side.[201] The German Ambassador to the Holy See, Ernst von Weizsäcker, in discussing the peaceful exchange that took place in Rome, gave "chief credit to the ceaseless quiet activity of the Pope."[202]

Both the Italian king and the prime minister had fled to safety in southern Italy when the Germans invaded. Mussolini, having been ousted as dictator, was in northern Italy. As such, during the occupation and at the time of liberation, the pope was the only authority figure in Rome. Thousands who had been in hiding ran out into St. Peter's Square for the first time in nine months and embraced the soldiers.[203] That evening, families joined other families in a massive, joyous march up to Vatican City to thank God and Pope Pius for bringing them through the war.[204]

The Romans considered Pius "their bishop."[205] They proclaimed him *Defensor Urbis* and *Defensor Civitatis* (Urban Defender).[206] They had no doubts about where the pope stood. Books had already been written and speeches had been made documenting the Vatican's support of the Allies and work with the Jewish victims of the Nazis.[207] Crowds streamed into the square and called for Papa Pacelli, who appeared on the loggia. He thanked God for saving Rome. "Every phrase of his was punctuated with thunders of applause. . . . He said that whereas yesterday Rome was still fearful for the fate of her children, today she rejoiced. . . ."[208] He gave a blessing to the crowd and left the balcony. The crowd continued to acclaim him.[209] Mussolini, who had sided with the Nazis, would receive a very different reception the following year.

The pope's standing with Jewish soldiers from the United States is reflected in the bulletin put out by the "Jewish Brigade Group" (U.S. 8th Army). The June 1944 edition carried a front-page editorial which proclaimed: "To the everlasting glory of the people of Rome and the Roman Catholic Church we can state that the fate of the Jews was alleviated by their truly Christian offers of assistance and shelter."[210] The Jewish chaplain of the Fifth Army explained: "If it had not been for the truly substantial assistance and the help given to Jews by the Vatican and by Rome's ecclesiastical authorities, hundreds of refugees and thousands of Jewish refugees would have undoubtedly perished before Rome was liberated."[211] The Committee on Army and Navy Religious Activities of the American Jewish Welfare Board wrote to the pope:

> Word comes to us from our army chaplains in Italy telling of the aid and protection given to so many Italian Jews by the Vatican and by priests and institutions of the Church during the Nazi occupation of the land. We are deeply moved by these stirring stories of Christian love, the more so as we know full well to what

dangers many of those exposed themselves who gave shelter and aid to the Jews hunted by the Gestapo.

From the bottom of our heart we send to you, Holy Father of the Church, the assurance of our unforgetting gratitude for this noble expression of religious brotherhood and love.[212]

Davar, the Hebrew daily of Israel's Federation of Labor, quoted a Jewish Brigade officer shortly after Rome's liberation: "When we entered Rome, the Jewish survivors told us with a voice filled with deep gratitude and respect: 'If we have been rescued; if Jews are still alive in Rome come with us and thank the pope in the Vatican. For in the Vatican proper, in churches, monasteries and private homes, Jews were kept hidden at his personal orders.'"[213]

On July 31, 1944, in front of fifty thousand people at Madison Square Garden, Judge Joseph Proskauer, the president of the American Jewish Committee said, "We have heard ... what a great part the Holy Father has played in the salvation of refugees in Italy, and we know ... that this great Pope has reached forth his mighty and sheltering hand to help the oppressed of Hungary."[214] That same month, Dr. Israel Zolli, the chief rabbi of Rome, "made a solemn declaration in the Roman synagogue, paying tribute to the Holy See for having condemned the anti-Semitic laws and diminished their effects."[215] Today, in Vatican City, where one enters the porticos of the Sacred Congregation for Bishops just off St. Peter's Square, is a square called "The Square of Pius XII, the Savior of the City."[216] "Savior of the world," is the way some Jewish survivors have preferred to describe him.[217]

"COLOURED TROOPS"

Critics have one issue that they like to discuss about the liberation of Rome. Just before it took place, the British ambassador to the Vatican, Francis D'Arcy Osborne, cabled to England that "the pope hoped that no allied coloured troops would be among the small number that might be garrisoned at Rome after the occupation."[218] Critics take this as evidence that the pope was a racist.[219]

Actually, the pope's concern was not about "coloured troops," but specific French Moroccan troops who were known to the Vatican to have engaged in acts of violence.[220] As reflected in an American intelligence report of the time, this misunderstanding stems from a report the pope received about French Moroccan troops that had committed horrible acts of violence in areas where they were stationed.[221] As bishop of Rome, Pius did not want those soldiers stationed in his city (or anywhere else).[222] Pius expressed his concerns about these specific men (he spoke of "Marocchini," not "coloured troops") to Osborne, who broadened the statement in his cable back to London, perhaps in order to avoid insulting French allies.

That the pope was concerned about specific French Moroccan troops is made clear in a now-declassified confidential memorandum from the Office of Stategic Services, Washington, D.C.,[223] an article that appeared in *l'Osservatore Romano* on October 4, 1944,[224] and a message sent from the Vatican to its representative in France.[225] None of these documents makes reference to race, just the pope's concern over these specific French Moroccan troops. The lack of any other records relating to the request confirm that this was not a racial matter, especially when considered in light of the pontiff's other statements, actions, and appointment of minority bishops.

The ss journal, *Das Schwarze Korps*, published an article arguing that it was a crime against nature to permit black soldiers to fight against white races. It attacked the French for "following the creed of the Vatican, believing that baptism can transform the soul of a man." Vatican Radio replied:

(a) That it is sufficient for a black man to be a human being in order to be able to claim a human soul and human dignity. The black race has proved... that it has been able to fill the gap between the primitive state and civilization. Black men have given proof that they can be a real asset to human culture.

(b) The allegation that it is a crime to allow colored people to fight against the white race reminds us that Germany made Negroes fight during the last war in East Africa.

(c) The movement of the black peoples towards the Catholic Church is becoming very considerable. There are at present over seven million black persons who have embraced the Catholic Faith, and they are among its most valuable members. According to the statement of a well-known missionary... the deep faith and high morals he found in Africa are beyond comparison."[226]

In paragraph 45-50, of his first encyclical, *Summi Pontificatus* (*Darkness Over the Earth*) Pius dealt with racial matters and expressed his belief that the Church could not discriminate against any given race of people. He expressly stated that all races and nationalities were welcome in the Church and had equal rights as children in the house of the Lord. In paragraph 48, he put meaning to his anti-racist statements by naming new bishops of different races and nationalities. Two weeks later, in *Sertum Laetitiae* (*On the Establishment of the Hierarchy in the United States*), Pius wrote of a "special paternal affection" for black Americans.

Shortly after World War II, a pastor in Indianapolis, Indiana assured this congregation that "no Negro will ever come to Holy Angels parish." When word of this made its way to Rome, Pope Pius XII immediately had the pastor removed.[227] About this same time (May 27, 1946), Pius addressed the American Negro Publishers Association on the importance of interracial justice and brotherhood.[228]

Against all of this and more, the critics cite only a secondary source that, by all of the best evidence, mis-reports the pope's actual request. Once again, a fair analysis of the evidence suggests that the critics are far too willing to accept bad evidence when it meets with their preconceived notions.

POST-WAR STATEMENTS

Critics including Susan Zuccotti, Michael Phayer, John Cornwell, and Daniel Goldhagen claim that even after the liberation of Rome, Pius remained "silent" about Jews and anti-Semitism. In making this argument, they ignore or dismiss not only several of Pope Pius XII's statements, but also Vatican condemnations of anti-Semitism that were issued in 1916,[229] 1928,[230] 1930,[231] 1942,[232] and 1943.[233]

Upon the liberation of Rome in 1944, Pius made one of his most fervent pleas for tolerance. "For centuries," he said, referring to the Jews, "they have been most unjustly treated and despised. It is time they were treated with justice and humanity. God wills it and the Church wills it. St. Paul tells us that the Jews are our brothers. Instead of being treated as strangers they should be welcomed as friends."[234]

The following year, to an audience in St. Peter's Square, Pius gave a warning to those who had sympathized with Nazi brutality: "To those who allowed themselves to be seduced by apostles of violence, who are now beginning to waken from their illusions, shocked to see where their servility has led them, there remains no way of salvation but to forswear once and for all the idolatry of absolute nationalism, the pride of race and blood, the lust for mastery in the possession of the world's goods, and to turn resolutely to a spirit of sincere brotherhood, founded on the worship of the divine Father of all men."[235]

In a major address to the College of Cardinals on June 2, 1945, after the surrender of Germany, Pius XII called National Socialism "a conception of state activity that took no account of the most sacred feelings of humanity and trod underfoot the inviolable principles of the Christian faith."[236] He spoke of the "satanic specter of Nazism" and of the background and impact of the anti-Nazi encyclical *Mit brennender Sorge*: "In these critical years, joining the alert vigilance of a pastor in the long suffering patience of a father, our great predecessor, Pius XI, fulfilled his mission as Supreme Pontiff with intrepid courage. But when, after he had tried all means of persuasion in vain . . .

he proclaimed to the world on Passion Sunday, 1937, in his encyclical *Mit brennender Sorge* what National Socialism really was: the arrogant apostasy from Jesus Christ, the denial of His doctrine and of His work of redemption, the cult of violence, the idolatry of race and blood, the overthrow of human liberty and dignity."[237] As for his own efforts, the pope explained:

> Continuing the work of Our Predecessor, We never ceased during the war (especially in broadcast messages) to oppose Nazi doctrine and practice the unshakable laws of humanity and Christian faith. This was for Us the most suitable, We may even say the only effective, way of proclaiming in the sight of the world the unchanging principles of the moral law among so much error and violence, to confirm the minds and hearts of German Catholics in the higher ideals of truth and justice. Nor was it without effect. We know in fact that Our broadcasts, especially that of Christmas 1942, were in spite of every prohibition and obstacle studied by diocesan conferences and expounded to the people.[238]

On November 29, 1945, a group of Jewish refugees returning from captivity came to the Vatican to express gratitude for the way the Church's charity had transcended egoism and racial passion. In an audience he granted them, Pius spoke of "the brotherhood of man":

> Your presence, gentlemen, is an eloquent reflection on the psychological changes, the new directions that the war has brought to maturity. The gulfs of discord and hate, the folly of persecution, which were created among peoples and races by false and intolerant doctrines, opposed to human and Christian spirit, have devoured many innocent victims, including non-combatants. The Apostolic See, faithful to the principles of natural right inscribed by God in every human heart, revealed on Sinai and perfected by the Sermon on the Mount, has never left in doubt at any moment however critical that it repudiated those ideas which history will list among the most deplorable and dishonorable travesties of human thought and feeling.[239]

Pius explained: "the Church, remembering her religious mission, must maintain a wise reserve about particular questions of political and territorial character. But this does not prevent her proclaiming the great principles of humanity and brotherhood which must underlie the solutions of such questions."[240] The pope went on to note that "In your own persons you have felt the evil and harm of hatred, but in the midst of your trials you have also experienced and benefitted from the consolation of love—that love which does not draw its inspiration and nourishment from earthly sources, but from a profound faith in the eternal Father Whose sun shines upon all of every tongue and race. . . ."[241]

Pius named many new cardinals after the war, expanding the College of Cardinals from thirty-eight to seventy, and transforming the College of Cardinals into a "more truly international body."[242] Italian cardinals were outnumbered for the first time in recent history.[243] Many of the nominees were also notorious opponents of the Nazis. The *New York Times* reported: "The three new German Cardinals were all outspoken critics of the Nazi regime. The outstanding nominee in France is the venerable Archbishop Saliège of Toulouse, noted for his defiance of the Germans and the collaborationists. Archbishop Sapieha of Cracow is a courageous patriot who shared all the suffering of his people. Archbishop Mindszenty of Hungary was a prisoner of the Nazis."[244] Pius xii's comment was: "This Church does not belong to one race or to one nation, but to all peoples."[245]

On August 3, 1946, Pius said the following to a delegation of Palestinian Arabs: "There can be no doubt that peace can only come about in truth and justice. This presupposes respect for the rights of others and for certain vested positions and traditions, especially in the religious sphere, as well as the scrupulous fulfillment of the duties and obligations to which all inhabitants are subject." He continued: "That is why, having received again during these last days numerous appeals and claims, from various parts of the world and from various motives, it is unnecessary to tell you that We condemn all recourse to force and to violence, from wherever it may come, as also We have condemned on several occasions in the past the persecutions which a fanatical anti-Semitism unleashed against the Jewish people.[246]

Pius condemned racism until the end of his life. In 1957, he received a delegation from the American Jewish Committee. The Committee's representatives described the pope as a "great friend" in the battle against racism and anti-Semitism in the United States. The pope, in turn, praised the Committee's work, and issued a statement condemning anti-Semitism.[247]

Shortly after the war, Catholic philosopher Jacques Maritain, who is often presented as a critic of Pius XII's wartime policy, wrote a letter to the papal assistant Giovanni Battista Montini on the need for the Church to address the issue of post-war anti-Semitism. In a key part of the letter, dealing with the war years, Maritain went out of his way to praise "the tireless charity with which the Holy Father has tried with all his might to save and protect the persecuted," and he praised Pius XII's "condemnations against racism that have won for him the gratitude of Jews and all those who care for the human race." Maritain hailed the pope's wartime diplomacy on behalf of persecuted Jews, recognizing that it was founded upon "very good reasons, and in the interests of a higher good, and in order not to make persecution even worse, and not to create insurmountable obstacles in the way of the rescue that he [Pius XII] was pursuing."[248]

In a related matter, Susan Zuccotti claims that there was a great deal of criticism of Pius XII during and after the war. Almost no one else sees it that way. Peter Novick wrote: "As far as I know, the only comment on Pius's silence during the Holocaust that was made at the time of his death came from a writer for the French Communist newspaper *L'Humanité.*"[249]

> Among the very many tributes to Pope Pius XII printed or mentioned by the Times, there was only one negative, coming from Paris. The Communist official organ *L'Humanité* accused the late Pope of allowing his doctrinal condemnation of Marxist atheism

"to be transformed into an arm of anti-Soviet policy in Europe and the world." While the Pope had spoken out against the arms race, the Communist paper contended, criticism should be made against the Pope "for not having taken a stand against the Nazi concentration camps during the War." . . . The origin of the false accusation that Pope Pius xii had been silent concerning the Holocaust, was Soviet Russia. It was propaganda for Communist ends.[250]

There is simply no legitimate excuse for ignoring the evidence the way that modern papal critics have done.

TRIBUTES

Jewish organizations took note of Pius xii's efforts, and they turned to him in times of need. In June, 1943, Grand Rabbi Herzog wrote to Cardinal Maglione on behalf of Egyptian Jews expressing thanks for the Holy See's charitable work in Europe and asking for assistance for Jews being held prisoner in Italy. The Rabbi, in asking for assistance, noted that Jews of the world consider the Holy See their "historic protector in oppression."[251] The following month he wrote back thanking Pius for his efforts on behalf of the refugees that "had awoken a feeling of gratitude in the hearts of millions of people."[252] On August 2, 1943, the World Jewish Congress sent the following message to Pope Pius: "The World Jewish Congress respectfully expresses gratitude to Your Holiness for your gracious concern for innocent peoples afflicted by the calamities of war and appeals to Your Holiness to use your high authority by suggesting Italian authorities may remove as speedily as possible to Southern Italy or other safer areas twenty thousand Jewish refugees and Italian nationals now concentrated in internment camps . . . and so prevent their deportation and similar tragic fate which has befallen Jews in Eastern Europe. Our terror-stricken brethren look to Your Holiness as the only hope for saving them from persecution and death.[253]

Later that same month, *Time* reported: ". . . no matter what critics might say, it is scarcely deniable that the Church Apostolic, through the encyclicals and other Papal pronouncements, has been fighting totalitarianism more knowingly, devoutly, and authoritatively, and for a longer time, than any other organized power."[254] In fact, that same article went on to note that the Catholic Church "insists on the dignity of the individual whom God created in his own image and for a decade has vigorously protested against the cruel persecution of the Jews as a violation of God's tabernacle."[255]

In September 1943, a representative from the World Jewish Congress reported to the pope that approximately four thousand Jews and Yugoslav nationals who had been in internment camps were removed to an area that was under the control of Yugoslav partisans. As such, they were out of immediate danger. The report went on to say: "I feel sure that the efforts of your Grace and the Holy See have brought about this fortunate result, and I should like to express to the Holy See and yourself the warmest thanks of the World Jewish Congress. The Jews concerned will probably not yet know by what agency their removal from danger has been secured, but when they do they will be indeed grateful."[256] In November, Rabbi Herzog again wrote to Pius expressing his "sincere gratitude and deep appreciation for so kind an attitude toward Israel and for such valuable assistance given by the Catholic Church to the endangered Jewish people."[257] Jewish communities in Chile, Uruguay, and Bolivia also sent similar offers of thanks to the pope.[258]

After the war, Israel's first foreign minister (and the second prime minister), Moshe Sharett, was received by Pius XII for an audience. He told the pope: "that my first duty was to thank him, and through him the Catholic Church, on behalf of the Jewish public, for all they had done in various countries to rescue Jews."[259]

Many who try to document historical attitudes cite the *New York Times*. That paper, of course, heaped praise upon the pope during World War II. Susan Zuccotti and (to a lesser extent) Daniel Goldhagen, however, have challenged the *New York Times* as a biased source.[260] While one might seriously question the critics' assertions, positive evaluations of Pius can be found in many other sources. For instance, the *Times* of London ran the following editorial: "A study of the words which Pope Pius XII has addressed since his accession in encyclicals and allocutions to the Catholics of various nations leaves no room for doubt. He condemns the worship of force and its concrete manifestation in the suppression of national liberties and in the persecution of the Jewish race."[261]

The *Jewish Chronicle* (London) editorialized that "The Pope's action is . . . a striking affirmation of the dictum of one of the Pope's predecessors that no true Christian can be an anti-Semite."[262] The 1943-1944 *American Jewish Yearbook* reported that Pius XII "took an unequivocal stand against the oppression of Jews throughout Europe."[263] Following the war, the *Jerusalem Post* reported that: "Thousands of Jews in Italy owe their lives to Italian citizens and the Catholic Church."[264] This was virtually a universal perception of Pius XII, with good reason.

By September 1957, *Wisdom* magazine (not a Catholic or even a religious periodical) was able to editorialize: "Of all the great figures of our time, none is more universally respected by men of all faiths than Pope Pius XII."[265] Following a meeting with Pius, Winston Churchill reportedly said: "I have spoken today to the greatest man of our time."[266] Churchill admired Pius XII's "simplicity, sincerity and power."[267] Some months after Pius XII's death, Elio Toaff, the Chief Rabbi of Rome, said: "More than anyone else, we have had the opportunity to experience the great compassionate kindness and the magnanimity of the late Pope, during the years of persecution and terror, when it seemed that there was no more hope for us."[268]

In 1955, when Italy celebrated the tenth anniversary of its liberation, Italian Jewry proclaimed April 17 as "The Day of Gratitude." That year, thousands of Jewish people made a pilgrimage to the Vatican to express appreciation for the pope's wartime solicitudes.[269] The Israeli Philharmonic Orchestra even gave a special performance of Beethoven's Ninth

Symphony in the Papal Consistory Hall as an expression of gratitude for the Catholic Church's assistance in defying the Nazis.[270]

Before the celebration, a delegation approached Msgr. Montini, the director of Vatican rescue services who later became Pope Paul VI, to determine whether he would accept an award for his work on behalf of Jews during the war. He was extremely gratified and visibly touched by their words, but he declined the honor: "All I did was my duty," he said. "And besides I only acted upon orders from the Holy Father. Nobody deserves a medal for that"[271] (Later, as Pope Paul VI, Montini made other statements defending Pius XII's wartime record.)[272]

Critics sometimes ask why there is not more written evidence of papal involvement and why so many witnesses waited twenty years to come forward. Some, particularly Susan Zuccotti, have even argued that had there been papal involvement in rescue activities, people would have saved written evidence to protect Pius XII's reputation.

Actually, anyone who cared for the pope would have destroyed written evidence of his involvement in rescue activities. It was extremely dangerous to keep papers related to anti-Nazi efforts, and few who worked in the underground did. Italian Senator Adriano Ossicini, founder of the "Christian Left" in Italy was arrested by Mussolini's Fascists in 1943. Upon his release, he thanked Pius for his intervention with Mussolini and apologized to the pope because one of the reasons for his arrest was that he was carrying a document which showed how strongly Pius opposed racial laws.[273]

Similarly, in the spring of 1940 there was a group of German generals who wanted to oust Hitler and make peace with the English. Needing a way to communicate with the Allies (mainly the British), they approached Pope Pius XII.[274] Not only did he help with the negotiations,[275] he actually went so far as to inform the Allies about German troop movements.[276] There are, however, no documents on this in the Vatican's published collection. The documents were found only in the British archives.[277] During Pius XII's pontificate, and particularly during the war, important matters were not kept on paper: "For every form of communication used within the Roman Curia—memo, letter, phone call, encyclical, Papal bull and smoke signal—the whispered word outranks them all. Millions of words are put to paper or sent over wire. But urgent truths and hot gossip go out by whisper, shot anywhere from two inches to one foot from the ear of the listener."[278] Any Vatican papers related to the planned coup, like any relating to other anti-Nazi or rescue efforts, were undoubtedly hidden or destroyed. This direct involvement by the Pope in an attempted coup is far more telling than mere words ever could have been.[279]

More importantly, no one at the time thought Pius XII's reputation would need to be protected. As rescuer John Patrick Carroll-Abbing wrote in his 1965 book: "Never, in those tragic days, could I have foreseen, even in my wildest imaginings, that the man who, more than any other, had tried to alleviate human suffering, had spent himself day by day in his unceasing efforts for peace, would—twenty years later—be made the scapegoat for men trying to free themselves from their own responsibilities and from the collective guilt that obviously weights so heavily upon them."[280]

In his earlier book, Carroll-Abbing wrote of being inspired by the "luminous sublime example of the Holy Father."[281] He also reported assistance being given to Jews, and the pope's order that "no one was to be refused" shelter.[282] In an interview given shortly before his death, Carroll-Abbing said: "I can personally testify to you that the Pope gave me direct face-to-face verbal orders to rescue Jews." Asked about the thesis that the rescuers like himself acted without papal involvement, he denied it and added: "But is wasn't just me. It was also the people I worked with: Father Pfeiffer and Father Benoît and my assistant, Monsignor Vitucci and Cardinals Dezza and Pallazzini, and of course Cardinals Maglione and Montini and Tardini. We didn't simply assume things; we acted on the direct orders of the Holy father."[283]

Although she later changed her argument, in 1987 even Susan Zuccotti acknowledged that "Any direct personal order would have had to be kept very quiet to protect those who were actually sheltered."[284]

6

"The Jews Are Our Brothers"

It is understandable why the death of Pope Pius xii
should have called forth expressions of sincere grief
from practically all sections of American Jewry.
For there probably was not a single ruler of our
generation who did more to help the Jews in their
hour of greatest tragedy, during the Nazi occupation
of Europe, than the late Pope.
Jewish Post (1958)[1]

AS THE CHURCH'S EFFORTS to oppose Nazism in Germany and Italy become ever more clear, critics have turned to Austria, Czechoslovakia, France, Poland, Denmark, Croatia, and elsewhere to find issues on which to build their cases. Careful study does reveal the occasional Catholic official who did not live up to the example set by the leadership in Rome, but those were the exceptions. When such cases became known to the Vatican, Pius xii and his assistants took corrective action to minimize the damage done to the victims. Moreover, officials of the Holy See engaged in outreach activities that brought much comfort and protection to victims of many nations.

AUSTRIA

One of the first examples of the Vatican disciplining a local prelate who appeared to be getting too close to the Nazi war machine comes from Austria. That nation was annexed and made a part of the Third Reich in 1938 (the "Anschluss"). Shortly after the annexation, the Archbishop of Vienna, Cardinal Theodor Innitzer, met with Hitler and essentially welcomed the Anschluss. A report of this event, translated into English, was sent to Ambassador Joseph P. Kennedy by Cardinal Pacelli, who strongly disassociated it from the Vatican's position.[2] Austrian bishops also issued a public statement praising the achievements of Nazism. This was in accord with much of the feeling throughout Austria, where the German troops had been greeted as heroes rather than conquerors. Vatican Radio, however, immediately broadcast a vehement denunciation, and Pacelli ordered the archbishop to report to Rome.[3]

Before meeting with the pope, Innitzer met with Pacelli. This has been called one of the "most tempestuous" meetings of the whole pontificate.[4] In the words of the British Minister to the Holy See, Innitzer "was severely hauled over the coals by the Vatican" and "told to go back and eat his words."[5] He was made to sign a new statement, issued on behalf of all of the Austrian bishops, which provided: "The solemn declaration of the Austrian bishops on 18 March of this year was clearly not intended to be an approval of something that was not and is not compatible with God's law."[6] The Vatican newspaper also reported that the bishops' earlier statement had been issued without approval from Rome.

A German official in Rome, who saw Innitzer shortly after his meetings, reported: "I have the impression that the Cardinal, who seemed very exhausted from the conversations in the Vatican, had had a hard struggle there."[7] The same official reported later the same day that the retraction of the earlier statements "was wrested from Cardinal Innitzer with pressure that can only be termed extortion."[8] Before long, however, Innitzer was recognized as a true enemy of the Nazis.[9]

POLAND

When the Nazis invaded Poland, the world could barely imagine the brutality that would take place. The Vatican, however, took immediate steps to present the facts. On September 28, 1939, Vatican Radio broadcast the voice of the primate of Poznan, exiled Polish Cardinal Hlond: "Martyred Poland, you have fallen to violence while you fought for the sacred cause of freedom. . . . On these radio waves . . . I cry to you. Poland, you are not beaten."[10] On January 22, 1940 Pope Pius XII read a report on Vatican Radio in which he spoke of a "violent assault on justice and decency . . . a persecution which is one more contemptuous to the law of nations, one more grievous affront to the moral conscience of mankind."[11] The Nazis tried to restrict Church activities, but Pius sent a message that said: "The Church will go on as before. The Nazi machine is making war on the Church. The Church will fight with its own weapons."[12] The Vatican ordered its Polish priests to "assist all who need help regardless of race or creed."[13]

Upon receiving the Vatican's orders, Bishop Fulman of Lublin called together the priests from his and other nearby dioceses. He told them that "the new Jewish reserve the Nazis have set up here in Lublin is a sewer. We are going to assist those people as well as our own, as well as any man, woman or child, no matter of what faith, to escape; and if we lose our lives, we will have achieved something for the Church and for God."[14] Bishop Fulman's activities led to severe retaliation from the governor-general of Occupied Poland, Dr. Hans Frank. Bishop Fulman was incarcerated, and he saw many of his priests die in the concentration camp. Following one execution, Hans Frank addressed Fulman:

> "We shall exterminate all enemies of the Reich, including you, Bishop, down to the lowest of your kind. When we have finished with Poland, when we have finished with Europe, not one of you will be left . . . Not one. No Pope. No priest. Nothing. *Nichts.*"
>
> "God have mercy on you," Bishop Fulman [replied].

"God better have mercy on you," Frank mocked. "You obey the orders of the Vatican, and for that *all* of you will die."[15]

Indeed, many Catholic priests, religious, and laypersons did pay with their lives for following directives from the pope.[16]

Early in the war, Archbishop Sapieha (who headed the Catholic Church within Poland) asked the pope for a forceful statement in support of Poland and against the Nazis.[17] In 1942, Pius had a letter smuggled into Poland to be read from the pulpits. Pius XII's messenger, Monsignor Quirino Paganuzzi reported what happened next:

> As always, Msgr. Sapieha's welcome was most affectionate. . . . However, he didn't waste much time in conventionalities. He opened the packets [from Pius XII, with statements condemning Nazi Germany], read them, and commented on them in his pleasant voice. Then he opened the door of the large stove against the wall, started a fire, and threw the papers on to it. All the rest of the material shared the same fate. On seeing my astonished face, he said in explanation: "I'm most grateful to the Holy Father . . . no one is more grateful than we Poles for the Pope's interest in us . . . but we have no need of any outward show of the Pope's loving concern for our misfortunes, when it only serves to augment them. . . . But he doesn't know that if I give publicity to these things, and if they are found in my house, the head of every Pole wouldn't be enough for the reprisals Gauleiter Frank will order."[18]

Sapieha declined to release the letter because he realized that such a statement would have no lasting positive impact and could bring about severe repercussions.

Pius later cited his experience with the message to Sapieha in a letter that he wrote to Bishop Preysing of Berlin: "We leave it to the local bishops to weigh the circumstances in deciding whether or not to exercise restraint, to avoid greater evil [*ad maiora mala vitanda*]. This would be advisable if the danger of retaliatory and coercive measures would be imminent in cases of public statements by the bishop. Here lies one of the reasons We Ourselves restrict Our public statements. The experience We had in 1942 with documents which We released for distribution to the faithful gives justification, as far as We can see, for Our attitude."[19]

Pius did not, however, completely decline to talk about Poland. On June 2, 1943 (the feast day of St. Eugenio), in an address to the cardinals which was broadcast on Vatican Radio and clandestinely distributed in printed form within Poland, the pope, at the request of Archbishop Sapieha, expressed in new and clear terms his compassion and affection for the Polish people and predicted the rebirth of Poland[20]: "No one familiar with the history of Christian Europe can ignore or forget the saints and heroes of Poland . . . nor how the faithful people of that land have contributed throughout history to the development and conservation of Christian Europe. For this people so harshly tried, and others, who together have been forced to drink the bitter chalice of war today, may a new future dawn worthy of their legitimate aspirations in the depths of their sufferings, in a Europe based anew on Christian foundations."[21]

Archbishop Sapieha wrote from Krakow that "the Polish people will never forget these noble and holy words, which will call forth a new and ever more loyal love for the Holy Father . . . and at the same time provide a most potent antidote to the poisonous influences of enemy propaganda."[22] He also said that he would try to publicize the speech as much as possible by having copies printed, if the authorities would permit it.[23] After the war, Pius named Sapieha a cardinal.

On April 19, 1943, Jewish residents of Warsaw staged a desperate uprising in the ghetto. The Nazis countered with a block-to-block search, but they found it difficult to kill or capture the small battle groups of Jews, who would fight, then retreat through cellars, sewers, and other hidden passageways. On the fifth day of the fighting, Himmler ordered the ss to comb out the ghetto with the greatest severity and relentless tenacity. General Juergen Stroop decided to burn down the entire ghetto, block by block. Many victims burned or jumped to their death, rather than permit themselves to be caught by the Nazis.

The Jews in Warsaw resisted for a total of twenty-eight days. On May 16, General Stroop reported that "the former Jewish quarter of Warsaw is no longer in existence. The large-scale action was terminated at 2015 hours by blowing up the Warsaw synagogue. . . . Total number of Jews dealt with 56,065, including both Jews caught and Jews whose extermination can be proved."[24] (About twenty thousand Jews were killed in the streets of Warsaw and another thirty-six thousand in the gas chambers.) Polish sources estimated that three hundred Germans were killed and about one thousand were wounded.

On May 5, 1943, the Vatican secretariat issued a memorandum expressing the reaction of the Roman authorities:

> The Jews. A dreadful situation. There were approximately four and a half million of them in Poland before the war; today the estimate is that not even a hundred thousand remain there, including those who have come from other countries under German occupation. In Warsaw a ghetto had been established which contained six hundred and fifty thousand of them; today there would be twenty to twenty-five thousand. Some, naturally, have avoided being placed on the list of names. But there is no doubt that most have been liquidated. The only possible explanation here is that they have died. . . . There are special death camps near Lublin (Treblinka) and Brest-Litovsk. It is said that by the hundreds they are shut up in chambers where they [are] gassed to death and then transported in tightly sealed cattle trucks with lime on their floors.[25]

Not only in Warsaw, but throughout Poland, Jewish people were in hiding. About two hundred convents hid more than fifteen hundred Jewish children, mainly in Warsaw and the surrounding area.[26] This was especially difficult, because Polish nuns in German-occupied areas were often persecuted and forced into hiding themselves. (In a small town near Mir, Poland, the Nazis executed twelve nuns in one day for suspicion of harboring Jews.)[27] Nuns who lived in Soviet-occupied areas did not have it much better. They were sent to work for the Soviets, in areas as far away as Siberia. The courage of the priests and nuns who provided shelter to Jewish people was truly admirable.

Why did people take these risks? Roncalli (the future Pope John XXIII) and Montini (the future Pope Paul VI) both gave all credit to Pope Pius XII.[28] At the end of World War II, Pius "enjoyed near-universal acclaim for aiding European Jews through diplomatic initiatives, thinly veiled public pronouncements, and, very concretely, an unprecedented continent-wide network of sanctuary."[29] As the *New York Times* reported, he made hiding Jews on the run the thing to do.[30]

Daniel Goldhagen asserts that the Polish ambassador pleaded with Pius in vain for the Jews, and that by 1944 Pius XII was so "sick" of hearing about the Jews that he got angry with the ambassador. Goldhagen gives no documentation for this charge. This is hardly surprising, since it is untrue.

The Polish ambassador to the Holy See during the War was Casimir Papée. His book, *Pius XII e Polska* (*Pius XII and Poland*), comprehensively analyzed—and supported—Pius XII's wartime policies.[31] Moreover, in a postwar interview he made clear that his pleas were made on behalf of all Poles, not expressly on behalf of Jewish victims, as Goldhagen would have his readers believe.[32]

FRANCE

As early as 1933, when Hitler first rose to power in Germany, Cardinal Archbishop Saliège of Toulouse declared:

> Not only do I feel myself struck by the blows that are falling on
> the persecuted, but I shudder with all the more distress when I
> find that it is not some confused idea that is misunderstood and
> ridiculed . . . but that living, personal being whose breath has run
> through and borne the entire history of Israel: Yahweh, he whom
> I call "the good God," the Just One par excellence. . . . I cannot

forget that there it was in Israel that the tree of Jesse flowered and that there it brought forth its fruit. The Virgin, Christ, the first disciples were of the Jewish race. How could I not feel bound to Israel like a branch to the trunk that bore it! . . . Catholicism cannot agree that belonging to a particular race places men in a position that entitles them to fewer rights. It proclaims the essential equality of all races and individuals.[33]

In his pastoral letter for Lent 1939, Saliège again denounced "the new heresy of Nazism, which shatters human unity and places a superhuman value in what it considers to be privileged blood."[34]

From the summer of 1941 on, foreign Jews were rounded up and deported from Vichy with the full cooperation of Vichy officials.[35] Eventually, some forty thousand citizens were murdered and sixty thousand more deported to concentration camps for "Gaullism, Marxism or hostility to the regime." One hundred thousand others were deported on racial grounds. On August 1, 1941, Vatican Radio reported: "A great scandal is presently taking place and this scandal is the treatment suffered by the Jews; it is why I desire that a free voice, the voice of a priest, should be raised in protest. In Germany the Jews are killed, brutalized, tortured because they are victims bereft of defense. How can a Christian accept such deeds . . . these men are the sons of those who 2,000 years ago gave Christianity to the world."[36] When the first mass deportations began from the unoccupied zone in the summer of 1942, Archbishop Saliège lodged the first public episcopal protest.[37]

As soon as deportations began, Papal Nuncio Valerio Valeri contacted Henri-Philippe Pétain, head of the Vichy government, demanding that they be put to an end. Pétain reportedly said: "I hope that the Pope understands my attitude in these difficult circumstances." The nuncio replied: "It is precisely that which the Pope cannot understand."[38] Vatican Radio condemned "this scandal . . . the treatment of the Jews."[39]

Vatican secretary of state, Luigi Cardinal Maglione, told the French Ambassador to the Vatican "that the conduct of the Vichy Government toward Jews and foreign refugees was a gross infraction" of the Vichy Government's own principles, and was "irreconcilable with the religious feelings which Marshal Pétain had so often invoked in his speeches.[40] As reported by the *Tablet* (London), on July 10, 1942, Pope Pius XII "spoke with exceptional decisiveness against the over-valuation of blood and race."

Responding to the arrest of thirteen thousand Jewish Parisians in July 1942, the French bishops issued a joint protest: "The mass arrest of the Jews last week and the ill-treatment to which they were subjected . . . has deeply shocked us. There were scenes of unspeakable horror when the deported parents were separated from their children. Our Christian conscience cries out in horror. In the name of humanity and Christian principles we demand the inalienable rights of all individuals. From the depths of our hearts we pray Catholics to express their sympathy for the immense injury to so many Jewish mothers."[41] The text was delivered immediately to Pétain, and each bishop was charged with communicating it to his clergy. The *Jewish Chronicle* reported that "Catholic priests have taken a leading part in hiding hunted Jews, and sheltering the children of those who are under arrest or have been deported to Germany."[42]

Daniel Goldhagen says that Pius XII "clearly failed to support" this protest. This is yet another falsehood.[43] At the direction of the pope, the protests were broadcast and discussed for several days on Vatican Radio.[44] Statements such as "he who makes a distinction between Jews and other men is unfaithful to God and is in conflict with God's commands" were broadcast into France, in French, on Vatican Radio.[45] Pierre Cardinal Gerlier, a French Catholic bishop who condemned Nazi atrocities and deportation of the Jews, explicitly stated that he was obeying Pius XII's instructions when he made these statements.[46]

In August 1942, Archbishop Jules Gérard Saliège, from Toulouse, sent a pastoral letter to be read in all churches in his diocese: "There is a Christian morality that confers rights and imposes duties. . . . The Jews are our brothers. They belong to mankind. No Christian can dare forget that!"[47] At the express request of Pius XII, Vatican Radio broadcast Saliège's letter twice and made comments on it for six consecutive days.[48] As the Vatican newspaper put it, "Saliège became a national hero, a symbol of spiritual resistance and courage."[49] (When the war ended, the American Jewish Committee gave him an award for saving so many Jews, and Pope Pius XII named him a cardinal.)[50]

Pius also instructed his nuncio to issue another protest and recommended that religious communities provide refuge to Jewish people.[51] On August 7, 1942, Nuncio Valeri sent a ciphered message to Maglione reporting: "I have spoken quite frequently to the foreign minister... and with the head of state himself (Pétain) about this very sad problem."[52] This was sent just a day after a *New York Times* headline proclaimed: "Pope Is Said to Plead for Jews Listed for Removal from France."[53] Three weeks later, a headline in the same paper told the sad story: "Vichy Seizes Jews; Pope Pius Ignored."[54]

On September 10, 1942, D'Arcy Osborne, the British ambassador to the Vatican, cabled Anthony Eden, the British foreign secretary, detailing the Italian Fascist press attacks and threats against the Church, which Osborne wrote were "a reproach for the Vatican's protest against the anti-Jewish policy of the Vichy Government."[55] Two days later, on September 12th, Osborne telegrammed the British Foreign Office: "The Pope today confirmed to me that the Nuncio at Vichy had protested against persecution of Jews in France."[56] In fact, the American press reported that the pope protested to the Vichy government three times during August 1942.[57] The protests, unfortunately, angered the new Vichy leader Pierre Laval, and he reaffirmed his decision to cooperate in the deportation of all non-French Jews to Germany.[58]

The *Canadian Jewish Chronicle* ran the following headline on September 4, 1942: "Laval Spurns Pope—25,000 Jews in France Arrested for Deportation." In an editorial dated August 28, 1942, the *California Jewish Voice* called Pius "a spiritual ally" because he "linked his name with the multitude who are horrified by the Axis inhumanity." In a lead editorial, the London *Jewish Chronicle* said that the Vatican was due a "word of sincere and earnest appreciation" from Jews for its intervention in Berlin and Vichy."[59] The editorial went on to say that the rebuke that Pius received from "Laval and his Nazi master" was "an implied tribute to the moral steadfastness of a great spiritual power, bravely doing its manifest spiritual duty."

According to the *Geneva Tribune* of September 8, 1942, Vichy ordered the French press to ignore Pope Pius XII's protests concerning the deportation of Jews.[60] Despite this order, word spread rapidly due to the courageous attitude of the Catholic clergy. In fact, just weeks later, the *New York Times* reported: "The moral prestige of Marshal Pétain is undermined by the mounting resistance of French Bishops and clergy to Vichy's surrender to German pressure notably expressed in resistance to the deportation of refugee Jews."[61]

On September 14, 1942, the Vatican Radio theme in France was "Let us not betray our brothers." There was no doubt about who was to be considered a brother: "Jesus-Christ. . . . first turns his attention to the flock of his own beloved Jewish people, to all those of his race who helped to save the world, among them his mother, his friends, his disciples. He gazed at the Jewish people with an everlasting love."[62] Similarly, a broadcast from a few weeks earlier asked the anti-Semites: "Why this vicious campaign, why always lash out against the harmless and not the ferocious? Really did the former do everything? Did he carry the weight of Israel's crimes? Are you sure? Of course not. You know that it isn't. And yet you lie and mislead your fellow man."[63]

When Lord Bishop Bruno de Solages from Montauban spoke up against the deportation of Jews, he made clear that he considered Vatican Radio to be the authentic voice of the pope. A French Jesuit priest, Fr. Michel Riquet, who was imprisoned for his work in support of Jews later said: "Throughout those years of horror when we listened to Vatican Radio and the Pope's messages, we felt in communion with the Pope, in helping persecuted Jews and in fighting Nazi violence."[64] That helps account for all of the rescuers who have cited Vatican Radio as one of their inspirations. Leaders of the resistance even produced an underground newsletter, *La Voix du Vatican*, which reprinted transcripts from these broadcasts.[65]

French Catholic philosopher Jacques Maritain was in the United States in 1940 when his nation fell to Germany. That autumn he wrote *France My Country, Through the Disaster* to counter the collaborationist propaganda in Vichy France. The U.S. Army Air Corps airdropped copies into Vichy, and it became the "first breviary of the Resistance."[66] He continued to write and speak against the Nazis and the Holocaust. As he explained in a Vatican Radio broadcast: "What the world gives us to contemplate in the great racist prosecutions is that Israel is itself engaged on the way of Calvary, because is activates and stimulates earthly history, and because the slave masters do not pardon it for the demands it and its Christ have introduced into the heart of the temporal life of the world, for they will always say No to tyranny and to the triumph of injustice."[67] Following the war, Maritain moved to Rome, as France's envoy to the Holy See.

As it did in other nations, the Church in France helped produce thousands of false documents that were used to deceive the Germans, and special efforts were made to protect Jewish children. Working with Jewish groups, French Christian organizations saved thousands of Jewish children in France.[68]

At one point, a force of Protestant and Catholic social workers broke into a prison in Lyon and "kidnaped" ninety children who were being held with their parents for deportation. The parents were deported the next day. The children were sheltered in religious institutions under the protection of Cardinal Pierre Gerlier with the assistance of Father Pierre Chaillet, a member of the cardinal's staff. When Gerlier refused an order to surrender the children, Vichy leaders had Chaillet arrested. He served three months in a "mental hospital" before being released.[69] On April 16, 1943, the *Australian Jewish News* ran an article quoting Gerlier to the effect that he was simply obeying Pius XII's instruction to oppose anti-Semitism.[70] In June, 1943, Vatican Radio warned its listeners in France that "He who makes a distinction between Jews and other men is unfaithful to God and in conflict with God's commands."[71]

Despite all of these efforts, critics routinely turn to a document known as the Bérard Report, in order to paint the Vatican in a bad light. This matter began in August 1941, when Pétain asked the French ambassador to the Holy See, Léon Bérard, to ascertain the views of the Vatican on the collaborationist Vichy government's efforts to restrict the Jews through anti-Jewish legislation.

Henri Cardinal de Lubac, who lived through the German occupation of France, has two chapters about the Bérard Report in his book, *Christian Resistance to Anti-Semitism: Memories from 1940-1944*. Lubac explains that Pétain was being pressured by the Catholic hierarchy in France to abandon the anti-Semitic laws, and he wanted a statement from the Vatican that he could use to silence French Catholics. In a letter dated August 7, 1941, he asked for a report on the Holy See's attitude towards the new legislation.

The response came in a long memorandum from Bérard, the key phrase of which is: "As someone in authority said to me at the Vatican, it will start no quarrel with us over the statute for the Jews." Bérard assured Pétain that "the Holy See had no hostile intention." He claimed that the Vatican did not wish to "seek a quarrel."[72]

Rather than providing the official position of the Holy See, Bérard cited "someone in authority" and gave a long justification for that position, based on Church history, including the writings of St. Thomas Aquinas. It is, of course, highly suspect for a diplomatic report to go into historic Church teaching rather than relying on diplomatic sources. Moreover, the historic discussion omitted many more recent authoritative statements against anti-Semitism. Those authoritative statements, however, would not have served Pétain's purposes.

As others have concluded, Bérard drafted this memorandum to meet Pétain's needs, not to reflect the Church's actual position. As Lubac says, "[i]f the ambassador had been able to obtain from any personage at all in Rome a reply that was even slightly clear and favorable, he would not have taken so much trouble to 'bring together the elements of a well-founded and complete report' obviously fabricated by himself or by one of his friends."[73]

Bérard's report was dated Sept. 2, 1941. On September 13, at a reception at the Parc Hotel in Vichy, Nuncio Valeri criticized the anti-Semitic legislation and said that the Holy See had made clear its opposition to racism. Citing the Bérard report, Pétain suggested that the nuncio might not be in agreement with his superiors.

Bishop Valeri immediately wrote the Vatican's secretary of state, Cardinal Maglione, and asked for more information. Then, around September 26, Valeri called upon Pétain and was given a copy of the Bérard report. In exchange, the nuncio gave Pétain a note concerning the "grave harms that, from a religious perspective, can result from the legislation now in force."

On September 30, Valeri wrote to Maglione, enclosing a copy of the Bérard Report. He explained the conversation at the Parc Hotel as follows: "I reacted quite vigorously. . . . I stated that the Holy See had already expressed itself regarding racism, which is at the bottom of every measure taken against the Jews."

Maglione wrote back to Valeri on October 31 explaining that Bérard had made exaggerations and deductions about Vatican policy that were not correct. He fully approved of the note that Valeri had given to Pétain and encouraged him to continue efforts to discourage the rigid application of the anti-Semitic laws. Valeri then drafted a note of protest that he sent to Pétain.[74]

What we know for certain is the following: if Pétain ever thought that Bérard's account was legitimate, the Vatican's true position was immediately—and before the commencement of mass deportations—brought to his attention. As Lubac concludes, "from the very first day . . . the opposition between the orientation of the Vichy government and the thought of Pius XII was patent."[75]

Charles De Gaulle returned to liberated Paris in August 1944. As part of the new government's procedures, he expelled all diplomats who had represented their countries to the Vichy government, including Nuncio Valeri. De Gaulle, however, informed the former nuncio that he was aware of all the good things that he had done for France and he regretted his departure. He even awarded Valeri the Grand Cross of the Legion of Honor and had military honors paid to the departing diplomat.

Valeri was replaced by Monsignor Angelo Roncalli, the future Pope John XXIII. One of Roncalli's first tasks was to undertake a ten-month long investigation into allegations of collaboration with the German occupiers. Of the seventy-eight bishops whom he investigated, Roncalli found evidence against only three of them (a far smaller percentage than that of the public in general).[76] He had them removed from office.

Rabbi Stephen S. Wise, the leading Jewish voice in the United States during the war, wrote in 1942: "It appears to be more than rumor that his Holiness Pope Pius XII urgently appealed through the papal nuncio to the Vichy government to put an end to deportations from France, and the appeal of the Pope is said to have been reinforced by petition and protest from the Cardinal Archbishops of Paris and Lyons. . . . If such papal intervention be factual, then Pius XII follows the high example set by his saintly predecessor, whose word in reprobation of anti-Semitism, 'spiritually we are all Semites,' will never fade out of the memory of the people which does not forget but forgives."[77]

BELGIUM

Belgium's Cardinal Joseph-Ernest Van Roey was one of the staunchest opponents of the Nazis during the war. In 1938, with encouragement from Pius XI, he publicly condemned Nazi racial theories, arguing that "the racial doctrine is nothing but the most abject materialism and it is destructive of the traditional conception of law as something rising above special interests and offering a common measure for all individuals and peoples." The "doctrine of blood," he concluded, "must be denounced as deadly delusion; totalitarianism deriving from it and vesting itself in the interests and exigencies of the race is a doctrine absurdity and an immense moral danger."[78]

On August 11, 1941 Van Roey delivered an address in Wavre Notre Dame. Not only did he directly order Catholics not to collaborate with the Nazi's, but he ordered them to resist: "It is wrong for Catholics to collaborate in the establishment of a tyrannical regime. Indeed, they have an obligation to work with those who try to resist such a regime."[79] Priests in Belgium, Holland, and France "immediately went to war against the invader."[80]

The priests established an underground network that helped British soldiers escape back to England.[81] One case involved four priests from Antwerp. The Nazis were systematically killing off the Jewish population by sending carloads of people off to concentration camps. The priests knew that they were obliged to help the victims, but they went to Cardinal Van Roey to ask about their obligation in this case. His reply was: "Our orders are quite clear. You must help these men to escape."[82]

The priests ultimately set up an escape route from Belgium, through France, and into Switzerland or Spain. The plan was relayed to Cardinal Van Roey, and he later informed Pope Pius about it. While the pope's reaction is unknown, the escape route remained in place throughout the war, indicating that neither the pope nor the cardinal ordered it to be stopped. It is known that Pius instructed Van Roey: "Ensure that there is no distinction made between men, that all who need help are given it irrespective of their faith."[83] Van Roey did that.

In the spring of 1942, a Vatican Radio broadcast quoted Van Roey on his view of Nazi race theory: "Blood, a material element, cannot be the only source of a superior existence. The individual has his or her own worth, it is permanent and immortal. . . . But the individual is never subordinated to race. All races are perfectible. . . . If the races are perfectible they are therefore fundamentally equal because they all have the same origin."[84] When the Nazis threatened him with death, he replied: "I take my orders from the Holy Father in the Vatican, not from Berlin."[85]

Bishop Lamiroy of Bruges was also a strong opponent of the Nazis. When a known collaborator was killed, Lamiroy refused to grant him a Catholic funeral. "By selling himself to the Nazi cause, this man betrayed his nation and his Church. In the face of an order from the Holy Father himself, he went against the Church and turned to the enemy. He died without the comfort of the Church; he shall be buried without the Church."[86]

Leon Degrelle, quisling and leader of the Rexist party in Belgium, made his opinion clear: the Vatican was fighting a war against the Third Reich. He told high-placed Nazis in Belgium that they had better shoot all the priests or send them to concentration camps. Otherwise they would be forced to capitulate. "You can fight England and win, but I believe the church is too strong for you. You will lose against the church."[87]

THE SOVIET UNION

In March 1937, Pope Pius XI issued the encyclical *Divini Redemptoris* (*Of the Divine Redeemer*, although it is better known by its subtitle, *On Atheistic Communism*) in which he attacked Communism, which was beginning to spread throughout Europe and other parts of the world. He wrote that Communism was historically evil, that Communist governments were out to destroy religion, were Godless, were violent, denied the individual and the family, and reigned by terror. He concluded that "Communism is intrinsically wrong, and no one who would save Christian civilization may collaborate with it in any undertaking whatsoever."[88] Later, his successor, Pope Pius XII, helped stave off a Communist takeover of Italy.

In the early and mid-1930s, Hitler and Mussolini were seen by many world leaders (including some officials of the Holy See) as the best defense against the spread of Communism. This was, after all, the time of Stalin's show trials and other measures of mass terror, and it was long before the worst Nazi atrocities. Moreover, today it is clear that Church leaders were right to fear Communism. After the Allied victory, the Soviets expanded their sphere of influence (and their persecution of the Church) throughout most of Eastern Europe, including half of Germany.[89] They murdered millions of people.

The well-established Catholic opposition to Communism led critic John Cornwell to argue that Pope Pius XI and Secretary of State Pacelli were determined that "no accommodation could be made with Communism, anywhere in the world." Others have charged that anti-Communist feelings caused Pius XII to favor the Germans over the Allies. Again, the critics are wrong.[90]

Pope Pius XI, through Pacelli, tried to obtain a concordat with the Soviet Union in the mid-1920s,[91] and he did conclude one with the predominantly Socialist government of Prussia in 1929.[92] In fact, in 1926, Pacelli consecrated a Jesuit bishop in Berlin, Fr. Michel d'Herbigny, whose task it was to go into the USSR to consecrate several bishops secretly and to inform them officially of their appointments as apostolic administrators.[93]

Despite his concern over the spread of Communism, Pius XII also recognized that Nazism presented a similar threat. He still condemned Communism during the war, but as an observer of that time noted, "(w)ith it he bracketed Nazism in the same breath, for it strikes, no less ruthlessly, at the individuality of the home, the very heart of religion. Both are tyrannically pagan."[94] In 1942, Pius XII told Fr. Paolo Dezza, SJ (made a cardinal in 1991): "The Communist danger does exist, but at this time the Nazi danger is more serious. They want to destroy the Church and crush it like a toad."[95] When the Allies sought to have him speak out against Nazi Germany, he said he was unwilling to do so without also condemning the atheistic government of the Soviet Union, but he also refused Axis requests to bless their "crusade" into the god-less Soviet Union.[96] In fact, at the request of President Roosevelt, he stopped all mention of the Communist regime in the Soviet Union.[97] He did, however, provide aid to Soviet prisoners of war.[98] President Roosevelt's representative to the Pope, Myron Taylor, reported that Pius XII's concern about the Soviet Union would present no problem to the American war effort.[99]

In the British Public Record Office, there is a short message dated May 10, 1943, from the British Embassy in Madrid. It reports on a message that had been forwarded by a member of the Spanish Ministry of Foreign Affairs. According to this report, "In a recent dispatch the Spanish Ambassador reported that in conversation with the Pope[,] the latter informed him that he now regarded Nazism and Fascism, and not Communism, as he used to, as the greatest menace to civilization and the Roman Catholic Church."[100] Others were also aware of the pope's view. According to a post-war interrogation of Joachim von Ribbentrop, Hitler thought that the Catholic Church sometimes worked with the Communists.[101] U.S. papal representative Harold Tittmann said that "Pius XII himself had joined the President in admitting that Hitlerism was an enemy of the Church more dangerous than Stalinism and that the only way to overcome the former was an Allied victory, even if this meant assistance from Soviet Russia."[102] As such, the record simply does not support the conclusion that hatred of Communism blinded Pius XII to the evils of Nazism.[103]

In April 1943, Hungarian Prime Minister Nicholas de Kallay met with Pius XII. He recorded: "His Holiness brought up the matter of conditions in Germany. He depicted the conditions prevailing in Germany, which fill him with great sadness, in dramatic words. He finds incomprehensible all that which Germany does with regard to the Church, the Jews, and the people in occupied territories. . . . He is quite aware of the terrible dangers of Bolshevism, but he feels that, in spite of the

Soviet regime, the soul of the large masses of the Russian people has remained more Christian than the soul of the German people."[104]

In fact, by cooperating with Franklin Roosevelt's request to support extension of the lend-lease program to the USSR, Pius actually gave economic and military aid to the Soviets, even though this seemed to be in conflict with Pope Pius XI's 1937 encyclical *Divini Redemptoris*, which strictly prohibited Catholics from collaborating with Communists.[105] (Later, Pius XII's appeals on behalf of Ethel and Julius Rosenberg again revealed his ability to look beyond the "Communist" issue.)[106] The failed Catholic-Jewish study group found no evidence to support the conclusion that Pius favored the Germans over the Soviets.[107]

CROATIA

Many papal critics point to Croatia—where wartime details are less well known—to raise questions about the Church's relationship with the Nazis. As more and more is learned about the Church's role in this nation, however, the critics' arguments make less and less sense.

Croatia came into being during the war. On March 25, 1941, Italy, Germany, and Yugoslavia signed an agreement bringing Yugoslavia into the Axis. Two days later, a group of Serbian nationalists seized control of Belgrade and announced that they were siding with the Allies.[108] As a result, Hitler invaded Yugoslavia. Croat Fascists then declared an independent Croatia. The new Croat government was led by Ante Pavelic and his group, the Ustashi.

There had been a long history of hatred in this part of the world between Croats (predominantly Catholic) and Serbs (mainly Orthodox). The Ustashi government exacted revenge against the Serbs for years of perceived discrimination. According to some accounts, as many as 700,000 Serbs were slaughtered.[109] Among the charges against the Catholic Church in Croatia are that it engaged in forcible conversions, that Church officials hid Croat Nazis after the war, that Nazi gold made its way from Croatia to the Vatican, and that Catholic leaders in Croatia supported the government's brutality toward the Serbs.

While some of these charges are recent in origin (and from suspect sources), there is no credible evidence that the pope or the Vatican behaved inappropriately. As for the allegations regarding gold and money taken abroad from the independent Croatian state during 1944-45, Professor Jere Jareb, an expert on the history of Croatia, examined all the relevant documents. He found no evidence that Pavelic and his Croatian Fascists deposited stolen gold at the Vatican, much less that Pius XII approved of such criminal acts.[110]

Regarding forcible conversions, the Holy See expressly repudiated them in a memorandum, dated January 25, 1942, from the Vatican Secretariat of State to the Legation of Yugoslavia to the Holy See.[111] In August of that year, the Grand Rabbi of Zagreb, Dr. Miroslav Freiberger, wrote to Pius XII expressing his "most profound gratitude" for the "limitless goodness that the representatives of the Holy See and the leaders of the Church showed to our poor brothers."[112] In October, a message went out from the Vatican to its representatives in Zagreb regarding the "painful situation that spills out against the Jews in Croatia" and instructing them to petition the government for "a more benevolent treatment of those unfortunates."[113] In December 1942, Dr. Freiberger wrote again, expressing his confidence "in the support of the Holy See."[114]

The secretary of state's notes reflect that Vatican petitions were successful in getting a suspension of "dispatches of Jews from Croatia" by January 1943, but Germany was applying pressure for "an attitude more firm against the Jews."[115] Cardinal Maglione went on to outline various steps that could be taken by the Holy See to help the Jews.[116] Another instruction from the Holy See to its unofficial representatives (since there were no diplomatic relations) in Zagreb directing them to work on behalf of the Jews went out on March 6, 1943.[117]

Croatian Archbishop Alojzij Stepinac originally welcomed the Ustashi government, but after he learned of the extent of the brutality, and after having received direction from Rome,[118] he condemned its actions.[119] A speech he gave on October 24, 1942, is typical of many that he made refuting Nazi theory: "All men and all races are children of God; all without distinction. Those who are Gypsies, Black, European, or Aryan all have the same rights. . . . for this reason, the Catholic Church had always condemned, and continues to condemn, all injustice and all violence committed in the name of theories of class, race, or nationality. It is not permissible to persecute Gypsies or Jews because they are thought to be an inferior race."[120] The Associated Press reported that "by 1942 Stepinac had become a harsh critic" of that Nazi puppet regime, condemning its "genocidal policies, which killed tens of thousands of Serbs, Jews, Gypsies and Croats."[121] He thereby earned the enmity of the Croatian dictator, Ante Pavelic.[122]

Stepinac's bravery is reflected in an incident that took place during the German occupation. Hans Frank, the Nazi official in charge of the occupation continually hinted that he wanted to be invited to dinner at the archbishop's residence. Presumably, this would help legitimize Frank's position. Finally the invitation came. When Frank sat down to dine with the archbishop, he was served a meager meal of black bread (made in part from acorns), beet jelly, and ersatz coffee. Stepinac calmly explained that this was the only food he could obtain with the ration coupons provided by the Nazis, and he certainly could not risk his own arrest or the arrest one of his household servants by trading on the black market.[123]

Although critics argue that the Holy See recognized the Ustashi government, in actuality the Vatican rebuked Pavelic and refused to recognize the Independent State of Croatia or receive a Croatian representative.[124] When Pavelic traveled to the Vatican, he was greatly angered because he was permitted only a private audience rather than the diplomatic audience he wanted.[125] He might not even have been granted that privilege, if the extent of the atrocities had been known.

In 1944-45, Communist partisans under Josip Broz Tito conquered the Balkans, occupied Zagreb, and established the Socialist Federation of Yugoslavia. That government immediately undertook severe prosecution of the Catholic Church, confiscating property, closing seminaries and schools, banning Masses, and persecuting clergy. Before coming to power, the Communists had "used Cardinal Stepinac's speeches in their propaganda, as the Cardinal always spoke against the Nazi occupation and against the violation of human rights committed by Pavelic. Stepinac cried out against all injustice, especially against racism."[126] Now that they had power, however, Stepinac was a threat.

The Communists put Stepinac on trial for allegedly supporting the Ustashi government. Pope Pius publicly protested the prosecution, noting that the cardinal had saved thousands of people from the Nazis. The president of the Jewish Community in the United States, Louis Braier, said: "This great man was tried as a collaborator of Nazism. We protest this slander. He has always been a sincere friend of Jews and was not hiding this even in times of cruel persecutions under the regime of Hitler and his followers. He was the greatest defender of the persecuted Jews."[127] During the war, Meir Touval-Weltmann, a member of a commission to help European Jews, wrote a letter of thanks for all that the Holy See had done and enclosed a memorandum which stated: "Dr. Stepinac has done everything possible to aid and ease the unhappy fate of the Jews in Croatia."[128]

Stepinac was sentenced to sixteen years of hard labor, but due to protests and indignation throughout the democratic world, and Jewish testimony about the good work he had done, he was moved to house arrest in 1951. Almost immediately, Pope Pius XII raised him to the cardinalate. He died under house arrest in 1960.[129] In 1985, Jakov Blazevic, the man who conducted Stepinac's trial, admitted that the cardinal had been framed.[130]

Croatia's Jewish community credited Stepinac with helping many Jews avoid Nazi persecution. In fact, one of the first acts of Parliament in the newly independent state of Croatia in 1992 was to issue a declaration condemning "the political trial and sentence passed on Cardinal Alojzij Stepinac in 1946."[131] Stepinac was condemned, declared the

Parliament: "because he had acted against the violence and crimes of the communist authorities, just as he had acted during the whirlwind of atrocities committed in World War ii, to protect the persecuted, regardless of the national origin or religious denomination."[132] He was beatified on October 3, 1998, at which time Pope John Paul ii described him as a man who had the strength to oppose the three great evils of our century—Fascism, Nazism, and Communism.[133]

Daniel Goldhagen ends his grossly inaccurate portrait of Croatia by making the outrageous assertion that "Forty thousand . . . perished under the unusually cruel reign of 'Brother Satan,' the Franciscan friar Miroslav Filopovic-Majstorovic. Pius xii neither reproached nor punished him . . . during or after the War."

Actually, the so-called "Brother Satan" was tried, defrocked, and expelled from the Franciscan order before the war ended.[134] In fact, his expulsion occurred in April 1943, *before he ran the extermination camp* (April-October 1943). For Pius xii to have punished him "after the war" would have been difficult indeed. This renegade priest was executed by the Communists in 1945.[135] Other Croatian priest-collaborators were also punished by the Church (though critics like Goldhagen overstate the number of such priests).[136]

ROMANIA

The Holy See was quite active on behalf of the Jews of Romania, particularly through its papal representative, Archbishop Andrea Cassulo.[137] As soon as Romania's brutal dictatorial regime, led by Marshal Ion Antonescu, allied itself with Nazi Germany and began employing Nazi racial measures, Cassulo protested deportations, welcomed Jewish converts as a means of defending them under the Holy See's concordat with Romania, visited and brought assistance to interned Jews, intervened for orphaned Romanian Jewish children, and worked tirelessly with Romania's Jewish leaders for the reduction, if not elimination, of anti-Semitic measures.

As the *Actes et Documents* reveal,[138] Cassulo's activities were carried out with the closest collaboration of Vatican officials, especially Pope Pius XII, with whom Cassulo met in the Fall of 1942, and who gave him financial aid. Even Fr. John Morley, who is critical of Pope Pius XII, says of Cassulo: "the Jewish community . . . considered him their greatest ally in time of peril, and it was to him that they gave the credit for the safety of the majority of Romanian Jews."[139] Both during the war and after, Romania's Jewish leaders, particularly Chief Rabbi of Bucharest Alexander Safran, were effusive in their praise of Cassulo and the Church.[140]

DENMARK

The Danes have received considerable praise for their resistance to the Nazis anti-Semitic campaign.[141] Daniel Goldhagen writes that "Rychlak and the Pope's other defenders fail to discuss the famous and most relevant case for assessing the efficacy of acting on behalf of Jews: the case of Denmark." He is wrong. Page 137 of my *Hitler, the War, and the Pope* reports: "On April 9, 1940, German troops swept across the Danish border. Danes, including King Christian X, Catholic bishops, priests, and students, demonstrated solidarity with the Jews by wearing the yellow star in public. Privately, the Danes hid and eventually smuggled almost the entire Jewish population of eight thousand to safety. The Catholic Church played an important role in this rescue, and Pius XII was noted for his contribution to the effort." Footnotes direct the reader to three different references for this information.[142]

It turns out that King Christian may not have ever actually worn the yellow star. Some writers also say that he never even threatened to do so.[143] "In fact, under Pius XII's pontificate, many Catholic clergymen and nuns took greater risks and suffered far more on behalf of the Jews than did King Christian of Denmark"[144] Legend has it, however, that the King defied the Nazis, and I certainly did not conceal this information.

As Goldhagen himself concedes, eventually the Germans deported about five hundred Jews from Denmark. Fortunately, many others had escaped by that time. Those who were deported were for the most part sent to a "show" camp at Theresienstadt, where about 90 percent of them survived. Of course, those Jews displaced others who had been living at Theresienstadt. They were sent on to death camps, so the net effect was not what Goldhagen would lead his readers to believe.

HUNGARY

In March 1944, Germany invaded Hungary on the pretext of safeguarding communications, and the last great nightmare of the war began.[145] Hungary had been a haven for refugee Jews, but the Nazis immediately issued anti-Jewish decrees.[146] From almost the first day, Nuncio Angelo Rotta worked to help improve the treatment of the Jews. He was the first foreign envoy to submit a formal diplomatic objection, and he issued baptismal certificates and passports that enabled thousands of Jews and converted Jews to leave Hungary.[147] The Holy See also informed other nations about the conditions in Hungary, and this brought international pressure on the Hungarian government.[148]

Early in the occupation, Rotta received a letter of encouragement from Pius XII in which the pope termed the treatment of Jews as "unworthy of Hungary, the country of the Holy Virgin and of St. Stephen."[149] From then on, acting always in accordance with instructions from the Holy See and in the name of Pope Pius XII, Rotta continually intervened against the treatment of the Jews and the inhuman character of the anti-Jewish legislation.

On June 25, Pius himself sent the well-known open telegram to the Regent of Hungary, Admiral Nicholas Horthy:

> Supplications have been addressed to us from different sources that we should exert all our influence to shorten and mitigate the sufferings that have for so long been peacefully endured on account of their national or racial origin by a great number of

unfortunate people belonging to this noble and chivalrous nation. In accordance with our service of love, which embraces every human being, our fatherly heart could not remain insensible to these urgent demands. For this reason we apply to your Serene Highness appealing to your noble feelings in the full trust that your Serene Highness will do everything in your power to save many unfortunate people from further pain and suffering.[160]

Pius XII also sent a telegram to Hungarian Cardinal Justinian Séredi asking for support from the Hungarian bishops.[151] Serédi responded by issuing a statement of his own: "We would forfeit our moral leadership and fail in our duty if we did not demand that our countrymen should not be handled unjustly on account of their origin or religion. We, therefore, beseech the authorities that they, in full knowledge of their responsibility before God and history, will revoke these harmful measures."[152] This strong statement, issued pursuant to a request from the Pope, was read publicly in the Catholic churches until Nazi authorities confiscated all copies.[153] It helped lead to the postponement of deportations that "saved the lives of tens of thousands of Hungarian Jews."[154]

On June 28, Archbishop Francis Spellman of New York broadcast a strong appeal to Hungarian Catholics deploring the anti-Jewish measures, which, he said, "shocked all men and women who cherish a sense of justice and human sympathy." These measures were, he said, "in direct contradiction of the doctrines of the Catholic faith professed by the vast majority of the Hungarian people." He called it incredible "that a nation which has been so consistently true to the impulses of human kindness and the teachings of the Catholic Church should now yield to a false, pagan code of tyranny."[155] *Time* magazine reported: "This week listeners at Europe's thirty-six million radio sets might have heard New York's Archbishop Francis Joseph Spellman preaching civil disobedience. The Archbishop's ... broadcast ... eloquently urged Hungary's nine million Catholics to disobey their government's new anti-Semitic decrees."[156] The Allies dropped printed copies of it over

Hungary.[157] Spellman later confirmed that he had made the statement at the express request of Pope Pius XII.[158] According to the Italian periodical *Regime fascista*, Spellman was an "agent of American Jews, someone who sends any amount of dollars to the Vatican in exchange for an anti-fascist policy approved by the Holy See."[159]

Admiral Horthy complained to the Germans that he was being bombarded with telegrams from the Vatican and others and that the nuncio was calling on him several times each day.[160] In the face of these protests, Horthy withdrew Hungarian support from the deportation process, making it impossible for the Germans to continue. Horthy's reply cable to the pope, dated July 1, 1944 said: "It is with comprehension and profound gratitude that I receive your cable and request you to be convinced that I shall do all within my power to make prevail the demands of Christian humanitarian principles."[161] Horthy agreed to work against the deportations, and he even signed a peace agreement with the Allies. For once it appeared that Pius XII's pleas on behalf of the victims might actually have had a positive effect. The Germans, however, would not be dissuaded by mere words.

The Germans arrested Horthy in October, put Hungary under the control of Hungarian Nazis, and the deportations resumed.[162] The pope and his representatives then made many more protests to German authorities, issued a report documenting the Vatican's work with the Jews of Hungary, and encouraged Catholics to help the victims.[163] In October, Pius joined in an effort to raise money to support Hungarian refugees, urging the faithful to redouble their efforts on behalf of all victims of the war, regardless of their race.[164] Almost every Catholic church in Hungary provided refuge to persecuted Jews during the autumn and winter of 1944.[165]

On November 10, 1944, Nuncio Rotta protested to the German foreign ministry, saying that "from a humanitarian perspective but also to protect Christian morality, the Holy See protests the inhumane attitude adopted toward the Jews."[166] When Nazi officials suggested that Jews were merely being sent to Germany to work, not for any evil purpose, Rotta sarcastically responded: "When old men of over seventy and even over eighty, old women, children, and sick persons are taken away, one wonders for what work these human beings can be used? . . . When we think that Hungarian workers, who go to Germany for reasons of work, are forbidden to take their families, we are really surprised to see that this great favor is granted only to Jews."[167]

The nunciature in Budapest had been bombed and half destroyed, communications with the Vatican were extremely difficult, and the lives of those Catholic officials still in the city were in constant danger. Nuncio Rotta sent a message to Rome asking what to do. The reply from Pope Pius was: "If it is still possible to do some charity, remain!"[168]

The Germans were finally forced out of Budapest two days before Christmas, 1944. Despite the terrible losses that had taken place during their occupation, most of the Jews in Budapest were saved from the gas chamber.[169]

The World Jewish Congress, at its December 1944 war emergency conference in Atlantic City, sent a telegram of thanks to the Holy See for the protection it gave "under difficult conditions to the persecuted Jews in German-dominated Hungary."[170] Similarly, the American Jewish Committee sent an expression of deep thanks to Pius and Cardinal Maglione for having helped stop the deportations from Hungary.[171] On May 25, 1945, Nuncio Andreas Cassulo informed the Vatican: "[Chief] Rabbi Safran has expressed to me several times . . . his gratitude for what has been done for him and for the Jewish community. Now he has begged me to convey to the Holy Father his feelings of thankfulness for the generous aid granted to prisoners in concentration camps on the occasion of the Christmas festivities. At the same time, he told me he had written to Jerusalem, to the Chief Rabbi [Herzog], and also elsewhere, in America, to point out what the nunciature has done for them in the time of the present difficulties."[172] Chief Rabbi Safran also told other Jewish leaders about the Catholic Church's efforts to protect Jewish people.[173]

SLOVAKIA

In attempting to implicate Pius XII in the atrocities carried out in the Nazi satellite states of Slovakia, Daniel Goldhagen mentions the work of Livia Rothkirchen, a respected authority on the annihilation of Slovak Jewry, but he fails to mention that in documenting and appropriately condemning the savageries committed by anti-Semitic Slavs, Rothkirchen emphasized that this was done in spite of, not because of, Pope Pius XII.[174] In fact, she concludes, in her major work on the subject, that the several letters of protest delivered by the Vatican during the years 1941-1944 "prove sufficiently that the Vatican objected to the deportation of Jews from Slovakia."[175]

Goldhagen also suggests that Vatican action in Slovakia came only after it was clear that the Allies would win the war.[176] In fact, the Nuremberg race laws were introduced in that country on September 9, 1941. Two days later the Vatican's *chargé d'affaires* in Bratislava (the capital of Slovakia), went to see President Jozef Tiso to stress "the injustice of these ordinances which also violate the rights of the Church."[177] Shortly thereafter, Slovakia's representative to the Vatican received a written protest from the Holy See that these laws were "in open contrast to Catholic principles."[178]

Because Tiso was a priest, some critics have argued that the Vatican supported him despite his collaboration with the Nazis. Actually, the available evidence demonstrates just the reverse. On the day that Tiso was chosen as the first president of the Slovak Republic (September 26, 1939), the Vatican released a statement expressing its "grave misgivings," and warning that this move would corrupt the relationship between Church and State. The Holy See pointed to the Nazi connection: "Owing to Slovakia's subservience to Germany it is not doubted that President Tiso will have to visit Berlin and most likely be seen and even photographed with Chancellor Hitler, whom the Vatican regards as a persecutor of Catholics. . . . It was recalled in this connection that the Vatican, prompted by a similar consideration, refused to sanction the appointment some months ago of a priest as Ambassador to the Holy See from a South American Republic, and the candidate had to be withdrawn."[179]

Despite Pius XII's concern that this move might have a Catholic priest pictured with Hitler, Tiso assumed the office in defiance of the pope, not with his support: "What followed was strictly according to the Nazi pattern. Persecution of the Jews and imprisonment of every democratic voice; the creation of an Iron Guard to shoot down strikers and saboteurs; the Germanization of the school system; the expropriation of property, the confiscation of grain and foodstuffs; and the dispatch of Slovak youth to the Russian front. From Rome came the thunders of the Holy Father, denouncing these outrages, but Tiso paid no heed to the voice of the Holy Father."[180]

When Jews were deported from Slovakia in 1942, the Vatican secretary of state immediately filed a protest.[181] On March 21, 1942, a pastoral letter was read by episcopal order in all Slovak churches. The letter spoke of the "lamentable fate of thousands of innocent fellow citizens, due to no guilt of their own, as a result of their descent or nationality."[182] Under direct orders from Pius XII, the Slovak Minister to the Holy See was summoned and requested to take immediate action with his government.[183] The Vatican also instructed the chargé d'affaires in Bratislava once again to contact Tiso and seek relief.[184] Catholic prelate Paval Machàcek, vice president of the Czechoslovak State Council, said in a broadcast to the Slovak people: "It is impossible to serve simultaneously God and the devil. It is equally impossible to be at the same time a good Christian and an anti-Semite."[185]

Between 1941 and 1944, the Vatican sent six official letters and made numerous oral pleas and protests regarding the deportation of Jews from Slovakia.[186] A letter sent from Pius XII, dated April 7, 1943, could not have been more clear:

> The Holy See has always entertained the firm hope that the Slovak government, interpreting also the sentiments of its own people, Catholics almost entirely, would never proceed with the forcible

removal of persons belonging to the Jewish race. It is therefore with great pain that the Holy See has learned of the continued transfers of such a nature from the territory of the Republic. This pain is aggravated further now that it appears from various reports that the Slovak government intends to proceed with the total removal of the Jewish residents of Slovakia, not even sparing women and children. The Holy See would fail in its Divine Mandate if it did not deplore these measures, which gravely damage man in his natural right, merely for the reason that these people belong to a certain race.[187]

The following day, a message went out from the Holy See instructing its representative in Bulgaria to take steps in support of Jewish residents who were facing deportation.[188] Shortly thereafter, the secretary of the Jewish Agency for Palestine met with Archbishop Angelo Roncalli "to thank the Holy See for the happy outcome of the steps taken on behalf of the Israelites in Slovakia."[189]

7

The Hidden Pius XII

*Pius XII was the most warmly humane, kindly,
generous, sympathetic (and, incidentally, saintly)
character that it has been my privilege to meet in the
course of a long life. I know his sensitive nature was
acutely and incessantly alive to the tragic volume of
human suffering caused by the War and, without the
slightest doubt, he would have been ready and glad to
give his life to redeem humanity from its consequences.*
Sir Francis D'Arcy Osborne,
British Minister to the Holy See[1]

CRITICS OF POPE PIUS XII are unable to establish their point by sticking to the facts, so they often resort to presenting a shallow caricature of the wartime pontiff. He is depicted as rude, aloof, cold, uncaring, and sometimes downright evil. In the motion picture *Amen,*[2] he was seen as presiding over opulent dinners while peasants starved in Nazi concentration camps. This caricature, of course, is ridiculously off of the mark.

During his life, Pius XII was widely regarded as a warm man and a brilliant conversationalist.[3] The Vatican reporter for the *New York Times* described the new pope in 1939:

> His personality is even more impressive than his precision. No member of the Sacred College so perfectly looks the part of a prince of the church. His tall, slender figure has remarkable dignity. His face is thin and ascetic, with long features and deepset, questioning eyes.
>
> He has the manner of a great gentleman, simple, modest and assured. He speaks English clearly and well. His expression is much more lively than the photographs indicate.[4]

Noting that he had a reputation for being austere, she went on to explain that she found him to be "smiling, warm, and vivacious."[5]

Until failing health forced him to restrict his activities, he was extraordinarily accessible. He celebrated more public masses and held more private audiences than any of his recent predecessors had, and each week he held a special audience just for newlyweds.[6] He shifted the time of certain services, to permit more people to attend.[7] He also used television and radio to reach out directly to the people. As the *New York Times* reported, he "exchanged views with more laymen of different creeds and nationalities than any pontiff of modern time."[8] Because of all this, he was known as the "least stuffy" of Popes.[9]

Pius was able to "introduce an extraordinary intimacy, gentleness, a sense of love into his work and writings.... [He] has been described as a Franciscan with a love for nature and animals."[10] An article in the March 1939 edition of *Reader's Digest* explained: "Pope Pius XII seems cold and austere, cloaked in an impenetrable dignity, until he comes within five feet of you. Then you see that his blue eyes are wells of understanding, his thin lips turn up slightly at the corners, features that appeared stern become warm and gentle. And when he speaks and uses his hands in gesture he is magnetic and charming. In conversation, his mind and tongue are keenly alive."[11]

Monsignor Hugh Montgomery, an English priest who knew Pope Pius XII well, wrote of him in the *Catholic Herald*: "It must seem absurd to anyone who knew 'Papa Pacelli' at all to hear him described as 'cold.' He had a boyish eagerness of manner which was most attractive and a radiant smile."[12] That personality served him well for the twenty-two years prior to becoming pope that he spent as an international diplomat in service to the Holy See.[13]

As a young boy, Eugenio Pacelli was small, but he loved swimming, hiking, canoeing, and horseback riding. He collected coins and stamps. He also learned to play the violin and developed a love of music that continued throughout his life. He enjoyed having stories read to him. Many of the stories, of course, were religiously oriented. One day, when he was very young, his uncle told him the story of a missionary priest who was persecuted and ultimately crucified by his tormentors. Eugenio told his uncle that he too would like to be a martyr, "but—without the nails!"[14]

The Congregation for the Causes of Saints has an essay that Eugenio wrote when he was probably thirteen or fourteen years old. In it, he comments on his body, his moral character, and his attitude toward life. "I am of normal height," he writes, "my body thin, my face somewhat pale, my hair dark brown and soft, my eyes very dark, my nose aquiline. There's not much to be said about my chest, which, in all frankness, is not broad and powerful. Lastly, as for my legs they are long and thin; my feet cannot be called small." He sums up: "Physically, I am pretty much an average boy."[15] The teenaged Pacelli goes on to note that he is sometimes overly excitable, but he is working on controlling that. He adds that he does not like to be corrected, but that he quickly forgives those who offend him, because he is striving to attain more fully a spirit of generosity.

A former classmate once described the young Eugenio: "You would not call him a genius, but rather a consistent worker. . . . He was a lovable and courageous boy."[16] When he was in the seminary, Eugenio "found time for the lighter moments of student life," including a starring role in the play seminarians put on during carnival time.[17]

Friends say that everyone who spent any time around Pius heard him tell a story about his younger days. The future pope used to ride from one town to another in a carriage. Halfway through the trip, the driver would stop for a pint of wine. He always bought a pint for the horse as well. One night the man was too ill to drive the carriage, but he let young Eugenio drive himself. The horse stopped at the pub. Thinking that it would be a special treat, Eugenio gave both pints to the horse. The result, of course, was that the horse fell asleep, and the future pontiff had to travel the rest of the way on foot.[18]

The story sounds apocryphal, but that makes it even more interesting. Pius repeatedly told a self-effacing story, probably because it got a good laugh. He "often laughed at his own foibles."[19] When he was a monsignor, the future pope told another story: "A certain abbess, the head of a female monastery, insisted that the priest chaplain of the monastery kiss her hand when meeting her. He refused. The matter was referred to Rome, which gave this decision, translated from Latin: 'The chaplain is not bound to kiss the abbess, but let him make merely a slight inclination of the head as to an old relic.'"[20] This certainly reflects a sense of humor not typically seen in depictions of Pope Pius XII.

Pius called laughter a gift from God and said that: "laughter has no religion. . . . There should be more of it in the world."[21] As his friend Domenico Cardinal Tardini remembered him:

> Pius XII appeared also to be—and was in reality—happy. He took pleasure in lively conversation, and appreciated fine literary phrases . . . As a true Roman, he loved and relished with, and was quick to see the humorous, so often hidden in the inexhaustible variety of human affairs.
>
> When he laughed, with his wide mouth open, his eyes flashing, and his arms raised, he looked—allow me to say so, for I cannot find any other comparison—like a happy child.[22]

As a true Roman indeed, Pacelli understood the predilections and habits of the Italians, and he did not try to change them. When he was in Berlin as papal nuncio (where he was known as an avid bridge player),[23] he was one day asked why Italians did not follow the same strict discipline that was common in German churches. Specifically he was asked why Romans behaved in church as if they were in the theater. He replied: "For the same reason that Germans behave in the theater as if they were in church."[24]

Even in difficult times, Pius xii's humor came through: "To his own friends, the Cardinal was the same warm, sincere, humor-loving person he had always been."[25] In 1933, when Hitler's government forced the Vatican into an agreement that the Nazis never intended to honor, then-Secretary of State Pacelli remarked: "well, at least they probably can't violate all of the terms at the same time."[26] Later in the 1930s, Pacelli (who is often depicted as being overly devoted to Germans and Germany) was quoted as having said: "I have lived for too long among Germans not to value highly social relations with Frenchmen."[27]

In 1936, Secretary of State Pacelli toured the United States by plane. The flight attendant called him "the most considerate passenger I ever had."[28] One report of a reception given in his honor while he was in New York states: "To all, the Cardinal guest of honor gave his smiling attention, his ready wit, and his serious consideration, and America loved him for it."[29] In her memoirs, Rose Kennedy, mother of John F. Kennedy, wrote about traveling with the Cardinal:

> He was not a handsome man, yet his eyes shone with such inten-
> sity and compassion, in his bearing there was an unearthly sense
> of important purpose that I truly felt I was in the presence of a
> mortal who was very close to God.
>   At Hyde Park there were cars waiting to take us the additional
> few miles to the President's home. . . . Suddenly, about halfway
> there, there were hundreds of children—from local and nearby
> parochial schools—lining the road, all rosy cheeked and excited

and waving their little U.S. and papal flags. The cardinal could have waved and smiled and passed by; but instead that humane and godly man stopped our caravan, left his car and—with the red robes of his cardinalate moving with the shift of autumn breezes—passed among the children, smiling and patting heads, and with his right hand making the Sign of the Cross or raised in a gesture of benediction. I shall never forget the future Pope Pius XII striding in his robes among those children on a rural roadside near the Hudson River in apple-and-pine tree country in New York State. It was such a happy and spontaneous gesture.[30]

As the future Pope traveled the United States, it became a custom for him to grant a holiday to students at Catholic schools where he spoke. After accepting an honorary degree at Fordham University, he announced: "I grant you a holi-day." Due to his accent, it sounded like "holy day," and there was no reaction. This alarmed the cardinal, who waved his hands in the air and shouted: "Free day!" This time it sounded like "three days." The applause was deafening! From then on, again in a self-effacing way, whenever visitors came from Fordham he would ask whether they remembered his "terrible mistake."[31]

At another university in South Bend, Indiana, students wondered how the prelate would pronounce the name of their institution. He stood on the stage, and "In a decided South Bend accent, all heard him speak the flat English Name, 'Noter Dame!' The students went wild; a new hero had appeared on their horizon, and Cardinal Pacelli was 'all right.' Of course, he gave them a holiday in honor of his presence and to his own delight."[32] Before Pacelli left the U.S., President Franklin D. Roosevelt—who had just won a landslide victory for a second term—invited the Cardinal to his home. Afterwards, Pacelli joked with reporters: "I enjoyed lunching with a typical American family."[33]

The future pope developed a great fondness for the United States and liked to reflect on his trip to America. "He spoke of his airplane flight across the great American Continent and of the largeness of the view, the tolerance, the free atmosphere of America. Evidently the freedom struck him most. No other atmosphere, he implied, was so conducive to the free practice and free growth of religion."[34]

At some point after his trip to the United States, Cardinal Pacelli repaid the hospitality of the Americans by hosting visitors from the United States. After an early morning Mass, he invited them to his apartment for breakfast:

> But if his breakfast was meager, it was more than compensated for by the sparkling conversation at the table. . . . It was a merry, witty interlude. Shielded behind heavy glasses, his eyes played such hide and seek that often it was difficult to discover when he was joking, but no humorous slip or opportunity for a jest was allowed to pass without his pouncing on it.
>
> The young guest summed it up in these words: "He is the most impressive man I have ever met—intensely spiritual, but his mind is so keen that he misses nothing of all that is going on around him."[35]

On another of his long voyages as secretary of state, Pacelli took an ocean liner to South America. Relaxing on a deck chair, he laid aside his golden cross and red moire cape. Soon thereafter a young boy grabbed them and began to run up and down the deck with these symbols of majesty. A horrified father witnessed the scene and rushed to grab the items from his young son. "Let him be," said Cardinal Pacelli. "Little children bless all they touch."[36]

The cardinal remembered how he had been as a boy. One day he returned to Chiesa Nuova, the church in Rome where he had served as an altar boy. Pointing to a hook on the wall in the sacristy he said: "There is the hook toward which I used to fling collar, tie, and cassock before running home. They didn't always make the hook."[37]

In 1939, Pope Pius XI passed away, and Pacelli—much to the dismay of the German government—was elected his successor. Even in the hectic days between the election and the coronation, the new Pope's personality shone through: "Characteristically, in the midst of universal acclaim, the new Pope did not forget to pay a visit to his former colleague and devoted friend, Cardinal Marchetti-Selvaggiani, Vicar of Rome, who was ill. The ailing Cardinal tried to raise himself to bow and whisper: 'Holy Father.' But the Pope said: 'Ah, not for tonight—let me still be Eugenio to your Francesco.'"[38]

There was not much light banter around the Vatican during World War II. The war took a serious toll on the pope. Although he could have lived the style of a king (as suggested by the movie *Amen*),[39] he survived on the same wartime rations that were available to everyone in Rome (little food, no coffee, and no heat). By the end of the war, although he was more than six feet tall, he weighed only 130 pounds. That did not, however, dull his wit. A few days after Rome's liberation, Lieutenant General Mark Clark, Commander of the Fifth Allied Army, apologized for the noise made by his tanks. Pius XII smiled and replied: "General, any time you come to liberate Rome, you can make just as much noise as you like."[40]

After the war, servicemen and celebrities from all around the world came to see the pope. He tried to talk to everyone. Field Marshal Earl Alexander wrote: "I well remember that, when the Allies were in occupation of Rome, crowds of our soldiers went to the Vatican to see the Pope, who daily gave them his blessing. Thinking that it might be too great a strain on him I said one day: 'I hope that all these Allied soldiers are not too great a burden for your Holiness,' and added, 'although of course, so many of them are Catholics,' He replied: 'No! No! Let them all come to me—I love them all.'"[41] "This was the period of 'open house' at the Vatican when Pius XII met more Americans than any other Pontiff in history or any living ruler."[42]

One time a soldier dropped his hat, and the pope smilingly picked it up for him.[43] Another soldier told the pope that they shared something in common: "We both used to be Cardinals." Pius asked how that could have been. Joe "Ducky" Medwick of the St. Louis Cardinal baseball team's famed "gas house gang" then let the pope in on his joke. "I guess I really walked into that one," said a smiling pope.[44] Pius also enjoyed the time a group of enthusiastic GIs got carried away during an audience and sang, "For He's a Jolly Good Fellow."[45] Excited Polish soldiers, after presenting the pope with a beautifully decorated shield, sought permission to carry him on the *sedia gestatoria.*[46]

Many children came to see the pope. They "pressed close to him and offered him gifts of candy and flowers. His love for these small ones of his flock was very evident in his smiling, affectionate gaze."[47] It was said that he "made himself a child with children."[48] A young mother at a papal audience once asked another woman to hold her crying baby while she approached Pius XII. She returned a moment later, saying: "Let me have him. His Holiness says he doesn't care if the baby does cry."[49]

Pius went out of his way to meet with handicapped visitors. A Swiss Guard reported in his memoirs: "Well I remember a cripple in the audience hall. Unnoticed he squatted behind hundreds at the entrance of the room. He was happy to see the Holy Father from the distance. Pius XII stood up from his throne, approached him with great strides and treated him like a poor brother whom one has not seen for years and who has come back to his home, ill in body and soul."[50] He also paid special attention to the many widows who brought their children to meet him at an audience.[51] Anne O'Hare McCormick, the *New York Times* correspondent at the Vatican, wrote: "Pius XII is not tired by the innumerable audiences he gives, because he likes people."[52]

"Movie stars, sports heroes, celebrities of every stripe, creed and discipline flocked to [Pius XII's] audiences."[53] "Among prominent Americans he has received are Dwight D. Eisenhower (when he was still in uniform), ex-Presidents Truman . . . and Hoover and Secretary of State Dulles."[54] When the Harlem Globetrotters visited the Vatican, Pius was filmed tapping his foot to "Sweet Georgia Brown."[55] When Clark Gable came to visit, the pope discarded his schedule to spend time with his favorite movie star (keeping Angelo Roncalli—the future Pope John XXIII waiting for two hours).[56] Robert Murphy, U.S. undersecretary of state, had—along with Pacelli—been a diplomat in

Germany during the mid-1920s. When they met after the war, Murphy reminisced about how they both had reported to their governments that Hitler would never amount to anything. In response, the pope smiled, raised a finger, and joked: "Remember, back then I was not infallible."[57]

One time a group of altar boys visiting the Vatican got lost and ended up in the papal apartment. They were quite surprised to learn that the kindly man they asked for directions was the pope.[58] Similarly, a lady waiting for an audience with the pope asked Pius to hold her baby while she primped. He did so gladly.[59] Pius always enjoyed telling these stories on himself. Once, when a non-Catholic wondered aloud whether he should have come to a papal audience, Pius "smilingly asked him to accept the blessing, not of the Pope, but of an old man!"[60]

In keeping with tradition, Pius xii normally ate his meager meals alone, but kept little plates of bird seed on the table for his pet canaries, that would sometimes light on his shoulder.[61] He also spoke "familiarly" with his attendants and had reports read to him.[62] He was the first pope to use the telephone or an electric razor.[63] He took walks in the garden and used the gymnasium (complete with electric horse, rowing machine, and punching bag) that he had installed in the Vatican Palace when he was secretary of state.[64] He also loved to ride in fast cars; it was suspected that he left late for meetings so that his driver would have to have to drive fast.[65] It was said that under Pius xii, "the fabric of St. Peter's became as modern as the fabric of New York."[66]

Pius was known for making highly informed presentations to representatives from all types of professions. He amazed listeners with his knowledge of various technologies. The pope worked hard and cared deeply about his research. Illustrating the importance that he attached to accurate citation of authority, he liked to tell the story of one professor who said to another: "I congratulate you. In your latest book—which is really excellent—I found one accurate quotation."[67]

About four years before he died, Pius suffered a very serious illness and almost died. From that point on, he was more withdrawn than he had been when he was younger and healthier. This is the picture that too many people have in their memory of Pius XII and the one that his critics try to exploit. He was, indeed, a pious man. There was, however, much more to his personality than just that.

During World War II, it was written that Pius XII possessed "the nobility of Leo the Great, the courage of Gregory VII, the learning of Benedict XIV, the culture of Leo XIII, the pastoral zeal of Pius X, the acumen of Benedict XV, and the firmness of character of Pius XI."[68] He was both brilliant and able to relate to children: "Pius XII's intelligence entered into details: That was his charm; he refined and cultivated it. He really learned new languages. He spoke of agriculture with agriculturists, of atomic science with atomic scientists, of obstetrics with midwives, of the law with solicitors. He made himself a child with children. And, inversely, as if to compensate for this incarnation in a technique, a profession, a circumstance, a case, he rose up to Tabor. He gazed at heaven. He *saw*."[69]

When remembering Pope Pius XII, it is good to remember his piety, his strength, and the warm, caring personality who brought comfort to those around him, not the false caricature offered by his critics.

8

Illogical Arguments and Manufactured Evidence

Never, in those tragic days, could I have foreseen, even in my wildest imaginings, that the man who, more than any other, had tried to alleviate human suffering, had spent himself day by day in his unceasing efforts for peace, would—twenty years later—be made the scapegoat for men trying to free themselves from their own responsibilities and from the collective guilt that obviously weighs so heavily upon them.
Rescuer John Patrick Carroll-Abbing (1965)

IN RESPONDING TO THE VARIOUS CRITICISMS of the Catholic leadership during World War II, I have made an effort to address them thematically. In other words, I organized this book around issues, not specific critics. That is often easy to do, since many critics repeat the same or similar allegations. Some charges, however, are so peculiar, and some arguments are so strained, that it makes best sense to answer them in the context of discussing the particular critics who make them.

JOHN CORNWELL'S DOCTORED EVIDENCE

The surest sign that an advocate does not have a good case is that he resorts to illogical arguments or, even worse, manufactures evidence. Critics of Pope Pius XII have resorted to brazen fabrications and outrageous interpretations of facts. Moreover, in violation of typical historical analysis, they attribute improper motivation without any evidence to support their conclusions. Apparently they know that their case lacks merit.

The first cause for suspicion about John Cornwell's book, *Hitler's Pope*, is its cover. The dust jacket of the British edition shows Nuncio Pacelli leaving a reception given for German President Hindenburg in 1927. The photograph, a favorite of those who seek to portray Pius in an unfavorable light,[1] shows the nuncio dressed in formal diplomatic regalia (which could easily be confused with papal garments), as he exits a building. On each side of him stand soldiers of the Weimar Republic. In front of him stands a chauffeur saluting and holding open the square-looking door, typical of automobiles from the 1920s. Those who do not recognize the differences in uniform details could easily confuse the Weimar soldiers with Nazi soldiers because of their distinctive helmets associated with Nazi-era German soldiers.

Use of this photograph, especially when coupled with a provocative title such as *Hitler's Pope*, gives the impression that Pope Pius XII is seen leaving a meeting with Hitler.[2] Making matters even worse is the caption from inside the dust jacket on early British editions of the book, which labels the photograph as having been taken in March 1939.[3] By this time, Hitler was chancellor of Germany, and this was the month Pacelli was elected pope. A fair-minded person reading the caption could easily conclude that Cardinal Pacelli paid a visit to Hitler immediately prior to being elected pope.

The American version of *Hitler's Pope* never had the wrong date, but—given that the date might have been an honest error—it is far more revealing about the intentional misinformation that went into the marketing of this book. The U.S. edition uses the same photograph as the British edition, but it is cropped to eliminate two important points of reference: the soldier nearest the camera and the square door of the automobile. Both of those images provide clues to the true date of this photo (1927), and Cornwell apparently did not want that known.[4] The photo also has been significantly darkened, giving it a more sinister feel.[5] Even more telling is the intentional blurring of the background. Looking at this cover, Nuncio Pacelli is in clear focus, but the soldier to his left and the chauffeur are both badly blurred, so badly that it is impossible even for a well-trained observer to recognize that the soldier wears a Weimar uniform rather than a Nazi uniform. The chauffeur, due to the blurring and cropping that eliminates the car door, takes on the appearance of a saluting ss officer. Even a civilian in the background could seem to be a Nazi official.

Since none of the images on the British edition are blurred, and since Nuncio Pacelli's face is in focus on the U.S. cover but the other images are blurred, the only logical conclusion is that the photo was intentionally altered to support Cornwell's thesis. Unfortunately, this is not the only dishonest aspect of the book.

Inside *Hitler's Pope*, before the text, Cornwell presents a quotation from Thomas Merton, a well-known contemplative monk whose writings have inspired many people. As butchered by Cornwell, the quotation says: "Pius XII and the Jews. . . . The whole thing is too sad and too serious for bitterness . . . a silence which is deeply and completely in complicity with all the forces which carry out oppression, injustice, aggression, war." This is a fairly shocking condemnation of the Pope from an esteemed Catholic thinker. If Merton had actually written this, it would indeed give one pause. Actually, however, this is not a true quotation. Cornwell manufactured it.

Cornwell gave no citation, so his deception was hard to uncover.[6] The full quotation, which was written by Merton in his personal journal, is a complaint that he had been ordered not to publish his essay on nuclear war. The "silence" about which he complained was the "silence" that had been imposed upon him. It was unrelated to Pius XII. Merton actually wrote:

> A grim insight into the stupor of the Church, in spite of all that has been attempted, all efforts to wake her up! It all falls into place. Pope *Pius XII and the the Jews*, the Church in South America, the treatment of Negroes in the U.S., the Catholics on the French right in the Algerian affair, the German Catholics under Hitler. All this fits into one big picture and our contemplative recollection is not very impressive when it is seen only as another little piece fitted into the puzzle. *The whole thing is too sad and too serious for bitterness.* I have the impression that my education is beginning—only just beginning and that I have a lot more terrible things to learn before I can know the real meaning of hope.
>
> There is no consolation, only futility, in the idea that one is a kind of martyr for a cause. I am not a martyr for anything, I am afraid. I wanted to act like a reasonable, civilized, responsible Christian of my time. I am not allowed to do this, and I am told I have renounced this—fine. In favor of what? In favor of *a silence which is deeply and completely in complicity with all the forces that carry out oppression, injustice, exploitation, war.* In other words silent complicity is presented as a "greater good" than honest, conscientious protest—it is supposed to be part of my vowed life, it is for the "Glory of God." Certainly I refuse complicity. My silence itself is a protest and those who know me are aware of this fact. I have at least been able to write enough to make that clear. Also I cannot leave here in order to protest since the meaning of any protest depends on my staying here."[7]

Cornwell linked the italicized phrases with ellipses.

Not long after the release of *Hitler's Pope*, the Vatican issued a statement on Cornwell's work in Rome. It denied Cornwell's claim to have been the first person to have access to the archives that he used, denied his claim that he had worked "for months on end" in these archives,[8] denied his claim that a letter he had found had been kept secret prior to his efforts (noting that it had been published in full several years earlier), and stated that these falsehoods had been revealed "to put readers on guard about Cornwell's claims."[9]

When he was asked about these claims in *Brill's Content* magazine, Cornwell replied: "Nowhere in the book do I claim that I spent months on end in the Secretariat of State archive. The quote is taken from a sub-editorial conflation in a newspaper article and was an error of strict fact that actually turns out to be essentially true." This was a brazen effort to obfuscate the issue. Cornwell completely neglected to mention that the newspaper article was one that *he* had written about his book. Moreover, he repeated the claim in a piece that *he* wrote about his book for *Vanity Fair* magazine.[10]

Cornwell's supposed "new information" came not from secret files, but from the open pre-1922 archives of the Vatican's Secretariat of State. This would account for the only "new" pieces of evidence offered in his book, both of which are dated before 1920.[11] He also saw Pius xii's beatification deposition transcripts,[12] but they were also not secret.[13]

Cornwell claimed that these beatification deposition transcripts were "explosively critical matter" and "a priceless biographical resource" that Fr. Peter Gumpel (relator for the cause of beatification of Pius xii) had made available to him "at great risk." In fact, he said that "in the absence of a devil's advocate [the testimony of Pacelli's younger sister, Elisabetha] should be heeded."[14] One might expect to find controversy in the materials. However, as one plows through the ninety-eight deposition transcripts (not seventy-six, as Cornwell writes), they turn out to be not at all controversial. No witness gave "shocking" testimony. Many spoke of Pius xii's concern for and help given to Jewish people, both before and after he became pope.

The original handwritten transcripts fill just over seventeen hundred pages in seven volumes; the printed set, two volumes in the *Positio,* is just over nine hundred pages (not one thousand pages, as Cornwell says). Yet Cornwell has only thirty citations of this material in which he references only twelve of the ninety-eight witnesses. More telling are the contents of the testimony that he found so devastating.

Cornwell was able to uncover a bit of disharmony between the pope's housekeeper and his sister (who wanted to be his housekeeper), but other than some petty jealousy—not on the part of Pius—the testimony is not in the slightest negative.[15] Much of it relates to matters such as Pius XII's height, weight, health problems, and the like. Cornwell attempts to present these transcripts as controversial by quoting statements favorable to the pope, then arguing against them. As the Congregation for the Causes of Saints concluded, *Hitler's Pope* is neither scholarly nor honest.[16] The clear message from each and every witness is that Eugenio Pacelli—Pope Pius XII—was an honest, holy, and charitable man–even saintly.

Below is a chart that covers every citation that Cornwell has to the deposition transcripts. The headings indicate the location of the citation in *Hitler's Pope* (by chapter and page), the page number of the location of the testimony in the printed transcripts , the witness, and a thumbnail sketch of the testimony.

Hitler's Pope Chapter	Note # in *Hitler's Pope*	Vatican Transcript Page	Witness	Subject Matter of Testimony
Intro.		229	Carlo Pacelli (nephew)	Height and weight of Pius.
1	7	30	Guglielmo Hentrich (professor)	No heat in Pacelli's childhood home.
1	14	109	Pascalina Lehnert (housekeeper)	Young Pacelli had unusual sense of control over self.

1	20	3	Elisabetha Pacelli (sister)	Family brought him food when he was in seminary.
2	4	255-56	Maria Teresa Pacelli (cousin)	Young cousin felt that she could confide in him.
2	5	256	Maria Teresa Pacelli	Older, the same cousin, found him open, modest, humble, reserved but cheerful, and marked by simplicity.
5	26	6	Guglielmo Hentrich	1920s problem between members of Nuncio Pacelli's domestic staff.
5	27	6	Guglielmo Hentrich	Pacelli pleased when accusations of a romance between him and his housekeeper were disproved.
5	28	69	Suora Ignazia Caterina Kayser (member of religious order)	Priest-Assistant thought nuncio Pacelli should fire his housekeeper.
6	18	54	Hans Struth (journalist)	Pacelli blessed crowds as he left Germany.
7	12	6	Elisabetha Pacelli	Domestic quarrel between housekeeper and staff.
11	13	12	Guglielmo Hentrich	Pacelli's nephew took photo of housekeeper in an embarrassing position with a man.

15	3	31	Guglielmo Hentrich	Pius slept no more than 4 hours/night during the war.
16	22	85	Pascalina Lehnert	Pius decides to burn notes of condemnation due to news of persecution of baptized Jews in Holland.
17	31	831	Gen. Karlo Otto Wolff (ss commander)	Wolff talks with Hitler about occupation of Vatican.
17	32	832-33	Gen. Karlo Otto Wolff	Hitler makes "dark threats" against Vatican.
17	33	832	Gen. Karlo Otto Wolff	Hitler orders occupation of Vatican and kidnaping of Pope.
17	34	834	Gen. Karlo Otto Wolff	Wolff tries to thwart Hitler's plans.
17	35	836-37	Gen. Karlo Otto Wolff	Wolff urges Hitler to drop plans against Vatican.
18	14	340	Quirino Paganuzzi (worked in Vatican)	Pius got on knees and apologized to priest with whom he had been sharp.
20	3	102	Pascalina Lehnert	Pius says that a Pope must be perfect, but not others.

20	4	334	Quirino Paganuzzi	Pius stayed up late to return books and files to their proper place.
20	8	89	Pascalina Lehnert	Companion did not share the vision seen by Pius.
20	10	219	Carlo Pacelli	There was a rumor that Pius XII's housekeeper interrupted an important meeting.
20	13	37	Guglielmo Hentrich	Pius did not think beauty contests were good for women.
20	14	249	Virginio Rotondi (journalist)	Pius rejected a candidate for sainthood due to his use of obscene language.
20	15	210	Giacomo Martegani (radio and newspaper man)	Pius warned priests to avoid temptation by avoiding trips with young women.
20	23	229	Carlo Pacelli	Pius had dental problems.
20	26	276	Cesidio Lolli (newspaper writer)	Pius XII's health problems.
20	27	227	Carlo Pacelli	Pius changed doctors.

Not only did all of these witnesses have favorable things to say about Pope Pius XII, even the portions of testimony cited by Cornwell are not critical of Pius, despite Cornwell's arguments to the contrary. One need not view the deposition transcripts to verify this summary. Just look at Cornwell's citations and compare them with his text. The testimonies "are without any exception, positive with regard to the life, activity, and virtue of Pius XII."[17]

In the April 2000 issue of *Brill's Content* magazine, Cornwell addressed the fact that these depositions contain nothing that could possibly put an honest person into a state of moral shock. His only reply was that: "[Pius XII's sister] tells us that he was accused of having had an affair with his housekeeper nun and that the housekeeper in turn had been engaged in a flirtation with the Vatican architect. Is that not explosive?" That testimony (which actually was that Pius immediately ordered an investigation when he heard this rumor and was pleased when it was disproved) has nothing to do with Hitler, the Jews, the Nazis, or the Holocaust. Cornwell's claim of having been left in a "state of moral shock" is preposterous.[18]

CORNWELL'S RELIANCE ON KLAUS SCHOLDER

While Cornwell has only thirty citations to the deposition transcripts, he has about twice that many citations to Klaus Scholder's two volumes on *The Churches and the Third Reich* (Fortress Press, 1988). In fact, Cornwell says that his "greatest debt, and indeed homage, is to the magisterial scholarship of the late Klaus Scholder." According to Cornwell, Scholder's reputation as a church historian is "unchallenged in German scholarship," but scholars at the Holy See have overlooked him. On both counts, Cornwell is demonstrably wrong.

Scholder has been most seriously challenged by Konrad Repgen. In several works, Repgen has particularly contested Scholder's assertion that there was a connection between the dissolution of the Center Party and the concordat negotiations between the Third Reich and the Holy

See in 1933.[19] Ludwig Volk's work, though published prior to Scholder's, also refutes the latter's contentions, in particular Scholder's claim that the initiative for the concordat came from the Vatican.[20] Other scholarship also undercuts Scholder's claim that the push for the concordat came from the Vatican instead of the Germans.[21] In fact, the editors of a collection of Scholder's papers that was published after his death even admitted in the introduction that Scholder's anti-Pacelli thesis could not be supported from the available records.[22]

As for the Vatican's failure to consult Scholder's work, Cornwell reports that in a conversation, Fr. Peter Gumpel admitted "that not only had he not read Klaus Scholder's extensive and crucial scholarship on the Reich Concordat, but that he was unaware of its existence." Gumpel, of course, has read Scholder's writings.[23]

Gumpel attributes Cornwell's error to a misunderstanding that took place when Cornwell visited Rome. "He has a very bad pronunciation of German," Gumpel explained. "He may have asked whether I knew of Scholder's work, but mispronounced the name so badly that I did not recognize it." Gumpel has also explained why Cornwell relies so heavily on Scholder: "Scholder's work relating to the various concordats is 'largely surpassed' by other standard works, but Scholder better supports Cornwell's thesis."[24]

INFLUENCING THE FUTURE OF THE CHURCH?

The last chapter of *Hitler's Pope* is entitled "Pius XII Redivivus." In it, John Cornwell argued that the late John Paul II represented a return to a more highly centralized, autocratic papacy, as opposed to a more diversified Church. He wrote about early signs of a titanic struggle between the progressives and the traditionalists, with the potential for a cataclysmic schism, especially in North America. Cornwell argued that John Paul II was leading the traditionalists as the Church moved toward this struggle, and he said that "canonization of Pius XII is a key move in the attempts to restore a reactionary papal absolutism."[25]

Any doubt about Cornwell's intent to denigrate Pope John Paul II was resolved in March 2000, at the time when the pontiff made an unprecedented and historic trip to the Holy Land. At that time, as Christians and Jews were coming closer together, Cornwell described John Paul as "aging, ailing, and desperately frail as he presides over a Vatican that is riven by cliques, engulfed in scandal, and subject to ideological power struggles."[26] To Cornwell, the Vatican was "a nest of nepotism and corruption, sexual depravity, gangsterism, and even murder." Quoting an unidentified "Vatican insider," Cornwell described the Vatican as "a palace of gossipy eunuchs. . . . The whole place floats on a sea of bitchery."[27]

In *Breaking Faith* (2001), Cornwell made charges against Pope John Paul II similar to those that he made against Pius XII in *Hitler's Pope*. Cornwell argued that centralization of power under John Paul's authoritarian rule had brought about a fundamental breakdown in communications between hierarchy and laity. "Bullying oppression," Cornwell wrote, was driving people away from the Catholic Church. He blamed virtually all of the Church's modern problems on "the harsh centralized rules of Wojtyla's Church." He called the pope a "stumbling block" for "a vast, marginalized faithful" and said that the Holy Father had "encouraged an oppressive intellectual culture." Cornwell warned that if a conservative pope succeeds John Paul II, the Church will "deteriorate" and push "greater numbers of Catholics toward antagonism, despair and mass apostasy."[28]

In *The Pontiff in Winter* (2005), Cornwell argued that John Paul II had "taken a bit of the Iron Curtain with him" to the Vatican to mold a rigid, authoritarian papacy. Cornwell not only blamed John Paul for the spread of AIDS, but also for global terrorism. He also said that John Paul had developed a "medieval patriarchalism" towards women and his "major and abiding legacy . . . is to be seen and felt in various forms of oppression and exclusion." Cornwell criticized the pope's positions on the September 11 attacks, the clash between Islam and Christianity, and statements regarding Mel Gibson's *The Passion*. His strongest criticisms, however, related to the Church's teaching on homosexuality, abortion, AIDS, the sexual abuse crisis, divorce, and the ordination of women. Cornwell charged that the Catholic teachings voiced by the pontiff have "alienated generations of the faithful" and that "John Paul's successor will inherit a dysfunctional Church fraught with problems."[29]

Cornwell's continuing theme across all of these books is that the Church needs to decentralize its authority. Mainly, however, he advances the typical laundry list of liberal Catholic demands, including married clergy, women priests, a bigger role for the laity in running the Church, and inclusive language in the Mass.[30] He is deeply offended by the Church's teachings on sexuality, particularly Pope Paul VI's encyclical *Humanae Vitae*. Cornwell thinks that contraception, homosexuality, divorce, and essentially all extramarital sex are matters to be decided by consenting adults,[31] and he would like the Church to change its position on these matters.

In the first few pages of *Breaking Faith*, Cornwell explained why he worked so hard to prove his credentials as a good, practicing Catholic with the release of *Hitler's Pope* and why he hid his earlier hostility towards the Church: "there is a world of difference between an authentic believing Catholic, writing critically from within, and a 'Catholic bashing' apostate who lies about being a Catholic in order to solicit an unwarranted hearing from the faithful." Although Cornwell assures us that he is an "authentic believing Catholic," his expressed faith is not in the teachings of the Catholic Church.

At the same time that he lodged criticism from the left, in *Breaking Faith* Cornwell also raised many of the objections that one usually hears only from critics on the right. In fact, one fairly conservative American Catholic magazine, *Crisis*, gave him a friendly profile, noting that many of his objections were in line with complaints regularly made in that periodical.[32] Thus, Cornwell claimed to be concerned about "dumbed-down populism" and wrote negatively of overblown signs of peace, dancing girls at Mass, and a lack of reverence for the

Holy Eucharist. He questioned modern music, the architecture of modern church buildings, and criticized the number of annulments granted to divorced Catholics. Of his return to Catholicism, he wrote: "Mostly I was appalled at what I encountered. Something was badly wrong with the singing, the translations of the Latin rite, the manner of participation."

When an entity is criticized from two different directions, one might assume that it is somewhere in the middle, probably doing a pretty good job. What, however, is one to make of an individual who criticizes the Catholic Church from both the left and the right at the same time? The only constant seems to be that each pope since Pius XI (with the exception of John Paul I, who did not live long enough to offend Cornwell) is criticized. Pius XII was suspicious of democracy,[33] and he suppressed Catholic thinkers. John XXIII was an "archconservative when it came to seminary training." In fact, seminarians, including Cornwell, "could not wait" for the "better days to come" after John's papacy. Paul VI, of course, committed the ultimate sin of authoring *Humanae Vitae* and reasserting traditional Christian teaching against contraception. John Paul II has taken all types of authoritarian actions that are reportedly destroying the Church. Cornwell takes every opportunity that he can find to criticize the Catholic Church, regardless of inconsistencies in his argument.

Instead of consistent arguments, Cornwell reviews opinion surveys suggesting that Catholics have difficulty with Church teachings on contraception, abortion, divorce, and homosexuality. He interprets this as resistance to papal authority, and the only solution that makes sense to him is to weaken the papacy and change the Church teachings. That, however, is not the Catholic way. As historian Paul Johnson has written: "Catholicism is not a market-research religion. It is not in business to count heads or take votes. . . . Dogma and morals are not susceptible to guidance by opinion polls. The truth is paramount and it must be the naked truth, presented without cosmetics and exercises in public relations. . . . The Catholic Church has not survived and flourished over two millennia by being popular. It has survived because what it taught is true. The quest for popularity, as opposed to the quest for truth, is bound to fail."[34]

In contrast to Cornwell's warped approach to Catholicism is that of John Henry Newman, who was made a cardinal by Pope Leo XIII in 1879. "Newman would not have condemned any view more strongly than the one holding that opinion polls decide the truth. Nothing would have shocked him more than the thought that the faithful and not the Magisterium decide what is to be believed."[35]

Pope John Paul II, perhaps better than anyone else, recognized the parallels between his efforts and those of Pius XII.[36] John Paul, of course, did not have a horrible world war to contend with, nor was he threatened with the possibility of Vatican City being invaded, but given those differences, the approach each leader took was similar. As John Paul II explained: "Anyone who does not limit himself to cheap polemics knows very well what Pius XII thought of the Nazi regime and how much he did to help countless people persecuted by the regime."[37]

John Cornwell recognized divisions in the Catholic Church today and the similarities between Pius XII and John Paul II, but rather than trying to discuss them honestly, he picked a target that he thought would be easy to attack, created a far-fetched theory, and ignored all evidence contrary to his thesis. Along the way, he revealed a basic misunderstanding of modern history. His books, which purport to be genuine scholarship, are unfortunately much less than that.

SUSAN ZUCCOTTI'S OVERLOOKED EVIDENCE

Susan Zuccotti went through parish archives throughout Italy. Time after time she found that Catholic bishops, priests, nuns, and laypersons fed, sheltered, and clothed Jewish refugees. She claimed, however, to find no evidence of papal help with this rescue work. When overwhelming oral evidence of papal support was pointed out to her, she rejected anything except contemporaneous written evidence. Not finding any, and assuming that the Vatican would have published any such documents if they existed, she concluded that there was no valid evidence of papal involvement in rescue efforts.[38] She was wrong.

To begin with, Zuccotti's thesis is illegitimate. She builds her case not on evidence, but on a lack of evidence.[39] In doing this, she violates the Talmudic rule: "not to have seen is not yet a proof."[40] This has also been called "rule one" of archaeology: "Absence of evidence is not evidence of absence."[41] The same maxim applies to legal analysis.[42] No honest historian should make such an argument.

Holocaust denier (and researcher for Rolf Hochhuth) David Irving once offered a reward for anyone who could find a document from Hitler linking him to the extermination of Jews. Serious historians rightfully rejected his argument. A lack of existing written evidence is not sufficient to prove that Hitler lacked responsibility for the Holocaust. Everyone who arrested a Jew, informed on those who sheltered refugees, or helped run a concentration camp knew that Hitler approved of this work.[43] By the same token, everyone who helped rescue Jews knew that they were fulfilling the pope's wishes. He inspired them and encouraged them.[44]

Zuccotti frequently notes that Pope Pius XII allowed his underlings to carry out life-saving work on behalf of the Jews. For instance, on page 214 of *Under His Very Windows,* she reports: "He may not always have known the extent of the rescue work, but . . . [he] did not prohibit these activities." On page 188 she writes: "he allowed Benedetto's [rescue] activities to continue." On page 236 she informs the reader: "Pius XII did not prohibit [rescue operations in north Italy]." On 299 one reads: "Pius XII and his advisors undoubtedly knew what Bernardini was doing, and approved." On page 243, she even goes further, saying that rescuers "may have been encouraged" by Pius XII's public statements or by articles about his work that appeared in local parish bulletins. Unfortunately, like Irving, she rejects overwhelming evidence simply because she could not find the written order. Zuccotti's theory is bad logic for a Holocaust denier, and it is bad logic for her.

One problem with her argument is that in order for it to be valid, the researcher must have scoured every potential source. Zuccotti assured her readers that she did just that, but subsequent discoveries have established that she did not find all the evidence.

In southern Italy, Giovanni Palatucci was known as "The Policeman Who Saved Thousands of Jews." He was named by Yad Vashem, Israel's Holocaust Martyrs' and Heroes' Remembrance Authority, as a "Righteous Gentile" for helping save five thousand Jewish lives. Palatucci worked in close collaboration with his uncle, Giuseppe Maria Palatucci, bishop of Campagna, a small town where the largest internment camp in southern Italy was located. In 1940, Bishop Palatucci received two letters from the Vatican.

The first letter, sent to the bishop on October 2, 1940, reported that Pope Pius XII had agreed to grant to him the sum of 3,000 lire. The letter, which was signed by Cardinal Maglione, Pius XII's secretary of state, stated: "This sum is preferably to be used to help those who suffer for reason of race" (*questo denaro e preferibilmente destinato a chi soffre per ragioni di razza*). The choice of language at this time and place in history was a clear reference to Jews.

In a second letter, the future Pope Paul VI, Giovanni Battista Montini, then an official in the Vatican's Secretariat of State, notified Bishop Palatucci that Pope Pius XII had granted him the sum of 10,000 lire "to distribute in support of the interned Jews" (*da distribuirsi in sussidi agli ebrei internati*). These two letters are very clear, and they completely contradict Zuccotti's thesis.[45]

Pacelli is now also known to have written a letter complaining about the Nazis as early as 1923. On November 14, 1923, Pacelli wrote to Cardinal Pietro Gasparri to report that "followers of Hitler and Ludendorff" were persecuting Catholics.[46] The attacks "were especially focused" on Michael Cardinal Faulhaber, who "had denounced the persecutions against the Jews."[47]

Similarly, on April 4, 1933, the Holy See sent a letter, signed by Secretary of State Pacelli, to Cesare Orsenigo, the nuncio in Germany.

It said that some requests had come to the pope asking for his "intervention against the danger of anti-Semitic excesses in Germany." The letter continued: "Given that it is part of the traditions of the Holy See to carry out its mission of universal peace and charity toward all men, regardless of the social or religious condition to which they belong, by offering, if necessary, its charitable offices, the Holy Father asks your Excellency to see if and how it is possible to be involved in the desired way."[48] As others have concluded: "The letter is of decisive value in the debate launched by those who say that Eugenio Pacelli, the future Pius XII, never spoke in favor of the Jews, to the point of labeling him 'Hitler's Pope.'"[49]

In some cases, Zuccotti simply misconstrues the evidence. For instance, she gives considerable attention to a Jewish family's request for permission to stay in an Italian convent.[50] She discusses Montini's note of October 1, 1943, concerning this matter and his efforts on behalf of the Jewish family, but she says nothing of Pius XII's own involvement, which is confirmed by a notation at the bottom of that note (Ex. Aud. SS.mi. 1.X.43).[51] The abbreviation stands for "Ex Audientia Sanctissimi, 1 Oct. 1943," meaning that it was discussed with the Pope on that date.[52] The term "Sanctissimi" stands for His Holiness—in this case Pius XII.

In fact, below this indication that the matter was discussed with the pope is a further notation: "*Si veda se possible aiutarlo.*" The phrase means roughly "See if he can be helped." Following the notation of the meeting with the pope, this is an indication of his permission for the convent to admit a male Jew, despite a normal prohibition on men in the convent. Thus, this very document shows direct papal involvement in the sheltering of Jews even prior to the notorious roundup of October 16, 1943.[53] Again, one cannot overlook or fail to understand written exhibits like this and then build a legitimate case arguing that there is a lack of evidence.

Zuccotti criticized my work because I had noted Monsignor Hugh O'Flaherty's rescue work in Rome during the Nazi occupation. She says that I "exaggerated claims" because the authors that I cited (Hatch and Walshe) did not say that O'Flaherty sheltered Jews, only that he helped *refugees*. Technically, she has a point. Hatch and Walshe did not specifically note that Jews were among O'Flaherty's group. They called him the "Conrad Hilton of the underground" because he had more than sixty apartments (some with as many as twelve rooms) in which he kept refugees. In order to find proof that many of the refugees were Jewish, one only had to consult any of numerous other sources.

The evidence shows that O'Flaherty took care of "aristocrats, *Jews*, and anti-Fascists who were in danger. He found them clothes and food."[54] He also "earned the title 'the Oscar Schindler of Killarney' by hiding four thousand Jews and escaped Allied prisoners."[55] In fact, O'Flaherty first began smuggling and hiding refugees in the fall of 1942, when the Italians cracked down on prominent Jews and anti-Fascist aristocrats. He later broadened his operation to include escaped British POWs. As the war went on, O'Flaherty did not ask about faith or race. He took care of Jews or anyone else who needed assistance.[56] According the author J. P. Gallagher: "On the day of the liberation of Rome, the Pimpernel [O'Flaherty] and his associates were looking after about 4,000 people—British, South African, Russian, Greek, American and a score of other nationalities, *quite apart from an uncounted number of Jews whom O'Flaherty personally saved.*[57] A downed British airman, who was protected by Monsignor O'Flaherty during the war wrote an account explaining how Allied soldiers, Jewish refugees, and escaped war prisoners were sheltered in the basements and attics of Catholic seminaries and universities throughout Rome. In fact, he quoted O'Flaherty complaining to British soldiers: "Between you fellows and all my Jews, I can't get my work done."[58]

Zuccotti also notes that I, like many other authors, have translated the Italian word *stirpe*, which was used in several official Church statements, as meaning "race."[59] On page 2 of her book, she argues that *stirpe* does not exactly correlate with the English word race, but should be understood as meaning descent. Her clear suggestion is that when the pope or various Church officials used the word *stirpe*, they were not saying *race* and therefore were not speaking on behalf of Jewish people. She thus argues that those who have defended the pope were wrong.

In fact, the Church did not view people as being racially distinct in the way that the Nazis did. Jewish people were defined by their faith. When it was necessary to refer to them as a group, the well-established practice at the Vatican had been to use the word *stirpe*.[60] Moreover, *Cassell's Italian Dictionary* (1979), gives the following as the definition of the Italian *stirpe*: "stock, race, descent, lineage, extraction." ("Race" precedes "descent.") The *Zanichelli New College Italian and English Dictionary* gives: "stock, race, family, lineage, ancestry." ("Descent" is not given as an option.)[61] Of greatest importance, the *Nuovo Dizionario della Lingua Italiana*, published in Milan in 1924 (therefore best reflecting Italian usage when Pius XII was a young man) gives *schiatta* ("race") as an exact synonym of *stirpe*. It even provides as an illustration of the word's meaning the phrase: "*la stirpe semitica*," ("the Semitic race").[62]

Pope Pius XI's anti-Nazi encyclical, *Mit brennender Sorge*, used a German word that Dr. Zuccotti does translate as meaning race (*rasse*). This time, however, her analysis is changed. She argues that since the Church did not actually consider Jews as a distinct race, rather as a religion, "it is unlikely that any reference to observant Jews was intended."[63] Thus, regardless of the word used, she finds a basis for her criticism of the pope and the Church. Her effort to dismiss numerous war-time statements with this analysis should be rejected.[64]

Several quotations in Zuccotti's book seem to have been truncated to eliminate any evidence that might show the pope's concern for Jewish victims. For instance, pursuant to Pope Pius XII's request, Secretary of State Maglione met to lodge a protest with German Ambassador Weizsäcker after the notorious October 16, 1943, roundup of Jews.[65] Weizsäcker was known to be a friendly voice within the German leadership in Rome, and he was embarrassed about the Nazi treatment of the Jews. Maglione began his memo about the meeting by writing:

> ***Having learned that this morning the Germans made a raid on the Jews,*** I asked the Ambassador of Germany to come to me and I asked him to try to intervene on behalf of these unfortunates. I talked to him as well as I could in the name of humanity, in Christian charity.
>
> ***The Ambassador, who already knew of the arrests, but doubted whether it dealt specifically with the Jews, said to me in a sincere and moved voice: I am always expecting to be asked: Why do you remain in your position?***

Unfortunately, Zuccotti deleted the italicized clauses, thereby eliminating the cardinal's first two express references to the victims being Jewish. She also omitted the entire concluding paragraph, which recounted Maglione's last words to Weizsäcker:

> ***In the meantime, I repeat: Your Excellency has told me that you*** [Weizsäcker] ***will attempt to do something for the unfortunate Jews. I thank you for that. As for the rest, I leave it to your judgement. If you think it is more opportune not to mention our conversation*** [to the German high command due to fear of retaliation], ***so be it.***[66]

So, even though Cardinal Maglione referred explicitly to "Jews" three times, Zuccotti's readers never saw those references; they were all deleted.[67] She apparently did not want to show Vatican officials protesting on behalf of Jewish victims, preferring to leave the impression that they considered Jews as abstract people who had no specific worth.[68]

Similarly, Zuccotti quotes a report written by Nuncio Valerio Valeri to Cardinal Maglione, dated August 7, 1942. This memorandum related to the deportation of Jews from France to unknown areas, probably in Poland. Zuccotti accuses Valeri of manufacturing papal interventions on behalf of the Jews elsewhere in the world, but she deletes the crucial first line of Valeri's report where *he* mentions that *he* had used *his* position to *frequently* intervene for Jews in the name of the pope.[69] This testimony, which would be hard for her to discount, is simply omitted.

Zuccotti also quotes Cardinal Tisserant, claiming that in 1939 he questioned whether Eugenio Pacelli was strong enough to be pope. She does not, however, mention that Tisserant later praised Pius xii's wartime conduct. The full facts are that Cardinal Tisserant sent a private letter to Cardinal Emanuel Suhard, the Archbishop of Paris, in 1940 (two years before the infamous Wannsee conference at which Nazi leadership decided upon the "Final Solution" for the Jews), in which he wrote "I fear that history will reproach the Holy See for having followed a policy of comfort and convenience, and not much else." The letter, never meant for public consumption, was seized by the Gestapo in Paris; and later found in their archives. It was made public in 1964 by those seeking to damage the reputation of the wartime pontiff. Tisserant immediately issued a statement unequivocally clarifying his remarks: "The pope's attitude was beyond discussion. My remarks did not involve his person, but certain members of the Curia. In the dramatic period of the War, and what a period that was, Pius xii was able to guide the Church with invincible strength."[70] He also told the *New York Times* that: "It seems evident to me that the principles, reaffirmed by Pope Pacelli in his first encyclical, and repeated forcefully at every circumstance, above all in the Christmas messages of the war years, constitute the most concrete condemnation of the Hitlerian type of absolutism."[71] Robert Graham later interviewed Tisserant about the whole affair, and Tisserant admitted that he had written his 1940 letter in anger ("*ab irato*") and that it was perhaps even unfair to the people in the Curia whom he was criticizing. He underscored that it was written in 1940 when Pius could not "have dealt with the tragedy which was yet to unfold."[72]

Similarly, Zuccotti tells us that French priest-rescuer Fr. Marie-Benoît received virtually no support from Rome, but he is on record as saying just the opposite. In 1976, on the centennial of Pius XII's birth, Fr. Benoît prepared a statement which spoke in glowing terms of the Holy Father and his undertakings on behalf of Jews.[73] Benoît noted that Pius listened to his plan to save Jews with great attention and promised to take care of the matter personally. "An AFP report which came out of the Vatican as recently as March of 1976 indicates that Benoît spoke in glowing terms of the Holy Father. In fact on the occasion of the centenary of Eugenio Pacelli's birth, he sent a report which praised the various undertakings of the Pope on behalf of the Jews during the war"[74]

Among the published documents, Zuccotti encountered evidence that the Vatican provided money to help Benoît.[75] She claims it is difficult to interpret and supposes that the amount must have been "exceedingly sparse."[76] Yet Fernande Leboucher, who worked with Fr. Benoît as perhaps his closest collaborator, wrote a book about their rescue work. She even called upon him for help in putting the book together.[77] Leboucher estimated that a total of some four million dollars was channeled from the Vatican to Benoît and his operation.[78] The evidence is certainly not as Zuccotti would have us believe.

Actually, the Nazis noted the coordinated efforts of Catholic officials in different areas and speculated that they were acting pursuant to a larger plan. A German Foreign Office agent named Frederic was sent on a tour through various Nazi-occupied and satellite countries during the war. He wrote in his confidential report to the German Foreign Office on September 19, 1943, that Metropolitan Sheptytsky, from the Ukraine, remained adamant in saying that the killing of Jews was an inadmissible act. Frederic went on to comment that the Metropolitan made the same statements and used the same phrasing as the French, Belgian, and Dutch bishops, as if they were all receiving instructions from the Vatican.[79]

Zuccotti even mischaracterizes Pius XII's first encyclical, *Summi Pontificatus*, saying that it "never mentioned Jews. Indeed, despite references to the unity of the human race, it seemed to single out Christians, or perhaps Catholics, for special consideration."[80] In fact, Pius did use the word "Jew" in the context of explaining that there is no room for racial distinctions in the Church.[81]

On April 16, 1943, the *Australian Jewish News* quoted Cardinal Gerlier as saying that he was obeying instructions from Pius XII by opposing France's anti-Semitic measures. Since that claim is not supported by a written order from Pius, it does not meet Zuccotti's demand for written documentation. It should be noted, however, that she applies that standard quite inconsistently.

Even Zuccotti agrees that Catholic rescuers "invariably believed that they were acting according to the pope's will."[82] He encouraged, inspired, and authorized them to do what they could to help, but in conformity with the Catholic social doctrines of subsidiarity and solidarity,[83] details were usually left to be decided at the local level.[84] That is not to say, however, that Pius was uninvolved in rescue efforts. In August 1944, Pulitzer-winning *New York Times* reporter, Anne O'Hare McCormick, wrote from liberated Rome that Pius enjoyed an "enhanced" reputation because during the Nazi occupation he had made "hiding someone 'on the run' the thing to do" and had given Jews "first priority."[85]

Between 1967 and 1974, ninety-eight witnesses who knew Pope Pius XII personally gave sworn testimony, under oath, about his life.[86] This evidence, unlike published Vatican documents, focuses directly on Pope Pius XII's personal efforts on behalf of Jews and others. In other words, these transcripts contain exactly the type of evidence that Zuccotti was seeking.

No less than forty-two witnesses, including five cardinals, spoke directly of Pius XII's concern for and help given to Jewish people.[87] Some witnesses spoke of papal orders to open buildings. Others testified that Pius knew of and approved of the sheltering of Jews in church buildings. The vice-director of the Vatican newspaper testified that Pius personally opened Vatican buildings, and he authorized convents and monasteries to welcome outsiders. The clear message from each and every witness was that Pope Pius xii was honest, holy, and charitable.[88]

It may be understandable that a researcher would not consult the deposition transcripts. They have not been translated or widely published. One cannot, however, legitimately overlook this most relevant testimony and then turn around and build a case based upon an alleged lack of evidence.[89]

In a related manner, Zuccotti leads her readers to believe that none of the rescuers credited Pius for supporting their work. Again, she is mistaken. Pius has a long list of very credible witnesses on this matter, including two popes.

In 1955, the Israeli Philharmonic Orchestra played a concert of thanks to the pope in Vatican City.[90] While they were there, a delegation from Israel approached Archbishop Montini, the future Pope Paul vi, to determine whether he would accept an award for his work on behalf of Jews during the war. He declined the honor: "All I did was my duty," he said. "And besides I only acted upon orders from the Holy Father. Nobody deserves a medal for that."[91] Angelo Roncalli (the future Pope John xxiii) made a very similar statement when he was offered thanks for his efforts to save Jewish lives in Istanbul: "In all these painful matters I have referred to the Holy See and simply carried out the Pope's orders: first and foremost to save human lives."[92]

Cardinal Pietro Palazzini, then assistant vice rector of the Seminario Romano, hid Italian Jews there in 1943 and 1944. In 1985, Yad Vashem honored the cardinal as a Righteous Gentile. In accepting the honor, Palazzini stressed that "the merit is entirely Pius xii's, who ordered us to do whatever we could to save the Jews from persecution."[93] Palazzini also credited Pius for the "great work of charity" of sheltering anyone who needed refuge during the war.[94] In fact, Palazzini wrote that: "Amidst the clash of arms, a voice could be heard—the voice of Pius XII. The assistance given to so many people could not have been possible without his moral support, which was much more than quiet consent."[95]

Cardinal Paolo Dezza, head of one of the institutions that sheltered Jews, quoted Pius as saying to him: "Avoid helping the military . . . but as for the others, help them willingly, especially help the poor, persecuted Jews."[96] Fleeing soldiers were sheltered at another Vatican institution, the Palazzo Callisto.

Jewish historian Michael Tagliacozzo, head of the Center on Studies on the Shoah and Resistance in Italy, told about how he was rescued from the Nazis and hidden in the Pope's building in Vatican City. He also said that Pius himself ordered the opening of convents and that Pius was the only person to intervene when the Nazis rounded up Roman Jews on October 16, 1943.[97]

Hungarian rescuer Tibor Baranski was honored by Yad Vashem as a Righteous Gentile for his rescue work in Hungary during World War II. As executive secretary of the Jewish Protection Movement of the Holy See, Baranski officially saved three thousand Jews. During the war, he worked closely with Angelo Rotta, papal nuncio in Hungary (who was also recognized by Yad Vashem as a Righteous Gentile).

Baranski makes clear that these life-saving activities were not the lone actions of himself or Nuncio Rotta. "I was really acting in accordance with the orders of Pope Pius XII." Charges that Pius was not involved are "simple lies; nothing else," and claims that Pius should have done more for the Jews are "slanderous."

Baranski reports that he personally saw at least two letters from Pius XII instructing Rotta to do his very best to protect Jews but to refrain from making statements that might provoke the Nazis. He adds: "These two letters were not written by the authorities at the Vatican, but they were hand-written ones by Pope Pius himself." He goes on to note that "all other Nuncios of the Nazi-occupied countries received similar letters." Italian Jews, for instance, were sheltered in monasteries, seminaries, and other Church buildings on the "direct instruction of the Vatican."

Baranski explained that for Pius, the first and foremost concern was saving human lives. "It was precisely because [Pius] wanted to help the Jews" that he refrained from making repeated public condemnations. Pius "intervened in a very balanced way," trying to save lives without provoking retaliation. He did not, however, behave differently depending upon the status of the victims. Baranski noted that these same concerns prevented the pope from making repeated public appeals when the Nazis killed thousands of Catholic priests.

"The Pontiff did not only encourage the Nuncio to protect Vatican [baptized] Jews," explains Baranski, "but as many persecuted persons as possible, in the ghetto or elsewhere." The nuncio kept Pius well informed of efforts undertaken in collaboration with other embassies, including close work with Swedish diplomat and rescuer Raoul Wallenberg, who also was declared a Righteous Gentile by Yad Vashem.

Baranski, who says that he was "fantastically near" to Wallenberg, argues that were he alive today, Wallenberg would defend Pope Pius XII and commend the Catholic Church for its work in collaboration with him. "Look, there was not problem or disagreement whatsoever between the Catholic Church and Wallenberg. I personally arranged unofficial, private meetings between Wallenberg and Nuncio Rotta." Baranski reports that Wallenberg "knew Pius was on his side." Rotta, Baranski, Wallenberg, and—yes—Pius XII worked together as a team. Baranski believes that, like the others, Pius XII should be honored as a Righteous Gentile.[98]

Another witness to Pius XII's orders to help Jews was Righteous Gentile Don Aldo Brunacci. Zuccotti spoke to him as part of her research. He told her that the Vatican sent a letter instructing Catholics to assist Jews during the Nazi occupation of Italy, but she discounted his testimony because he did not read the letter of instruction that came from the Vatican; it was read to him by Bishop Giuseppe Nicolini of Assisi. Brunacci, interviewed after Zuccotti's book was published, disputed her analysis:

Q: In her book . . . Susan Zuccotti, who says that she interviewed you, maintains that you never actually saw the text of the letter from the Vatican to Bishop Nicolini.

BRUNACCI: Ah, Zuccotti! Yes, I did speak with her. What should I say? It is true, I did not make a photocopy of the text.

Q: Did you actually see the letter?

BRUNACCI: I did not actually see the text of the letter, but look, I was alone with the bishop in the room, he held the letter up and showed it to me. He said he had received the letter from Rome, and he read what it said—that the Holy Father wanted us to see to it in our diocese that something would be done to ensure the safety of the Jews—and the bishop wanted to consult with me on what to do.

Q: So you never actually read the letter?

BRUNACCI: No, the bishop read the letter to me.

Q: Then, as Zuccotti suggests in her book, it might be possible that the letter was not what Bishop Nicolini told you it was, that he was in some way deceiving you?

BRUNACCI: (Laughs.) Impossible, impossible. (Laughs again.) It is not possible that Bishop Nicolini was deceiving me. I am certain of that. Look, we were alone in the room and he read the letter to me. It was clearly from the Vatican, there is no doubt of that. Not from the Pope himself, personally, but from the Secretariat of State.

It was a letter asking the bishop to do all he could to help the Jews, and the bishop wanted me to advise him on the best way to carry out that request. In fact, this same order went out to many other diocese in Italy. . . .

The work of Pope Pius xii was a majestic work, a work of deeds, not of words. Zuccotti doubts that Pius xii could have issued such an order because she is persuaded by the campaign launched against Pius in 1963. But that campaign has been filled with slanders and calumnies. Still, Signora Zuccotti is persuaded by it, and so cannot accept that this letter was sent out, and she has to invent the story that the bishop deceived me to explain it away. But the letter was sent out. I saw it with my own eyes, in my bishop's hands, as he read it to me. It was a letter from the Vatican asking the bishop to take measures to help protect the Jews. And we took the measures.

Don't take Zuccotti too seriously. . . .[99]

Italian Senator Adriano Ossicini, founder of the Italian "Christian Left,"[100] and Sr. Maria Corsetti Ferdininda,[101] both told similar stories. In her book *Yours Is a Precious Witness*, Sr. Margherita Marchione writes that in interview after interview she was told that, "at the request of Pope Pius xii, doors of convents and monasteries were opened to save the Jews when the Nazis occupied Italy."[102]

Author Antonio Gaspari recounts several instances of Pius xii intervening in his personal capacity, through the Vatican state secretariat, to save Jews.[103] In one case, one thousand German Jews wanted to emigrate to Brazil, and the pontiff paid out of his own pocket the $800 each needed for the trip. In 1939, Pius organized special operations inside the Vatican Information Office to help Jews persecuted by Nazism. Regarding Zuccotti's thesis that Catholic rescue activity took place without papal support, Gaspari expressly says: "This is a thesis that is impossible to defend."[104]

So how does Zuccotti argue that Pope Pius xii had no role in rescue efforts, when so many witnesses testified that he did? The answer is that—time and time again—she discounts or dismisses the testimony of people who were there. In so doing, she denies the legitimacy of the gratitude of the Jewish victims and denies "the credibility of their personal testimony and judgement about the Holocaust itself."[105]

On page 264, she discusses a bishop who claimed to have been holding a letter from Pius in his hands, but she suggests that the bishop falsified this claim because he "may have considered it useful to make his assistants believe that they were doing the Pope's work."

On page 193, Zuccotti suggests that nuns who credited the pope for having ordered their convents opened to Jewish refugees were "eager that Pius XII receive credit for the work of their order." (She does, however, concede that Pius probably knew these nuns were sheltering Jews.)

On page 143, she discusses a letter from A. L. Eastman, of the World Jewish Congress, thanking the pope for helping free imprisoned Jews. Zuccotti however, dismisses this testimony by saying, "Eastman must have known better."

On page 103, she quotes the papal nuncio in Vichy, praising Pope Pius XII for condemning the persecution of Jews and others. Zuccotti accuses him of fabricating the papal responses.

On page 301, she discusses gratitude from Jewish people to the Pope following the war. She attributes their attitude to "benevolent ignorance."[106]

On page 302, in an even more disturbing analysis, she suggests that Jewish chaplains simply lied because they were "anxious to protect and preserve the fragile goodwill between Jews and non-Jews that seems to be emerging from the rubble of the war in Italy."

At other points along the way she dismisses letters of thanks from Jewish people because "The Holy See had done nothing more for the Jewish Internees than for non-Jews" (p. 85). Favorable accounts of the pope's efforts to help Jews are dismissed as "less than honest" (p. 272). Testimony from the future Pope Paul VI is dismissed because, according to Zuccotti, he "knew perfectly well" that his statement was wrong (p. 169).

Zuccotti does not show a lack of papal involvement in rescue efforts. All she has shown is that she does not believe the limited amount of evidence that she has reviewed.[107] She has also engaged in unfair and selective analysis of the evidence:

> It simply will not do for the beneficiaries of freedom to come after the event and either to disregard the ambiguities and veiled communications or to pick out one of the meanings of a deliberately ambiguous utterance and that *not* the one meant to be conveyed (with as much benefit and immunity as possible in the circumstances) at the time of the transaction, but one that fits a later case.
>
> Much of the conflict about the church has been of that kind. People have picked out not only the documents but parts of documents, even parts of meanings of single sentences or of words that suited them.[108]

At the end of the day, we have Zuccotti on one side arguing that there is no evidence of papal involvement.[109] On the other side we have a mountain of testimony from rescuers, victims, Germans, Jews, priests, nuns, the *New York Times* (and other papers), seven cardinals, and two popes. We also now have the written, archival confirmation of papal involvement in the rescue of Jews that Zuccotti thought did not exist. In other words, the evidence all weighs in favor of Pope Pius xii. To ignore that evidence is to deny history.[110]

GUENTER LEWY'S CRISIS OF CONSCIENCE

Guenter Lewy was one of the first authors to criticize Pope Pius xii. His work has been often cited by contemporary critics. For instance, despite her insistence on original sources, Susan Zuccotti's only source for the old canard holding that Pius xii was unwilling to speak out against the Nazis because this would create a conflict of conscience for the German soldiers is Lewy. There is no document to back this story up, and no one who has spent any time trying to know Pope Pius xii can believe that this was a significant influence upon him.

The story, according to Lewy, is that a correspondent for the Vatican newspaper in Berlin, Eduardo Senatra, at a public discussion in Berlin in 1964, said that Pius had told him this.[111] The problem is that Senatra was not from the Vatican newspaper, but from an Italian (Fascist) newspaper. He had no particular relationship with Pope Pius. Senatra, who had never made such a claim in his own newspaper, later wrote a letter correcting statements attributed to him at that 1964 occasion. Nevertheless, and despite the lack of any supporting documents, this unbelievable story is repeatedly told by those who want to present the worst possible portrait of Pope Pius XII and the Catholic Church.[112]

Lewy, like some critics who followed him, used quotations very selectively. For instance, he quoted the German theologian, historian, and sociologist Ernst Troeltsch (1865-1923) in attempting to explain the Catholic Church's role in society. Lewy wrote: "To use the sociological categories of Ernst Troeltsch, Catholicism is an example of 'that type of organization which is overwhelmingly conservative . . . it becomes an existing part of the existing order, . . . [and which knows to attain her end] by a process of adaption and compromise.'"[113] The ellipses and bracket commentary is provided by Lewy. In fact, the second ellipse covers eight pages of Troeltsch's writings![114]

Beate Ruhm von Oppen, writing on this bit of scholastic sleight of hand, explained that if one were to reject the very notion of sacraments (which, of course, would mean rejecting Catholicism) one might go on to argue, as did Lewy, that the Catholic Church has "usually been unable to separate her ideal aims from her interest in survival and she has often found her own gospel a liability rather than a source of strength. She has therefore from time to time retreated behind the cloister walls, and instead of being the salt of the earth has become the force tragically upholding injustice and tyranny."[115] Von Oppen goes on to note, however, that "one cannot use Troelsch for that argument," as Lewy attempted to do with the misleading quotation.[116]

DANIEL GOLDHAGEN: CHRISTIANITY AS ANTI-SEMITISM

Daniel Goldhagen seems to seek nothing less than a renunciation of Christianity. He accuses Pope Pius XII of collaborating with the Nazis and, like James Carroll, treats the Cross as a symbol of oppression. He lectures about how portions of the New Testament were fabricated and asserts that the very term "New Testament" is offensive.[117] Goldhagen writes that the Catholic Church's claim to be the people of God is the source of ideological anti-Semitism.[118] His agenda-driven approach, coupled with sloppy fact-checking and poor analysis, results in one of the most unjust broadside attacks launched against Christianity in several generations.[119]

One of Goldhagen's main assertions is that the guilt of all Jews for the crucifixion was a "central Catholic doctrine" and that during the 1940s it was taught as "official Catholic Church doctrine." He provided no evidence for this serious charge, nor could he. The *Catechism of the Council of Trent*, published in 1566 and approved by many popes thereafter, was the authoritative statement of Catholic doctrine during the Nazi period. It states that "*All sinners* were the authors of Christ's Passion" (emphasis added).

Goldhagen and similar critics focus on those passages of the New Testament that can be misunderstood. For instance, they cite the Gospel of John, chapter 8. Here Jesus is instructing people to reject Satan and follow him to the Father. "If you remain in my word, you will truly be my disciples, and you will know the truth, and the truth will set you free." Of those who reject him, however, Christ says: "You belong to your father the devil and you willingly carry out your father's desires. He was a murderer from the beginning and does not stand in truth, because there is no truth in him. When he tells a lie, he speaks in character, because he is a liar and the father of lies. But because I speak the truth, you do not believe me." Goldhagen argues that these words are anti-Semitic because Jesus is calling "Jews" the "children of the devil."[120]

The Gospel does say that Jesus was talking to a group of Jews, but that—in context—is like saying he was talking to any group of people who were not his followers.[121] After all, Jesus was born into a Jewish family. His mother was Jewish. His early followers were all Jewish, and the people who first heard him were Jewish. At his triumphal entry into Jerusalem, the crowds thronging around him were made up almost exclusively of Jews.[122] In John, chapter 8, he was trying to convince a group of those people to follow him. Jesus's words, as recorded in scripture, were not anti-Semitic.[123]

Critics are also concerned about Matthew 27:24-25, where Jesus is handed over to the Roman authorities, ultimately to face crucifixion. Pontius Pilate offers to free one of the "criminals," and the crowd calls for Barabbas. As Matthew reports: "So when Pilate saw that he was gaining nothing, but rather that a riot was beginning, he took water and washed his hands before the crowd, saying, 'I am innocent of this man's blood; see to it yourselves.' And all the people answered, 'His blood be on us and on our children!'"[124] Goldhagen argues that Matthew here falsely attributes blame for the crucifixion to all Jews for all times, that this instilled a hatred of Jews into the European psyche, and that Hitler merely had to exploit this pre-existing attitude to his own perverted ends.

The Catholic Church, of course, does not read Matthew or John the way that the critics suggest. A popular Catholic educational book published in 1903 told the story of Pope Pius IX coming upon an unconscious Jewish man, giving him a ride home, and later sending his personal physician to care for the man. This was done to illustrate the lesson that: "It is unworthy of a Christian to refuse aid to any one because he is of a different creed or nationality."[125]

At the Second Vatican Council, the Church reaffirmed its centuries-old teaching by explaining that guilt for Jesus' death is not attributable to all the Jews of that time or to any Jews of the current times.[126]

In fact, at every Mass, whether they recite the Apostles' Creed or the Nicene Creed, Catholics identify only the Roman leader Pontius Pilate when it comes to the passion of Christ.[127] As Pope Pius XI said in 1938: "Spiritually, we are all Semites."[128]

Critics who try to force an anti-Semitic interpretation on the Gospels have selected a particularly difficult target in the Catholic Church. Catholics have an authority, a history of scholarship, and a Magisterium. The Holy See's Pontifical Biblical Commission has devoted significant attention to this issue. In a document entitled *The Jewish People and Their Sacred Scriptures in the Christian Bible*, the commission discussed the charges that the New Testament is anti-Semitic.[129] As explained in the introduction, "the reproofs addressed to Jews in the New Testament are neither more frequent nor more virulent than the accusations against Israel in the Law and the Prophets, at the heart of the Old Testament itself. They belong to the prophetic language of the Old Testament and are, therefore, to be interpreted in the same way as the prophetic messages: they warn against contemporary aberrations, but they are essentially of a temporary nature and always open to new possibilities of salvation."

This document, which is 105 pages long, goes on to discuss the long and generally close relationship between Catholics and Jews. "[T]he main conclusion to be drawn is that the Jewish people and their Sacred Scriptures occupy a very important place in the Christian Bible. . . . Without the Old Testament, the New Testament would be an incomprehensible book, a plant deprived of its roots and destined to dry up and wither." Quoting Pope John Paul II, the commission explains: "The Jewish religion is not 'extrinsic' to us, but in a certain manner, it is 'intrinsic' to our religion. We have therefore a relationship with it which we do not have with any other religion." All of this, of course, is at odds with what the critics would have their readers believe about the Catholic faith.

It is easy enough to find sloppy interpretations of the Bible or hate-mongers who bend it for their own purposes, but that is not to be found in the official teachings of the Catholic Church.[130] Unfortunately, critics often appear to be unfamiliar with the existing scholarship.[131] Goldhagen, for instance, says that Catholic teaching has always "revised" its essential beliefs. That is certainly not true, and it reflects a fundamental ignorance of the topic on which he purports to write.[132] The documents of Vatican II maintain a clear and unqualified connection with the original Deposit of Faith.[133] The Catholic Church, according to its own teaching, does not have the authority to rewrite scripture or deny the ultimate divinity of Christ. (Imagine the divisions that would take place within Christianity if it tried to do so.)[134]

Certainly no one would suggest that Christians and Jews have gotten along well at all times throughout history. Prior to 1870, when popes had real temporal power, Jews were sometimes treated with religious and political contempt. Many Catholic officials of this period were fearful that Jews would lead Christians away from Christ, or worse.[135] They found reason for their fear in Old Testament passages such as Joshua 6:21 (Jews "observed the ban by putting to the sword all living creatures in the city: men and women, young and old, as well as oxen, sheep and asses."), Deuteronomy 20:17 ("You [Jews] must doom them all...."), and Deuteronomy 7:1-5: "When the LORD, your God, brings you [Jews] into the land which you are to enter and occupy . . . and you defeat them, you shall doom them. Make no covenant with them and show them no mercy. . . . Tear down their altars, smash their sacred pillars, chop down their sacred poles, and destroy their idols by fire. For you are a people sacred to the LORD, your God; he has chosen you from all the nations on the face of the earth to be a people peculiarly his own."

Additionally, the "imprecatory" sections of the Scriptures contain prayers or songs for vengeance upon the enemies of the Jewish nation or which end in triumphant praise at their destruction (Psalm 5:11; Psalm 10:15; Psalm 18:38-43; Psalm 31:18-19; Jeremiah 15:15; Jeremiah17:18).[136] In 1564, Pope Pius IV announced that the Talmud could be distributed only on the condition that the portions offensive to

Christians were erased.[137] Earlier popes had, at times, banned it altogether.

The incorrect understanding of scripture did, indeed, breed suspicion and mistrust between Christians and Jews, but even papal critics acknowledge that throughout even the worst periods popes regularly condemned violence directed against Jews and offered protection when they could.[138] "A papal bull of Pope Calixtus II (1190) condemning violence against the Jews and attempts to baptize them under constraint was confirmed at least twenty-two times up to the middle of the eighteenth century."[139] Catholic "anti-Judaism" was a matter of religion, not race. In fact, the more common charges arising out of this history related to efforts directed towards encouraging Jews to convert—*to become Catholics.*

To take one oft-cited example from the past, on Good Friday Catholics used to pray for the conversion of the "perfidious Jews."[140] This is offensive to the modern ear, but what was it saying?[141] It was a request to God that these people who did not believe in Jesus as savior be converted so that they could share in eternity. While describing this act of "anti-Semitism," critics never point out that when this prayer was placed into the Good Friday service, "perfidious" did not have the pejorative connotation that it now carries—it simply meant "non-believing."[142]

By contrast, Nazi racial anti-Semitism did not encourage Jews to "join the party." This "scientific" position drew support from biological arguments and the absence of religion. Nazis showed films equating Jews, handicapped persons, and other "undesirables" with vermin that needed to be exterminated. This grew out of a Darwinian-scientific ideal and was in direct contradiction to everything that the Catholic Church had always taught about the fundamental dignity of all human life.[143]

Does this mean that it was impossible for Hitler to lay claim to Christian teachings as he advanced his evil agenda? Of course not. In *Mein Kampf,* Hitler went to great length about misusing religious imagery to inspire and inflame the masses. Hitler also played to a populist mentality, a racist mentality, a socialist mentality, a chauvinistic mentality, a nurturing-mothering mentality, a scientific mentality, and just about any other mentality that he could think of. Are they all to be condemned because they were capable of being manipulated by Hitler (who also planned to eliminate largely-Catholic Poland)? The answer is equally clear: of course not.

Goldhagen seems to think the pope should have set aside all of his intelligence and adopted a confrontational approach to the Nazis—in each and every location. That, of course, would have been foolish.[144] The pope knew of the retaliation following *Mit brennender Sorge*. He had the example from Holland. He had sent an express condemnation into Poland to be read, but the Archbishop of Krakow, Adam Sapieha, burned it, saying that it would bring too many reprisals.[145] In fact, the Nuremberg report documents case after case of retaliation against clergy (Catholic and Protestant) following statements or other agitation against the Nazi regime.[146]

Rather than endangering others with grand public gestures, Pius used churches, convents, monasteries, seminaries, and the Vatican itself to run a rescue operation for all victims, without any distinction based on race, religion, or nationality. The last thing a rescue operation wants is attention, particularly when it is likely to bring about reprisals. Goldhagen focuses only on potential reprisals against Jewish people. Such reprisals occurred; but the pope was also concerned about Catholics. For one thing, Catholic rescue efforts could be harmed, causing further suffering for Jews. More importantly, as Pius said, martyrdom cannot be imposed on someone, but must be voluntarily accepted.[147] Catholic doctrine would not permit the pope to sacrifice some lives to save others, even if a utilitarian equation might suggest that would be appropriate. The Church did not, however, vary its approach based upon the identity of the victim. Goldhagen's speculations notwithstanding, the Vatican under Pope Pius XII acted in the same way whether the victims were Catholic priests or Jewish peasants.

Marcus Melchior, the Chief Rabbi of Denmark during the war, well understood this situation. He explained that Pius had no chance of influencing Hitler: "I believe it is an error to think that Pius XII could have had any influence whatever on the brain of a madman." He added that if he had been more confrontational, "Hitler would have probably massacred more than six million Jews and perhaps ten times ten million Catholics, if he had the power to do so."[148] Similarly, the Chief Rabbi in Rome during the German occupation, Israel Zolli, said that "no hero in all of history was more militant, more fought against, none more heroic, than Pius XII."[149]

The historical facts show that sometimes a confrontational approach worked with the Nazis, but other times it did not. Robert M. W. Kempner, the Deputy Chief U.S. Prosecutor at the Nuremberg war trials, explained that a public protest against persecution of the Jews could only lead to "partial success when it was made at a politically and militarily opportune moment."[150] He added that Pius made such protests through nuncios when and where possible. Confrontation with Hitler would not, however, have been advisable. "Every propaganda move of the Catholic Church against Hitler's Reich," he wrote, "would have been not only 'provoking suicide' . . . but would have hastened the execution of still more Jews and priests."[151]

Goldhagen also asserts that Pius did not privately instruct cardinals, bishops, priests, and nuns to save Jews. Catholic rescuers—including people such as Cardinal Pietro Palazzini and Tibor Baranski who were later recognized by Israel as Righteous Gentiles—testified that they received precisely such orders from the pope.[152] Several other witnesses also testified that such instructions were sent out in the form of letters.[153] Still others, including Fr. Marie-Benoît, Carroll-Abbing, Pope John XXIII, and Pope Paul VI, all testified that they received such instructions from Pope Pius XII in face-to-face meetings, or through other direct channels.[154]

Goldhagen even tries to link the Vatican and Pacelli with the notorious anti-Semite Julius Streicher. Streicher's venomous writings tell a different story. He railed against the pope's support for Jewish people: "The Jews have now found protection in the Catholic Church, which is trying to convince non-Jewish humanity that distinct races do not exist. The Pope has made his own the false conception of racial equality—and the Jews, with the help of Marxists and Freemasons, are doing their best to promote it. But the Pope's attitude will surprise no one who is familiar with the shrewd schemes of Vatican politics."[155]

Pacelli's opposition to Streicher's worldview was well-known. In *Three Popes and the Jews*, Pinchas Lapide cited a public address by Pacelli in Rome which repeated Pope Pius XI's eloquent statement that "spiritually we are all Semites."[156]

THE POPE PIUS XII STUDY GROUP

In 1998, the Vatican released a long-awaited statement on the Holocaust. Entitled *We Remember: Reflections on the Shoah*, the statement was addressed to all Catholics, and sent to Jewish leaders around the world. It acknowledged that centuries of anti-Jewish attitudes in the Church may have contributed to Christians' lack of resistance to Nazi policies: "We deeply regret the errors and failures of those sons and daughters of the Church. This is an act of repentance, since, as members of the Church, we are linked to the sins as well as the merits of all her children."

The fourteen-page text, prepared by the Pontifical Commission for Religious Relations with the Jews and at the request of Pope John Paul II, did not, however, acknowledge any culpability on the part of Pope Pius XII. In fact, it said: "During and after the war, Jewish communities and Jewish leaders expressed their thanks for all that had been done for them, including what Pope Pius XII did personally or through his representative to save hundreds of thousands of Jewish lives."

Reactions to *We Remember* were mixed. While some saw it as a step toward better relations between Jews and Catholics, others saw problems, especially in the section on Pope Pius XII. Abraham Foxman, national director of the Anti-Defamation League, said: "This document rings hollow. It's mostly an apologia, a rationalization for Pope Pius and the church during the Shoah."[157] Phil Baum, executive director of the American Jewish Congress, lamented the Vatican's reluctance to "impose moral culpability on some leading church authorities . . . who were either indifferent or in some cases actually complicit in the persecution of Jews."[158] Israel's chief rabbi, Meir Lau, a Holocaust survivor, even demanded an "explicit apology for the shameful attitude of the pope at the time."[159]

In an effort to get to the truth, and heal the developing rift between Jews and Catholics, Cardinal Edward Cassidy, then president of the Holy See's Commission for Religious Relations with the Jews, and Seymour D. Reich, Chairman of International Jewish Committee for Interreligious Consultations announced the appointment of a study group charged with examining the 11 volumes of the *Actes et Documents du Saint Siège Relatifs à la Seconde Guerre Mondiale* (ADSS).[160] The three Catholic scholars were Gerald Fogarty, SJ, of the University of Virginia, theologian Eva Fleichner, emeritus professor at Montclair State University, and Rev. John F. Morley of the Seton Hall University. The Jewish scholars were Michael Marrus of the University of Toronto, Robert S. Wistrich of Hebrew University in Jerusalem, and Bernard Suchecky, a researcher who had been affiliated with the Free University in Brussels, Belgium.[161]

A report on the contents of the eleven volumes could have been a tremendous service for those in search of the truth. A careful study of those documents makes clear that Pope Pius XII was very concerned with the welfare of all people, including Jews. In fact, these volumes contain enough information to refute all recent slanders against the wartime pope. Unfortunately, from the very beginning, some members of the study group acted as if they were more interested in getting into secret archives than in learning what took place during the war.[162]

At the time of the group's formation, Leon Feldman, Emeritus Professor of History at Rutgers University and Jewish coordinator for the study group said he thought there was a "smoking gun" in the archives and that was the reason the Vatican kept them closed. Prior to being named to the study group, Robert Wistrich of Hebrew University said: "Pius XII did not perform in a way that reflects any credit on the Vatican or on the Catholic church. He wound up in a position where he was complicit [sic] in German policy."[163] Later, when he was named to the study group, Wistrich said that to read the volumes without having access to the archives would be "a farce." The clear implication was that the four Jesuit editors may have refused to publish incriminating documents.[164]

In assenting to the mandate to study the ADSS, members of the study group agreed to pursue their work in a clearly defined way. Ultimately, however, that is not what they did. The demand for full access to the archives was placed ahead of the desire to study the ADSS. This became most evident when the group traveled to Rome to meet with Vatican officials.

In April 2000, the group called Peter Gumpel, SJ, relator (independent, investigating judge) for the cause of Pius XII's sainthood, wanting to set up a meeting. Gumpel agreed, but he asked that any questions be submitted to him in advance so that he would have time to prepare his answers with supporting documentation. Members of the study group came to Rome in October 2000. About two weeks prior to their arrival, they sent ahead forty-seven questions for Gumpel. The questions were presented as a "preliminary report." The charge given to the group, however, had not called for a preliminary report.

When Gumpel saw the forty-seven questions, he thought that the study group wanted them answered, and he worked very hard to prepare himself to answer the questions. He felt that it would take several days to address them all. As it ended up, however, he spent only three hours with the group. As such, he was able to address only a handful of questions. The vocal representatives of the group, however, made clear that they were not interested in answers to the questions. They wanted Gumpel to join in their call for the opening of the archives.

Gumpel pointed out that while it is legitimate for a historian to seek archival information, there was sufficient information already available to answer the questions that the study group had presented to him. He set about answering the forty-seven questions, with references to available Vatican documents, books, memoirs, and other archival sources.

At one point, Seymour Reich said that Gumpel could not possibly answer the group's questions, because the questions did not ask what happened, but what the archives indicated had happened. At another point in the meeting, Rabbi Leon A. Feldman said that he personally remembered Eugenio Pacelli, the papal nuncio in Germany and future Pius XII, not doing anything as he watched the Nazis burn books in Berlin in 1933. Gumpel politely explained that this was impossible since Pacelli had left Berlin in 1929 to become the Vatican Secretary of State and never returned.[165]

Gumpel complained about previous breaches of confidentiality on the part of the study group. He was given assurances that the group itself was outraged and that steps had been taken to assure that there would be no further "leaks."[166] Unfortunately, while the team was still in Rome, the "preliminary report," with all forty-seven questions, was leaked to the press and published around the world.[167]

Gumpel's meeting was cut short, but he reports placing several calls to the group to try to set up further meetings. Unfortunately, according to Gumpel, the group was tied up in meetings related to the leak. This same problem kept two members of the group from meeting with Fr. Pierre Blet, the sole surviving member of the team that put together the ADSS.[168]

The Associated Press called the preliminary report "explosive." The *New York Times* said that the report expressed the dissatisfaction of the six panel members with Vatican records. *Le Monde* of Paris said it pointed to failures of the Pope and Church.[169]

Having expressed regret for earlier leaks, one might have expected the study group to have issued a condemnation of this breach. Perhaps

Bernard Suchecky, who was responsible for this leak,[170] might have been suspended from the group. Instead, certain members of the team were emboldened. Professors Marrus and Wistrich were both widely quoted as saying that the ball was now in the Vatican's court. Reich, Wistrich, and Marrus all publicly said how they were still waiting for the Vatican to reply to the report. Wistrich even attacked Gumpel and the Vatican in the German magazine *Der Spiegel* (Apr. 24, 2001) and told the *Jerusalem Report* (July 2, 2001) that the Vatican had acted in "bad faith" by refusing to open the archives.[171] They had posed their forty-seven questions, and they would await the Vatican's reply. No mention was made of answers that were provided by Fr. Gumpel, Cardinal Cassidy, Cardinal Laghi, and then-Archbishop (now Cardinal) Mejía, all of whom met with the study group in Rome.

In point of fact, many of the questions from the preliminary report were not hard to answer. Certainly they should not have been hard for scholars who had been studying Pope Pius XII for a significant period of time. For the most part, the study group asked for additional documents, suggesting that the documentation supplied in the ADSS was lacking, or that more existed in the archives. The group also asked in many cases for "confirmation" about questions as to which numerous witnesses had already supplied testimony.

In 2001, Cardinal Cassidy stepped down from his post as president of the Holy See's Commission for Religious Relations with the Jews, and he was replaced by Cardinal Walter Kasper, a German theologian. Cardinal Kasper was not influenced by the history that had shaped the study group up until this point. He looked at what was taking place, and he did not like it.

In an interview published June 21, 2001, Cardinal Kasper said: "The commission failed to do what it was charged to do—to read the Vatican's 11 published volumes on Pius' pontificate. They must read the 11 volumes; they have never done the work they were asked to do in a proper way." Regarding the leaks, he called them unacceptable, "unethical" behavior.[172]

On the same day that the interview was published, Cardinal Kasper sent a letter to the study group asking for a "final report on this project." He noted that he did not expect the final report to provide the whole answer to these issues, nor would it signal the end of discussion on this matter. It would, however, fulfill the mandate given to the study group. Cardinal Kasper also noted that some of the forty-seven questions had been answered by Fr. Gumpel and that others had been forwarded to the Vatican Secretariat of State, which controls the archives. The cardinal also made clear that the group would not be granted access to sealed Vatican archives.

On July 20, in a letter to Cardinal Kasper, the five remaining scholars on the team (Dr. Eva Fleischner had resigned for personal reasons) suspended their work, saying that they could not complete their assignment without "access in some reasonable manner to additional archival material."[173] This is when everything really began to fall apart.

Although Cardinal Kasper did no more than restate the agreement that had been in place from the very beginning of the project, Professor Wistrich imputed bad faith to the Holy See: "The Vatican is not really interested in allowing us to pursue our work further. Whatever expectation they had of the panel—that we would give carte blanche to Pius's beatification, or that the situation would be defused without probing too deeply—they were wrong. . . . They moved the goalposts."[174] Seymour Reich, expressed "deep disappointment" that the Vatican would not open all its wartime archives to the scholars and suggested that the letter from the scholars was a form of protest.[175]

Fr. Fogarty then issued a statement disassociating himself from what Reich had said. Eugene Fisher also condemned "Reich's attempt to twist the statement of the scholars to say what it did not intend to say." He called it "inexplicable and inexcusable."[176] Unfortunately, the mainstream press picked up on Wistrich's and Reich's accusations, not on the rebuttals and disclaimers.

The truth, as explained by Fogarty, was that "there were two different sets of expectations and two different agendas from the very beginning, and they finally clashed."[177] Some members of the study group viewed the project as a vehicle to press for open access to the archives, but that was never their charge. They were supposed to conduct a thorough study of the ADSS. "It is a fact, we could not work together with some people wanting greater access and others saying we can do more work; there was no point in saying we could work together as a group," Fogarty explained.[178]

Had the group carried out its assignment without delving into polemics and political posturing, it could have answered almost all of the questions about Pope Pius XII's conduct during the war.[179] Those documents, which were meticulously edited by world-renowned scholars, make clear that the pope was not silent, that he assisted the Allies, opposed Nazi racial atrocities, and that the Church fed, sheltered, and clothed victims of all races, religions, and nationalities.[180]

A historian might legitimately ask whether a different approach to the situation would have worked better to oppose the Nazis, but the documents leave no doubt about where the Holy See stood. Pope Pius did everything that he thought possible and appropriate to help Jews and other victims of the Nazis. Had the group carried out its assignment, that would have been made clear, and that would have gone a long way toward healing the division between Catholics and Jews. Unfortunately, that is not what happened.

Rather than seeking truth, too many people put their personal desires to enter the sealed archives above the agreed aim of the project. They did this at the expense of both truth and the continued viability of the project. The results that they obtained only raised suspicions and doubts.[181]

THE RIEGNER MEMO

Gerhard Riegner was critical of the Vatican in his final years. One reason was that his memorandum to the Holy See, dated March 18, 1942, described Nazi persecution of Jewish people, but it was not published in the *Actes et Documents*. Some critics, including Riegner and John Cornwell, have argued that this shows that the Vatican was trying to coverup its knowledge of the Holocaust.[182] By the same token, however, the letter of thanks that Riegner sent to Nuncio M. Philippe Bernadinion on April 8, 1942 was also not published in the *Actes et Documents*. In that letter, Riegner stated:

> We also note with great satisfaction the steps undertaken by His Excellence the Cardinal Maglione, with authorities of Slovakia on behalf of the Jews of that country, and we ask you kindly to transmit to the Secretariat of State of the Holy See the expression of our profound gratitude.
>
> We are convinced that this intervention greatly impressed the governmental circles of Slovakia, which conviction seems to be confirmed by the information we have just received from that country. . . .
>
> It appears . . . that the Slovak Government finds it necessary to justify the measures in question. One might therefore conclude that it might be induced–in the application of these measures–to conform more closely to the wishes expressed by the Holy See which desired to revoke the recent measures against the Jews.
>
> In renewing the expressions of our profound gratitude, for whatever the Holy See, thanks to your gracious intermediation, was good enough to undertake on behalf of our persecuted brothers, we ask Your Excellency to accept the assurance of our deepest respect.[183]

The reason that neither the memo nor the letter of thanks were printed in the *Actes et Documents* collection is that they were classified as *unofficial*. "Acting on a traditional principle, the editors included only those documents that originated in one of their own diplomatic service's offices, or related ecclesiastic structures, and hence did not print, but only made reference in a footnote to other documents, however significant [they may have been]."[184] If all correspondence from all sources had been published, the collection would have been far too large. Moreover, the Riegner memo did not report a definite source of information, but reported on persecutions that were "more or less known to the public at large."[185]

It is very important to note that at the time the *Actes et Documents* collection was published, the Riegner memo had already appeared in print. The *Actes et Documents* made note of the Riegner memo.[186] In fact, a footnote was added just to draw attention to receipt of the memo. It was certainly never hidden, concealed, or missing.

THE KATZ LAWSUIT

Robert Katz was another early critic of Pope Pius XII. Katz first leveled charges against Pope Pius XII in his 1967 book *Death in Rome* and then again in his 1969 book *Black Sabbath*. He also authored the screenplay for a movie entitled *Massacre in Rome*. In each of these works, Katz severely criticized Pope Pius XII for failing to take a more firm stand in opposition to the Nazis.[187]

One of his important claims, which was followed by critics Cornwell and Zuccotti, relates to the slaughter of 335 Italian citizens.[188] On March 23, 1944, the group GAP (Gruppi di Azione Patriottica),[189] comprised mainly of Communist students, planted a bomb which exploded as a German unit was marching down Via Rasella in Rome.[190] Thirty-three German soldiers were killed. In accordance with Nazi policy that was well known to everyone in occupied areas, the High Command in Berlin ordered the immediate execution of ten Italians for every soldier who had been killed.[191] According to a direct order from Adolf Hitler, the reprisal was to be completed within twenty-four hours.[192]

By noon on March 24, a convoy that included men, women, Christians, Jews, one Catholic priest, and two fourteen-year-old boys—none of whom had anything to do with the bomb—was directed to some man-made caves (the Ardeatine Caves) on the outskirts of Rome, among the catacombs of the Appian Way.[193] Under the direction of SS Lt. Col. Herbert Kappler, these 335 Italians were shot and killed.

German engineers then blew up the entrances to the caves, sealing the evidence inside. Months passed before the identities of all the victims were known.[194]

The critics claim that Pius had special advance notice about the retaliation, that he failed to intervene in any meaningful way with the Nazi occupying forces, and that when he finally did speak, his only advice was to caution the Italians against striking back against the Nazis.[195] This time, the critics are 0 for 3.

As for the claim that Pius had advance notice, the truth is that everyone knew about the threat of Nazi retaliation. They posted signs to warn the population, and announcements had been widely published. Katz and those who follow him, however, argue that Pius had special knowledge because a memo received at the Vatican just hours before the executions put him on notice that executions were about to begin.

Katz reprinted this memo in *The Battle for Rome*, and he suggested that it was important, new evidence proving papal knowledge.[196] The memo, however, was not new. It was first published by the Vatican in 1980, and it had been discussed in previous books.[197] Moreover, while in his text Katz claimed that the memo was from "an authoritative source," buried in an endnote he admitted that the author has never been identified by anything other than the name reported on the memo.[198] It was, essentially, an anonymous letter.

There is no indication that this notice—received at the Vatican only hours before the slaughter—made it all the way to the pope prior to the executions. The Vatican is notorious for chains of command. A memo like this would have gone to several lower ranking prelates before it was shown to the pope (if it ever was shown to him). Moreover, the memo would not have been rushed to the pope; it provided no new details.[199] Hitler had threatened retribution in an Italian radio broadcast on September 11, 1943. Pius had discouraged acts of violence against Nazi occupying forces precisely because he knew that it would only bring about bad results.[200]

Evidence that the pope did not know in advance about this act of revenge comes from Cardinal Nasalli Rocca, a papal representative who visited prisoners of the Nazis on a daily basis. He was also confessor for those condemned to die. He wrote: "I remained at the prison until 7 AM the next morning, March 25 [the day after the massacre]. I then went to see Pope Pius XII and related everything I had found out at the prison. The Holy Father cupped his head in his hands and, obviously stunned and overwhelmed, said to me, 'what are you talking about? It is not possible, I cannot believe it.'"[201] Despite this eyewitness testimony, Katz still argues that the pope had advance knowledge of the massacre.

Even though it was too late to truly matter, Pius was not inactive. After learning of the arrests, but before he received the report of the slaughter from Rocca, he sent his special liaison officer, Fr. Pancratius Pfeiffer, SDS Superior General, to plead with the German command.[202] According to some accounts, Pius also sent his nephew, Prince Carlo Pacelli, to investigate.[203] Unfortunately, the Vatican officials were too late to intercede. The German diplomatic corps withdrew into discreet silence, and on March 29 the German ambassador's office said that inquiries about persons taken by the Germans should be addressed to the headquarters of SS Lt. Col. Herbert Kappler, the Nazi chief of police in Rome. As Kappler confessed years later, it was a waste of time to come to him; by then the people had all been killed.[204]

The claim that Pius spoke only to caution the Romans not to retaliate against the Germans is also wrong. It is true that an article appearing on the front page of the March 25 issue of the Vatican newspaper noted the recent tragedy and cautioned against retaliation.[205] The March 25 issue of l'Osservatore Romano, however, had been printed by about 2:00 PM on March 24.[206] The article in question would have been written and edited probably before noon on the 24th. Thus, this plea for peace came after the attack on the Nazis but before the pope could have known about the slaughter at the caves. In other words, this was not—as the critics always argue—a caution to the populace not to retaliate against the Nazis. Rather, it was an unsuccessful plea to the Nazis that they not retaliate against civilians for the attack that had killed the thirty-three German soldiers.[207]

In 1974, Pope Pius XII's niece, Elena Pacelli Rossignani, commenced a legal action against Katz, movie producer Carlo Ponti, and director George Cosmatos, charging that they had unfairly defamed the memory of the late pope. Central to that suit was Katz's charge about the slaughter at the caves.[208]

On November 27, 1975, Katz was found guilty of defamation. The court ruled that "Robert Katz wished to defame Pius XII, attributing to him actions, decisions and sentiments which no objective fact and no witness authorized him to do." He was fined 400,000 Lire, given a thirteen-month suspended prison sentence, and required to pay various expenses related to the plaintiff's lawyers.[209] Katz appealed the judgment, and on July 1, 1978, an appellate court absolved him, ruling that he could not be punished due to his right to free speech and expression. Since Katz could not be punished, neither could the filmmakers.

The General Procurator of Rome appealed this ruling, and on October 19, 1979, the *Corte di Cassazione* (the highest court) held that the sentence could not be enforced against the film due to a general amnesty that had been put in place in 1970.[210] As for the action against Katz based upon his book, the Court remanded the case to the appellate court for a new hearing.

On July 7, 1981, the appellate court held that even though the Italian edition of Katz's book was first published in 1967 (thus pre-dating the 1970 amnesty and therefore not being punishable), other editions had been published with Katz's consent after 1970, so the amnesty was not applicable. The new editions constituted a continuation of defamation against Pius XII. Essentially, the 1975 sentence condemning Katz was confirmed and he was ordered to pay a fine of 400.000 lire, plus legal expenses, and to be held in jail for thirteen months.[211]

Katz again appealed. On September 29, 1983, the *Corte di Cassazione* rejected Katz's appeals on the merits. It noted that Katz had consented to have his book published in Italy and did not limit himself to a true historic study, but set in motion an unjustified effort to defame Pope Pius XII's person and moral dignity by attributing to him a callous, uncaring refusal to intervene in favor of human lives. As such, the finding on the merits remained. In judging Pius XII's conduct, the court said that Katz had adopted criteria that were contrary to fair historical analysis. Moreover, the court found that Katz had altered the truth.

Nevertheless the Court concluded that the legal action was foreclosed by amnesties that had been issued in the 1970s and the 1980s. Katz was therefore not criminally responsible. He was, however, ordered to pay court costs. Importantly, the court rejected all of Katz's arguments that related to the merits of the case.[212]

The long and short of it is that Katz eventually benefitted from a general amnesty, but that does not negate the findings on the merits against Katz, and those findings should be sufficient to warn readers—much less researchers—about the legitimacy of (and motivation behind) his work.

THE "RAT-LINE" TO SOUTH AMERICA

One oft-repeated charge is that the Vatican under Pope Pius XII helped Nazis escape justice in Europe and make their way to South America, via the so-called rat-line. This claim was most fully developed by the self-styled "investigative journalists" Mark Aarons and John Loftus. They first brought it up in their 1991 book, *Unholy Trinity: The Vatican, the Nazis, and the Swiss Banks*. In a later book, *The Secret War Against the Jews* (1994), Aarons and Loftus expanded their argument and asserted that almost every entity in the world—from the Vatican to the Bush family—is at war with the Jews.[213] Commenting on their argument, Anti-Defamation League director Abraham Foxman called it "so exaggerated, so scantily documented, so overwrought and convoluted in its presentation, that Loftus and Aarons render laughable their claim to offer 'a glimpse of the world as it really is.'"[214]

The Vatican has acknowledged that Bishop Alois Hudal of Austria, a Nazi sympathizer stationed in Rome, helped war criminals. Evidence shows, however, that this was done without approval from Vatican authorities.[215] In 1976, Hudal's memoir, *Römische Tagebücher*, was posthumously published. In that book, Hudal admitted that he helped war criminals, but he made it clear that this was done without the encouragement or knowledge of the pope. Similarly, in a letter published in the *New York Times* on March 13, 1984, Nazi hunter Simon Wiesenthal admitted that there was no evidence that Pius XII knew of Hudal's activities. Recently-opened archives show that Hudal "acted without Rome's permission or knowledge."[216]

Many writers, including Michael Phayer, have alleged that Hudal enjoyed a close relationship with Pius XII.[217] In his memoirs, however, Hudal frequently complains of the Vatican's "pro-Allied bias" during World War II and how Pius XI, Pius XII, and Montini, mistreated him throughout his career. The fact that Hudal, unlike many of the pope's close friends, was never elevated to cardinal shows that they did not enjoy a friendly relationship. In fact, recently-opened archives indicate that he was "kept at arms length" from positions of responsibility because the pope and his secretary of state did not trust him.[218]

Phayer cited Uki Goni's *The Real Odessa* (2002) for his argument. Goni asserted that papal assistant Monsignor Giovanni Montini (the future Pope Paul VI) asked the government of Argentina, to shelter war criminals and cited a letter by him to Argentina's embassy at the Vatican as proof. Professor Igancio Klich, however, the coordinator of the Comision Para el Esclarecimiento de las Actividades Del Nazismo en la Republica Argentina (CEANA), the historical commission that looked into Argentina's role in sheltering war criminals, has denied that Montini's letter requested help for war criminals. Rather, the letter asked Argentina to keep its doors open to all immigrants and refugees.

There were hundreds of thousands of refugees made homeless by the war and displaced persons fleeing persecution from Communist countries in Eastern Europe at the time.[219] The Vatican was trying to help these people start new lives in other countries as quickly as possible.

The Vatican recently permitted Professor Matteo Sanfilippo, a member of CEANA, to examine Hudal's personal papers. Sanfilippo found no evidence that the pope encouraged Hudal's unsavory activities.[220] In fact, Sanfilippo uncovered a letter from Montini to Hudal expressing outrage at his suggestion that the Vatican should help members of the ss and the Wehrmacht.[221]

Like the Vatican, the International Red Cross has been identified as having helped Nazis escape from justice.[222] It is, however, inconceivable that the Nazis revealed their background to the Church or Red Cross officials. It is even less likely that any such information would have reached the upper echelons of these organizations.[223] The logistics of the massive relocation programs simply made it impossible to investigate most individuals who sought help.[224]

In an interview, Monsignor Karl Bayer, who was liaison chaplain responsible for the 250,000 prisoners of war in the north of Italy explained:

> "If there really was a screening," he said, "an attempt at detailed research by examining each of the people concerned, it would have required at least a dozen German-speaking priests. I knew them all. There were, of course, quite a few, but they were incredibly busy—too busy, I think, for the kind of supervision of the many people [they dealt with]. . . .
>
> "Well, of course we asked questions," he said. "But at the same time, we hadn't an earthly chance of checking on the answers. In Rome, at that time, every kind of paper and information could be bought. If a man wanted to tell us he was born in Viareggio—no matter if he was really born in Berlin and couldn't speak a word of Itallian—he only had to go down into the street and he'd find dozens of Italians willing to swear on a stack of Bibles that they knew he was born in Viareggio—for a hundred lire.[225]

In a situation like that, it is hard to fault any relief agency for being deceived.

A 1947, Top Secret Department of State memorandum entitled *Illegal Emigration Movements in and Through Italy* identified the Vatican as the largest single organization involved in the illegal movement of emigrants. "Jewish Agencies and individuals" were identified as the second largest group. The memo, however, made clear that all of the agencies, including the International Red Cross, worked in collaboration with one another and that anyone could take advantage of these programs. In fact, the memo indicated that the Church had no way to identify the politics of the people in the program. Moreover, the memo reported that Vatican and Red Cross passports were easily and commonly falsified by changing the pictures on them.[226]

In his 1944 Christmas message, Pope Pius XII defended the punishment of war criminals, though he objected to the collective punishment of nations. In fact, the Vatican actually helped prosecute Nazi war criminals.[227] In 1946 the Vatican handed over many of its documents to the International Military Tribunal in Nuremberg, which used them as evidence against the Nazis for persecuting the Catholic Church before and during the war. Although he asked for clemency for some criminals, including Prime Minister Tojo in Japan, the pope refused to intervene on behalf of the Nazis who were sentenced to death at Nuremberg. The critics' arguments do not stand up to analysis.

In the end, it must be concluded that the Church, like the Red Cross, was interested in ending suffering. Undoubtedly, some Nazis took advantage of the Vatican's efforts to help dislocated people move about the world.[228] In the chaos of postwar Europe, many war criminals used false names and forged papers to obtain exit visas and travel documents from many civilian relief agencies, including those run by the Church. There is, however, no indication that the Holy See was intentionally involved in trying to help Nazis escape justice following the war.[229] Critics who make this charge have ignored the evidence to advance their case.[230]

DISCOUNTING JEWISH SCHOLARS

Several of the papal critics have labeled certain authors as being biased, particularly the Jewish scholars Joseph Lichten and Pinchas Lapide. Lichten was the director of the Inter-cultural Affairs Department of the Anti-Defamation League of B'nai B'rith. He wrote a blistering response to the allegations made in *The Deputy*, and set forth what had been the dominant Jewish view of Pius XII up until that time. Naturally, his work embarrasses contemporary papal critics.

Susan Zuccotti asserts, without evidence, that Lichten deliberately sacrificed the truth in order to foster good relations between Israel and the Holy See. She argues, for instance, that Lichten "wrote without evidence" that the Vatican offered Jewish scholars teaching posts to protect them from Fascist persecution. In fact, not only did Lichten have supporting evidence, this matter was very well-publicized.[231]

As for Lapide, Zuccotti claims that there is "no evidence offered" for his assertion that Bishop Hudal wrote a letter of protest, at the urging of the pope, on behalf of Rome's Jews, during the Nazi roundup of October 16, 1943. In fact, Hudal's own memoirs reveal that his letter of protest was prompted by Pope Pius XII's personal agent—his nephew Carlo Pacelli.[232] Moreover, the letter was delivered to German General Stahel by Fr. Pancratius Pfeiffer, Pius XII's personal emissary to the Germans.[233] Lapide documents the intervention by citing an article on Fr. Pfeiffer's life-saving efforts (accomplished under the direction of Pius XII) published in the June 28, 1964 *L'Osservatore della Domenica*.

The most controversial figure surrounding these Jewish authors is the estimate relating to the number of Jewish lives that were saved by the Holy See under Pope Pius XII. Following months of research at the Yad Vashem archives, Lapide came up with the estimate that Pius saved 700,000 to 860,000 Jews.[234] While critics have challenged this number, others have produced similar or higher tallies.[235] Moreover, Lapide's credentials are (or should be) above question.

Lapide, a journalist and diplomatic official of the Israeli government, knew both Pope Pius XI and Pope Pius XII. He was the author of at least nine books, and he wrote extensively on religious affairs for journals throughout the world. In World War II, he fought with the British Eighth Army in the North African and Italian campaigns. While serving in southern Italy he found a group of peasant converts to Judaism, and he spent twenty years serving as their spiritual advisor. His book *The Prophet of San Nicandro*, which tells this story, was translated and published in eight different languages. The Jewish Book Guild of America awarded him a literary prize for it. Lapide also worked for a time with the prime minister's office in Jerusalem and wrote *A Pilgrim's Guide to Israel* and *An Israeli's Introduction to Christianity*, both of which helped the interfaith movement in Israel.

Lapide attributed his estimated number of Jewish lives saved to "The Holy See, the nuncios, and the entire Catholic Church." Seen that way, and recognizing that he was an Israeli diplomat, who spent months researching the issue in the Yad Vashem archives, it is not surprising that his figures have become so widely accepted, despite protests from the critics.[236]

THE ATTACK ON FR. PETER GUMPEL

Daniel Goldhagen's lowest blow is directed at Fr. Peter Gumpel, SJ. An official of the Congregation for the Causes of Saints, Gumpel is the relator or independent, investigating judge—by papal appointment—for the cause of Pius XII's sainthood. Goldhagen writes: "Perhaps the Church protects Fr. Gumpel in his post because only an anti-Semite and a historical falsifier can be counted on to present Pius XII in the glowing manner required for canonization."[237]

Gumpel is a warm man, though he can seem rather formal to those who do not know him. He is a German Jesuit, in his eighties, with English as his fifth or sixth language. (He is fluent in English, German,

Dutch, French, Italian, and nearly fluent in Spanish. He also reads Danish, Portuguese, Latin, classical Greek, and Hebrew.) He has great knowledge and a great love for his Church.[238]

He was born in 1923 to a distinguished German family. He was still a boy when Hitler came to power. His family stood in opposition to the Nazis, and this led the Nazis to kill his grandfather as well as other relatives.[239] As a young boy, he saw Nazi persecution first-hand. He was so distressed that he could not do his school work.[240] Gumpel himself was twice sent into exile for his own protection. The first time he went to France; later he went to Holland. There, he became active in the underground, putting his life at risk to help escort Jews across the Belgian border.[241]

One night, a teenaged Gumpel received a phone call saying that the Nazis had captured his mother and that she would be killed. Fortunately, a German officer who had been a friend of Gumpel's grandfather intervened and saved his mother's life.[242] The horror of that night has, however, never left him, nor has his abhorrence of Nazism and anti-Semitism. One can sense it in the scorn with which he pronounces the word "Nazi."

Gumpel's experiences during World War II led directly to his decision to enter the priesthood, and he joined the Jesuits in 1944. He studied in England for four years and earned several degrees, including a doctorate in the history of dogma. He began teaching at the Pontifical Gregorian University in Rome, and in 1972 he was assigned to the Congregation for the Causes of Saints. He also served on the faculty at the Gregorian and at the Pontifical Oriental Institute.

That critics like Goldhagen would disregard the facts and call this good man an anti-Semite is depressingly unsurprising. His evidence in this case comes from truncated quotations that have been taken out of context.[243] In fact, Gumpel has repeatedly condemned anti-Semitism and affirmed his allegiance to the teachings of Vatican II.[244]

The charge that Gumpel is a "historical falsifier" is perhaps even more outrageous than calling him an anti-Semite. Goldhagen provides no evidence to support it. Indeed, he leaves the reader entirely in the dark about what it is that Gumpel is alleged to have falsified. This practice of blackening someone's reputation by publicly making unspecified and unsubstantiated charges in a situation where the person has little chance of offering a defense is nothing short of slander.

9

A Righteous Gentile

From the bottom of our hearts we send to you,
Holy Father of the Church, the assurance of our
unforgetting gratitude for your noble expression
of religious brotherhood and love.
National Jewish Welfare Board (1944)[1]

THE HORROR OF THE HOLOCAUST is so difficult to comprehend that people are constantly trying to spread the blame. Consider Robert Wistrich's *Hitler and the Holocaust* (2001). The first half of this book does a credible job discussing the forces that shaped Hitler's belief in a "Jewish menace" that had to be eradicated. Wistrich brings particular insight to Jewish life in the ghetto and aptly contrasts Nazi terror with Soviet terror. Unfortunately, the second half of this book plays the "blame game."

Wistrich finds collaboration all over Europe, indifference to the Jewish plight among the Allies, and lack of compassion from the Christian churches. President Roosevelt, Winston Churchill, Pope Pius XII, German clergy, and Croatian Cardinal (now Blessed) Alojzije Stepinac are particularly targeted, but no one escapes blame, not even other Jews. Wistrich argues that world leaders and people in occupied nations should have taken a more openly confrontational position against the Nazis. He thinks that this might have reduced the number of Jews who died in the camps, but he never discusses the very real possibility that such actions might also have made things worse.[2]

An example of the problem faced by those who might have considered a public denunciation of Hitler can be found in what Wistrich writes about Hungary. In 1942, Prime Minister Miklos Kallay rejected German demands to expropriate all Jewish wealth, to impose the yellow star, and to deport Jews to the east. Wistrich reports that this "was almost certainly a factor in the German invasion of Hungary nearly one year later." With the invasion came Jewish deportations, which were carried out with Hungarian assistance. Eventually, the Hungarian government "did buckle to pressure from the Western Allies, Pope Pius xii, the king of Sweden, and other dignitaries" and stopped the deportations. This, in turn, caused the Germans to overthrow the existing government and appoint a new, terribly violent government which "tormented and butchered" twenty thousand Hungarian Jews. More would have been killed, Wistrich notes, if not for the good work of the papal nuncio, Swiss diplomats, and Swedish diplomat Raoul Wallenberg.[3]

This illustrates the problem with the argument in favor of more direct confrontation: resistance to the Nazis often made things worse for the victims. Moreover, as Wistrich judges others with 20/20 hindsight, he completely overlooks the real and legitimate fear of Nazi retaliation, which obviously influenced these matters.

In an essay published in the *Times Literary Supplement*, Wistrich picked up where his book left off.[4] Accepting without question the charges that appear in some of the more notorious recent anti-Catholic books, Wistrich claimed that not just Pius xii, but a succession of popes encouraged and promoted "the rise of modern anti-Semitism as a political ideology." The culmination of papal policy, according to

Wistrich, came during the Nazi Holocaust, when Pope Pius xii did virtually nothing to aid the Jews.

Efforts to portray Pius xii as an anti-Semite are contradicted by an abundance of evidence—beginning with the fact that in the critical six months between his election as pope (March 1939) and the outbreak of the war (September 1939), he made six public appeals to prevent the catastrophe that was about to claim millions of innocent victims. In his book, Wistrich notes that war made the Holocaust possible. He seems, however, to have missed the important implication stemming from that insight: efforts to bring about peace were also efforts to end (or prevent) the Holocaust.

Wistrich, like many papal critics, is convinced that Pius should have broadcast dramatic public appeals on behalf of the victims and in opposition to the Nazis. "At the very least," Wistrich writes, "a public protest by Pius would have enhanced the moral integrity and reputation of the Papacy."[5] Pius himself once speculated along these same lines: "No doubt a protest would have gained me the praise and respect of the civilized world, but it would have submitted the poor Jews to an even worse fate."[6] Accordingly, he decided to provide moral guidance with actions and carefully tailored messages, rather than repeatedly using the bully pulpit. But no one was confused about where he stood.

Pius made many statements in opposition to the Nazis and in support of the Jews. His first encyclical, *Summi Pontificatus* (*Darkness Over the Earth*), released just weeks after the outbreak of war, expressly mentioned Jews and urged solidarity with all who profess a belief in God.[7] Allied forces later dropped thousands of copies behind enemy lines for propaganda purposes. In his 1942 Christmas statement, Pius said that mankind owed this vow to all victims of the war, including "the hundreds of thousands who, through no fault of their own, and solely because of their nation or race, have been condemned to death or progressive extinction."[8] Pius xii's 1943 encyclical, *Mystici Corporis Christi*, explained: "Our paternal love embraces all peoples, whatever their nationality or race." Christ, by his blood, made Jews and Christians one "breaking down the middle wall of partition . . . in his flesh by which the two peoples were divided."[9]

In addition to these and other statements, Pius used his representatives throughout Europe to intervene on behalf of Jewish victims. He sent open telegrams complaining to collaborating governments and commiserating with the persecuted.[10] He also established the Pontifical Relief Commission, which distributed food, medicine, and clothing in forty countries during the war, and he created the Vatican Information Office, which supplied information about missing persons and helped reunite families—all without any discrimination on the basis of race, religion, or nationality.[11]

Catholic rescuers drew inspiration from the knowledge that they were carrying out the pope's will. Many of them expressly noted the repeated appeals in support of Jews that were broadcast on Vatican Radio. Some even testified to direct papal orders.[12] The pope's attitude, like his means of inspiring the resistance, were well understood by the press during the war. According to a *New York Times* account written after the liberation of Rome: "What the Pope did was to create an attitude in favor of the persecuted and hunted that the city was quick to adapt, so that hiding someone 'on the run' became the thing to do. This secret sharing of danger cleared away fascism more effectively than an official purge. The Vatican is still sheltering refugees. Almost 100,000 homeless persons from the war zone and devastated areas are fed there everyday."[13] Empty words could not possibly have been as effective.

The Nazis also understood Pius xii's position during the war. There are numerous instances of Nazi leaders complaining bitterly about the Pope's statements. They even spied on him and many of his assistants, in an effort to render any protests ineffective.[14] This culminated in an order from Hitler (later retracted at the urging of his staff) to invade the Vatican itself.[15]

Responding to the observation that a more confrontational position might have made things worse for Hitler's victims, Wistrich writes: "I find this argument bizarre as well as speculative." Of course, it is no more speculative than the conclusion that such a position would have made things better.[16] That certainly was a serious concern for Pope Pius XII. American diplomat Harold Tittmann reported back to Washington: "The Holy See is apparently still convinced that an open denunciation by the Pope of the Nazi atrocities, at least as far as Poland was concerned, could have no more result but the violent death of a great many more people."[17] The deputy chief U.S. prosecutor at Nuremberg, Dr. Robert Kempner, agreed: protests did not stop the Nazis and they often made things worse.[18] As reported by the Congregation for the Causes of Saints following a thirty-nine-year investigation: "Loud protests achieve nothing and only cause damage ... The only means to save the Jews was, therefore, secret but efficient ways to shelter them, provide them food and clothing, and move them to neutral countries. Pius XII did this in a manner unequaled by any state or organization, as was attested by many Jewish authorities and individuals."[19]

That is the crux of the dispute when it comes to Pope Pius XII. He outlined a course of action in his first encyclical, and he stuck with it. He felt that this was the best way to help save lives, minister to all, and achieve peace. It was also in keeping with papal tradition.

Decisions like this are always subject to after-the-fact speculations, and it is impossible to prove whether a different course of action would have been better or worse. Papal critics, however, do more than ask whether the pope made the correct decision. They suggest that he did not care about the victims, that he was anti-Semitic, or that he was "Hitler's Pope." They attribute to him evil intentions. In doing this, they cease writing history and instead engage in character assassination.[20] They also do a terrible disservice to the truth.

In a letter to the president of the Pontifical Committee of Historical Sciences, Pope John Paul II wrote: "Historical research, free of

prejudices and linked uniquely to scientific documentation, has an ir-
replaceable role in breaking down barriers among peoples. Often, great
barriers have been built up throughout the centuries due to partiality
of historiography and of reciprocal resentment. The consequence has
been that even today misunderstandings persist which are an obstacle
to peace and fraternity among men and peoples."[21] Too often, however,
critics of the Catholic Church during World War II are not "free of
prejudices" and their works are not based upon valid documentation.
In advancing their arguments, they contribute to the misunderstandings that become obstacles to peace and brotherhood.

The evidence clearly shows that Pius was appalled by the Nazis and
sympathized with their victims. He intervened where he could, in ways
that he thought would be most effective. The Vatican under his rule was
certainly more outspoken than it had been under Benedict during the
First World War.[22] Pius XII's decisions were not based on affection for
Hitler, hatred of the Communists, dislike for the Jews, fear for his own
safety, or any of the malicious reasons suggested by the critics. Nor
were they made without serious reflection. Historical questions about
his approach are fair, though his decisions are certainly defensible.[23]
When the critics resort to ad hominem attacks against Pope Pius the
man, however, they simply raise the heat and not the light.

Unfortunately, it may be that some critics are indeed more interested in raising the heat. John Cornwell, James Carroll, Gary Wills, and
Daniel Goldhagen have all—in one way or another—called upon the
Church to reform itself.[24] They are critical not only of Pope Pius XII,
but also Pope John Paul II, Pope Benedict XVI, traditional Catholic
doctrines of papal supremacy, the all-male priesthood, and, especially,
Catholic sexual teachings.[25] In fact, the critics recognize that the Catholic Church stands as perhaps the preeminent voice advancing the very
concept of ultimate truth, and that makes it their target. What Robert
Louis Wilken said of James Carroll's *Constantine's Sword* could be applied to the work of many of the contemporary critics of Pius XII:

> At the end of the day, in spite of the enormous effort to lay bare
> the sins of the Church over two millennia, *Constantine's Sword*
> is not really a book about Christian theology of the Jews. Its
> subject is Christian theology *tout court*, and its polemic springs
> from the currently fashionable "ideology of religious pluralism"—
> what might be termed horror at strong opinions. Carroll wants
> a Christianity that celebrates a "Jesus whose saving act is only
> one disclosure of the divine love available to all," and calls for a
> pluralism of "belief and worship, of religion and no religion, that
> honors God by defining God as beyond every effort to express
> God." What we have, then, is a rather conventional cultural cri-
> tique of Christianity. The Jews are the victims *par excellence* of
> the excesses of revealed religion. But what Carroll forgets is that
> Jews, too, believe in revelation. . . . In Carroll's brave new world
> there will be neither Jews nor Christians.[26]

The critics focused on Pope Pius XII because he seemed to be an easy
target for their anger at the Catholic Church and organized religion
in general.[27] They were wrong.

Pope John XXIII, shortly after being elevated to the papacy, indicated that Pius would not only one day be named a saint, but would
also be declared a Doctor of the Church.[28] Pope Paul VI nominated
Pius for sainthood,[29] and Pope John Paul II called him "a great Pope."[30]
In 1962, the president of the foreign correspondent association in Italy,
Barrett McGurn, concluding an extended study of the pontificate of
Pius XII, offered the opinion that "Pius, an exceptional man in a line of
such men, merited the title of 'great' which the Catholic Church only
rarely bestows on its pontiffs."[31]

The Congregation for the Causes of Saints in Rome has now been
presented with the results of the historical research into Pius XII's life.
The authors of the report, who shared their work with me as I completed this manuscript, believe it to be one of the strongest cases that
they have seen in the more than forty years that they have been doing
this kind of work. They expect the cause to move forward quickly on
the merits.[32] The designation which would go farthest in terms of

resolving this debate, however, is not a declaration of sainthood by the Catholic Church, but it is a different title to which Pius XII is also entitled.

Since 1963, a commission headed by an Israeli Supreme Court justice has been charged with the duty of awarding the title "Righteous among the Nations" to those who rescued Jews during World War II. The commission is guided in its work by certain criteria and meticulously studies all pertinent documentation, including evidence from survivors and other eyewitnesses. In order to arrive at a fair evaluation of the rescuer's deeds and motivations, the commission takes into consideration all the circumstances relevant to the rescue story, including the following:

1. How the original contact was made between the rescuer and the rescued.
2. A description of the aid extended.
3. Whether any material compensation was paid in return for the aid, and, if so, in what amount.
4. The dangers and risks faced by the rescuer at the time.
5. The rescuer's motivations, in so far as this is ascertainable; e.g., friendship, altruism, religious belief, humanitarian considerations, or others.
6. The availability of evidence from the rescued persons.
7. Other relevant data and pertinent documentation that might shed light on the authenticity and uniqueness of the story.

In general, when the data on hand clearly demonstrate that a non-Jewish person risked his or her life, freedom, and safety in order to rescue one or several Jews from the threat of death or deportation to death camps without exacting in advance monetary compensation, the rescuer qualifies for serious consideration to be awarded the "Righteous Among the Nations" title. Based on the record that we already have, Pope Pius XII fully deserves that designation, and fairness dictates that it should be bestowed upon him.[33]

Such recognition from a major, international Jewish organization—based upon full and honest research—would remove Pope Pius XII (and by extension the official actions of the Catholic Church during World War II) from most debate. Catholics and Jews could then focus on their joint efforts and shared heritage. Working together, they could concentrate on efforts to make certain that horrors such as the Holocaust do not happen again. That, not a revision of Catholic doctrine or social teaching, is the important result that should come from honest research into the Catholic Church during the Nazi era.

Notes

1 *Due Process*

1 S.K. Padover, *Nazi Scapegoat Number 2*, Reader's Digest, February 1939 at 1 (condensed from *The Forum*). A similar account appears in the religion section of Newsweek, May 29, 1937 (discussing "four years of Church-state strife" in Germany). *See also The Persecution of the Catholic Church in German-Occupied Poland; The Persecution of the Catholic Church in the Third Reich.*

2 *See* Congregation for the Causes of Saints, *Positio*, appendix 25 at 236. Hochhuth was a disciple of Erwin Piscator, founder of the school of drama known as "Political Theatre," whose method was to put living or recently deceased political persons on stage for either pillorying or praise. He has been described as "a young German with the gifts of a Goebbels." Oppen at 396.

3 Congregation for the Causes of Saints, *Positio*, appendix 25 at 236. Hochhuth's credibility was seriously damaged when his next play claimed that Winston Churchill had ordered the murder of Polish General Wladyslaw Sikorski and (later) the pilot who crashed Sikorski's plane. Unbeknownst to Hochhuth, the pilot was still alive, and he won a libel judgment that badly damaged the theater in London that had staged the play. *Pilot of General Sikorski's Aircraft Claims Libel Damages from German Playwright*, The Times (London), May 3, 1972, at 3; *£50,000 Award to General Sikorski's Pilot*, The Times (London), May 4, 1972, at 1; *$130,000 Awarded to Pilot for Libel in Hochhuth Play*," New York Times, May 4, 1972, at 48; Joseph Bottum, *The End of the Pius Wars*, First Things, April 2004, at 19. "David Frost, the well-known television interviewer, has stated that possibly his best performance ever was the night he fairly thoroughly dismantled Hochhuth before the cameras, above all for waiting until Churchill's death to make such a foul slander; he also waited until Pius xii was dead. . . ." O'Carroll at 151. Hochhuth "ignores, falsifies, misinterprets and misrepresents those facts that contradict or fail to support his preconceived thesis and invents or twists others to suit it." Desmond Fisher at 46.

4   A number of war-time diplomats publicly rejected Hochhuth's characterization of Pope Pius XII, including Wladimir d'Ormesson (a member of the French Academy), Sir Francis D'Arcy Osborne (British Minister to the Holy See during the war), Ambassador Grippenberg (from Finland), Ambassador Gunnar Haggelof (from Sweden), and Minister Kanayama (from Japan). See Congregation for the Causes of Saints, *Positio*, appendix 25 at 237-38. In 1963, Albrecht von Kessel, aide to the German Ambassador to the Holy See during the war, wrote: "We were convinced that a fiery protest by Pius XII against the persecution of the Jews would have in all probability put the Pope himself and the Curia into extreme danger, but *would certainly not have saved a single Jew*. Hitler, like a trapped beast, would react to any menace that he felt directed against him, with cruel violence." *Die Welt*, April 6, 1963 (emphasis added); O'Carroll at 21, 81.

5   *See* Congregation for the Causes of Saints, *Positio*, appendix 25 at 237 (discussing Paul's defense of Pius that appeared in *The Tablet* and in *L'Osservatore Romano* on June 29, 1963).

6   Congregation for the Causes of Saints, *Positio*, Statement of the relator, p. 9. Like most world governments, the Holy See keeps records confidential for an extended period of time to make certain that secret governmental information will not be revealed and that living people will not be embarrassed by disclosure of private information. Only recently were most (not all) of the American OSS World War II files made public, and similar French and British files also remain secret.

7   Volume three is split into two books, which accounts for occasional references to 12 volumes.

8   *Quoted in Positio*, appendix 25 at 251, note 3.

9   Oppen at 400.

10   Wills, *Papal Sin: Structures of Deceit* (2000).

11   Carroll, *Constantine's Sword: The Church and the Jews: A History* (2001).

12   Zuccotti, *Under His Very Windows: The Vatican and the Holocaust in Italy* (2001).

13   Phayer, *The Catholic Church and the Holocaust, 1930-1965* (2001).

14   Goldhagen, *A Moral Reckoning* (2002).

15   Kertzer, *The Popes Against the Jews* (2001).

16   Wistrich, *Hitler and the Holocaust* (2002).

17   Cornwell, *Breaking Faith* (2001). In *The Pontiff in Winter* (2004), Cornwell did not focus on Pope Pius XII, but he retracted the central thrust of *Hitler's Pope*.

18   Katz, *The Battle for Rome. See also* Katz, *Black Sabbath*; Katz, *Massacre in Rome*.

19   Lewy, *The Catholic Church and Nazi Germany* (1964); Morley, *Vatican Diplomacy and the Jews during the Holocaust 1939-1943* (1980).

20   *See* Ronald J. Rychlak, *The Church and the Holocaust*, The Wall Street Journal (Europe), March 28, 2002 (reviewing *Amen*).

21   Sánchez, *Pius XII and the Holocaust: Understanding the Controversy* (2002); Steigmann-Gall, *The Holy Reich: Nazi Conceptions of Christianity, 1919-1945* (2003); Godman, *Hitler and the Vatican : The Secret Archives that Reveal the Complete Story of the Nazis and the Vatican* (2004); *Pope Pius XII and the Holocaust* (Rittner & Roth, 2002).

22   Rychlak, *Hitler, the War, and the Pope* (2000); McInerny, *The Defamation of Pius XII* (2002); Burleigh, *The Third Reich: A New History* (2001); Stephen M. DiGiovanni, *Pius XII and the Jews: the War Years* (monograph, 2000); Gaspari, *Gli ebrei salvati da Pio XII* (2001); Lawler, *Popes and Politics: Reform, Resentment, and the Holocaust* (2002); Löw, *Die Schuld: Christen und Juden im Urteil der Nationalsozialisten und der Gegenwart* (2003); Marchione, *Pope Pius XII: Architect for Peace* (2000); Marchione,

Man of Peace: Pope Pius xii (2003); Marchione, *Pope Pius xii* (2003); Marchione, *Shepherd of Souls: A Pictorial Life of Pope Pius xii* (2002). Andrea Tornielli, *Pio xii. Papa degli ebrei* (2001).

23   *See, e.g.,* Daniel J. Goldhagen, *What Would Jesus Have Done?*, The New Republic, January 21, 2002.

24   F. David Dalin, *Pius xii and the Jews*, The Weekly Standard, February 26, 2001, at 31-39. *See also* Ronald J. Rychlak, *Misusing History to Influence the Future*, Forum Focus, Summer 2002.

25   *See* Fr. Martin Rhonheimer, in *The Holocaust: What Was Not Said*, First Things, November 2003.

26   Oliver Wendell Holmes, Jr., *The Path of the Law*, 10 Harvard Law Review 457 (1897).

27   *See* Phayer at 1, 3, 4, 6, 23, 57, 58, 60.

28   "In making the sort of charges he did the onus should be on the accuser to produce his evidence. This Hochhuth has failed to do." Desmond Fisher at 12.

29   In cases where evidence is hard to obtain, assignment of the burden of proof can decide the case. For example, one author, commenting on my review of Daniel Goldhagen's work, suggested that I had accepted Goldhagen's claim that the Norwegian Catholic Church concerned itself only with "five Christian families that included converts from Judaism." Andy Lamey, *Hyping the Church and the Holocaust*, National Post, June 4, 2002. That is not true. I simply had not addressed the issue because I had no evidence one way or the other. I seriously question the charge, but the burden should be for Goldhagen to prove his charge. I do not think that he has met that burden. (For the record, I should note that Lamey was generally complimentary about my review of Goldhagen.)

30   *See Berger v. United States*, 295 U.S. 78 (1935).

31   Of course, when there is reason to doubt the newspaper evidence, it can be kept away from the jury.

32   *See Spinelli v. United States*, 393 U.S. 410 (1969); *Illinois v. Gates*, 462 U.S. 213 (1983).

33   The origin of this story seems to be in the following statement: "There is finally the report that in the months preceding his death he was given Hochhuth's play *The Deputy* to read and then was asked what one could do against it. Whereupon he allegedly replied: 'Do against it? What can you do against the truth?'" Hannah Arendt, *Men in Dark Times* 63 (Harcourt Brace: New York, 1968).

34   Felicity O'Brien, *Letter to the Editor*, The Catholic Times [Manchester, England], July 20, 1997.

35   Private correspondence from Loris Francesco Capovilla to the relator of Pius xii's sainthood cause, dated May 18, 2002.

    With regard to the actions in favor of the Jews, affected particularly in Istanbul in the years 1935-1944, which was recognized and praised by Hebrew communities in Jerusalem, Istanbul, and the United States, it is obligatory to recognize that Roncalli was and declared himself the executor of the thought and the directives of Pius xii. He repeated, in fact: "The papal representative is the eye, the ear, the mouth, the heart and the effective hand of the Pope." *Id.* Capovilla continued that Roncalli's rescue efforts on behalf of Jews make sense "only if they are referred above everything else to Pius xii, of whom Roncalli was the careful and most faithful interpreter. Any strictly personal action, even though it be heroic, of Roncalli himself, would otherwise be inconceivable." *Id.*

36   In *Hitler, the War, and the Pope*, I reported that John said the Pope's order was

"first and foremost to save Jewish lives." I gave the quote the way it was reported in O'Carroll at 20, and I cited O'Carroll. O'Carroll cited Pinchas Lapide for his authority, but Lapide says "human lives." After this was brought to my attention, I contacted O'Carroll through a friend. He stands by the accuracy of his quote, saying that in context there is no difference in the two terms. He also says that his information came not only from Lapide, but also from Chief Rabbi Isaac Herzog of Israel. O'Carroll reports that Herzog was close to Pius XII and heard him give orders to save Jewish lives.

　　　O'Carroll has a point about the context of the quote, but frankly, I think it more appropriate for the Pope to have said "human lives" without distinction. A Pope should not give priority to a particular group of people in need. Certainly an order "first and foremost" to save "human lives" encompasses saving Jews. So, I think the "human lives" quote actually speaks better for Pope Pius XII than does the quotation that I originally used.

37　　McGurn at 88. "In the autumn of 1958 the world showed little doubt that one of its great ones had departed, and none showed less doubt than Angelo Roncalli [the future John XXIII]." Purdy at 7.

38　　McGurn at 99.

39　　Discorsi I, p. 101.

40　　McGurn at 36, 39.

41　　Discorsi I, p. 101. It should be noted that only a saint can be declared a Doctor of the Church. *See Days of Devotion* at 12 ("Pope John's programme and its concern for the modern world naturally enough found much of its inspiration in Pope John's predecessor under whom he served for 19 years, and from whom came much of the intellectual foundation on which the Council is built. No one was more generous in acknowledging this debt than Pope John himself.")

42　　*The New Catholic Treasury of Wit and Humor* 193-94 (Meredith Press, New York: 1968, Paul Bussard, ed.).

43　　Lewy at 303-04. *See* pages 233-34.

44　　*See* pages 240-44.

45　　*See Harris v. New York*, 401 U.S. 222 (1954).

46　　Critics say that true feelings of anger were disguised during and after the war to preserve good will, but a wartime, inter-office memo of the World Jewish Congress, apparently not intended for release to the public, reported: "The Catholic Church in Europe has been extraordinarily helpful to us in a multitude of ways. From Hinsley in London to Pacelli in Rome, to say nothing of the anonymous priests in Holland, France and elsewhere, they had [*sic*] done very notable things for us." *Quoted in* a World Jewish Congress memorandum dated March 24, 1959 and enclosed in a letter from Monty Jacobs of the World Jewish Congress to Dr. Edgar Alexander, also dated March 24, 1959.

47　　See Susan Estrich, *Real Rape: How the Legal System Victimizes Women Who Say No* (Cambridge, MA: Harvard University Press, 1987).

48　　With the opening of new archives in 2003, we are finding even more documents showing that Pope Pius XI and Secretary of State Pacelli were very concerned about the Nazi persecution of Jewish people. *See* Ronald J. Rychlak, *Reopening the Case*, Crisis, April 2004, at 44-45 (reviewing Godman's *Hitler and the Vatican*).

49　　In fact, an Italian court found critic Robert Katz did not limit himself to a true historic study, but set in motion an unjustified effort to defame Pope Pius XII's person and moral dignity. *See* pages 240-44.

50 *See* Joshua Dressler, *Understanding Criminal Law* 201-04 (2001).
51 Similarly, Jewish law does not justify killing someone, even under duress. *Jewish Law*, 1 S'Vara: A Journal of Philosophy and Judaism 51-73 (1990) at 56.
52 *See Great Untold Stories of World War II* (Phil Hirsch ed. 1963) (reporting that Pope Pius XII once counseled against an act of sabotage because it was virtually certain to result in the slaughter of 400 innocent hostages, but also noting that "the Holy Father can see no objection" to doing the same thing at a later date when hostages would not be at risk).
53 *Pius XII Gave Instructions Specifically to Save and Protect Jews: Magazine to Publish 2 Wartime Letters*, Zenit News Service, January 29, 2003. Famed Italian bicyclist Gino Bartali helped rescue 800 Jews at the direction of Pope Pius XII, according to other newly-discovered documents. *Pius XII's Directive Helped Save 800 Jews in 3 Cities, Papers Reveal*, Zenit News Service, April 8, 2003. *See also* Gallo at 140. For more on Giovanni Palatucci, *see*, Piersandro Vanzan, *La Shoah e Giovanni Palatucci: L'avvio della Causa di beatificazione*, La Civiltà Cattolica, 2003, vol. 1, at 149-58; *Cause Under Way for Policeman who Saved Jews*, Zenit New Agency, October 14, 2002.
54 The Vatican archive reference is: Sacra Congregazione Degli Affari Ecclesiastici Straordinari, Germania, Anno: 1933-1945, Posizione 643, Fascicolo 158.
    As for the translation, most accounts have referred to anti-Semitic "excesses." The actual word used by Pacelli was "eccessi," which can be translated as "rage" or "extremes"–as in "andare agli eccessi"—"to go to extremes;" or "dare in eccessi"—"to fly into a rage"– these are the examples given by *Langenscheidt's Standard Italian Dictionary* 143 (Munich, 1990). Thus, Pacelli should not be seen as tolerating a limited amount of anti-Semitic behavior but opposing an excessive amount. Rather, he is condemning the abuse of Jews by the Nazis, which he considers outrageous.
55 *New Proofs of Pius XII's Efforts to Assist Jews: 1933 Letter Targets "Anti-Semitic Excesses" in Germany*, Zenit News Service, February 17, 2003. *See also* Godman at 37-38 ("Orsenigo read the Catholic vice-chancellor, Franz von Papen a lesson on how the legislation represented 'an offense against the divine law.'")
56 Erich Ludendorff had been a leader of the German Army, especially at the end of the First World War. He was a strong supporter of the Nazi Party and agreed to become head of the German Army in Hitler's government.
57 The identification of this letter in the Vatican archives is: Archivio Nunziatura Monaco, #28961, Busta 396, Fascicolo 7, Foglio 6r-7v.
58 *Historian Sir Martin Gilbert Defends Pius XII; Goebbels Saw in Him an Enemy of Nazism*, Zenit News Service, Feb. 20, 2003 ("the test for Pacelli was when the Gestapo came to Rome to round up Jews. And the Catholic Church, on his direct authority, immediately dispersed as many Jews as they could.") "Hundreds of thousands of Jews saved by the entire Catholic Church, under the leadership and with the support of Pope Pius XII, would, to my mind, be absolutely correct." *The Untold Story: Catholic Rescuers of Jews*, Inside the Vatican, August 2003, at 31 (interview with Gilbert, conducted by William Doino).
59 *American Intelligence and the German Resistance to Hitler: A Documentary History* (Jürgen Heideking, ed., Westview Press, 1996), document 65.
60 *Memorandum to General Donovan from Fabian von Schlabrendorff. See also* Schlabrendorff, *The Secret War Against Hitler*. Müller was later imprisoned by the Nazis, kept in chains, and "forced to eat his food like a dog, from a plate on the stone floor of his prison cell, with his hands tied behind his back." *They Almost Killed Hitler* at 5.

61 *Dietrich Bonhoeffer: Letters and Papers from Prison* 214 (Eberhard Bethge, ed., Collier Books, New York, enlarged ed., 1971).

62 *Id.* at 267, n.152. This important evidence of contact between Pius XII and the resistance may have been missed by previous researchers because the letter refers only to "the Pope," not to Pope Pius XII, and the index of names mis-identifies the pope in question as Pius XI. *Id.* at 428. Leiber, by the way, was one of Pius XII's closest advisors, and he was known as a strong opponent of the Nazis. Sereny at 61. *See also American Intelligence and the German Resistance to Hitler: A Documentary History*, (Westview: Boulder, Colorado, Heideking, Frey, & Mauch, eds., 1996), document 65 (report on the O.S.S. confidential interview with Fr. Leiber after the liberation of Rome, on August 18, 1944 discussing coordination between the Vatican and the German resistance).

63 *See* Andrea Tornielli, *Pio XII. Papa degli ebrei* (Piemme, 2001); *see also* Zenit Daily Dispatch, *Eichmann's Diary Reveals Church's Assistance to Jews*, March 1, 2000.

64 Ashley Parrish, *Nun's past a slice of WWII history*, Tulsa World, 2002.

65 *See* pages 32-37.

66 *Stephen S. Wise, Servant of the People*. In letters, Wise was critical of Austrian Cardinal Theodor Innitzer, Neville Chamberlain, American Jews, *The Christian Century* (a Protestant magazine), Fr. Charles Coughlin, Rabbi Louis Wolsey, Rabbi William Fineschriber, Rev. Martin Niemoeller, and others. He praised Pope Pius XI, Cardinal Michael von Faulhaber, Cardinal Arthur Hinsley, and unnamed Catholic priests in France and Poland. The quotation about Pius XII appeared in a column Wise wrote regarding papal efforts in France. *Christendom and the Jews*, The Jewish Chronicle (London), Sept. 11, 1942. *See* Wise, *As I See It* (reprinting the 1942 article).

67 *See* Ronald J. Rychlak, *A "Righteous Gentile" Defends Pius XII*, National Catholic Register, Oct. 28, 2002 and in 32:11 Briefing 8 (November 2002) (Catholic Bishops' Conferences of England & Wales and Scotland). Rev. Martin Niemoeller was a noted German Protestant leader who spent seven years in concentration camps for his opposition to Hitler and the Nazis. A friend and fellow inmate in the concentration camps, himself a Jew, wrote that: "Pastor Niemoeller counted on the resistance of the Catholic Church to weigh heavily on the ultimate overthrow of Hitler." Stein at 129.

68 Tittmann at 213. Additionally, a newly released document, written in 1945, shows that Protestant resistor Dietrich Bönhoffer cooperated with Joseph Müller, the Vatican's main contact with the resistance in Germany. "This way the struggle of the Catholic and of the Protestant Church were coordinated." *Memorandum to General Donovan from Fabian von Schlabrendorff*.

69 The Catholic News, November 21, 1942 (reprinting the entire statement). *See* Rychlak, *Hitler, the War, and the Pope* at 175.

70 *See Holy Father Extends Thanks to American Catholics for Aid*, The Catholic News, November 21, 1942 (the bishops' letter is reprinted in this issue, along with the Pope's note of thanks for their collaboration).

71 Charles R. Gallagher, *'Personal, Private Views:' A newly discovered report from 1938 reveals Cardinal Pacelli's anti-Nazi stance*, America, September 1, 2003. Klieforth, an American diplomat, went to Rome on the pretext of taking a vacation. He spent a long time with Secretary of State Pacelli and according to Klieforth's son: "what was divulged was critical, sensitive information because among other things, it proved that the pope-to-be was anti-Nazi and hated Hitler." Ann Aubrey Hanson, *San Diego Diplomat Defends Pope Pius XII*, The Southern Cross, January 15, 2004, at 2 (quoting Alexander Klieforth, son of Alfred Klieforth). "Cardinal Pacelli thought the whole

Nazi ideology an abomination because it persecuted the Jews and persecuted the Church." *Id.*

72   Gallagher, *Personal, Private Views.*

73   *Id.*

74   John Thavis, *Jesuit journal cites new evidence that Pius xii helped save Jews,* Catholic News Service, December 4, 2003; Giovanni Sale, *La Civilta Cattolica,* December 5, 2003.

75   *Id.*

76   National Public Radio, Morning Edition, *Father Don Aldo Brunacci discusses his efforts to save 200 Jews during World War II,* March 31, 2004. *See also* Mae Briskin, *Rescue Italian Style,* The Jewish Monthly, May 1986, at 22 (similar quote from Brunacci). Fr. Brunacci was arrested by the Nazis, but they moved him to Rome shortly before its liberation, and he spent less then three weeks in captivity. *Id. See also* Congregation for the Causes of Saints, *Positio,* appendix 25 at 280.

77   *Inside the Vatican of Pius xii.*

78   *Id.* at 122-23.

79   *Id.* at 95.

80   *See Exonerated,* National Catholic Register, Jan. 23-29, 2005, page 1 ("the author most responsible for spreading the 'Hitler's Pope' myth admits he was wrong.") Cornwell still faults Pius for not being more outspoken following the end of the war. For more discussion of that charge, see chapter five.

81   *See also* Joseph Bottum, *The End of the Pius Wars,* First Things, April 2004, at 23 ("As far as I can tell, all this recent information breaks in favor of Pius xii.")

82   Such a study is undertaken on every candidate for sainthood, though due to the length of his papacy and the complexity of the issues involved, this study took somewhat longer than most.

83   The volumes that make up the Positio were prepared by the Postulator, Fr. Paul Molinari, with the help of various collaborators. The work was carried out under the supervision of the relator, Fr. Peter Gumpel. At the time that I reviewed the report, it had been printed but not yet bound.

84   These are the same transcripts that I used in *Hitler, the War, and the Pope* (pages 289-90).

85   *La campagna denigratoria nei riguardi della persona e dell'opera di Pio xii,* Congregation for the Causes of Saints, *Positio,* appendix 25 at 236-93; *see id. Statement of the Relator,* at 1-2, 13-14.

86   Congregation for the Causes of Saints, *Beatificationis et Canonizationis Servi Dei Pii xii (Eugenii Pacelli) Summi Pontificis (1876-1958): Positio Super Vita, Virtutibus et Fama Sanctitatis* (Rome, 2004). The Positio was assembled with a view to the discussions to be carried out by theologians, cardinals, and bishops as to the heroic virtue of Pope Pius xii's life. It will one day be made public, but until the decisions are made as to Pius xii it remains confidential. I was given extraordinary access and permission to quote from the document due to my previous work on the subject.

87   The historians found that there was a campaign to denigrate Pius xii. *La campagna denigratoria nei riguardi della persona e dell'opera di Pio xii,* Congregation for the Causes of Saints, *Positio,* appendix 25 at 236-93; *see id. Statement of the relator* at 1-2, 13-14. This should not, I think, be taken as an orchestrated campaign of critics working in conjunction. Rather, many of the critics share a view of the world that runs counter to the Catholic Church, and they have tried to advance their view and discredit the Church by denigrating Pope Pius xii. These critics are not really trying to find the truth; they are advancing a political agenda. *See* F. David Dalin, *Pius*

XII and the Jews, The Weekly Standard, February 26, 2001, at 31-39; Justus George Lawler, *Review Symposium: Proleptic Response*, 20 U.S. Catholic Historian at 89; Ronald J. Rychlak, *Misusing History to Influence the Future*, Forum Focus, Summer 2002. Other critics seem to have acted in good faith but were either deceived by ill-motivated authors, wrote before all of the evidence was available, or misunderstood the evidence that they saw.

88   *La campagna denigratoria nei riguardi della persona e dell'opera di Pio XII*, Congregation for the Causes of Saints, appendix 25 at 236-93; *see id. Statement of the Relator*, p. 1-2, 13-14. On March 8, 1999, Cardinal Secretary of State Angelo Sodano spoke against "the calumnies launched after the war against the Servant of God Pius XII of venerable memory.... This is a deceitful, treacherous persecution." *Id.*, appendix 25 at 272 (reprinting Peter Gumpel, *Cornwell's Cheap Shot at Pius XII*, Crisis, December 1999). The papal critics specifically identified as being involved in this campaign include: Rolf Hochhuth, Günter Lewy, Saul Friedländer, Robert Katz, John Cornwell, and Susan Zuccotti. *Id. Statement of the Relator*, at 14. *See id.*, appendix 25 at 276 (noting that the list could be longer). One footnote suggests: "We should, however, be lenient with respect to the excess and lack of understanding shown by Saul Friedländer, an inexperienced author, using only very unilateral documentation, seeing that he has dedicated his work 'to the memory of my parents, killed at Auschwitz.'" *Id.*, appendix 25, p. 250, note 3.

89   The *Positio* even has a separate appendix dealing with the question of Pius XII and nepotism. *Id.*, appendix 24 at 229-35.

2 Achille Ratti: Pope Pius XI

1   *See* Phayer at 1-6. *See also* Zuccotti, *The Holocaust, the French, and the Jews* at 23 (noting that Catholic-Jewish relations improved under the leadership of Pius XI.).

2   One of the first critics to turn on Pope Pius XI was David Kertzer. In his book on papal anti-Semitism, he discussed the ancient and false charge that during the Passover Jews ritually murdered Christian children to get their blood. In fact, he devoted far too much attention to this subject for a book about papal anti-Semitism. The "blood libel" was not an invention of Catholics, and Popes frequently condemned it. It was certainly not thought valid at the time of Pope Pius XI. *See* W.F.P. Stockley, *Popes and Jewish "Ritual Murder,"* Catholic World, July 1934 (quoting British Cardinal Bourne: "As you say, the Catholic Church has, so far as I am aware, always recognised that such accusations had no foundation whatever in the religious belief or practices of the Jewish people.")

     Similarly, discussing the treason trial of Alfred Dreyfus, Kertzer emphasized the French Catholics who contributed to the persecution of an innocent man, but he failed to mention the papacy's opposition to this anti-Semitic campaign. In a book about papal anti-Semitism, this was a rather serious oversight. *See* Ronald J. Rychlak, *The Popes and the Jews* (reviewing Kertzer, *The Popes Against the Jews*) Catalyst, Dec. 2001.

3   "Instructed by Pope Benedict to direct the distribution of Catholic relief in postwar Poland, Ratti gave considerable funds not only to Catholics but also to impoverished Jews who had lost their homes and businesses in the pogroms." David Dalin, *Truths and Falsehoods in the History of Catholic-Jewish relations*, The Weekly Standard, November 5, 2001.

4   Pius XI served as Pope from 1922 until his death in 1939. Over the course of his pontificate, he published thirty encyclicals, covering subjects as diverse as education,

marriage, and social problems. Along the way he condemned contraceptive birth control, abortion, and eugenic sterilization. His 1931 encyclical, *Quadragesimo Anno* (*On Reconstruction of the Social Order*) called attention to the fortieth anniversary of Pope Leo XIII's encyclical *Rerum Novarum* (*On the Capital and Labor*), and in so doing it brought Catholic social teaching to life.

While he was known for promoting the Catholic intellectual life, Pius was also an excellent mountain climber. He modernized Vatican City by helping develop an efficient railroad system and installing telephones, elevators, electric kitchens, and modern plumbing in Vatican buildings. He also commissioned Guglielmo Marconi to build the Vatican radio station. In fact, Pius XI was the first Pope ever to speak on the radio or to appear in a talking motion picture. In Rome, his vigor and strength caused him to be known as "a born Pope." McCormick at 70. He was "the rock" against which nothing prevailed. *Id.* at 95.

5   Mussolini donated a library collection to the Vatican, restored the crucifix to the schools, went to Mass, and "made instruction in Christian doctrine an integral part of the Fascist educational system." McCormick at 59. Later, however, when Mussolini tried to give additional land to the Holy See as part of a negotiated settlement, Pius declined, saying: "The Church wants independence, not territory." *Id.* at 75.

6   *See* Rychlak, *Hitler, the War, and the Pope* at 35 - 41.

7   *See id.* at 22.

8   McCormick at 74, 77.

9   At this same time, Mussolini was being favorably profiled in various American publications. *See* Samuel Nisenson & Alfred Parker, *Minute Biographies: Intimate Glimpses into the Lives of 150 Famous Men and Women* 113 (1931).

10 Daniel Goldhagen made this charge. He was probably fooled by James Carroll's *Constantine's Sword*. Carroll artfully stated that the concordat was Nazi Germany's first "bilateral" treaty. *See* Ronald J. Rychlak, *At Cross Purposes* (reviewing James Carroll, *Constantine's Sword: The Church and the Jews*), The Washington Post, February 12, 2001 at C3. Although deceptive, Carroll was technically correct.

11 Two days later, Pius XI made an explicit reference to it in a speech, noting that it was an indication that the international community thought it was necessary to try to negotiate with Germany for the sake of peace. *See Principles for Peace: Selections From Papal Documents, Leo XIII to Pius XII* at 475. Thus, the Vatican was well aware of other countries formally signing an agreement with Germany before the concordat was signed.

12 John Jay Hughes, *The Pope's "Pact With Hitler:" Betrayal or Self-Defense?*, 17 Journal of Church and State 63, 69 n.28 (1975).

13 Gotto, *Die Katholiken und das Dritte Reich.*

14 *Hitler's Rise to Power* at 26, n.d; *see generally* Carr, *A History of Germany.*

15 The official German and Italian texts are published in *Acta Apostolicae Sedis*, XXV (1933), at 389-413.

16 Congregation for the Causes of Saints, *Positio*, appendix 25 at 269 (reprinting Peter Gumpel, *Cornwell's Cheap Shot at Pius XII*, Crisis, December 1999).

17 Pacelli, frequently accused of being overly concerned about the Soviet threat, carried out this attempt. He also, as papal representative in Germany during World War I, brought comfort to Soviet prisoners of war. *Pope Pius XII: Beloved Spiritual Leader*, Wisdom, September 1957, at 12.

18 Purdy at 62.

19 Congregation for the Causes of Saints, *Positio*, appendix 25 at 269 (reprinting Peter Gumpel, *Cornwell's Cheap Shot at Pius XII*, Crisis, December 1999). On June 2, 1945,

Pope Pius XII [Pacelli] said : "As the offer [to negotiate] came from the Reich Government, the responsibility of a refusal would have devolved upon the Holy See." Lapide at 101. *See also* Tittmann at 40 (Pius XII told Tittmann that the concordat "had been asked for by the Germans"). Former German Chancellor Franz von Papen (a Catholic) later claimed that the concordat was necessary to protect the Church from Hitler's aggression. *Office of United States Chief of Counsel*, vol. II, at 935-36 (indicating that the prosecutors thought his testimony may have been self-serving).

20 Lapide at 102-03; Congregation for the Causes of Saints, *Positio*, appendix 25 at 270 (reprinting Peter Gumpel, *Cornwell's Cheap Shot at Pius XII*, Crisis, December 1999).

21 William M. Harrigan, *Pius XII's Efforts to Effect a Détente in German-Vatican Relations, 1939-1940*, The Catholic Historical Review, July 1963, at 173.

22 *Mr. Kirkpatrick (The Vatican) to Sir R. Vansittart*, August 19, 1933, *Documents on British Foreign Policy*, Series II, vol. V, London, 1956, no. 342, p. 524. *See also* John Jay Hughes, *The Pope's Pact with Hitler*, 17 Journal of Church and State 63 (1975) (arguing that the Vatican had no real choice but to negotiate); William M. Harrigan, *Pius XII's Efforts to Effect a Détente in German-Vatican Relations, 1939-1940*, The Catholic Historical Review, July 1963, at 174 (Pacelli "had been offered a choice between concessions, which were greater than any previous German Government would have agreed to, and the threat of virtual elimination of the Catholic Church in Germany."); McCormick at 91 (because of the concordat, Catholics had a legal basis for their protests that Protestants did not have). During negotiations, Hitler put pressure on the Vatican by arresting 92 priests, searching 16 Catholic Youth Clubs, and shutting down nine Catholic publications, all within three weeks. R. Stewart at 17.

23 *Telegram from the German Embassy in Italy to the Foreign Ministry*, July 4, 1933, in *Documents on German Foreign Policy 1919-1945*, Series C (1933-1937), vol. I, no. 352.

24 Lewy at 77.

25 *Mit brennender Sorge*, paragraph 3. For a detailed discussion of this encyclical, *see* Congregation for the Causes of Saints, *Positio* (*Vita Documentata: L'Enciclica "Mit brennender Sorge"*), pages 583-621.

26 Lapide at 101.

27 Holmes at 107.

28 *Let's Look at the Record*, Inside the Vatican, October 1999, at X.

29 *See* Gallin, *German Resistance to Hitler: Ethical and Religious Factors* (arguing that the concordat helped the Vatican by providing it with a legal basis for its arguments); John Jay Hughes, *The Pope's Pact with Hitler*, 17 Journal of Church and State 63 (1975) (without the concordat, Hitler would have been able to persecute the Church without restriction).

30 The concordat "was simply the culmination of efforts Pacelli had begun long before with the Weimar Republic." Purdy at 22, 252.

31 Benns at 266.

32 Darragh at 15 (quoting Knox, *Nazi and Nazarene* at 9) (emphasis in original); *see also* Henri Daniel-Rops, *A Fight for God: 1870-1939* 308 (Dutton: New York, 1965) (similar); Desmond Fisher at 20 (a concordat "is never a friendship pact, as so many non-Catholics believe, but a sign of tension....")

33 Godman at 50.

34 *Chronicle of the 20th Century* at 422; Cornwell, *Hitler's Pope* at 153.

35 Benns at 266.

36 *Ai Margini del Concordato tra la Santa Sede e il Reich Germanico, L'Osservatore Romano,* July 26, 1933 at 1; *Ancora a proposito del Concordato tra la Santa Sede e il Reich Germanico,* July 27, 1933, at 2; Congregation for the Causes of Saints, *Positio,* appendix 25 at 270 (reprinting Peter Gumpel, *Cornwell's Cheap Shot at Pius XII,* Crisis, December 1999).

37 *Why "Hitler and the Vatican" Fails as History: Interview with Father Peter Gumpel, Postulator of Pius XII's Cause,* Zenit News Service, March 3, 2004. Gumpel is actually the relator, not the postulator of Pius XII's cause. The protests were published in the collection: *Der Notenwechsel zwischen dem Heiligen Stuhl und der Deutschen Reichsregierung - I. Von der Ratifizierung des Reichskonkordats bis zur Enzyklika 'Mit brennender Sorge'* Bearbeitet von Dieter Albrecht. VKZ A 1, Mainz (1965).

38 William M. Harrigan, *Pius XII's Efforts to Effect a Détente in German-Vatican Relations, 1939-1940,* the Catholic Historical Review, July 1963, at 186.

39 Stein at 128 (also noting that the concordat was influential in helping the Church oppose other propaganda, including the anti-Semitic book, *The Myth of the Twentieth Century.*)

40 *Hitler's Secret Conversations 1941-1944* at 449.

41 *See* Godman, *Hitler and the Vatican* at 89 (noting the extensive violations by the Nazis).

42 Micklem at 80-82.

43 *Hitler's Secret Conversations* at 449.

44 Shirer, *Berlin Diary* at 296. *See also* Office of the United States Chief of Counsel, Supp. B, at 1238 (Ribbentrop's testimony as to his desire to obtain a new agreement with the Vatican but that "thing's didn't come off.").

45 *Pope is Emphatic About Just Peace; His Stress on Indispensable Basis for End of Hostilities Held Warning For Reich; Jews' Rights Defended; Pontiff in von Ribbentrop Talk Spoke on Behalf of Persecuted in Germany and Poland,* The New York Times, March 14, 1940.

46 *See* Lapide at 185; Hatch & Walshe at 150-51. Ribbentrop "took home nothing but 'a delicate snubbing' and a nervous breakdown." *Current Biography, 1941* Maxine Block, ed., the H.W. Wilson Co., 1971 re-issue, at 673.

47 *See* Godman at 50; McCormick at 91 (the concordat did not prevent retaliation by the Nazis against Catholic priests).

48 Critic Daniel Goldhagen has asserted that a "secret annex" to the concordat gave the Church's approval to German rearmament. This bewildering argument must have been drawn from a misreading of the supplemental protocol. One provision stated that if Germany were to revive its army, Catholic soldiers would have access to chaplains. In other words, it was exclusively a matter of protecting the sacraments, not approving German rearmament. *See* Congregation for the Causes of Saints, *Positio,* appendix 25 at 270 (reprinting Peter Gumpel, *Cornwell's Cheap Shot at Pius XII,* Crisis, December 1999).

49 *Chronicle of the 20ᵗʰ Century* at 456.

50 In December 1935, the *New York Time's* Vatican reporter explained: "Add to this the special interest the present Pontiff takes in the Ethiopians. The only college within the confines of Vatican City has been built for students from Ethiopia, forty of whom now study in peace and safety in the heart of enemy country, under the direct protection of the Pope. Pius XI has been on cordial terms with the [emperor of Ethiopia] ever since, as Ras Tafari, the present Emperor of Ethiopia visited the Vatican ten years ago." McCormick at 79.

51 *Id.* at 77.

52 Darragh at 6; Hatch & Walshe at 115.

53 Henri Daniel-Rops, *A Fight for God: 1870-1939* 312 (New York: E.P. Dutton and Co., 1965).

54 Darragh at 7-8.

55 McCormick at 67.

56 *Id.* at 77.

57 Congregation for the Causes of Saints, *Positio*, appendix 25 at 273 (reprinting Peter Gumpel, *Cornwell's Cheap Shot at Pius XII*, Crisis, December 1999). For the official Latin text of the decree, see the Acta Apostolicae Sedis, volume XX, pp.103-04.

58 *The Pope's Desire to Help*, Jewish Chronicle of London, May 12, 1933, at 28.

59 *The Pope Denounces Anti-Semitism*, Jewish Chronicle of London, September 1, 1933.

60 *See* Rychlak, *Hitler, the War, and the Pope* at 92-94.

61 *The World's Great Catholic Literature* at 263. The same version was printed in a later edition of the same book. *The World's Great Catholic Literature: A Magnificent Treasury of Catholic Writing* 289 (George N. Shuster, ed. 1965).

62 *Mit brennender Sorge*, paragraph 42. Some critics point out that the complaints focused more on Nazi persecution of Catholics than of Jews, but in 1937, no one "could dream of what would develop" in terms of Nazi persecution of Jews. Sereny at 294.

63 This same month, Pius also issued an encyclical on Communism entitled *Divini Redemptoris* (On Atheistic Communism). In it, he explained that "Communism is intrinsically wrong and no one who would save Christian civilization may collaborate with it in any undertaking whatsoever." *See* Rychlak, *Hitler, the War, and the Pope* at 160-61.

64 Congregation for the Causes of Saints, *Positio* (*Vita Documentata: L'Enciclica "Mit brennender Sorge"*), p. 595.

65 *Religion: Nazis: An American Cardinal Champions Pope Pius' Cause*, News-Week, May 29, 1937, at 18.

66 Congregation for the Causes of Saints, *Positio* (*Vita Documentata: L'Enciclica "Mit brennender Sorge"*), p. 592-93 (quoting Prof. Robert d'Harcourt).

67 "Pope Pius' encyclical soon precipitated a fight to the finish. Five weeks later, government-controlled newspapers announced a nationwide campaign to "clean up" Catholic monasteries, schools, and charity institutions. Screamer headlines proclaimed: THE CLOISTERS HAVE BECOME SINKS OF VICE. Lurid screeds ranted on the immorality of the "sexual criminals in priestly robes." One thousand more of Germany's 13,900 Catholic monks and lay brothers were rounded up and charged with sex crimes." *Religion: Nazis: An American Cardinal Champions Pope Pius' Cause*, News-Week, May 29, 1937, at 18.

68 Lapide at 110; *see* Martin, *Spiritual Semites*.

69 *Quoted in* Lapide at 110.

70 *Id.*

71 *Documents on German Foreign Policy 1918-1945*, Series D (1937-1945), vol. I, no. 633.

72 *The Nazi Master Plan: The Persecution of the Christian Churches*; Congregation for the Causes of Saints, *Positio* (*Vita Documentata: L'Enciclica "Mit brennender Sorge"*), p. 593; Burleigh, *The Cardinal Basil Hume Memorial Lectures* at 18 (noting that the encyclical particularly infuriated Hitler because he hated being laughed at, and this document said he was being laughed at in heaven).

73 *Religion: Nazis: An American Cardinal Champions Pope Pius' Cause*, News-Week, May 29, 1937, at 18.
74 *Id.*
75 William M. Harrigan, *Pius xii's Efforts to Effect a Détente in German-Vatican Relations, 1939-1940*, the Catholic Historical Review, July 1963, at 176.
76 *Religion: Nazis: An American Cardinal Champions Pope Pius' Cause*, News-Week, May 29, 1937, at 18.
77 *Id.* The article went on to report that "Any other attitude would have made Pius an inconsistent Pope." Other authors noted that Pius xi "needlessly irritated the German government by praising the zeal of Cardinal Mundelein. William M. Harrigan, *Pius xii's Efforts to Effect a Détente in German-Vatican Relations, 1939-1940*, The Catholic Historical Review, July 1963, at 177.
78 *Religion: Nazis: An American Cardinal Champions Pope Pius' Cause*, News-Week, May 29, 1937, at 18.
79 William M. Harrigan, *Pius xii's Efforts to Effect a Détente in German-Vatican Relations, 1939-1940*, The Catholic Historical Review, July 1963, at 176.
80 David Kertzer, in *The Popes Against the Jews*, not only portrays Pius xi as hostile to Jews, he contends that modern anti-Semitism was "embraced" and "actively promulgated" by Popes from Pius vi (1775) through Pius xi (1923-1939). Whereas Kertzer asserts that the future Pope Pius xi only met once with Poland's Jews when he was the papal representative in Poland, other reports have documented that he greeted and assisted Jews throughout his three-year appointment. Incorrectly arguing that Pius XI made "no direct attack on anti-Semitism," Kertzer cites no words of Pius (such as *Mit brennender Sorge* or the "Spiritually we are all Semites" speech), but *Hitler's Pope* by John Cornwell. Convicting Pius xi "of anti-Semitism would seem to be a pretty difficult task, and Kertzer does not even come close. The wonder is that he thought it necessary to try." Whitehead, 31 The Political Science Reviewer at 384. "Kertzer's aim of turning the popes into anti-Semites fails in virtually every instance." *Id.* at 346.
81 This theme was developed by Susan Zuccotti in a debate that I had with her at Trinity College, Hartford Conneticut, on February 26, 2001. She claims to have read the relevant issues of *L'Osservatore Romano* and found nothing. Her ability to read these issues without finding the relevant articles is indicative of an amazing propensity to overlook evidence that conflicts with her thesis. Throughout 1938 there were numerous articles opposing anti-Semitism. *See* Ronald J. Rychlak, *Comments on Zuccotti's Under His Very Windows*, 7 J. Modern Italian Studies 218 (2002), cited at the definitive response to Zuccotti in Congregation for the Causes of Saints, *Positio*, appendix 25 at 279.
82 Stille at 70.
83 *L'Osservatore Romano*, July 17, 1938, at.1; *New York Times*, July 17, 1938, at 1.
84 *L'Osservatore Romano*, July 23, 1938, p. 1; *New York Times*, July 22, 1938. *See also* Cianfarra at 133-34 ("As the enslaved Italian press obeyed Fascist Party instructions to vilify the Jews, Pius XI fought with truly amazing vigor.... The papal appeal contained in the July 21 speech was a signal for a campaign throughout Italy against the racial laws").
85 *La parola del Sommo Pontefice Pio XI agli alunni del Collegio di Propaganda fide, L'Osservatore Romano*, July 30, 1938, at 1.
86 *Arresti e misure antisemite a Danzica, L'Osservatore Romano*, April 2, 1938 at 6.
87 *Parole del Santo Padre in un'udienza a Castelgondolfo, L'Osservatore Romano*, July 17, 1938, at 1 (sub-headline: *Errori e pericoli del nazionalismo*).

88 *Intorno alla Nationalità, L'Osservatore Romano*, July 21, 1938, at 2.
89 *Precisazione di Chamberlain sui colloqui di Wiedimann a Londra, L'Osservatore Romano*, July 23, 1938, at 5.
90 *Intorno alla Nationalità, L'Osservatore Romano*, August 13, 1938 at 2.
91 *Attuali problemi della Piccola Intesa, L'Osservatore Romano*, August 22-23, 1938 at 1 (sub-headline: *Questioni minoritarie*).
92 *Le controversie slovacco—ungheresi, L'Osservatore Romano*, October 17-18,1938 at 1.
93 *Colloquio di François Poncet con Hitler, L'Osservatore Romano*, October 20,1938 at 2.
94 *Mon curé chez les Nazistes, L'Osservatore Romano*, October 23, 1938 at 2.
95 *La situazione religiosa nel Reich, L'Osservatore Romano*, October 25, 1938 at 1.
96 *Attività spirituale e culturale dell'azione Cattolica Italiana a Città di Castello, L'Osservatore Romano*, October 26, 1938, at 4.
97 *La situazione religiosa nel Reich, L'Osservatore Romano*, October 27, 1938 at 2.
98 *La campagna antisemita nei Sudeti, L'Osservatore Romano*, November 3, 1938, at 2.
99 *Dopo le manifestazioni antisemite in Germania, L'Osservatore Romano*, Nov. 13, 1938 at 6.
100 *La ripercussione delle manifestazioni antisemite in Germania, L'Osservatore Romano*, November 14-15, 1938, at 6.
101 *La sorte degli ebrei in Germania, L'Osservatore Romano*, November 16, 1938, at 6.
102 *Dopo le manifestazioni antisemite tedesche, L'Osservatore Romano*, November 17, 1938, at 1.
103 *Per la soluzione della questione ebracia, L'Osservatore Romano*, November 19, 1938, at 1.
104 *Gli sviluppi della questione ebracia dopo manifestazioni antisemite nel Reich, L'Osservatore Romano*, November 20, 1938, at 6.
105 *La situazione religiosa nel Reich, L'Osservatore Romano*, November 21-22, 1938, at 2.
106 *Gli sviluppi della questione ebracia, L'Osservatore Romano*, November 23, 1938, at 1.
107 *Il Cardinale van Roey e il Cardinale Verdier illustrano la dottrina cattolica di fronte al "razzismo" L'Osservatore Romano*, November 24, 1938, at 2.
108 *Inasprimento della lotta antisemita in Germania, L'Osservatore Romano*, November 26, 1938, at 6.
109 *La situazione religiosa nel Reich, L'Osservatore Romano*, December 25, 1938, at 2.
110 *La situazione religiosa nel Reich, L'Osservatore Romano*, January 19, 1939, at 2. See* Passelecq & Suchecky at 293-97 (confirming the dates of many of the articles identified. above).
111 Dinneen at 201-02.
112 Purdy at 24.
113 A.C. Jemolo, *Chiesa e stato in Italia negli ultimi cento anni* 680-81 (Einaudi: Torino, 1948).
114 *Id.* at 703.
115 Nazareno Padellaro & Robert L Reynolds, *His Reign*, Wisdom, September 1957, at 26. Even critic Susan Zuccotti admits: "*L'Osservatore Romano* did object unequivocally and strenuously to the infamous Italian police order number five of December 1, 1943, which declared that all Jews in Italy were to be arrested by Italian police and carabinieri and interned in camps within the country. The objections were commendable." Zuccotti, *Under His Very Windows* at 306.
116 *Quoted in* Cianfarra at 143; Holmes at 115.
117 *Dopo le manifestazioni antisemite in Germania, L'Osservatore Romano*, Nov. 13, 1938.

118 *La ripercussione delle manifestazioni antisemite in Germania, L'Osservatore Romano,* November 14-15, 1938, at 6; *La sorte degli ebrei in Germania, L'Osservatore Romano,* November 16, 1938, at 6; *Dopo le manifestazioni antisemite tedesche, L'Osservatore Romano,* November 17, 1938, at 1; *Il Cardinale van Roey e il Cardinale Verdier illustrano la dottrina cattolica di fronte al "razzismo" L'Osservatore Romano,* November 24, 1938, at 2.

119 Lapide at 95.

120 *Id.*

121 *Pius XI Ordered Catholic Universities to Refute Nazi Racist Theories: 1938 Letter from Sacred Congregation for Seminaries* Zenit, March 4, 2003. The letter was published in Nouvelle Revue Théologique, Leuven (Volume 66), 1939. *See also* Gallo at 15; *The Inner Forum: Scholars at the Vatican,* The Commonweal, Dec. 4, 1943, at 187 ("When he engaged Jewish scholars for the libraries and academies of the Vatican, Pius XII followed in the footsteps of his illustrious predecessor. . . .").

122 *Quoted in The Inner Forum: Scholars at the Vatican,* The Commonweal, Dec. 4, 1943, at 188.

123 *Id.* (noting that Pope Pius XII was guided by the same concerns).

124 His successor, Pope Pius XII, let his opposition to the Italian racial laws be known from the very outset of his papacy: "At the beginning of World War II, Pius XII arranged a meeting at the Quirinal Palace with the King of Italy, and specifically excluded Mussolini from the session . . . the pope's words [were]: 'I don't want anyone present at the meeting who signed the racial laws.'" *L'Avvenire,* June 27, 1996 (as recounted by Adriano Ossicini, a personal friend of Pius XII and an anti-Fascist leader); *More Echoes on Pope Pius XII, Nazi Holocaust,* Zenit News Agency, June 27, 1996.

125 For the original text as it was delivered in French, see the Belgian publication: *La Libre Belgique* (September 14, 1938); the original text also was reproduced in the French documentary news service: La Documentation Catholique, vol. 39, no. 885 (December 5, 1938, columns 1459-60).

126 Critics sometimes complain that various papal statements were not reported in the Catholic press. Sometimes they even note articles that appear to be anti-Semitic in Catholic publications. One must be careful, however, when looking at Catholic publications in Nazi-controlled countries. As one author explained: "Father Leiber went on to say that although the final clause of the Concordat assured the Catholic Church the right freely to disseminate its ideology, he had found no one in Germany who believed that this privilege could in fact be exercised. Already, he said, it was impossible to get ideas or articles contrary to the opinion of the Party into even Catholic publications. If they included such an item, the Catholic editor was removed and replaced with a National Socialist, but the publication continued to appear as if under Catholic auspices (thereby obviously lulling the reader into a false security)." Sereny at 62.

127 Lapide at 118; Stewart at 21.

128 *The New York Times,* Dec. 12, 1938 at 1.

129 Maritain, *The Pagan Empire and the Power of God,* The Virginia Quarterly Review at 161, 167.

130 *Italy: Like Son, Like Father,* National Jewish Monthly, January 1939, at 157, 183.

131 Gallo at 303, n. 1 (citing the New York Times, January 17, 1939).

132 Das Schwarze Korps, January 19, 1939. *See* Rychlak, *Hitler, the War, and the Pope,* at 106.

133 *See* Gallo at 27.
134 F. Murphy at 57; Duffy at 261 ("stubborn old man"). In his final years Pius refused to let his deteriorating health slow him down. Working with his secretary of state, Eugenio Pacelli (the future Pope Pius XII), he investigated ways to preserve world peace, counter Nazi anti-Semitism, and protect the Church until he passed away on February 10, 1939. *See* McCormick at 73-74 (Pius XI saw the developing prospects for war earlier than other world leaders, and he tried to warn them).

3 The German Clergy

1 *Hitler's Secret Conversations* 624 (Signet edition, 1961).
2 Polish Catholic clergy also strongly resisted the Nazis. *See* Lukas, *Forgotten Holocaust* at 13-15. They suffered greatly for it. Of the 2,800 Polish priests sent to Dachau, only 816 survived until April 1945. Purdy at 45. *See also Recalling the Polish Clergy Imprisoned in Dachau: Interview With Archbishop Emeritus Majdanski of Stettino-Kamien,* Zenit News Org., May 2, 2004 ("I was arrested, as were other students and professors of the seminary, for wearing a cassock. The Germans who arrested us did not ask us for our particulars. So it can be said that I was arrested as a Catholic priest.... Our German executioners cursed God, denigrated the Church, and called us the 'dogs of Rome.' They wanted to force us to desecrate the cross and the rosary. To make a long story short, for them we were only numbers to be eliminated. . . . I saw so many priests die in a heroic way.") *See generally* Lenz, *Christ in Dachau.*
3 Eric Ludendorff had been a leader of the German Army at the end of the First World War. He was an early and strong supporter of what would become the Nazi Party.
4 They were not yet known as Nazis.
5 The letter's identification in the Vatican archives is: Archivio Nunziatura Monaco, #28961, Busta 396, Fascicolo 7, Foglio 6r-7v.
6 *See* Holmes at 110.
7 Gallin at 166-67.
8 *See* Lewy at 9-10; Holmes at 101; Gallin at 167-68.
9 Gallin at 168 ("At this early date, there was apparently unanimity among the bishops as to the incompatibility of Catholicism and National Socialism, and they were courageous in their denunciation of the errors inherent in the philosophy of which the latter was based."); Lewy at 10-11. Lewy claimed that after the Nazis obtained power, the German Catholic Bishops abandoned this noble record and began to placate, if not collaborate with, the Nazis. Since Lewy's book originally appeared, however, an abundance of new evidence has become available which has placed the German Catholic Bishops record in proper perspective. Heinz Hürten, *Deutsche Katholiken, 1918-1945* (Ferdinand Schöningh: Paderborn, 1992) completely contradicts the version supplied by Lewy and his uncritical followers like Daniel Goldhagen. *See also,* Ludwig Volk, *Zwischen Geschichtsschreibung und Hochhuthprosa: Kritisches und Grundsätzliches zu einer Neuerscheinung über Kirche und Nationalsozialismus,* in *Stimmen der Zeit,* volume 176 (1965) at 29-41.
10 Steigmann-Gall at 67.
11 Tinnemann at 334, citing Hans Müller, *Katholische Kirche und Nationalsozialismus, Dokumente 1930-1935,* 13-47 (Munich: Nymphenburger Verlagshandlung, 1963).
12 *Id.* at 334.
13 *Id.*
14 *Id.* at 339.
15 *Quoted in* Cornwell, *Hitler's Pope* at 179.

16 *Id.*
17 *Id.* at 179-80.
18 Tinnemann at 339, citing Hans Müller, *Katholische Kirche und Nationalsozialismus, Dokumente 1930-1935*, 13-47 (Munich: Nymphenburger Verlagshandlung, 1963).
19 *Id.*
20 *Id.*
21 William M. Harrigan, *Pius xii's Efforts to Effect a Détente in German-Vatican Relations, 1939-1940*, The Catholic Historical Review, July 1963.
22 *The Papal Secretary of State to the German Ambassador to the Holy See*, Oct. 19, 1933, in Documents on German Foreign Policy, 1918-1945, Series C (1933-1937), vol. II, no. 17, at 23 (enclosure); *see Controversial Concordats* at 226.
23 Graham, *Pope Pius xii and the Jews of Hungary in 1944* at 5-6. One of the German officials at the Foreign Office complained that "the Nuncio used to come to me nearly every fortnight with a whole bundle of complaints." Weizsäcker at 282. In December 1933, the German ambassador to the Holy See wrote to German Foreign Minister Neurath that he considered a clash with the Curia quite possible and that the lack of response to the Vatican's charges would look bad to the world. *Ambassador Bergen to Foreign Minister Neurath*, Dec. 28, 1933, in Documents on German Foreign Policy, 1918-1945, Series C (1933-1937), vol. II, no. 152.
24 Tinnemann at 337, 341.
25 *Memorandum to General Donovan from Fabian von Schlabrendorff*, Oct. 25, 1945. On Innitzer and the Vatican, *see* p. 151.
26 *Memorandum to General Donovan from Fabian von Schlabrendorff*, Oct. 25, 1945. *See also* Schlabrendorff, *The Secret War Against Hitler*.
27 Official Report by William Donovan, *The Nazi Master Plan; Annex 4: The Persecution of the Christian Churches*, July 6, 1945, reprinted in Stein at 272-73.
28 *Id. See also* Rychlak, *Hitler, the War, and the Pope* at 35-41; Congregation for the Causes of Saints, *Positio*, appendix 25 at 270 (reprinting Peter Gumpel, *Cornwell's Cheap Shot at Pius xii*, Crisis, December 1999). *See* cross reference.
29 Oppen at 396 (the world's press treated "the Pope and German Catholic bishops much like allies").
30 Tinnemann at 345. *See* pp. 54-55.
31 *Id.*
32 *Id.*
33 *Id.*
34 Oppen at 406.
35 *Id.*, quoting *Die Briefe Pius' xii. an die deutschen Bischöfe 1939-1944*, Herausgegeben von Burkhart Schneider in Zusammenarbeit mit Pierre Blet und Angelo Martini (Mainz, 1966) at 355-66.
36 Orsenigo was criticized for being too accommodating to the Nazis. Recently opened archives, however, indicate that he was not as friendly toward the Nazis as had been thought. Godman at 30-33, 80, 87. Ernst Von Weizsäcker, the German Ambassador to the Holy See, later wrote that Orsenigo carried out his duties properly, but that his efforts to avoid angering Hitler caused him to appear more sympathetic to the Nazis than he really was. Weizsäcker at 282-83; *see also* Rhodes at 343. In fact, Orsenigo intervened with leaders in Berlin on behalf of Nazi victims at least 300 times, but it was almost all in vain. Lapomarda at 128. *See* Rychlak, *Hitler, the War, and the Pope* at 325, n. 12. Moreover, when he was inclined to make overtures to the Reich government, Pacelli instructed him not to make friendly statements about Hitler and the Nazis. *See Vatican Told Nuncio to Forgo Praise of Hitler: Professor Sees Signs*

of Opposition to Nazism in 1930s Archives, Zenit News Service, May 1, 2003; Andrea Tornielli, *Interview with Prof. Matteo Luigi Napolitano*, Il Giornale (Milan, Italy), April 10, 2003. Pius XII also feared that if he recalled Orsenigo, the Germans would be unlikely to accept a new nuncio. This would cut off the Vatican's best source of information on the Nazi activities in Germany, including the many acts of persecution against the Church. Holmes at 149; Alvarez & Graham at 161; O'Carroll at 138, 150-51; *The Pius War* at 253 ("Most scholars believe that had Orsenigo been recalled... the Nazis would have prevented any nuncio from remaining in Germany, just as they banned the one in Poland.")

37 Oppen at 407.

38 Purdy at 254. For more on Rarkowski, see Gordon C. Zahn, *German Catholics and Hitler's Wars*, 143-72 (Notre Dame: Notre Dame Press, 1962).

39 Purdy at 254. *See* Lewy at 247, 390.

40 Purdy at 254 (noting that the broadcast brought a protest from the German Foreign Office).

41 *Akten Deutscher Bischöfe über die Lage der Kirche 1933-1945* (Matthias-Grünewald: Mainz, Stasiewski and Volk eds., 1968-1985) (correspondence and statements of the German Catholic bishops during the Nazi era; volume 1 contains material on the background of the concordat, showing how Pius XI, Cardinal Pacelli, and the German episcopacy coordinated their efforts; also included are the major anti-Nazi pastoral letters of the German bishops).

42 McCormick at 107.

43 *Quoted in* Saperstein at 43.

44 *Akten Deutscher Bischöfe über die Lage der Kirche, 1933-1945*, 6 volumes., edited by Bernhard Stasiewski and Ludwig Volk (Matthias-Grünewald-Verlag: Mainz, 1968-1985). These letters were misrepresented in Guenter Lewy's *The Catholic Church and Nazi Germany*, on which Daniel Goldhagen seems to have relied. For English translations of many of the Bishops statements, *see* Lothar Groppe, *The Church's Struggle with the Third Reich* at 12-15 and at 23-27; and Groppe, *The Church and the Jews in the Third Reich* at 18-27.

45 "Only the Church stood squarely across the path of Hitler's campaign for suppressing truth. I had never any special interest in the Church before, but now I feel a great admiration because the Church alone has had the courage and persistence to stand for intellectual truth and moral freedom. I am forced thus to confess, that what I once despised, I now praise unreservedly." *German Martyrs*, Time, Dec. 23, 1940, at 38 (statement of Albert Einstein).

46 Steigmann-Gall at 67.

47 *Id.* "The territories of the old Austro-Hungarian Empire of the Catholic Hapsburgs were where the majority of the concentration camps for Jews were located. The Hapsburgs rule ceased after the First World War, on the insistence of the United States and other nations. In a world 'made safe for democracy' a benign, free, centuries-old Catholic monarchy was not allowed to exist. Hitler hated the Catholic aristocracy and social order in Vienna, Prague, Budapest, and Krakow, which he regarded as pro-Jewish.

"In recent years, upon the death of the last Hapsburg Empress, who lived in exile, her body was returned to Austria and buried with a full state funeral. The Chief Rabbi of Vienna went to the Catholic monastery of Klosterneuberg to pay his respects to the Catholic Empress.

"There, before the assembled international press, he publicly thanked the Hapsburgs for their centuries of kind treatment and friendship with the persecuted Jews.

(This writer was an eyewitness of the event.) It was the removal of the Hapsburg's Catholic leadership that led in large measure to the wholesale persecution of the Jews in modern Europe under Hitler." Hugh Barbour, *Has the Church Ever Taught that the Jews Should be Persecuted and Segregated?*, Ad Veritatem, March 2004.

48 Steigmann-Gall at 67.

49 *Id.*

50 *See* Ulrich von Hehl, *Priester unter Hitler's Terror* (Matthias-Grünewald-Verlag: Mainz, 1984) (biographical and statistical survey documenting how up to one-third of the German Catholic clergy were persecuted by the Nazis, experiencing everything from interrogations to imprisonment and execution). Other than Jews and Gypsies, few segments of the German population were persecuted to the same extent as Catholic priests. *See* Irene Gut Opdyke, *In My Hands: Memories of a Holocaust Rescuer* (New York: Anchor Books, 2001) at 135, quoting a Nazi official: "You must know by now the Fuhrer wants all the Jews eliminated. Once we finish with them we'll eliminate the Poles and their tiresome Catholic Church."

51 *The Nazi Master Plan: The Persecution of the Christian Churches*, July 6, 1945. *See also* Burleigh, *The Cardinal Basil Hume Memorial Lectures*, 3 Totalitarian Movements and Political Religions at 29 ("the pastoral letters and sermons of the bishops were punctuated with protests against the myriad incremental measures which added up to systematic religious persecution. The density of complaint can be gauged from a rather impressive book, The Nazi Persecution of the Catholic Church, published in London in 1940.").

52 *The Nazi Master Plan: The Persecution of the Christian Churches*, July 6, 1945.

53 *Id.*

54 *Hitler's Secret Conversations* at 83.

55 *Id.* at 112.

56 *Id.* at 296.

57 *Id.* at 583.

58 *Id.* at 98-99.

59 *The Church and the Jews in the Third Reich*, Fidelity, November 1983, at 21.

60 *Hitler's Secret Conversations* at 389.

61 *Id.* at 48-49.

62 *Id.* at 624. Of course, it is impossible to identify a single "Nazi view" of Christianity. *See* Ronald J. Rychlak, Book Review: *The Holy Reich: Nazi Conceptions of Christianity, 1919-1945*, by Richard Steigmann-Gall, First Things, October 2003. Hitler's attitude can be deduced from several semi-private statements that he made: "There is something unhealthy about Christianity." *Hitler's Secret Conversations* at 397. "I shall never come personally to terms with the Christian life. . . . If my presence on earth is providential, I owe it to a superior will. But I own nothing to the Church that trafficks [sic] in the salvation of souls. . . . Our epoch will certainly see the end of the disease of Christianity." *Id.* at 330. "When one examines the Catholic religion closely, one cannot fail to realise that it is an almost incredibly cunning mixture of hypocrisy and business acumen, which trades with consummate skill on the deeply engrained affection of mankind for the beliefs and superstitions he holds." *Id.* at 398. "It is deplorable that the Bible should have been translated into German, and that the whole of the German people should have thus become exposed to the whole of this Jewish mumbo-jumbo." *Id.* at 482.

63 Johann B. Neuhäusler, *Kreuz und Hakenkreuz* (2 Volumes: Katholische Kirche Bayerns: Munich, 1946), especially volume 1, p.76. An English translation of many of the documents Neuhäusler compiled can be found in *The Persecution of the Catholic*

Church in the Third Reich; Facts and Documents translated from the German. See also George N. Schuster, *Catholic Resistance in Nazi Germany*, 22:84 Thought 12 (March, 1947); *The Anti-Christians*, The Tablet (London), January 4, 1941, at 12 (reviewing *The Persecution of the Catholic Church in the Third Reich*).

64   The formerly secret documents are collected in *American Intelligence and the German Resistance to Hitler.*

65   *See* p.14.

66   *Akten Kardinal Michael von Faulhaber, 1917-1945,* (edited by Ludwig Volk, Matthias-Grünewald-Verlag: Mainz, 1975-1978), vol. 1, at 705, 726 (these are the official papers of Cardinal Faulhaber). The letter is also cited in Hamerow at 75. Hamerow says of Faulhaber: "The Cardinal's private correspondence during the early months of the Third Reich reveals, moreover, that his sympathies were not confined to the Judaism of antiquity. In a letter to Alois Wurm, editor of a Catholic periodical, he condemned the new government's anti-Semitic campaign. 'This action against the Jews is so unchristian that every Christian, not only every priest, would have to stand up against it.' ... Clearly, Faulhaber cannot be accused of being an anti-Semite." *Id.* at 75.

67   *The Nazi Master Plan: The Persecution of the Christian Churches*, July 6, 1945.

68   *Id.*

69   *Id.*

70   *Id.*

71   *Id.*

72   *Id.*

73   Summi Pontificatus is central to Pius xii's approach to the war. *See* Rychlak, *Hitler, the War, and the Pope* at 273-77.

74   *The Tablet* (London), April 27, 1940, at 398. *The Tablet* reported that: "the Osservatore Romano, the Vatican's newspaper, published important extracts from Cardinal Faulhaber's recent outspoken pastoral on the Encyclical Summi Pontificatus." *See La figura e l'opera di Pio xii, L'Osservatore Romano*, April 14, 1940, at 1.

75   No documentation of this photo is provided, other than a reference, at the end of the book, which lists the illustration credits, to "Max Hollweg, courtesy of the USHMM [United States Holocaust Memorial Museum] Photo Archives."

76   Some critics have faulted the Holy See for leaving Orsenigo in Berlin. *See* pp.277-78.

77   Goldhagen-Buch; "Wissenschaftlich fragwuerdig," Focus Magazin, September 30, 2002.

78   *German court bars sale of book on Roman Catholic church during Nazi era after complaint about photo* (AP), Oct. 8, 2002.

79   They had been put on notice that Goldhagen's work was tainted. *See* Ronald Rychlak, *Goldhagen v. Pius xii*, First Things, June/July 2002, at 37-54.

80   Stein at 127.

81   *Id.*

82   *Memorandum to General Donovan from Fabian von Schlabrendorff* (noting that "quite a number of the lower clerics" who repeated his teachings "ended up in prison or in a concentration camp.") *See also* Schlabrendorff, *The Secret War Against Hitler.*

83   *Stephen S. Wise, Servant of the People: Selected Letters.* In a wartime editorial, he also spoke well of Pope Pius xii. *Christendom and the Jews*, The Jewish Chronicle (London), Sept. 11, 1942 (praising Pius XI and Pius xii); Wise, *As I See It* (reprinting the 1942 article).

84 Niemoeller himself, speaking of a meeting with Hitler [in 1931?], said: "I know that from that day on, until our eyes were opened, Hitler had the full support of the Protestant Church in Germany." Stein at 79 (later suggesting that Niemoeller's "eyes were opened" in January 1934).

85 Tinnemann at 342.

86 *The Nazi Master Plan: The Persecution of the Christian Churches*, July 6, 1945; *The Persecution of the Catholic Church in the Third Reich* at 421 (quoting Julius Streicher's *Stürmer*).

87 Congregation for the Causes of Saints, *Positio* (Vita Documentata: L'Enciclica "Mit brennender Sorge"), p. 587; *Pius XI und der Nationalsozialismus. Die Enzyklika 'Mit brennender Sorge' vom 14. März 1937*, edited by Heinz-Albert Raem (Ferdinand Schöningh: Paderborn, 1979); Portmann, *Cardinal von Galen*. For a discussion of *Mit brennender Sorge, see* pp. 32-37.

88 Oudendijk at 179.

89 *Id.*

90 For Pius XII's February 24, 1943 letter to von Galen, see the Holy See's *Actes et Documents*, volume 2, pp. 306-310. Even earlier, on February 2, 1942 Pius XII congratulated Cardinal Faulhaber for two bold sermons in the face of Nazism: *Actes et Documents*, volume 2, pp.236-237; *see also* Pius XII's April 30, 1943 letter to Bishop Konrad Preysing (of Berlin) and his March 3, 1944 letter to Archbishop Joseph Frings (of Cologne) on the difficulty of speaking out without risking reprisals: *Actes et Documents*, volume 2, pp. 318-327 and p. 365, respectively. Pius XII's wartime letters to the German bishops have been published as *Die Briefe an die Deutschen Bischöfe 1939-1944*, edited by Burkhart Schneider (Grünewald: Mainz, 1966).

91 *Quoted in* Beth A. Griech-Polelle, *Bishop von Galen: German Catholicism and National Socialism* (New Haven: Yale University Press, 2002).

92 This episode is central to the beginning of the motion picture *Amen. See* Ronald J. Rychlak, *The Church and the Holocaust*, The Wall Street Journal (Europe), March 28, 2002.

93 Congregation for the Causes of Saints, *Positio*, appendix 25 at 273-74 (reprinting Peter Gumpel, *Cornwell's Cheap Shot at Pius XII*, Crisis, December 1999).

94 Burleigh, *The Third Reich: A New History* at 400 (regarding the efforts of the Nazi leadership to compel the Church to tolerate euthanasia: "Negotiations collapsed when on 2 December 1940 Pope Pius XII unequivocally condemned the killing of 'life unworthy of life.'"). This statement was repeated on Vatican Radio (December 2) and in *L'Osservatore Romano* (December 6). Sereny at 74 (incorrectly reporting that the statement appeared in Latin instead of Italian). *See also* Gallo at 35 (noting that the Allies were heartened when they learned of this condemnation); Bishop Preysing of Berlin also read it from the pulpit of St. Hedwig's Cathedral on March 9, 1941. Sereny at 74. As early as 1930, in the encyclical *Casti connubii*, Pope Pius XI condemned sterilization (primarily in the United States) and asserted that the right of families to have children overrides the state's desire for eugenically perfect people. *See* Burleigh, *The Cardinal Basil Hume Memorial Lectures*, 3 Totalitarian Movements and Political Religions at 30.

95 A German euthanasia program was first proposed in 1933. "At that time, the German Catholic Church declared uncompromisingly that any kind of legally sanctioned euthanasia was incompatible with Christian morality." Sereny at 60. Cardinals Bertram and Faulhaber both spoke out against euthanasia in 1934 and again in 1940, and Archbishop Gröber did so in 1937. Id. at 72. Other German Catholic leaders also

filed protests: "Archbishop Gröber and Bishop Bornewasser von Trier, the Bishop of Limburg and of course the infinitely courageous Bishop of Münster, Count Galen–all in 1941; and finally a pastoral letter from all the German bishops, dated September 12, 1943, and certainly remarkable for the period, in which bishops protest not only against euthanasia but against the murder of 'innocent hostages, prisoners of war or penal institutions, and human beings of foreign race or extraction.'"*Id.* at 72 (quoting a circular letter from Bishop Johann Neuhäusler, Auxiliary Bishop of Munich, "an inveterate opponent of the Nazis who spent most of the war years in Dachau concentration camp, and whose own political integrity is beyond question.")

96   Graham, *The 'Right to Kill' in the Third Reich: Prelude to Genocide*, Lxii The Catholic Historical Review at 68. Pius always was close to Preysing, but beginning in 1942, he particularly began following Preysing's lead, even bypassing the papal nuncio to take advice from Preysing, a widely-recognized opponent of Nazism. *See* Oppen at 405 ("Preysing received far more correspondence than any of his colleagues; also, the Pope praised his outspoken stand for the rule of law and even-handed justice.") In April 1943, Pius wrote encouraging Preysing to continue his work on behalf of the Jews: "For the non-Aryan Catholics as well as for Jews, the Holy See has done whatever was in its power, with charitable, financial and moral assistance.... Let us not speak of the substantial sums which we spent in American money for the fares of emigrants.... We have gladly given these sums, for these people were in distress.... Jewish organizations have warmly thanked the Holy See for these rescue operations.... As for what is being done against non-Aryans in the German territories, we have said a word in our Christmas radio message." *Quoted in* Holmes at 167.

97   Graham, *The 'Right to Kill' in the Third Reich: Prelude to Genocide*, Lxii The Catholic Historical Review at 68-72; Holmes at 101. Several protests from bishops of this time period are reviewed in Groppe, *The Church's Struggle with the Third Reich* 24. *See also* Godman, *Hitler and the Vatican* (documenting numerous protests, but arguing that they should have been stronger).

98   Commenting on the mistaken notion that Galen's protests caused the Nazis to halt the "mercy-killing" program, Dr. Robert M.W. Kempner, deputy chief US prosecutor at Nuremberg, wrote: "'Open protests against the 'Final Solution' would certainly have been effective,' so it is now often asserted après le débâcle, this is proved by the 'success' of the German bishops protests against the so-called 'euthanasia' programme. This is not in accord with the facts, for even after the protests this programme of murder was strictly enforced in secret right up to the end of the war. For example, many thousands of victims were allowed to die of hunger, so that they died a 'natural death.' . . . A public protest against the persecution of the Jews could only lead to the partial success of gaining time when it was made at a politically and military opportune moment, like those of the nuncios in Slovakia and Romania...." Congregation for the Causes of Saints, *Positio*, appendix 25 at 239, 244 (quoting and reprinting the prologue to Levai, *Hungarian Jewry and the Papacy: Pope Pius did not Remain Silent*). Similarly, historian Michael Burleigh comments: "Galen's coruscating verbal assault... had no functional effects.... Although his sermon [condemning euthanasia in the summer of 1941] which enjoyed national and international notoriety, undoubtedly moved some Nazi leaders to contemplate murdering him, its effects on the 'euthanasia' programme were minimal. The medical killing of children continued unimpeded; gassing facilities were used to murder concentration-camp inmates; while the 'euthanasia' killing of adult psychiatric patients went on by other means down to the final days of the war." Burleigh, *The Third Reich: A New History* at 723;

see also Burleigh, *The Cardinal Basil Hume Memorial Lectures: Political Religion and Social Evil*, 3 Totalitarian Movements and Political Religions at 32-33.

99 *Three Sermons in Defiance of the Nazis Preached During 1941 by Bishop von Galen of Munster* at 5. Retaliation concerns are justified by statistics from Poland, where of the 828 priests in the diocese of Posen, 450 were put in camps and 74 were shot. Many of the others fled. Gallo at 34.

100 *Hitler's Secret Conversations* at 520. Hitler also vowed to send Nuncio Orsenigo home following the war. *Id.*

101 Congregation for the Causes of Saints, *Positio*, appendix 25 at 245 (reprinting the prologue to Levai, *Hungarian Jewry and the Papacy: Pope Pius did not Remain Silent*).

102 *The Nazi Master Plan: The Persecution of the Christian Churches.*

103 *Id. See also* Fredborg, *Behind the Steel Wall* at 138 (praising Galen's open opposition to Hitler and noting his widespread anti-Nazi reputation).

104 *Anti-Nazi Bishop a Step Closer to Beatification* (Zenit News, December 21, 2003).

105 *ADL Applauds Steps to Beatify Anti-Nazi Cardinal*, ADL press release, December 28, 2004.

106 Dietrich at 58.

107 Stehlin at 353.

108 Dietrich at 58.

109 *Quoted in* Dietrich at 58.

110 *Id.* at 58-59.

111 Stehlin at 20.

112 Oudendijk at 115.

113 Tinnemann at 335, citing Hans Müller, *Katholische Kirche und Nationalsozialismus, Dokumente 1930-1935*, 13-47 (Munich: Nymphenburger Verlagshandlung, 1963).

114 *Id.* at 342.

115 Dietrich at 164-65. *See also* Peter Godman, *Hitler and the Vatican* at 39, 109-11.

116 Tinnemann at 337, citing Hans Müller, *Katholische Kirche und Nationalsozialismus, Dokumente 1930-1935*, 13-47 (Munich: Nymphenburger Verlagshandlung, 1963); *Id.* at 338 ("members of the hierarchy cooperated positively for only a short period").

117 *Id.*

118 *Id.*

119 *See* pp. 14, 66

120 *Hitler's Secret Conversations* at 488.

121 Stein at 129.

122 This charge against Bertram has been made by Goldhagen and others, but it first surfaced when Klaus Scholder made the charge in the 1970s. At that time, Konrad Repgen, one of Germany's leading Catholic historians, investigated the allegation, examining Bertram's papers and interviewing his secretary. Repgen found the Requiem Mass story to be untrue. Repgen also rebutted many other of Scholder's accusations. At the time Goldhagen first made his accusations, Repgen confirmed the results of his investigation about Bertram, and he reaffirmed the baselessness of the accusation. A brief summary of Repgen's work can be found in *Controversial Concordats* at 236-38.

123 Scholder, *A Requiem for Hitler and Other New Perspectives on the German Church Struggle.*

124 S.K. Padover, *Nazi Scapegoat Number 2*, Reader's Digest, February 1939 at 1 (condensed from *The Forum*). A similar account appears in the religion section of News-

week, May 29, 1937 (discussing "four years of Church-state strife" in Germany). For an account of an Austrian nun who was beheaded for her opposition to the Nazis, *see* Hans Knight, *The Nun and the Nazis*, The Catholic Digest, February 1992, at 14.

125 *Quoted in* Matheson at 48-49.

126 Holmes at 108; Oppen at 407. Rev. Martin Niemoeller said: "I am convinced that if the Catholic Church had refrained from opposing Hitler it would have been permitted to handle its money affairs in the proper way. And I agree with the Pope that these laws are unethical. They were seized upon as a means of destroying the Catholic Church's prestige." Stein at 130 ("What Pastor Niemoeller said of the other charges could be no stronger from the lips of a Catholic priest.")

127 Oppen at 407.

128 William J. O'Malley, *The Priests of Dachau*, reprinted in *Pius XII and the Holocaust: A Reader* at 143. "[B]y 1942 over 400 German priests could be found at Dachau alone." William M. Harrigan, *Pius XII's Efforts to Effect a Détente in German-Vatican Relations, 1939-1940*, the Catholic Historical Review, July 1963, at 186-87. *See also* Lenz, *Christ in Dachau*.

129 Pius mentioned this and other sufferings of priests at Dachau in a 1945 address. Purdy at 45.

130 William J. O'Malley, *The Priests of Dachau*, reprinted in *Pius XII and the Holocaust: A Reader* at 143. Archbishop Juliusz Nowowiejski of Plock died in a concentration camp in May 1941, followed by his suffragan bishop, Leon Wetmanski. Bishop Kozal of Wloclawek was killed in Dachau. Szulc at 119. *See also* Lenz, *Christ in Dachau*.

131 O'Malley, *The Priests of Dachau*, reprinted in *Pius XII and the Holocaust: A Reader* at 143.

132 An English translation of this document can be found in *Nazi Conspiracy and Aggression* (Office of United States Chief of Counsel For Prosecution of Axis Criminality, 1946) vol. V, at 1018-1029.

133 A translation of this whole speech, as it was broadcast on Vatican Radio, can be found in *The Catholic Church and the Third Reich: Pope Pius XII Surveys an Heroic History*, The Tablet (London), June 9, 1945.

134 *Id.*

135 This observation alone serves to undercut the argument against Pope Pius XII set forth by Fr. Martin Rhonheimer, in *The Holocaust: What Was Not Said*, First Things, November 2003. Rhonheimer's theme was that historic anti-Judaism influenced the papal response to the Holocaust and the anti-Semitic activities that preceded it. The Vatican archives that were opened in February 2003, however, clearly show that Pope Pius XI and Secretary of State Pacelli were very concerned about the fate of German Jews. Drafts of statements, not issued on the advice of German clergy because of concern about Nazi retaliation, negate any inference of anti-Semitism or anti-Judaism. Those documents also dispel any notion that the Holy See was concerned only about "baptized Jews." *See* pp. 111-12. Of course, Rhonheimer himself backed off of the implication of his original article when responding to letters it generated. *See Martin Rhonheimer responds*, First Things, February 2004, at 4-5 ("my article was not about Pius XII and the Holocaust," the Church did far more to help the Jews than any other institution, and "The Church was certainly not responsible for the rise of Nazi anti-Semitism–indeed it did much to counter Nazi ideology.") Despite these backtracks, he suggests that some type of statement, made before the Holocaust had occurred to anyone, might have done some good. Of course, many such statements were made. *See*, e.g., pp. 32-37.

136 O'Carroll at 127.

137 Ronald J. Rychlak, *Guilty Collaborators, or Charitable Victims: The German Church and Forced Labor*, Our Sunday Visitor, October 15, 2000.

138 *German Catholic Church admits use of Nazi-era forced labour*, Agence France Presse, August 12, 2000.

139 Rychlak, *Guilty Collaborators, or Charitable Victims*. On August 20, 1942, the security department of the SS reported that the Catholic Church "in all parts of the Reich" tried to influence foreign laborers "by offering them special Masses or individual care." Nazi officials complained about the Church's "complete blurring of the racial and political borders" between foreigners and Germans. *Id.*

140 *German Church Denies Abuse of WW II Laborers, Offers Compensation*, America, September 9, 2000.

141 *Quoted in* Rychlak, *Guilty Collaborators, or Charitable Victims*.

142 *Germany's Catholic Church to pay own forced labour compensation*, Agence France Presse, August 29, 2000.

143 *Id.* Some workers may have been employed at Catholic parishes in order to keep them from being sent to the concentration camps. This technique of thwarting the Nazis was depicted in the motion picture, *Schindler's List*. Oskar Schindler, a Catholic, is today praised for using Jewish slave workers in order to keep them from the gas chambers.

144 *See generally* Scaperlanda, *Edith Stein*.

145 Eva Fogelman, *Conscience & Courage* at 172; Holmes, *The Papacy in the Modern World* at 165.

146 Fogelman, *Conscience & Courage* at 172; Holmes, *The Papacy in the Modern World* at 165.

147 Fogelman, *Conscience & Courage* at 172; Holmes, *The Papacy in the Modern World* at 165.

148 Fogelman at 172; Holmes at 165. A similar letter concerning the situation in the Third Reich was sent by German bishops on July 6, 1941. One of its provisions was: "Never, and under no circumstances, may a man, except in the case of war and legitimate defense, kill an innocent person." O'Carroll at 106.

149 Congregation for the Causes of Saints, *Positio*, appendix 25 at 246 (reprinting the prologue to Levai, *Hungarian Jewry and the Papacy: Pope Pius did not Remain Silent*).

150 Lothar Groppe, *The Church and the Jews in the Third Reich* at 23.

151 *Id.*

152 *Id.* ; *The Tablet*, August 29, 1942, at 103. The critics ignore this announcement.

153 Congregation for the Causes of Saints, *Positio*, appendix 25 at 246 (reprinting the prologue to Levai, *Hungarian Jewry and the Papacy: Pope Pius did not Remain Silent*). Reportedly, Pius XII was considering having *L'Osservatore Romano* publish a protest against Nazism when the events from Holland were reported back to him. There was no nuncio in Holland at the time, since he had been expelled by the Nazis, so Pius learned of these events from newspapers and radio accounts. He is said to have picked up two pages of writing that he had been working on and to have burned them. Congregation for the Causes of Saints, *Positio*, (Summarium) *Testimony of Sr. Pascalina Lehnert*, Oct. 29, 1968–Jan. 24, 1969, before the Tribunal of the Vicariate of Rome, on the beatification of Pius XII (Eugenio Pacelli), Part I, page 77, 85; Congregation for the Causes of Saints, *Positio* (Summarium) *Testimony of Maria Conrada Grabmair*, May 9, 1969–May 29, 1969, before the Tribunal of the Vicariate of Rome, on the beatification of Pius XII (Eugenio Pacelli), Part I, page 173, 174. *See* Rychlak, *Hitler, the War, and the Pope* at 301-02.

154 *Did Vatican Do Enough to Stop Holocaust?* CNN Sunday Morning, February 16, 2003 (comments of John Allen, CNN Vatican analyst).
155 *See* p. 14.
156 Critics often confuse this point, leading their readers to think that she was a Carmelite nun at the time of the letter. *See* Godman at 34.
157 *Self-Portrait in Letters 1916-1942*, vol. 5, at 327.
158 *Id.*
159 *See* pp. 32-37.
160 *Self-Portrait in Letters 1916-1942*, vol. 5, at 327.

4 *Eugenio Pacelli: Pope Pius XII*

1   A longer quote is provided in Congregation for the Causes of Saints, *Positio*, appendix 25 at 272 (reprinting Peter Gumpel, *Cornwell's Cheap Shot at Pius XII*, Crisis, December 1999).
2   "No choice could have been more welcome to this country [...] It is regarded as a sign, if not a guarantee, that the Vatican will continue to throw its worldwide influence against totalitarian ideas wherever they exist [...]" *British View the Election as Sign of Continued Resistance to Totalitarianism*, The New York Times, March 3, 1939. "Persons in official and semi-official life generally expressed gratification at the election of Cardinal Pacelli." *Washington Hails Pacelli Election*, The New York Times, March 3, 1939. From Paris, the *Times* correspondent reported: "The election of... Pacelli as Pope was received in France... with the greatest possible satisfaction. His elevation is regarded as a guarantee that the firm policies of Pius XI both in regards to spiritual matters and political ideologies will be vigorously defended by the Vatican." *France Applauds Choice of Pontiff*, The New York Times, March 3, 1939. According to the Jewish press: "Pius XII has clearly shown that he intends to carry on the late Pope's work for freedom and peace... we remember that he must have had a large part to play in the recent papal opposition to pernicious race theories and certain aspects of totalitarianism." Palestine Post, March 2, 1939. "The frantic attempts... by Nazis and Fascists to influence the election... in favour of a cardinal friendlier to Hitler and Mussolini... was ultimately foiled. The clumsy advice which... Germany's Ambassador to the Vatican, recently gave to the College of Cardinals... has already received an answer as unequivocal as the advice was arrogant. The plot to pilfer the Ring of the Fisherman has gone up in white smoke." Canadian Jewish Chronicle, March 10, 1939.
3   In 1939, the *New York Times* Vatican reporter, Anne O'Hare McCormick, explained that Pope Pius XII "has dedicated his pontificate to the search for peace. It is clear to any one to whom he speaks that he is driven by the sense that as Pope he must do something to save the human race from the awful catastrophe of war. It is clear that he believes, not that war is the worst of all evils, but that it will bring social and moral chaos in its train, disastrous to all he is commissioned to defend." McCormick at 104.
4   *See* pp. 248-49.
5   F. Murphy at 64. The executive editor of *Jewish Social Studies* wrote: "Never has the papacy spoken in such unmistakable terms against racialism and antisemitism as in the words and deeds of the present pope, Pius XII, and his predecessor, Pius XI." Koppel S. Pinson, *Antisemitism in the Post-War World*, in *Essays on Antisemitism*, 2nd ed. (New York: Conference on Jewish Relations, 1946).

6   After Holy Scripture, the writings of Pope Pius XII are the most cited source in the documents of Vatican II. *See* Congregation for the Causes of Saints, *Positio*, Appendix 18: *Documenti del Concilio Vaticano II nei quali si fa Riferimento a Testi di Pio XII*, p. 147-72 (reprinted from *Pie XII et la Cité: La pensée et l'action politiques de Pie XII*).

7   Congregation for the Causes of Saints, *Positio*, Statement of the relator, p. 1-2 (quoting Paul VI's tribute to Pius at the closing of Vatican II, Nov. 18, 1965).

8   *A Jewish Boyhood Friend*, Inside the Vatican, October 1999, at XXIV (special insert).

9   Padellaro, *Portrait of Pius XII*.

10 "Il Sinai del signor Marchi, su cui saliva per tuonare *non* contro ebrei duri di cuore, ma contro ragazzi duri di testa." Nazareno Padellaro, *Pio XII* 21 Editrice S.A.I.E. (Torino, 1956).

11 Ilse-Lore Konopatzki, *Eugenio Pacelli: Pius XII, Kindheit und Jugend in Dokumenten*, Universitätsverlag Anton Pustet, Salzburg und München (Salzburg, 1974) at 146.

12 William Rees-Mogg, *The Vatican's holy failure*, The Times (London), October 4, 1999.

13 José M. Sánchez & Kelly Cherry, *Pacelli's Legacy*, America, October 23, 1999, at 25.

14 As with all codification projects, the 1917 Code did slightly amend and clarify existing law. This was necessary to resolve conflicts and fill in gaps.

15 Cornwell elaborated this argument by saying that Pacelli spent the rest of his life trying to impose the code on Catholic Churches throughout the world by reaching agreements with civil governments. As these concordats were signed, according to Cornwell, local priests and bishops lost the ability to complain about injustices that they saw. "Political" disputes were instead handled through Rome.

16 Certainly if Austria had been granted the authority over these new areas, Serb nationalists would have been enraged. *See* William D. Rubinstein, *Books in Review: The Devil's Advocate*, First Things, January 2000, at 39, 40.

17 Sir Owen Chadwick, The Tablet (London), September 25, 1999.

18 Falconi at 102. *See also* William D. Rubinstein, *Books in Review: The Devil's Advocate*, First Things, January 2000, at 39, 43 ("It is, to put it mildly, extremely doubtful that the Serbian Concordat had a significant role in the outbreak of war. One wonders, for instance, if Britain's leaders even so much as heard of the Serbian Concordat. Cornwell's view of the role of the Concordat is simply absurd.")

19 On page 50, Cornwell cites Anthony Rhodes, *The Vatican in the Age of the Dictators* at 224.

20 Vatican SS [Segreteria di Stato] SRS [Sezione per i rapporti con gli stati]: Austria-Ungheria (1913-14), Fasc. 454, folios 21-22.

21 *Id.*

22 *Id.*

23 The idea that Pacelli sought to control and dominate the Vatican under Pope Pius XI is also contradicted by documents found in recently-opened archives. The documents show that the cardinal-secretary of state to Pius XI followed the orders of Pope Pius XII. Godman at 28-29, 40, 82-84, 164-65. *See also* Purdy at 20 (Pacelli "was to all appearances a punctilious collaborator of Pius XII, and enjoyed his complete confidence....").

24 "An interesting essay remains to be written on what Pacelli's sojourn in Germany contributed to German ecumenism, considered afterward so daring and advanced by many who regarded Pius XII as something of a symbol of intransigence." Purdy at 14.

25 *La Conciliazione Ufficiosa: Diario del barone Carlo Monti "incaricato d'affari" del governo italiano presso la Santa Sede (1914-1922)*, Vatican Press (Antonio Scotta, ed. 1997, Vatican City) at 51 (vol. I) (introduction by Giorgio Rumi).

26 *Id.* at 49-50.

27 The derogatory meaning of cult is reflected in the American Heritage Dictionary's secondary definition: "Obsessive devotion to a person or ideal; a group of persons sharing such devotion." As used by Pacelli, however, the word "was not a pejorative term." Marilyn Henry, *How pious was Pius XII?*, The Jerusalem Post, October 1, 1999, at 7B (quoting Eugene Fisher). "It has nothing to do with personal animosity toward Jews." *Id.*

28 *Hitler's Pope* at 174 (cult of St. Thérèse); *id.* at 344 (cult of the Assumption and cult of the Virgin Mary); *id.* at 345 (the Fátima cult); *id.* at 382 (noting that beatification "indicates that the Pope has sanctioned a local cult of the individual's sainthood").

29 *See* Bruno Walter, *Theme and Variations: An Autobiography* 221 (Knopf: New York, 1966) (Nuncio Pacelli helped a wrongly imprisoned Jewish musician during World War I).

30 Halecki & Murray at 46 (noting that no one was hurt). For a description of the havoc the Communist revolutionaries were causing in Germany at the time, *see* Kershaw at 109-16.

31 Martin, *The Decline and Fall of the Roman Church* at 219 (noting that several people had been killed, so the threat could not be taken lightly).

32 Pacelli had no food or money, having given it all to the poor of the city. Hatch & Walshe at 84.

33 *Id.*; Halecki & Murray at 47-48. *See* Rychlak, *Hitler, the War, and the Pope* at 296-98.

34 Nuncio Pacelli's letter of April 18, 1919, sent to Cardinal Secretary of State Gaspari.

35 *Id.*

36 *Id.*

37 *Id.*

38 *Id.*

39 Cornwell, *Hitler's Pope* at 74-75. Even worse were press reports that Pacelli described "Jews" (not a specific group of revolutionaries) as "physically and morally repulsive, worthy of suspicion and contempt." Cathy Lynn Grossman, *Catholic scholar casts Pius XII as 'Hitler's Pope'*, USA Today, September 7, 1999.

40 Therefore Daniel Goldhagen's statement that "the Communist revolutionaries, Pacelli averred, were 'all' Jews" is wrong. The word "all" appears only in Cornwell's mistranslation. (Levine himself, I have been told, was not actually Jewish.)

41 The German translation of *Hitler's Pope* has an even worse translation. "Rabble" is translated as "scum," so the passage at issue reads: "The boss of this female scum was Levien's mistress ...." *See* Rainer Decker, book review: John Cornwell. *Pius XII. Der Papst, der geschwiegen hat* H-Soz-u-Kult (February, 2000), on the Internet at <<www.h-net.msu.edu/reviews/showrev.cgi?path=4726951832799>>.

42 Cornwell claims that the letter was first brought to attention in his 1999 book, but the letter appears in Emma Fattorini, *Germania e Santa Sede. Le nunziature di Pacelli fra la Grande guerra e la Repubblica di Weimar* 322-25 (Società editrice Il Mulino: Bologna, 1992). *See* Congregation for the Causes of Saints, *Positio*, appendix 25 at 266.

43 The same holds true for Daniel Goldhagen and his publisher.

44 In an interview with a French newspaper, Pacelli described the situation in Munich in 1919: "I am one of the few non-German eye-witnesses of the Bolshevik régime

Notes to pages 82-83

that ruled Munich in April 1919. At the head of this "Soviet" government were native Russians; every idea of justice, freedom and democracy was suppressed; only the Soviet press was available. Even the nuncio's official residence was part of the republican government; armed bandits forced their way in here and when I protested energetically against this violation of international law, one of them threatened me with his pistol. I am well aware of the objectionable circumstances under which the hostages were massacred...." Sereny at 305, citing an interview with the French newspaper, *Le Matin*.

45 Cornwell continually argues that Pacelli was responsible for matters done in the name of Gasparri. *See Hitler's Pope* at 31 (they worked in tandem); *id.* at 38 (Gasparri was Pacelli's "boss and close confidant"); *id.* at 41 (Gasparri and Pacelli were "principal architects" of the Code of Canon Law); *id.* at 44 (an idea "became clear to Gasparri and Pacelli"); *id.* at 46 (Gasparri referring to Pacelli: "one of my trusty staff in the Secretariat of State, in whom I had particular confidence"); *id.* at 55 ("Gasparri, Pacelli's guide and mentor"); *id.* at 56 (Pacelli as Gasparri's "protégé"); *id.* at 61 ("Gasparri would not hear of Pacelli's leaving Rome until the new code had been published.").

46 *Cardinal Gasparri, Secretary of State, Replies to the Petition of the American Jewish Committee of New York*, February 9, 1916, in *Principles for Peace: Selections from Papal Documents, Leo XIII to Pius XII* at 198-99; *La Civiltà Cattolica*, April 28, 1916.

47 Cohen at 180, 214-15, 578. Cohen's sources are the archives of the American Jewish committee and statements by AJC members who were directly involved in Catholic-Jewish relations at the time. *See* Marchione, *Man of Peace* at 73, n.3.

48 *See* pp. 23-30.

49 According to Cornwell, Pacelli wanted to impose papal absolutism on the Church in Germany through the 1917 Code of Canon Law. The concordat itself, however, does not even mention the 1917 Code.

50 Cornwell, *Hitler's Pope* at 128. In general, voting patterns show that Catholics did not support Hitler during his rise to power. *See* Richard F. Hamilton, *Who Voted for Hitler?* (Princeton University Press: Princeton, 1982); Thomas Childers, *The Nazi Voter* (University of North Carolina Press: Chapel Hill, 1983).

51 Congregation for the Causes of Saints, *Positio*, appendix 25 at 270 (reprinting Peter Gumpel, *Cornwell's Cheap Shot at Pius XII*, Crisis, December 1999).

52 *Id. See* Cheetham, *The Keeper of the Keys* at 283-84; Kershaw at 478; Robert Leiber, *Reichskonkordat und Ende der Zentrumspartei*, in *Stimmen der Zeit: Monatschrift für das Geistesleben der Gegenwart*, Verlag Herder-Freiburg im Breisgau, 1960/61, at 213; *Telegraph from Mr. Newton (Berlin) to Sir J. Simon*, July 7, 1933, *Documents on British Foreign Policy 1919-1939*, Her Majesty's Stationary Office (E.L. Woodward, ed., London, 1956) (party members believe that dissolution will end arrests, sequestrations, and discrimination against the Catholic press).

53 Stehlin at 438. *See* Giovanni Sale, S.J., *Roma 1943: occupazione nazista e deportazione degli ebrei*, La Civilta Cattolicà, Dec. 6, 2003, at 417-429; *Archives Vindicate Vatican on Hitler's Appointment, Says Review* (Zenit News, Dec. 19, 2003) ("the archive sources attest that the Vatican was not informed ahead of time of negotiations that took place between Hitler and leaders of the Zentrum party on the question of the law of full powers.")

54 Congregation for the Causes of Saints, *Positio*, appendix 25 at 270 (reprinting Peter Gumpel, *Cornwell's Cheap Shot at Pius XII*, Crisis, December 1999).

55 Stehlin at 46-47 (Pius X "believed the mixture of politics and religion to be the most hybrid and dangerous possible for the Church"). In 1988, John Paul II wrote: "The

Church does not have technical solutions to offer for the problem of underdevelopment as such.... For the Church does not propose economic and political systems or programs, nor does she show preference for one or the other, provided that human dignity is properly respected and promoted, and provided she herself is allowed the room she needs to exercise her ministry in the world." *On Social Concerns* (Sollicitudo Rei Socialis) (1988). *See also Doctrinal Note on Some Questions Regarding the Participation of Catholics in Political Life*, by the Congregation for the Doctrine of Faith, Nov. 21, 2002 (especially section IV), available on the Internet through the Vatican's web page.

56   *See generally* Rhodes, *The Vatican in the Age of the Dictators: 1922-45.*

57   Pope Pius XI wrote *Quadragesimo Anno* in 1931. This was the first papal encyclical to use the term "social justice." Many modern Catholics equate that term with political action, but according to that encyclical, the Church has the right and duty "to interpose her authority... in all things that are connected with the moral law." This right and duty, however, is limited to issues of morality or natural law. Regarding political issues unrelated to morality, Pius wrote: "the Church holds that it is unlawful for her to mix without cause in these temporal concerns." Thus, two years before Hitler's rise to power, Pius XI set forth his thinking on the Church's political involvement.

The Second Vatican Council, in its *Pastoral Constitution on the Church in the Modern World* (Gaudium et Spes) reaffirmed this teaching: "At all times and in all places, the Church should have the true freedom to... pass moral judgment even in matters relating to politics." The ability of the clergy—of the Church itself–to become involved in politics is limited, however, to situations in which "the fundamental rights of man or the salvation of souls requires it."

58   Emphasis added.

59   *See Report from the British Legation to the Holy See*, Feb. 17, 1939, British Public Record Office, Fo 371/23789. Documents from recently opened archives show that the cardinal-secretary of state followed the orders of Pope Pius XI. Godman at 28-29, 40, 82-84,164-65. *See also* Purdy at 20 (Pacelli "was to all appearances a punctilious collaborator of Pius XI, and enjoyed his complete confidence....").

60   *Id.* "To Cornwell, Pius XII was too authoritarian, too monarchical, too powerful. It may be argued that the very opposite was true. Pius XII was not sufficiently confident of his power and of his situation." John Lukacs, *In Defense of Pius*, National Review, November 22, 1999.

61   Hatch & Walshe at 109; *see* Halecki & Murray at 65 ("closest possible co-operation"); McCormick at 98 ("As the Papal Secretary of State, Eugenio Cardinal Pacelli had admiration amounting to veneration not only for the person but the policy of his chief.")

62   *See* Godman at 28-29, 40, 82-84,164-65.

63   Congregation for the Causes of Saints, *Positio*, (Summarium) *Testimony of Cardinal Stefano Wyszynski*, October 18 & 25, 1968, before the Tribunal of the Vicariate of Rome, on the beatification of Pius XII (Eugenio Pacelli), part II, page 578; *Controversial Concordats* at 136.

64   Burleigh, *The Cardinal Basil Hume Memorial Lectures*, 3 Totalitarian Movements and Political Religions at 25 ("the once-mighty Catholic Centre Party was sent to the liquidators after it had voted for the March 1933 Enabling Act.")

65   *Justice for Jews*, reprinted in *Commonweal Confronts the Century: Liberal Convictions, Catholic Traditions* 193, 194 (Patrick Jordan and Paul Baumann, eds. 1999).

66   *Id. See* Dietrich at 105 ("Hitler's original intention had been to use a Concordat to dissolve the Center party, but the clergy themselves deserted the party, which by early July had dissolved itself."); Cheetham at 283-84; Kershaw, *Hitler: 1889-1936 Hubris* at 478; R. Leiber, *Reichskonkordat und Ende der Zentrumspartei,* in *Stimmen der Zeit: Monatschrift für das Geistesleben der Gegenwart,* Verlag Herder-Freiburg im Breisgau, 1960/61, at 213; *Telegraph from Mr. Newton (Berlin) to Sir J. Simon,* July 7, 1933, *Documents on British Foreign Policy 1919-1939,* Her Majesty's Stationary Office (E.L. Woodward, ed., London, 1956) (party members believe that dissolution will end arrests, sequestrations, and discrimination against the Catholic press).

67   *Positio, Appendix 25* at 270 (reprinting Peter Gumpel, *Cornwell's Cheap Shot at Pius XII,* Crisis, December 1999).

68   Cornwell himself noted that the Vatican could not control the party and that many German Catholics left the Center Party and joined the National Socialists. Cornwell also noted that the Catholic Center Party, including former Chancellor Heinrich Brüning, voted in favor of Hitler's Enabling Bill of 1933. *Hitler's Pope* at 135-36. That was an embarrassment to the Holy See and hardly suggests that the party was willing to battle Hitler to the end. *See id.* at 144, 197.

69   William Rees-Mogg, *The Vatican's holy failure,* The Times (London), October 4, 1999.

70   *See* Vazsonyi at 58, 148. While all of these points were popular with German people, the term "social justice" had particular meaning to Catholics. This term was regularly used in the United States by both Catholic social activist Dorothy Day and controversial radio personality Fr. Charles Coughlin.

71   Godman at 9, 39. German bishops at one point considered mediation of the disputes with the Reich, but Secretary of State Pacelli insisted that the concordat was with the Holy See, not German bishops. *Vice Chancellor Papen to Ambassador Bergen,* Nov. 11, 1933, in Documents on German Foreign Policy, 1918-1945, Series C (1933-1937), vol. II, no. 61 (margin note). The likely reason for this insistence is concern that the Nazis would bully local clergy into compliance.

72   The German bishops spoke out more brazenly than any other group in Germany. Groppe, *The Church's Struggle with the Third Reich.*

73   *See* Second Vatican Council, *Pastoral Constitution on the Church in the Modern World* (Gaudium et Spes).

74   Article 16 of the concordat contained a pledge required of new bishops that they "swear and promise to honor the constitutional government and to cause the clergy of my diocese to honor it." Article 32 of the supplementary protocol, however made clear that the German clergy was not prohibited or even limited in preaching about "the dogmatic and moral teachings and principles of the Church." *The Persecution of the Catholic Church in the Third Reich* at 522 (reprinting the supplementary protocol). *See Controversial Concordats* at 209; Groppe, *The Church's Struggle with the Third Reich.*

75   Rychlak, *Hitler, the War, and the Pope* at 35-41. *See* Cornwell, *Hitler's Pope* at 172.

76   *See The Persecution of the Catholic Church in the Third Reich* at 522 (reprinting the supplementary protocol); The Second Vatican Council, *Pastoral Constitution on the Church in the Modern World* (Gaudium et Spes); *see also* Pius XI, *On Reconstruction of the Social Order* (Quadragesimo Anno) (1931).

77   In 1943, for instance, the German bishops issued a statement saying: "The extermination of human beings is per se wrong, even if it is purportedly done in the interests of society; but it is particularly evil if it is carried out against the innocent

and defenseless people of alien races or alien descent." Saperstein at 43. Since this statement related to morality, it was not restricted by the terms of the concordat.

78 Joseph L. Lichten, *A Question of Judgment: Pope Pius and the Jews*, originally released in pamphlet form by the National Catholic Welfare Conference. It was reprinted in *Pius XII and the Holocaust: A Reader*. *See also* Michaelis, *Mussolini and the Jews* (some 5,000 Italian Jews sought baptismal papers in hopes of surviving the Holocaust).

79 Shortly thereafter, Pope Pius XI three times led a prayer for peace, with direct reference to the Italian-Ethiopian conflict. McCormick at 67.

80 Cardinal Pacelli's speeches as Secretary of State (1930-1939) appear in *Discorsi e Panegirici* (Società Editrice: Milan, 1939). *See also* F. Murphy at 59; Hatch & Walshe at 116-17 (longer quotation).

81 *Nazis Warned in Lourdes*, The New York Times, April 29, 1935.

82 R. Stewart at 18. "While Pacelli had been at great pains to stress that this was a religious visit with no political overtures whatsoever, his sermon in Notre Dame Cathedral on 13 July belied that assurance when, to the delight of all shades of French opinion, he condemned nazi statolatry." Kent at 596.

83 F. Murphy at 59-60.

84 *Documents on German Foreign Policy 1918-1945*, Series D (1937-1945), vol. I, no. 672.

85 *Id.*, vol. I, no. 673.

86 F. Murphy at 60.

87 *Principles for Peace* at 540-543.

88 Cornwell set forth a similar argument on pages 185-186 of *Hitler's Pope*, but even Cornwell conceded that Pacelli never referred to Jews by name.

89 *See* pp. 32-37.

90 "The present Italian Minister of the Italian Defense... has a note claiming that the Italian government archives show Pacelli as the instigator of the Vatican boycott of Hitler's visit to Rome in May 1938." Purdy at 22.

91 Daniel-Rops at 313; Purdy at 22. In what appears to be a self-serving fabrication, some German officials explained away the Pope's slight by saying that he was offended by Hitler's refusal to meet with him, and that is why he left town and closed the museums. Message from German Ambassador to the Holy See (Bergen) to the German Foreign Ministry, dated May 23, 1938, *Documents on German Foreign Policy 1918-1945*, Series D (1937-1945), vol. I, no. 710.

92 Holmes at 73; Message from German Ambassador to the Holy See (Bergen) to the German Foreign Ministry, dated May 5, 1938, *Documents on German Foreign Policy 1918-1945*, Series D (1937-1945), vol. I, no. 706 (relaying the anti-Nazi sentiments of the Pope).

93 *See* pp. 42-43.

94 The "hidden encyclical" was made public in 1972 by the National Catholic Reporter and again in 1973 by *L'Osservatore Romano*, not (as Cornwell reported) in 1995. Burkhart Schneider, *Un'enciclica mancata*, *L'Osservatore Romano*, April 5, 1973; National Catholic Reporter, Dec. 15, 1972.

95 Sereny at 294.

96 *See* Gallo at 326-27, n. 56.

97 Passelecq & Suchecky at 81 ("Grundlach was convinced that the new pope knew nothing about the encyclical project.... Fr. Maher informed LaFarge... that the new pope had not yet become acquainted with [preparatory documents]"); *id.* at 82 (Gundlach... once again expressed... his conviction that 'nothing was transmitted' to Pius XII, and, as a result, 'our project has gone the way of all earthly things.'")

98   *See* pp. 91-99.

99   LaFarge wrote glowingly about *Summi Pontificatus*. He did, however call it "dangerous" because it so obviously addressed the racism that was spreading across Europe. Lafarge, *Mankind is called to unity in Christ*, America, November 11, 1939, at 120-121. The Vatican correspondent for the *New York Times* later wrote: "Stripped of its religious references, the encyclical was tantamount to a declaration of war on Germany and Russia." Cianfarra at 199.

100   *See Principles for Peace* at 587-88.

101   *Id.*

102   *Id.* at 588-89.

103   *Id.* at 589-90.

104   François Charles-Roux, *Huit Ans au Vatican, 1932-1940* 351-52 (Flammarion: Paris, 1947).

105   *The Tablet* (London), April 27, 1940, at 398. *The Tablet* also reported that: "the Osservatore Romano, the Vatican's newspaper, published important extracts from Cardinal Faulhaber's recent outspoken pastoral on the Encyclical Summi Pontificatus." *See La figura e l'opera di Pio XII, L'Osservatore Romano*, April 14, 1940, at 1.

106   *See* Claire Hulme and Michael Salter, *The Nazi's Persecution of Religion as a War Crime: The OSS's Response Within the Nuremberg Trial's Process*, 3 Rutgers J. Law & Relig. 4 (2001/2002).

107   *The Nazi Master Plan: The Persecution of the Christian Churches. See also* Harrigan at 185 (it was read in the Catholic Churches but the Gestapo prevented further distribution).

108   O'Carroll at 53. The German-controlled Polish newspapers took advantage of the lack of communication with the outside world to distort and falsify the attitude of the Holy See. The encyclical *Summi Pontificatus* was circulated in corrupted versions which seemed to make the Pope blame the Poles for their own predicament. Graham, *The Pope and Poland in World War Two* at 34. *See* Holmes at 124.

109   *SS Group Leader Heydrich to Reich Minister and Chief of the Reich Chancellery Lammers*, Federal Archives (Germany), Koblenz, R 43 II/1504 c, typed copy with enclosure (June 22, 1940).

110   *Daily Telegraph* (London), Oct. 28, 1939.

111   *New York Times*, Oct. 28, 1939.

112   Congregation for the Causes of Saints, *Positio*, appendix 25 at 271 (reprinting Peter Gumpel, *Cornwell's Cheap Shot at Pius XII*, Crisis, December 1999); Chadwick, *Britain and the Vatican During the Second World War* at 83-85; Gallo at 32.

113   *Address to the Sacred College of Cardinals on December 24, 1939*, Acta Apostolicae Sedis, volume 32, at. 5-13; *L'Osservatore Romano*, December 26-27, 1939, at 1-2.

114   *Quoted in* Purdy at 34.

115   Drew Pearson and Robert S. Allen, *Peace by Spring... The Goal of the Pope and Roosevelt*, Look, March 26, 1940, at 33.

116   *Roosevelt Aims at Sound Peace*, Christian Science Monitor, December 27, 1939.

117   *The Goebbels Diaries 1939-1941* at 75 (entry for December 27, 1939).

118   *New York Times*, Dec. 25, 1941. *See* Cianfarra at 319-29.

119   *New York Times*, Dec. 25, 1942.

120   *Time*, August 16, 1943.

121   Herbert L. Mathews, *Happier Days for Pope Pius: Shadows of war are lifting for a Pontiff whose greatest interest is world peace*, New York Times, Oct. 15, 1944, at 8.

5 *"Charity That Fears No Death"*

1 Lapide at 269.
2 *See* Malachi Martin, *The Keys of This Blood* at 637 (Pius XII "personally saved over 1.5 million Jews"); Burleigh, *The Cardinal Basil Hume Memorial Lectures*, 3 Totalitarian Movements and Political Religions at 38 ("hundreds of thousands"); *Historian Sir Martin Gilbert Defends Pius XII; Goebbels Saw in Him an Enemy of Nazism*, Zenit News Service, Feb. 20, 2003 (about 500,000). *See also* pp. 248, 344-45.
3 Lapide at 269
4 *Historian Sir Martin Gilbert Defends Pius XII; Goebbels Saw in Him an Enemy of Nazism*, Zenit News Service, Feb. 20, 2003
5 P. Murphy at 203.
6 Zolli at 141; Holmes at 152. *See* Leon Poliakov, *Harvest of Hate* (Philadelphia, 1954) at 293 ("We do not know what were the exact instructions sent by the Holy See to the churches in the different countries, but the coincidence of effort at the time of the deportations is proof that such steps were taken."); Gallo at 143 ("The Vatican Secretary of State wrote to all superiors of religious orders on October 25, 1943, urging them to help all refugees.") Years later, when the Israeli press asked why Christian rescuers had risked their lives for others, they frequently referred to Vatican orders issued in 1942 "to save lives by all possible means." Lapide at 134-35.
7 Gallo at 143.
8 Holmes at 152; Fogelman at 172. A list of 155 religious houses used to shelter can be found in *Actes et Documents,* vol. IX, no. 548.
9 McCormick at 118 (from a *New York Times* dispatch of August 24, 1944).
10 *See* Lapomarda at 234-35, n. 17 (referring to a list of 4,447 Jews who had been sheltered by religious groups). *See generally* Cardinal Pietro Palazzini, *Il clero e l'occupazione tedesca di Roma* (Editrice Apes: Rome, 1955); Antonio Gaspari, *Nascosti in convento. Incredibili storie di ebrei salvati dalla deportazione, Italia 1943-1945*, Editrice Áncora (Milan, 1999).
11 Gallo at 144. The Vatican also helped Jews escape to unoccupied areas. *Id.*
12 The pontiff also granted audiences to German soldiers, many of whom suffered from guilty consciences, until an order from the German High Command prohibited them from entering the Vatican. In his diary, on April 5, 1942, Joseph Goebbels wrote that he urged the Führer to forbid German soldiers from visiting the Pope because Pius was using these opportunities for propaganda that was in conflict with Nazi aims. *The Goebbels Diaries 1942–1943* at 161. "The SS was certain that the Vatican was the center of anti-German espionage." Gallo at 146.
13 This rarely noted act was reported by Senator Adriano Ossicini, founder of the "Christian Left" in Italy, who was arrested in 1943 due to his opposition to the Fascist regime. *More Echoes on Pope Pius XII, Nazi Holocaust*, Catholic World News, June 27, 1996 ("On the eve of one massive police sweep... the hospital received direct orders from Pope Pius XII to admit as many Jews as possible immediately.")
14 Zolli at 187; Lapide at 132-33.
15 Blet, chapter 10.
16 Stille at 270.
17 *Id.* at 270-71. Stille tells the story of a woman who had not revealed that she was Jewish to the nuns sheltering her. The mother superior severely reprimanded her when she discovered this fact. The woman offered to leave, but the mother superior said: "No, it's not that, we just need to know so that if they come for you, we can

take you down a secret passageway." *Id.* at 216 ("the nuns were incredibly good and courteous to us.")

18 *See* Marchione, *Yours is a Precious Witness* (photo section).

19 Emilio Bonomelli, *I Papi in Campagna* 439 (Gherardo Casini Editore, Rome, 1953). When American soldiers (Special Forces) were housed in Castel Gandolfo, they "liberated" some of the Pope's furniture and other property. When the officers found out, they made sure that all of the property was returned. Robert H. Adleman & Col. George Walton, *The Devil's Brigade* 205-06 (1966).

20 Leboucher at 137.

21 Catholic World News, *Castel Gandalfo Celebrates 400 Years as Papal Residence*, December 31, 1996 ("During the pontificate of Pius xii in World War II, for example, 12,000 people took refuge in Castel Gandolfo, and the papal apartments were opened up to shelter pregnant women nearing the days of childbirth; some 40 infants were born there."); Jason Berry, *Papal Lives: Biographies of Pius xii and John Paul II examine 2 of the century's most controversial men of the cloth*, Chicago Tribune, October 24, 1999, section 14, p.1.

22 Marchione, *Pope Pius xii: Architect for Peace* at 134 (citing John S. Rader and Kateryna Fedoryka, *The Pope and the Holocaust*).

23 *From Hitler's Doorstep: The Wartime Intelligence Reports of Allen Dulles, 1942-1945* 237 (Pennsylvania State University Press, Neal H. Peterson, ed. 1996) (Document 3-43, Telegram 2341, March 9, 1944). This document is reprinted in the appendix.

24 Congregation for the Causes of Saints, *Positio*, (Summarium) Testimony of P. Guglielmo Hentrich, before the Ecclesiastical Tribunal of Rome, on the beatification of Pius xii (Eugenio Pacelli).

25 Lamb at 39.

26 Holmes at 153.

27 Mary DeTurris, *The Vatican and the Holocaust*, Our Sunday Visitor, May 18, 1997.

28 Fr. Peter Gumpel, the relator of Pope Pius xii's sainthood cause took part in this activity, escorting Jews from Holland to Belgium. *See* pp. 249-51.

29 Blet, Chapter 11; Rychlak, *Hitler, the War, and the Pope* at 365, n.94.

30 Gallo at 146. Critics often overlook this intimidation when speculating about what should have been done during the war.

31 Though at one point, Pius ordered the Swiss Guard to replace the pikes with machine guns. Rychlak, *Hitler, the War, and the Pope* at 202, 211.

32 "The Vatican itself at times contained more Jews than Christians, and paralegal means were found to protect Jews who could not be so accommodated. For example, there has existed for centuries an honorary institution of papal guards called the 'Palatine Guards,' membership which confers, automatically, Vatican citizenship. Because of the unusual immunities and privileges such citizenship implies, the number of Palatine Guards has always been kept to a minimum. In 1942, for instance, there were only some three hundred members. Between 1942, when the Germans began to apply pressure on Mussolini to enforce the anti-Semitic laws, and the end of 1943, when the persecution was at its most intense, the Germans noted that the Palatine Guard had grown to four-thousand members–all beyond the reach of the Gestapo. Their indignation knew no bounds when it was discovered that many hundreds of these papal guards were unbaptised Jews. At that point, fearing that Vatican citizenship might not be sufficient to protect the most desperately sought Jews among his guards, Pius xii ordered that some two hundred and fifty be quartered in the Vatican itself." Leboucher at 138.

33 *Actes et Documents*, Vol. IX, p. 501-02 (no. 364).

34 Of course, it is entirely possible that not all of these people actually went through baptism ceremonies. It was not unusual for Catholic officials to provide certificates to Jewish people solely to help them avoid Nazi persecution.

35 *See* Rychlak, *Hitler, the War, and the Pope* at 222.

36 John Thavis, *Jesuit journal cites new evidence that Pius xii helped save Jews*, Catholic News Service, December 4, 2003; Giovanni Sale La Civilta Cattolica, December 5, 2003.

37 *See* Rychlak, *Hitler, the War, and the Pope*, at 414-15, n. 61.

38 As a young priest, the future Pope John Paul ii refused to baptize a Jewish child who was being sheltered by a Catholic family for this very reason. *When Karol Wojtyla Refused to Baptize an Orphan*, Zenit News Service, Jan. 18, 2005.

39 Lapide at 210.

40 Tec at 187 (also noting that most Jewish survivors who had been sheltered by the Catholic Church "derived much comfort from the Catholic religion").

41 Elaine Sciolino & Jason Horowitz, *Saving Jewish Children, but at What Cost?*, The New York Times, January 9, 2005.

42 *See* Ronald J. Rychlak, *Postwar Catholics, Jewish Children, and a Rush to Judgment*, beliefnet.com (posted January 18, 2005) and reprinted in Inside the Vatican, March 2005; Mary Jo Anderson, Pius xii: *Saintly defender of European Jews*, WorldNetDaily, January 17, 2005.

43 *See* pp. 8-9.

44 Daniel Jonah Goldhagen, *If This Is a Saint...*, The Forward, January 2005. In this article and in the Italian newspaper *Il Corriere della Sera*, Goldhagen called for the establishment of an international commission to investigate the Catholic Church's handling of Jewish children. He used the new memo to call Pius xii an "anti-Semitic pope" who was "one of the most rampant would-be kidnappers of modern times." Goldhagen argued that the memo "reveals that the pope's and the church's policy was, in effect, to kidnap Jewish children, perhaps by the thousands.... Its plain purpose was to implement a plan that would cruelly victimize the Jews a second time by depriving these bodily and spiritually wounded survivors of the Nazi hell of their own children." He concluded by telling the Church of today that it "should cease efforts to canonize Pius xii." Rabbi Boteach wrote that "Pius ordered the mass kidnapping of hundreds of thousands of Jewish children...." Shmuley Boteach, *Pius xii: Collaborator and Kidnapper*, WorldNetDaily, January 13, 2005.

45 *See* Edward Pentin, *Pius xii Postulator Dismisses Jewish Baptism Document as 'Hoax'*, National Catholic Register, Jan. 23-29, 2005, at 4.

46 *Experts React to a Row Over Jewish Children Rescued by Church Doubts Raised About Alleged Vatican Document*, Zenit News Service, Jan. 11, 2005.

47 *1946 Document on Jewish Children Tells a Different Story: Undercuts Tale That Vatican Tried to Keep Them From Their Families*, Zenit News Service. Jan. 12, 2005.

48 Lapide at 209-10.

49 Hellman at 69.

50 *See* Ronald J. Rychlak, *Jewish Children after World War II: A Case Study*, beliefnet. com, January 18, 2004.

51 As this wording implies, to the Catholic Church, and in contrast with Nazi philosophy, Jewishness is a matter of religion, not race.

52 Joseph L. Lichten, *A Question of Judgement: Pope Pius and the Jews*, originally released in pamphlet form by the National Catholic Welfare Conference. It was reprinted in *Pius xii and the Holocaust: A Reader*, Catholic League Publications (Milwaukee, 1988). *See also* Meir Michaelis, *Mussolini and the Jews: German-Italian Relations and*

the *Jewish Question in Italy 1922-25*, 1978 (some 5,000 Italian Jews sought baptismal papers in hopes of surviving the Holocaust).

53 *See* p. 103.
54 Graham, *The Pope and Poland in World War Two* at 56.
55 *E.g.*, Lapide at 159; O'Carroll at 99. The official records indicate that 4,770 Jews were baptized in Budapest during this time, but that 80,000 baptismal certificates were distributed. Graham, *Pope Pius XII and the Jews of Hungary in 1944* at 17; O'Carroll at 104.
56 Godman at 33.
57 *Id.*
58 Irene Marinoff, *The Heresy of National Socialism* (Burns, Oates, & Washburn, "Publishers to the Holy See," 1941) (with a foreword by Archbishop Richard Downey of Liverpool).
59 *Current Biography 1941*, The H.W. Wilson Co. (Maxine Block, ed., 1971 re-issue).
60 Speaight at 3.
61 Gallo at 33. "On January 20, 1940, an American Jesuit became the first announcer in world radio to report the imprisonment of Jewish and Polish prisoners in 'sealed ghettos.' From that point on, Vatican Radio continued to feature stories on concentration camps and other Nazi torture chambers. From 1940 to 1946, Vatican Radio also ran an Information Office, transmitting almost 1.25 million shortwave messages to locate prisoners of war and other missing persons. Later the radio station combined its information services with the International Refugee Organization, forming a team Tracing Service to reunite war-torn families and friends." Marilyn J. Matelski, *Messages From the Underground* 6 (Praeger: Westport, 1997). *See also* Marilyn J. Matelski, *Vatican Radio: Propagation by the Airwaves* (Praeger: Westport, 1995). Vatican Radio broadcast 1.2 million shortwave messages asking for information about missing individuals. Margherita Marchione, *John Cornwell's Crusade Against the Papacy*, National Catholic Register, Jan. 23-29, 2005 at 9.
62 *See generally*, Speaight, *Voice of the Vatican*; Beales, *The Pope and the Jews.*
63 *La Civiltà Cattolica*, Jan. 17, 1976. *Actes et Documents*, vol. III, no. 102, at. 204 (Montini's notes on Pius XII's directives for Vatican Radio). *Pope Pius and Poland*, published by The America Press (New York) in 1942, covers Pius XII's many and explicit condemnations of Nazi atrocities in the first years of the conflict. It provides precise titles and dates of broadcasts and summarizes Vatican Radio's anti-Nazi broadcasts of January 13, 20, 27, April 25, December 20, 1940; and March 28 and April 4, 1941. *See also* Rychlak, *Hitler, the War, and the Pope* at 102, 119, 128, 135, 144, 149-51, 156-58, 167, 177, 187, 192, 195-96, 235 (various broadcasts).
64 *See* p. 119.
65 Alvarez & Graham, at 143. *See, e.g., Actes et Documents*, vol. IV, no. 140.
66 *Catholic Historian's Report Details Perils of 'Martyrs of Vatican Radio'*, The National Catholic Register, Feb. 1, 1976.
67 *Id. See also The Persecution of the Catholic Church in German-Occupied Poland: Reports by H.E. Cardinal Hlond, Primate of Poland, to Pope Pius XII, Vatican Broadcasts and Other Reliable Evidence.*
68 *See* Robert Graham, *La Radio Vaticana tra Londra e Berlino: Un dossier della guerra delle onde: 1940-1941*, in 1 *La Civiltà Cattolica*, 132 (1976); *Actes et Documents*, vol. III, no. 102, at. 204 (Montini's notes on Pius XII's directives for Vatican Radio).
69 *Catholic Historian's Report Details Perils of 'Martyrs of Vatican Radio'*, The National Catholic Register, Feb. 1, 1976.
70 *Actes et Documents*, vol. III, no. 102, at. 204 (Montini's notes on Pius XII's directives for Vatican Radio).

71   This same month, Pope Pius XII ordered the publication of a large volume (565 pages) of eyewitness accounts of the German efforts to crush the Church.

72   *Rome and Detroit*, American Israelite, March 14, 1940.

73   *"Let's Look at the Record"*, Inside the Vatican, October 1999, at XI.

74   Blet, Chapter 4 (quoting the *Manchester Guardian*).

75   Cornwell at 227. The Germans ultimately decided that due to the anti-German attitude of the Vatican's press and radio, Catholic priests and members of religious orders in occupied Poland would be prohibited from leaving that country. Blet, Chapter 4.

76   *Inside the Vatican of Pius XII* at 112.

77   *Id.*

78   *Vatican Radio Denounces Nazi Acts in Poland*, The Jewish Advocate (Boston, Mass.), January 26, 1940.

79   *Jewish Ledger* (Hartford, Conn), on Jan. 19, 1940.

80   Daniel Jonah Goldhagen, *What Would Jesus Have Done?* The New Republic, January 21, 2002.

81   *Vatican Radio Denounces Nazi Acts in Poland*, The Jewish Advocate (Boston), January 29, 1940, at 1. The entire text of the broadcast of January 21-22, 1940, intended for American broadcast, can be found in *The Persecution of the Catholic Church in German-Occupied Poland* at 115-17. The story was also reported in the January 23 edition of the *New York Times*, under the headline: "Vatican Denounces Atrocities in Poland; Germans Called Even Worse than Russians." A separate story in that same edition of the *Times* reported that a Soviet newspaper had labeled Pius the "tool of Great Britain and France." (At that time, the Soviets were still on better terms with the Germans than with the Allies.)

82   Blet at 99.

83   The broadcast said that "with violence and with singular ability, this literature has attacked Christianity and the Catholic Church both as a whole and in its personnel and institutions. It has even attacked the most essential dogmas of the Church. This attack has been carried out with the greatest possible efficiency, while the Church has been hindered from the self-defense it should properly have employed." It continued: "if National Socialism is a Christian movement as Alcazar alleges, what is the explanation of the fact that, whereas in 1933 almost the entire Catholic youth was educated in Catholic schools, the whole magnificent school organization is now practically non-existent?" The broadcast concluded with a broad hint to the Spanish Catholics: "There is not in Poland the flourishing religious life the writer of this report would have us believe. Rather the Catholics of Poland have grave need of the Catholics of the whole world to sustain them in their trial."

84   Quoted from a transcript of a Vatican Radio broadcast, in The Tablet (of London), April 5, 1941, at 264.

85   These pamphlets were published from 1940 until late 1942, with a suspension in publication between May and September of 1941. *See* René Bédarida, *La Voix du Vatican, 1940-1942, Bataille des ondes et résistance spirituelle*, in *Revue d'histoire de l'Eglise de France*, vol. 64 (July-Dec, 1978), pp.215-243. The original papers have been hard to find, because only a limited number of each issue was printed (800-900 at first, later about 1500) and few people kept them due to fear of persecution.

86   Mistiaen had close connections with high members of Pope Pius XII's staff. *See* Lapomarda at 242. *See also* Chadwick, *Weizsäcker, the Vatican* at 141-42.

87   *See Actes et Documents*, vol. 4, pages 18-29 (various German protests).

88 *The Tablet* (London) September 28, 1940, at 252. Nuncio Valeri also contacted Pétain, demanding that the deportations end.

89 Michel Riquet, *Chrétiens de France dans l'Europe enchaînée* 98 (SOS: Paris, 1973); Lacouture at 387 (footnote).

90 *La Voix du Vatican* # 23, Vatican Radio broadcast of April 29, 1942. *See* pp. 165-66. Similarly, on October 15, 1942 Fr. Mistiaen spoke on behalf of Jewish victims of the Nazis, saying: "All men are the children of the same Father.... They are no longer Jews, Greeks, gentiles, they are only candidates to the universal redemption brought by Jesus Christ." *La Voix du Vatican* # 30, Vatican Radio broadcast of October 15, 1942.

91 Holmes at 164-65. *See also* George Kent, *Shepherds of the Underground*, The Christian Herald, April 1945. Numerous other courageous statements from French bishops are set forth in Susan Zuccotti, *Pope Pius XII and the Holocaust: The Case in Italy*, in *The Italian Refuge*, at 257.

92 Lubac at 118-22.

93 *La Voix du Vatican* # 28.

94 *La Voix du Vatican* # 28, Vatican Radio broadcast of September 14, 1942.

95 Bruno de Solages, *Discours interdits* 80 (Spes: Paris, 1945).

96 *See Catholic Historian's Report Details Perils of 'Martyrs of Vatican Radio'*, The National Catholic Register, Feb. 1, 1976.

97 In 1943, Vatican Radio broadcast Croatian Cardinal Stepinac's sermons attacking the persecution of the Jews.

98 This was quoted in the *American Jewish Year Book, 1943-1944*, as well as *The New York Times* (June 27, 1943).

99 Wistrich at 144-45.

100 *Is the Catholic Church Anti-Social? A Debate Between G.G. Coulton and Arnold Lunn* 193 (The Catholic Book Club: London, 1947).

101 *The New York Times*, February 9, 1944, at 7.

102 Lubac, *Christian Resistance to Anti-Semitism* at 118-22.

103 Figaro, January 4, 1964. *See also Letters to the Editor: Pope Pius XII: An Eyewitness*, Inside the Vatican, January 2000 at 10 (a former seminarian in Rome tells of papal orders to shelter Jewish victims and of reports given on Vatican Radio).

104 Lapide at 254.

105 The President's Personal Representative to Pope Pius XII (Taylor) to the Cardinal Secretary of State (Maglione), Sept. 26, 1942, in *Foreign Relations of the United States, Diplomatic Papers, 1942, vol. III (Europe)*, United States Government Printing Office (Washington, 1961) at 775.

106 Telegram from the Minister in Switzerland (Harrison) to the Secretary of State, Oct. 16, 1942, in *Foreign Relations of the United States, Diplomatic Papers, 1942, vol. III (Europe)*, United States Government Printing Office (Washington, 1961) at 777 (going on to suggest that "there is little hope of checking Nazi barbarities by any method except that of physical force coming from without").

107 The Catholic News, November 21, 1942, *reprinted in* Secretariat for Ecumenical and Interreligious Affairs, National Conference of Bishops, *Catholics Remember the Holocaust*, United States Catholic Conference (Washington, 1998) at 17.

108 *Holy Father Extends Thanks to American Catholics for Aid*, The Catholic News, November 21, 1942.

109 *Id.*

110 Timothy A. Byrnes, *Catholic Bishops in American Politics*, Princeton University Press (Princeton, 1991). In 2002, I was given access to archives containing the papers of

Cardinal Spellman at St. Joseph's Seminary in Dunwoodie, New York. They reveal that Spellman played an important role in helping Pius XII coordinate efforts with President Roosevelt. For instance, in the autumn of 1942, Spellman (then archbishop) traveled to Washington, D.C. for a private meeting in the White House with President Roosevelt and Winston Churchill. *See* Florence D. Cohalan, *A Popular History of the Archdiocese of New York* 286 (U.S. Catholic Historical Society, 1983). On October 19, Myron Taylor (President Roosevelt's personal representative to Pius) sent a note to Spellman in which he said he would accept Spellman's advice and not take with him to Italy a certain manuscript that Spellman had given to him. Taylor was afraid that it might fall into Fascist hands. The note in question seems to be one contained in the Spellman archives that details Pius XII's close cooperation with Roosevelt.

The Nazis knew of Spellman's work for the Pope and against them, so they spied on him. Congregation for the Causes of Saints, *Positio*, appendix 25 at 245 (reprinting the prologue to Levai, *Hungarian Jewry and the Papacy: Pope Pius did not Remain Silent*). Ultimately, Cardinal Spellman was influential in selecting the scholars who would investigate the life of Pope Pius XII for the Congregation for the Causes of Saints. Congregation for the Causes of Saints, *Positio*, statement of the relator, p. 4.

111 *See* Gallo at 34 ("Those Bishops who had not fled from Poland begged the Pope not to make further protests because they felt it aggravated the situation and would only lead to further persecution.")

112 Blet, Chapter 6.

113 The British Chargé d'Affaires reported back to London that Pius felt that his broadcast of May 13 had already condemned the Nazis, and he had sent messages of consolation to various Polish priests. Pius did not see how he could do more. *Enclosure in Mr. Osborne's Dispatch No. 111 of September 11, 1942*, British Public Records Office, FO371/334148 56879; *Letter from Osborne to Mr. Howard*, July 12, 1942, British Public Records Office, FO371/33426 65042 (similar message).

114 *See* Telegram from the Minister in Switzerland (Harrison) to the Secretary of State, August 3, 1943, in *Foreign Relations of the United States, Diplomatic Papers, 1942, vol. III (Europe)*, United States Government Printing Office (Washington, 1961) at 772 expressing concern over the lack of a statement).

115 Mr. Harold H. Tittmann, Assistant to the President's Personal Representative to Pope Pius, to the Secretary of State, Oct. 6, 1942, in *Foreign Relations of the United States, Diplomatic Papers, 1942, vol. III (Europe)*, United States Government Printing Office (Washington, 1961) at 776.

116 *Outward Telegram*, FO 371/34363 59337 (January 10, 1943). *See also Political Distribution from Switzerland from Berne to Foreign Office*, January 5, 1943, FO 371/34363 59337 (similar).

117 *A Summary of the Conversations between His Holiness Pope Pius XII and Myron Taylor, Personal Representative of the President of the United States to His Holiness Pope Pius XII at Vatican City, September 19, 22, and 26, 1942*, p. 5. Posted on the Internet by the Franklin D. Roosevelt Library <<www.fdrlibrary.marist.edu/psf/box52/a467e01.html>>.

118 *Id.* at 5-6.

119 *Id.* at p. 11.

120 *Id.* at 13.

121 Wyman at 76. *See* Marchione *Pope Pius XII: Architect for Peace* (Church, Shoah, and Anti-Semitism) (suggesting that the Pope would have been reckless to have joined in the statement).

122 Of course, most careful observers saw through the official neutrality. Barrett McGurn, *A Reporter Looks at the Vatican* 92 (1962) ("On World War II and the East-West Cold War Pius was neutral in theory but warmly pro-Western in fact."). He "would not stay neutral in the sense of putting good and evil on the same footing." *Id.* at 93. In fact, there was "a virtual wholehearted endorsement of the Allies' World War II Atlantic Charter, Marshall Plan for postwar aid to Europe, the United Nations, the Atlantic Alliance, and the American-advocated drive to unite Western Europe economically and politically." *Id.* at 93.
　　Pius actually preferred the term impartiality to neutrality. He felt that neutrality implied passive indifference, while impartiality meant judging events according to the truth and justice. *Letter of Pius XII to Cardinal Faulhaber*, January 31, 1943, *Actes et Documents*, vol. 2, no. 96, p. 293. *See* Conway, *The Vatican, Germany and the Holocaust*, in *Papal Diplomacy in the Modern Age* at 111-12.

123 Additionally, to the extent that the appeal related to a statement for American consumption, Pius worked with the American bishops to help them make a very strong statement. The Catholic News, November 21, 1942, *reprinted in* Secretariat for Ecumenical and Interreligious Affairs, National Conference of Bishops, *Catholics Remember the Holocaust*, United States Catholic Conference (Washington, 1998) at 17. *See* p. 120.

124 *The Rights of Man*, broadcast of Pope Pius XII, Christmas 1942. The original Italian was published in the official Acta Apostolicae Sedis of 1943 (Volume 35, pp.5-8); *Pius XII: Selected Encyclicals and Addresses* 275-97 (Catholic Truth Society: London, 1949).

125 *The Rights of Man*, broadcast of Pope Pius XII, Christmas 1942.

126 This message was delivered on February 20, 1943. Blet, Chapter 4.

127 British Public Record Office, FO 371/34363 59337 (January 5, 1943).

128 Lapide at 201. For further details about the anti-Nazi Catholic Resistance in the Netherlands, see L. Bleys, *Resistance in the Netherlands*, The Tablet of London, October 14, 1944, at 186 (eyewitness account by a Dutch resistance priest, in which he provides details of how Pius XII communicated his support to Dutch Catholics fighting Nazism.) "In no other country, said the Pope, have the Bishops guided the faithful so clearly, so unanimously and so courageously in the battle against the errors of National Socialism." *Id.*

129 *New York Times*, December 25, 1942.

130 *A Vatican Visit*, The London Times, October 11, 1942. *See also* Gilbert, *The Righteous* at 357-358.

131 *Quoted in* Rhodes at 272-73 (citing German archives: A.A. Abteilung Inland, pak. 17, vol.I, January 22, 1943); *See also* Holmes at 140.

132 *Telegram from the Minister in Switzerland (Harrison) to the Secretary of State*, Jan. 5, 1943, in *Foreign Relations of the United States, Diplomatic Papers, 1943, vol. II (Europe)*, United States Government Printing Office (Washington, 1964) at 91.

133 *Telegram from the German Ambassador (Bergen) to the Reich Minister*, dated January 26, 1943, NARA, T-120, Roll 361, at 277668-70; Holmes, *The Papacy in the Modern World* at 140.

134 *See* pp. 211-12.

135 The full text of the address appears in Margherita Marchione, *Pope Pius XII: Architect for Peace* at 143-152. *See also* Office of the United States Chief Counsel, vol. I, at 285-86; Shirer, *The Rise and Fall of the Third Reich* at 324-25 (footnote); Purdy at 43.

136 *For Berlin, Pius XII Was a Subversive: Radio Operator's Experience of Spreading Papal Christmas Message*, May 14, 2002 (Zenit News Service).

137 Congregation for the Causes of Saints, *Positio* (Summarium), Testimony of Karl Otto Wolff, March 14, 1972, before the Ecclesiastical Tribunal of Munich, on the beatification of Pius XII (Eugenio Pacelli) at 825. Wolff "against Hitler's will and without his knowledge" played a decisive part in bringing about the surrender of the German armies in Italy. At the time of his first contact with Allied representatives, Wolff had promised to protect the lives of political prisoners in the area under his command. *They Almost Killed Hitler: Based on the Personal Account of Fabian von Schlabrendorff* at 4 (explaining that he did, indeed, protect the prisoners); Simpson at 186 (those in the Vatican knew it was possible that he would invade).

138 Rychlak, *Hitler, the War, and the Pope* at 264-66; Weizsäcker, *Memoirs of Ernst Von Weizsäcker* at 291; Holmes at 155-56; Payne at 485 (quoting Hitler: "Do you think I worry about the Vatican? We can wrap it up at once! The whole diplomatic corps will be there! I don't give a damn!... we'll apologize later. That's all right. There is a war on!")

139 Congregation for the Causes of Saints, *Positio* (Summarium), Testimony of Karl Otto Wolff, March 14, 1972, before the Ecclesiastical Tribunal of Munich, on the beatification of Pius XII (Eugenio Pacelli) at 825; Rychlak, *Hitler, the War, and the Pope* at 420-21, n. 145.

140 *See* Gallo at 48 (an "unequivocal condemnation of the Nazis 'euthanasia' program").

141 Lapide at 251.

142 The numerous translation errors created by papal critics reveal a particular problem with the normal approach to history. Knowledge of a language does not necessarily correlate with an understanding of the nuances of that language. *See* John L. Allen Jr., *All the Pope's Men: The Inside Story of How the Vatican Really Thinks* (2004). For instance, it seems likely that critic John Cornwell intentionally misrepresented Pacelli's 1919 letter back to Rome. *See* pp. 79-81. Critic Daniel Goldhagen seems not to have done any original work on this matter, and he just blindly accepted Cornwell's misrepresentation. Knowledge of language in situations like that makes little difference. On the other hand, it seems unlikely that Susan Zuccotti would have made such a major and ultimately foolish point over the Pope's use of the wore "stirpe" (*see* pp. 211-12) unless she thought that she understood technical differences in the meanings between very similar foreign words.

143 Mystici Corporis Christi also strongly condemned the forced conversions to Catholicism that were then occurring in Fascist Croatia, which critics like Daniel Goldhagen wrongly claim enjoyed Vatican support. *See* pp. 127-29.

144 The New York Times, June 27, 1943, at 16; *The American Jewish Yearbook, 1943-1944* 292 (Jewish Publication Society: Philadelphia).

145 Cianfarra at 315-16. Pius also embraced democratic ideals in his 1944 Christmas message. *See* McCormick at 125-27 (calling the papal message "a deeply pondered pontifical pronouncement in favor of democracy in the interests of the 'individual himself....'")

146 The Chief Rabbi of Rome, Israel (later Eugenio) Zolli, who approached the Vatican on behalf of the Jewish community for a loan of gold, wrote of this episode in his memoirs. Zolli at 160-61.

147 Susan Zuccotti, *Pope Pius XII and the Holocaust: The Case in Italy*, in *The Italian Refuge* at 254.

148 This message is the source of the title of one of Zuccotti's books. The memo was actually an attempt by Weizsäcker to convince Berlin not to launch an attack on the Vatican. He downplayed the papal reaction for that purpose. Congregation for the Causes of Saints, *Positio*, appendix 25 at 273 (reprinting Peter Gumpel, *Cornwell's Cheap Shot at Pius xii*, Crisis, December 1999); Ivo Herzer, *The Italian Refuge* 121 (Catholic University Press of America, 1989); Gallo at 136; Rychlak *Hitler, the War, and the Pope* at 208.

149 Katz, *Black Sabbath: A Journey Through a Crime Against Humanity* at 134-39. The Pacelli family later sued Katz for defamation. *See* pp. 240-44.

150 *See* Congregation for the Causes of Saints, *Positio*, appendix 25 at 264.

151 Ernst Von Weizsäcker, *Memoirs of Ernst Von Weizsäcker* (H. Regnery Co., Chicago, J. Andrews trans. 1951).

152 Congregation for the Causes of Saints, *Positio*, appendix 25 at 264 (quoting a *New York Times* book review from August 31, 1969). For the Vatican's record during the round-up, *see* Giovanni Sale, *Roma 1943: occupazione nazista e deportazione degli ebrei romani*, Civiltà Cattolica, 2003, vol. 4, at 417-29.

153 *See* Chadwick, *A History of Christianity* at 190; Owen Chadwick, *Weizsäcker, the Vatican, and the Jews of Rome*, 28 Journal of Ecclesiastical History 179 (April 1977) ("The pope was obviously surprised. He said that the Germans promised that they would not hurt the Jews, and knew of the 50 kilograms of gold."); Robert Graham, *La Strana Condotta di E. Von Weizsäcker ambasciatore del Reich in Vaticano*, La Civiltà Cattolica, June 6, 1970, at 455-471; Gallo at 134; Congregation for the Causes of Saints, *Positio*, appendix 25 at 260.

154 Princess Enza Pignatelli Aragona Cortés, taped interview for the documentary "History Undercover: Pope Pius xii and the Holocaust" (1997, A&E Home Video); Dan Kurzman, *The Race for Rome* (Doubleday: Garden City, 1975); , p. xxxi). *See also L'Osservatore Romano*, October 25-26, 1943 ("With the augmentation of so much evil, the universal and paternal charity of the Supreme Pontiff has become, it might be said, ever more active; it knows neither boundaries nor nationality, neither religion nor race."); Zuccotti, *Pope Pius xii and the Holocaust: The Case in Italy*, in *The Italian Refuge* at 255.

155 Congregation for the Causes of Saints, *Positio*, appendix 25 at 261; *Actes et Documents*, vol. IX, no. 368. An editorial in *The Jewish Chronicle* (London) of October 29, 1943, entitled *Jewish Hostages in Rome: Vatican Protests*, said: "The Vatican has made strong representations to the German Government and the German High Command in Italy against the persecution of the Jews in Nazi occupied Italy."

156 *Diplomatic (Secret) Telegram from Osborne to Foreign Office*, October 31, 1943, British Public Record Office, FO 371/37255 56879.

157 *Id.* ("Vatican intervention thus seems to have been effective in saving a number of these unfortunate people.")

158 Zenit Daily Dispatch, *Eichmann's Diary Reveals Church's Assistance to Jews*, March 1, 2000.

159 *Id.*

160 *See Dragnet: The Last Acceptable Bigotry*, This Rock, April 2000, at 7, 9 (quoting Eichmann's memoirs).

161 State of Israel Ministry of Justice, *The Trial of Adolf Eichmann: Record of Proceedings in the District Court of Jerusalem (Vol. I)* 83 (Jerusalem, 1992). A report from Rome to Berlin, dated October 26, 1943, confirmed that the "VATICAN has apparently for a long time been assisting many Jews escape. The fear is growing that further

actions to transport factory hands and workers are planned." *National Archives & Records Administration, CIA Selected Documents, 1941-1947*, Box 4, Group XIII/52, Rome to Berlin, RSS 210.26.19/43; Joseph Bottum, *The End of the Pius Wars*, First Things, April 2004, at 18, 34 (quoting this dispatch).

162 Gaspari, *Gli ebrei salvati da Pio XII*; Zenit News Service, *New Revelations on Jews Saved by Pius XII*, Feb. 16, 2001.

163 State of Israel Ministry of Justice, *The Trial of Adolf Eichmann: Record of Proceedings in the District Court of Jerusalem (Vol. IV)* 1504-05 (Jerusalem, 1992).

164 Antonio Gaspari, *The Jews Saved by Pius XII* (Gli ebrei salvati da Pio XII) (2001); Zenit News Service, *New Revelations on Jews Saved by Pius XII*, Feb. 16, 2001.

165 Zuccotti, *Under His Very Windows* at 169.

166 Congregation for the Causes of Saints, *Positio*, appendix 25 at 261; Andrea Tornielli, *Pio XII. Papa degli ebrei* (Piemme, 2001); *see also* Leonidas E. Hill III, *The Vatican Embassy of Ernst von Weizsäcker, 1939-1945*, 39 Journal of Modern History, 138, 148 (1967).

167 Congregation for the Causes of Saints, *Positio*, appendix 25 at 237 (noting that this was confirmed by one of Stahel's assistants in an interview with the German news agency KNA). *See also L'Osservatore Romano*, December 8, 2000, at 4.

168 *Actes et Documents*, vol. 9, no. 373, n.4 (emphasis added). As revealed in newly unsealed archives, Hudal, who helped Nazi war criminals escape justice at the end of the war, was not a supporter of the Nazis early in the war. Later, he was "kept at arms length" from positions of responsibility because the Pope and his Secretary of State did not trust him. Godman at 169.

169 *See Most of Rome's Jews Were Saved from Hitler's Final Solution, L'Osservatore Romano*, weekly edition in English, January 24, 2001 at 11 (translation of Kunkel's interview with KNA).

170 *Interview*, Zenit News Agency, Oct. 26, 2000 (emphasis added). *See* Congregation for the Causes of Saints, *Positio*, appendix 25, p 291.

171 *La strage degli innocenti, L'Osservatore Romano*, October 25-26, 1943.

172 Jewish Chronicle (London), October 29, 1943.

173 Gallo at 135 (quoting *L'Osservatore Romano* of October 25, 1943).

174 Professor Owen Chadwick of Cambridge dismissed Zuccotti's arguments as "not history but guesswork." *Pius XII's Terrifying Dilemma: Put Yourself in His Shoes*, The Tablet (of London), June 30, 2001, at 950-951.

175 Zuccotti, *The Italians and the Holocaust* at 127.

176 *Id.* at 303, n.69.

177 According to the Jesuit magazine *La Civiltà Cattolica*, the pope was informed of the roundup only after it had been completed. The pope immediately sent his a nephew to intercede with influential German church officials in Rome, to attempt to help the detained Jews and to prevent another such operation in the city. Whatever the reasons, the magazine reported that the roundup ended immediately and about 8,000 Roman Jews "miraculously had their lives saved." John Thavis, *Jesuit journal cites new evidence that Pius XII helped save Jews*, Catholic News Service, December 4, 2003; Giovanni Sale, *La Civiltà Cattolica*, December 5, 2003.

178 Cornwell, *Hitler's Pope* at 309 (citing Robert Katz, *Black Sabbath* at 259). In an example of circular scholarship, Cornwell and Zuccotti relied on Katz's work, which pre-dates the release of most relevant documents. In his newest book, Katz now relies on Cornwell and Zuccotti.

179 This is made clear in the diary of the Maestro di Camera (master of the chamber). The Maestro di Camera arranges audiences and pontifical ceremonies, and he keeps very detailed records of these matters. *See also* Note de Mgr. Tardini, *Actes et Docu-*

ments, vol. VII, p. 678, note 1 (noting Tittmann's mistake); *Actes et Documents*, vol. IX, p. 489-90 (noting the meeting on the 14th); Gallo at 323, n. 27.

180 *Nostre Informazioni, L'Osservatore Romano*, October 15, 1943, at 1. Tittmann's memoirs confirm that the resistance from within Germany encourage Pope Pius XII not to make more express condemnations regarding Nazi brutality. Writing in 1945 of German lawyer Joseph Mueller, who was very active in the resistance, Tittmann reported: "Dr. Mueller said that during the war his anti-Nazi organization in Germany had always been very insistent that the Pope should refrain from making any public statements singling out the Nazis and specifically condemning them and had recommended that the Pope's remarks should be confined to generalities only. Dr. Mueller said that he was obliged to give this advice, since, if the Pope had been specific, Germans would have accused him of yielding to the promptings of foreign powers and this would have made the German Catholics even more suspected than they were and would have greatly restricted their freedom of action in their work of resistance to the Nazis." Tittmann's ultimate conclusion was: "I cannot help but feel that the Holy Father chose the better path and thereby saved many lives."

181 *See* Rychlak, *Hitler, the War, and the Pope* at 214-15. Perhaps even worse than Cornwell's development of this argument is that critic Robert Katz repeated it several years after it had been exposed. Katz, *The Battle for Rome* at 113-14.

182 Gallo at 146, 316, n. 50.

183 Alan Schom, *Napoleon Bonaparte* 458 (Harper Perennial, New York, 1997).

184 Hochhuth at 351n. American document from 1943 suggests that most people in the Vatican at that time felt that Germany would not invade the Vatican unless Hitler had "a sudden outburst of anger against the church" and he overruled wiser counsel. The same report also noted that a minority was completely convinced that Hitler would invade the Vatican. Telegram from the Minister in Switzerland (Harrison) to the Secretary of State, Oct. 29, 1943, in *Foreign Relations of the United States, Diplomatic Papers, 1943, vol. II (Europe)*, United States Government Printing Office (Washington, 1964) at 951-52.

185 Clyde Haberman, *Magazine Says Hitler Planned to Abduct Pope*, New York Times, July 21, 1991, at sec. 1, p. 7. At other times, Hitler made similar threats about the Catholic Church in Germany. Consider the following statement made by Hitler in mid-July, 1941: "The ideal situation would be to leave the religions to devour themselves.... The heaviest blow that ever struck humanity was the coming of Christianity. Bolshevism is Christianity's illegitimate child. Both are inventions of the Jew. The deliberate lie in the matter of religion was introduced into the world by Christianity...." *Hitler's Secret Conversations* at 6. Goebbels wrote in his diary on November 1-2, 1941, that "The Catholic Church... has not lost contact with its Jewish origin." *The Goebbels Diaries 1942–1943* at 117.

186 Weizsäcker at 291; *Actes et Documents*, vol. IX, no. 355 & 474.

187 *See* Chadwick, *Weizsäcker, the Vatican, and the Jews of Rome* at 187-88, 195.

188 Holmes at 155-56.

189 Clyde Haberman, *Magazine Says Hitler Planned to Abduct Pope*, New York Times, July 21, 1991, at sec. 1, p. 7.

190 Michaelis at 377.

191 Stefano M. Paci, *Read Father Blet's book on Pius XII*, 30 Days, No. 4, 1998, 40; *see* Richard Lamb, *War in Italy 1943-1945: A Brutal Story* 45 (St. Martin's Press, New York, 1993) (similar quote).

192 Congregation for the Causes of Saints, *Positio*, (Summarium) Testimony of Karl Otto Wolff, March 14, 1972, before the Ecclesiastical Tribunal of Munich, on the

beatification of Pius xii (Eugenio Pacelli) at 832. In 1944, when the Allies liberated Rome, Wolff approached Pius xii to discuss a possible peace treaty. At that time Wolff provided Pius with documents regarding Hitler's plans to invade the Vatican. *Id.* The documents are reprinted along with Wolff's testimony in the *Positio. Id.* at 831. Peter Gumpel, S.J., the relator of the cause for Pope Pius xii's sainthood, told me that General Wolff was instrumental in freeing Gumpel's mother in 1938 when she was arrested by the Nazis.

193 *Id.*
194 Payne at 485. *See* Congregation for the Causes of Saints, *Positio,* (Summarium) Testimony of Karl Otto Wolff, March 14, 1972, before the Ecclesiastical Tribunal of Munich, on the beatification of Pius xii (Eugenii Pacelli) at 837; Toland at 851; Payne at 485. As Joachim von Ribbentrop explained in an interrogation during the Nuremberg war trials, maintaining good relations with the Vatican was an important part of the German foreign policy. Bad relations with the Vatican would negatively impact on Germany's relations with other nations, particularly in South America. Office of the United States Chief of Counsel, Supp. B, at 1236. Ribbentrop's concern over relations with the Vatican is reflected in a telegram he sent in January 1943. *Secret Telegram From Ribbentrop to the German Ambassador (Bergen),* dated January 13, 1943, Akten Zur Deutschen Auswärtigen Politik, 1918-1945, Series E, Band V, Vandenhoeck & Ruprecht in Göttingen (1978) no. 123.
195 *Great Untold Stories of World War II* at 95.
196 Congregation for the Causes of Saints, *Positio,* (Summarium) Testimony of Karl Otto Wolff, March 14, 1972, before the Ecclesiastical Tribunal of Munich, on the beatification of Pius xii (Eugenio Pacelli) at 836-37. Goebbels recorded in his diary on July 27, 1943, that Hitler at first intended to seize the Vatican, but decided against it when Ribbentrop and Goebbels pointed out the impact that such actions would have on world opinion. *The Goebbels Diaries 1942–1943* at 409.
197 *Il Giornale,* July 5, 1998. *See* Marchione, *Pope Pius xii: Architect for Peace* (Hitler's Plan).
198 Hochhuth at 324.
199 *The Pope's Solicitude,* The Jewish Chronicle, July 16, 1943; Robert A. Graham, *How to Manufacture a Legend: The Controversy over the Alleged "Silence" of Pope Pius xii in World War II,* in *Pius xii and the Holocaust: A Reader* at 22. Pius also took this opportunity to caution against the problems associated with unconditional surrender, which displeased President Roosevelt. Blet, Chapter 12; *id.* (conclusion).
200 Cornwell, *Hitler's Pope* at 321.
201 According to one account, this was the result of an order from Hitler. *Id.* The German Ambassador to the Holy See tried to approach the Allies through the Vatican to coordinate the transfer. He presented his proposal to the Vatican the night before the Allies moved into Rome. Weizsäcker at 292. *See* Smit at 237.
202 Weizsäcker at 293. "Although he failed to obtain any formal bilateral agreement, he did inspire both sides, as Weizsäcker wrote, with a type of reverential respect for Rome." Blet, Chapter 10.
203 Scrivener at 201.
204 *Id.* at 202 (placards all around town read: "Come to St. Peter's at six o'clock to thank the Pope.") German ambassador Weizsäcker noted how no one thought of the King of Italy. Chadwick, *Weizsäcker, the Vatican, and the Jews of Rome* at 183.
205 Nichols at 136.
206 Blet, Chapter 10.

207 *See* Cianfarra at 7; Marchione, *Pope Pius XII: Architect for Peace* (Church, Shoah, and Anti-Semitism) (quoting John W. Pehle, executive director of the United States War Refugee Board).
208 Scrivener at 203, *see* Blet, Chapter 10.
209 Scrivener at 203.
210 Lapide at 131; *see* Weizsäcker at 297.
211 Marchione, *Pope Pius XII: Architect for Peace* (2000) (The Jewish Community). See also Harrold J. Saperstein, *Witness from the Pulpit* (Lexington Books, 2002) at 233.
212 *Actes et Documents*, vol. X, p. 358 (no. 272).
213 Lapide at 131. The *Jewish News* (Detroit) reported on July 7, "It is gradually being revealed that Jews have been sheltered within the walls of the Vatican during the German occupation of Rome." An editorial in the July 14 edition of the *Congress Weekly*, the official journal of the American Jewish Congress, noted that the Vatican had provided kosher food.
214 Dimitri Cavalli, *How Pope Pius XII was made a villain*, Riverdale Press (Bronx, N.Y.), July 16, 1998, at A11. See also *Actes et Documents*, vol. X, no. 295, at 378 (Cicognani, the Apostolic Delegate to Washington, [writing] to Cardinal Maglione, August 9, 1944) (expressing thanks from the American Jewish Committee and the Committee to Save Jews in Europe to "the Holy Father and Your most Reverend Eminence for the decided improvement obtained in Hungary.... [T]he aforementioned committees recognize that everything is owed to the Holy Father."
215 Nazareno Padellaro & Robert L Reynolds, *His Reign*, Wisdom, September 1957, at 26.
216 In addition, as one enters St. Peter's Basilica, to the right just beyond Michelangelo's Pietá, stands a large statute of Pius XII.
217 Korn at 151. On October 29, 1944, elder survivors from a concentration camp in Ferramonti, Italy presented Pius a letter which said, in part:

> "Now that the victorious Allied troops have broken our chains and liberated us from captivity and danger, may we, the Jewish internees of Ferramonti, be permitted to express our deepest and devoted thanks for the comfort and help which Your Holiness deigned to grant us with fatherly concern and infinite kindness throughout our years of internment and persecution.
>
> "Your Holiness has as the first and highest authority upon earth fearlessly raised his universally respected voice, in the face of our powerful enemies, in order to defend openly our rights to the dignity of man.... When we were threatened with deportation to Poland, in 1942, Your Holiness extended his fatherly hand to protect us, and stopped the transfer of the Jews interned in Italy, thereby saving us from almost certain death. With deep confidence and hope that the work of Your Holiness may be crowned with further success, we beg to express our heartfelt thanks while we pray to the Almighty: May Your Holiness reign for many years on this Holy See and exert your beneficent influence over the destiny of the nations.
>
> "[signed] The President and community of Jewish internees of the former camp at Ferramonti-Tarsia."

> *Quoted in* Lapide at 129-30. *See also Actes et Documents*, vol. VIII, no. 294 (Vatican efforts on behalf of the internees at Ferramonti); *Actes et Documents*, vol. IX, no. 55 (Vatican concern over internees at Ferramonti); *Actes et Documents*, vol. IX, no. 228 (Vatican concern over Yugoslavian Jews interned in Italy). See also Blet, Chapter 7.

218 Cornwell, *Hitler's Pope* at 95.
219 *See* Robert G. Weisbord & Michael W. Honhart, *A Question of Race: Pope Pius XII and the "Coloured Troops" in Italy*, Historian, December 2002, at 403-17.
220 *Monsignor Tardini to the Nuncio in France, Roncalli*, February 26, 1945, *Actes et Documents*, vol. X at 410 ("It is known here that the French government has planned to occupy... northern regions of Italy with Moroccan troops. The Holy See has been sincerely asked to intervene... on account of the acts of violence already done by the above-mentioned troops in various parts of southern and central Italy.").
221 *Criminal Excesses, L'Osservatore Romano*, July 28, 1944 (report of brutality by Moroccan troops against women).
222 *Monsignor Tardini to the Nuncio in France, Roncalli*, February 26, 1945, *Actes et Documents*, vol. X at 410. In fact, Pius did not want any troops to engage in unlawful activities. He was critical of atrocities committed by white troops on both sides of the war. *E.g.*, O'Carroll at 18-19, 134-36.
223 Memo dated November 4, 1944 (stamp number 101307).
224 *Notizie Italiane*, October 4, 1944, at 1.
225 *Monsignor Tardini to the Nuncio in France, Roncalli*, February 26, 1945, *Actes et Documents*, vol. X at 410.
226 *The Tablet* (London), October 5, 1940 at 269; Speaight at 27.
227 Dan McFeely, The Indianapolis Star, June 2, 2003, at 1B.
228 This was reprinted in *L'Osservatore Romano* on May 27-28, 1946. *See also Pope Pius XII and the Negro*, Interracial Review, December 1939, at 179.
229 "The Catholic Church...considers all men as brothers and teaches them to love one another.... This law must be observed and respected in the case of the children of Israel, as well as of all others...." *Cardinal Gasparri, Secretary of State, Replies to the Petition of the American Jewish Committee of New York*, February 9, 1916, in *Principles for Peace* at 198-99.
230 On March 25, 1928, an official decree of the Holy Office condemned anti-Semitism: "Moved by the spirit of charity, the Apostolic See has protected the people [of Israel] against unjust persecutions, and since it condemns all jealousy and strife among peoples, it accordingly condemns with all its might the hatred directed against a people which was chosen by God; that particular hatred, in fact, which today commonly goes by the name anti-Semitism." For the official Latin text of the decree, see the Acta Apostolicae Sedis, Volume XX, pp.103-04.
231 On October 11, 1930, the Vatican' newspaper, *L'Osservatore Romano*, decreed in an editorial: "The Party of Hitler Stands Condemned by the Ecclesiastical Authorities.... Belonging to the National Socialist Party of Hitler is irreconcilable with the Catholic conscience."
232 *See* pp. 119-27. Out of disgust at the number of Jews that were released from Nazi-occupied areas due to Vatican pressure, the Third Reich circulated 10 million copies of a pamphlet saying that Pius XII inspired a lack of confidence in the Catholic world. *The Tablet* (London), October 24, 1942, at 202 (quoting the *Jewish Chronicle*).
233 As reported by *The Tablet* (London), Rabbi Lazaron "goes on to quote the Pope's condemnation of anti-Semitism, and the action taken by Bishops and priests throughout occupied Europe to protect Jews 'driven like animals' from their homes. 'They have shielded and healed them at the risk of their own lives, and indeed many priests have been killed and not a few killed in their effort. But it is more than a mere reciprocal gesture which prompts our prayers for His Holiness. We can place ourselves in the position of our Catholic friends.... We link our prayers with theirs. May God protect

and keep His Holiness in strength and all good." Quoted in *The Tablet* (London), December 25, 1943, at 306. Rabbi Morris S. Lazaron, writing in the *Baltimore Synagogue Bulletin*, affirmed that "The Pope has condemned anti-Semitism and all its works. Bishops of the Church have appeared in the streets... with the Shield of David on their arms.... Indeed, many priests and ministers have been jailed and not a few killed in their effort to protect Jews." *The Catholic Mind*, June 1964, at 26.

234 Halecki at 340; Joseph L. Lichten, *A Question of Judgment: Pius XII and the Jews*, in *Pius XII and the Holocaust: A Reader* at 127; Stewart at 60. Pius had a life-long Jewish friend, Dr. Guido Mendes. In 1939, Pius helped the Mendes family escape to Palestine. *The Jewish Chronicle*, October 11, 1963.

235 *Quoted in* Purdy at 42.

236 *Id.* The strength of this anti-Nazi statement was noted by U.S. Representative Harold Tittmann. *Inside the Vatican of Pius XII* at 213 (memo dated June 4, 1945 and referring to the Pope "attacking the Nazis in public").

237 Office of the United States Chief Counsel, vol. I, at 285-86; Shirer, *The Rise and Fall of the Third Reich* at 324-25 (footnote).

238 The full text of the address appears in Margherita Marchione, *Pope Pius XII: Architect for Peace* at 143-152. *See also* Office of the United States Chief Counsel, vol. I, at 285-86; Shirer, *The Rise and Fall of the Third Reich* at 324-25 (footnote); Purdy at 43.

239 *La vostra presenza*, November 29, 1945. Extracts were published in *Tablet*, December 8, 1945. *Quoted in* Purdy at 262; *Acta Apostolicae Sedis* 37 (December 23, 1945) at 317-18; *L'Osservatore Romano*, November 30, 1945, at 1; *Tablet*, December 8, 1945, at 277. *See also* Pius XII's address to representatives of the United Jewish Appeal, on relief work in Europe and Palestine, February 9, 1948, *L'Osservatore Romano*, February 9-10, 1948; *Tablet*, February 14, 1948, at 105; *New York Times*, February 10, 1948, at 13. *See Jewish Leaders Have Papal Audience*, Catholic World, January 1946, at 370.

240 *Jewish Leaders Have Papal Audience*, Catholic World, January 1946, at 370.

241 *Id.*

242 McCormick at 134 (from a *New York Times* dispatch of February 20, 1946). McCormick reports that Pius told her that he planned to accomplish this internationalization project well before the nominations were announced. *Id.*

243 The largest group of nominees came from the United States, and there were several from other North American countries, causing some Europeans to complain about the "Americanization" of the Church. McCormick at 131.

244 McCormick at 132 (from a *New York Times* dispatch of December 26, 1945).

245 James W. Demers, *The Last Roman Catholic?* 24 (1991), citing Francis X. Murphy, *The Papacy Today* 15 (1981); McCormick at 134 (similar quote).

246 *The Tablet* (of London), August 24, 1946, at 97 (excerpts). The full text of the allocution, entitled, *Nous sommes heureux*, appears (in its original French) in the Vatican's official *Acta Apostolicae Sedis*, Volume 38, 1946, pp. 322-323; also published, in Italian, in *L'Osservatore Romano*, August 15, 1946, and English excerpts in The *New York Times*, August 15, 1946, p. C-3.

247 The *New York Times*, June 29, 1957; Dimitri Cavalli, *The Good Samaritan: Jewish Praise for Pope Pius XII*, Inside the Vatican, October, 2000, at 76.

248 *Letter of July 12, 1946, to Montini*, quoted in *The Ecumenist* 39 (Spring 2002) at 1-3. Maritain went on to request a new Papal statement against anti-Semitism, and within weeks Pius XII issued his aforementioned August 3, 1946 condemnation.

249 Peter Novick, *The Holocaust in American Life* 316, n.77 (Houghton Mifflin, 1999); *Dulles to Attend Rites for Pontiff*, New York Times, October 11, 1958 at 2 (same).

250 DiGiovanni at 30 (noting that the Communist charge of papal silence was false). On February 2, 1944, the *New York Times* reported that the Soviet newspaper was setting forth false propaganda that Pius XII "had supported the Nazi Regime and had worked for the destruction of other states." The *Times* expressed consternation that anyone could believe the charges as anything other than Communist propaganda. *Id.*
  On February 4, 1944, the *Times* editorialized that the United States and Great Britain "have no doubt where the real sympathy of the Vatican lies in this struggle. They recognize the inescapable neutrality of the Pope's position; but they have had no difficulty in finding in his eloquent declarations clear evidence of his detestation for those who have violated the rights of the little nations who have committed bestial acts from one end of Europe to the other and who have attempted to elevate the dogma of Totalitarianism to the dignity of a new religion. [The Soviet] attack is damaging to the unity on which victory depends." *Id.* Pro-Communist agitators took their lead from the Soviet press and produced a whole body of anti-papal literature. *See e.g.,* Joseph McCabe, *The Pope Helps Hitler to World-Power: How the Cross Courted the Swastika for Eight Years* (Haldemon-Julius: Girard, Kansas, 1941); H.G. Wells, *Crux Ansata: An Indictment of the Roman Catholic Church,* (Agora: New York, 1944); Avro Manhattan, *The Catholic Church Against the Twentieth Century* (Watts: London, 1947); Edmond Paris, *Le Vatican Contre L'Europe* (Editions Fischbacher, Paris, 1959).

251 *Actes et Documents,* vol. IX, no. 247. *See also Actes et Documents,* vol. IX, no. 270, at 403-06 (The Grand Rabbi Herzog to Cardinal Maglione, July 19, 1943) (offering thanks and seeking help for the Jews in Poland).

252 Blet, Chapter 9.

253 *Actes et Documents,* vol. IX, no. 282.

254 *Peace & the Papacy,* Time, August 16, 1943, at 55, 60.

255 *Id.*

256 *Actes et Documents,* vol. IX, no. 346.

257 Blet, Chapter 9.

258 *Actes et Documents,* vol. IX, at 498, 501-02, 567.

259 Congregation for the Causes of Saints, *Positio,* appendix 25 at 272 (reprinting Peter Gumpel, *Cornwell's Cheap Shot at Pius XII,* Crisis, December 1999).

260 Zuccotti's argument is that during the war, editors at the *New York Times* wanted to court support from Catholics (and others) so they were less than honest in some reporting.

261 *A Vatican Visit,* The London Times, October 11, 1942.

262 *The Jewish Chronicle* (London), Sept. 11, 1942.

263 Similarly, the *Kansas City Jewish Chronicle* praised Pius XII in its March 29, 1940 issue because his actions showed "his disapproval of the dastardly anti-Semitic decrees." See Gallo at 33.

264 *Jerusalem Post,* January 22, 1946. Many other citations can be found in Antonio Gaspari, *The Jews Saved by Pius XII* (Gli ebrei salvati da Pio XII) 117-25 (2001).

265 *Acknowledging the Men and Women of Wisdom,* Wisdom, September 1957, at 2. *See also Vatican Radio Denounces Nazi Acts in Poland,* Jewish Advocate (Boston), January 26, 1940; *Laval Spurns Pope–25,000 Jews in France Arrested for Deportation,* Canadian Jewish Chronicle, September 4, 1942; *Vatican Gives Assurance of Aid to Jews,* California Jewish Voice, February 12, 1943; *Jewish Hostages in Rome: Vatican Protests,* Jewish Chronicle (London), October 29, 1943.

266 Anton J. Gahlinger, *I Served the Pope* 6 (The Mission Press, Techny, IL: 1952).

267 McCormick at 123 (from a *New York Times* dispatch of September 6, 1944). For his part, Pius described Churchill as "very able and large-minded." *Id.*

268 Gallo at 293; Lapide at 228.

269 Regarding a homeland for the Jews, Pope Pius XII was an early supporter of the concept. He did, however, fear that putting it in Palestine would create a great possibility of violence, as three religions quarreled over the geography.

270 "Conductor Paul Klecki had requested that the Orchestra on its first visit to Italy play for the Pope as a gesture of gratitude for the help his church had given to all those persecuted by Nazi Fascism." *Jerusalem Post*, May 29, 1955.

271 Similarly, Angelo Roncalli (the future Pope John XXIII), war time apostolic delegate in Istanbul, was thanked for his work on behalf of Jewish refugees. He replied: "In all these painful matters I have referred to the Holy See and simply carried out the Pope's orders: first and foremost to save human lives." Lapide at 181. The Nazis spied on Roncalli and tried to render his protests ineffective. Congregation for the Causes of Saints, *Positio*, appendix 25 at 245-46 (quoting and reprinting the prologue to Levai, *Hungarian Jewry and the Papacy: Pope Pius did not Remain Silent*).

272 *See* Pope Paul VI, *Heights of Heroism in the Life of Pope Pius XII*, St. Paul Editions, 1964 (the text of an address given by Paul at the dedication of a statue of Pius XII, in the Vatican Basilica, March 12, 1964); Rychlak, *Hitler, the War, and the Pope* at 266. During Paul VI's visit to Israel in 1964, he declared: "Everybody knows what Pius XII did for the defense of all those who were caught in [World War II's] tribulations, without distinction. And yet you know suspicions and even accusations have been leveled against this great Pontiff. We are happy to have the opportunity to state on this day and in this place that there is nothing more unjust than this slight against such a venerated memory. Those who intimately knew this admirable man know how far could go his sensibility, his compassion for human suffering, his courage, his delicacy of heart. Those who after the war came with tears in their eyes to thank him for saving their lives also knew it." 2 *Insegnamenti di Paolo VI* 53-54 (Libreria Editrice Vaticana: Città del Vaticano). *See also New York Times*, January 6, 1964, at 1 ("The pope's defense of Pope Pius XII's efforts to save Jews during World War II were widely and favorably commented on both privately and publicly [throughout Israel].")

273 Avvenire, June 27, 1996; CWN *More Echoes on Pope Pius XII, Nazi Holocaust*, June 27, 1996.

274 "Customarily the most deliberate of men, Pius XII on this occasion made up his mind with little of any hesitation." Deutsch at 120.

275 Congregation for the Causes of Saints, *Positio*, appendix 25 at 271 (reprinting Peter Gumpel, *Cornwell's Cheap Shot at Pius XII*, Crisis, December 1999). *See also* Jacques Nobécourt, *Le Vicaire et L'Histoire* 194 (Paris, 1964).

276 A very good account of this whole matter can be found in Conway, *The Vatican, the Nazis and the Pursuit of Justice*.

277 *See* Rychlak, *Hitler, the War, and the Pope* at 128-32; Gallo at 30-32.

278 Pepper at 77. *See also* Tittmann at 95 ("it was only rarely that records were kept by the Vatican officials of conversations the Pope had....")

279 In 1945, Fabian von Schlabrendorff, a Protestant member of the German resistance, wrote a memorandum to U.S. General William ("Wild Bill") Donovan, in which Schlabrendorff reported that: "Joseph Müller had orders from the Catholic Church to negotiate with representatives of the Protestant Church in order to harmonize their measures in the struggle against Hitler." *Memorandum to General Donovan from*

Fabian von Schlabrendorff, October 25, 1945 (Subject: Relationship of the German Churches to Hitler). *See also* Schlabrendorff, *The Secret War Against Hitler*. For more information on this episode, *see* Rychlak, *Hitler, the War, and the Pope* at 128-32.

280 Carroll-Abbing, *But for the Grace of God* at 48.
281 Carroll-Abbing, *A Chance to Live* at 77.
282 *Id.* at 141, 82. *See* Congregation for the Causes of Saints, *Positio*, appendix 25, p. 290.
283 William Doino, *The Witness of the Late Monsignor John Carroll-Abbing*, Inside the Vatican, July 12, 2001. Doino played portions of his tape recording of this interview for me. I note this because at a conference at Millersville University in 2002, Zuccotti raised the specter that Doino had fabricated the interview.
284 Zuccotti, *The Italians and the Holocaust* at 304.

6 "The Jews Are Our Brothers"

1 *The Jewish Post* (Nov. 6, 1958). Similarly, *The Jewish Chronicle*, in its October 10, 1958, edition said: "Adherents of all creeds and parties will recall how Pius XII faced the responsibilities of his exalted office with courage and devotion. Before, during, and after the Second World War, he constantly preached the message of peace. Confronted by the monstrous cruelties of Nazism, Fascism, and Communism, he repeatedly proclaimed the virtues of humanity and compassion."
2 Memorandum by the Vatican Secretary of State (Cardinal Pacelli) to the American Ambassador in the United Kingdom, April 19, 1938, in *Foreign Relations of the United States, Diplomatic Papers, 1938, vol. I (General)*, United States Government Printing Office (Washington, 1955) at 474.
3 Internal German records reflect that Nazi leadership wanted to "encourage Cardinal Innitzer and the Austrian bishops in their patriotic attitude." Message from German Ambassador to the Holy See (Bergen) to the German Foreign Ministry, dated April 2, 1938, *Documents on German Foreign Policy 1918-1945*, Series D (1937-1945), vol. I, no. 699 (also complaining about the Vatican Radio broadcast).
4 Cornwell, *Hitler's Pope* at 202. *See also* p. 46.
5 *Confidential Letter to Oliver Harvey from D'Arcy Osborne*, British Public Record Office, FO 371/67917 60675. *Memorandum to General Donovan from Fabian von Schlabrendorff*, Oct. 25, 1945. On Innitzer's original attitude towards the Nazis, *see* Sereny at 304.
6 Passelecq & Suchecky at 56.
7 Message from German Ambassador to the Holy See (Bergen) to the German Foreign Ministry, dated April 6, 1938, *Documents on German Foreign Policy 1918-1945*, Series D (1937-1945), vol. I, no. 701.
8 *Id.*, no. 702.
9 *See* pp. 46, 266. For an account of Sister Maria Restituta's resistance to the Nazis in Austria, that led to her being beheaded, *see* Hans Knight, *The Nun and the Nazis*, The Catholic Digest, Feb. 1992, at 14.
10 Alvarez & Graham at 142.
11 *Quoted in Great Untold Stories of World War II* at 84.
12 *Id.* at 85.
13 *Id.* at 80. *See generally The Pius War* at 268-270.
14 *Great Untold Stories of World War II* at 85.
15 *Id.* at 82.

16 For an account of life for priests in a concentration camp, *see* Lenz, *Christ in Dachau.*

17 Certain Poles, exiled in London, criticized the pope because it was thought that he had clearly spoken on behalf of the Jews, but not of Catholic Poles. *See* Gallo at 34. "The strongest complaint against the Pope came from Karol Radonski, Bishop of Wloclawek, who was in exhile in London and in contact with the Polish government in exile. When Maglione [the Cardinal Secretary of State during the War] chastised him for 'adding an additional cross' for the Pope to carry, Radonski replied that he had heard that the nuncio in France (Valeri) had told Pétain that the Pope had condemned the persecution of Jews.'Are we less deserving than the Jews?' he asked." Sánchez, *Pope Pius XII and the Holocaust* at 157. For the original correspondence between Radonski and Maglione, see the *Actes et Documents*, volume 3, at 633-636; 713-717; 736-739. For a refutation of the charge that Pius XII "turned his back on the Poles" during the war, see *Pius XII and Poland* published by the Jesuits at America Press in New York City (1942); Graham, *The Pope and Poland*; John Lafarge, *The Pope is True Holy Father to Poland's stricken people*, America, September 12, 1943 at 622-23.

18 *Vita*, April 15, 1964, as cited and translated by Carlo Falconi in The Silence of Pius XII, p. 149). *See Actes et Documents*, volume 3 (part 2), document 437, pp. 669-70 ("We very much regret that we cannot publicly communicate to our faithful your Holiness' letters, as this would only afford an opportunity for fresh persecutions; and the fact that we have been suspected of being in secret communication with the Holy See has already led to victimization"); Blet, chapter 4; Paci at 41; Rychlak, *Hitler, the War, and the Pope* at 368, n. 137.

19 *Actes et Documents*, volume 2, number 105, pp. 318-27; an English translation of the letter appears in Friedländer, *Pius XII and the Third Reich* at 135-143.

20 *See generally* Jakubowski, *Pope Pius and Poland* (documenting Pius XII's actions on behalf of Poland).

21 Toland at 864; Holmes at 132; O'Carroll at 131.

22 *Quoted in* Graham, *The Pope and Poland in World War Two* at 50.

23 Blet, Chapter 4.

24 *See* Gunther Deschner, *Warsaw Rising*, Ballatine Books (New York, 1972).

25 Blet, Chapter 7. On August 30, the United States Secretary of State expressed doubt about the whole matter, sending a message that "there exists no sufficient proof to justify a statement regarding executions in gas chambers." *Id.*

26 For a particularly interesting account of how one parish sheltered a Jewish Family, *see Great Untold Stories of World War II* at 86-87. *See also* Rychlak, *Hitler, the War, and the Pope* at 190-91.

27 Rychlak, *Hitler, the War, and the Pope* at 382, note 61.

28 *See* pp. 75, 106-07, 148, 263-64.

29 F. Murphy at 64.

30 Kevin M. Doyle, *Robert Graham, sj*, First Things, June/July 1997, at 16-17.

31 Papée, *Pius XII e Polska. See also* Sereny at 332 (quoting Papée: "He was in a very very difficult position.... He was–one must appreciate this–surrounded by Fascism: he had very little freedom of movement."); Jakubowski, *Pope Pius and Poland* (documenting Pius XII's actions on behalf of Poland).

32 Sereny at 333 (Papée pleaded for a statement on behalf of Poles, not Jews. He added: "I meant, of course all the Poles, including the Jews, most of whom, of course, by this time, were dead."). As discussed earlier, Pius prepared an express statement on behalf of all the Poles, but he was told by Archbishop Sapieha that it would only lead to bad repercussions. *See* pp. 153-54.

33 Lubac at 147-48. *See generally, The Pius War* at 250-52.

34 Lubac at 148.

35 French Catholics may have been particularly willing to oppose the collaborationist aspects of the Vichy government. In the 1790s, between 118,000 and 250,000 Catholics were brutally murdered in Vendée, a region of about 12,000 square kilometers in western France. This was done under the color of state law by the new, post-revolutionary secular government. The stories are horrific–"unparalleled until the advent of Stalin and Hitler." Anne Barbeau Gardiner, *The Heart of Darkness: How Visceral Hatred of Catholicism Turns into Genocide*, New Oxford Review, May 2004, at 39 (reviewing Michael Davies, *For Altar and Throne: The Rising in the Vendée (1793-1796)* (The Remnant Press) and Reynald Secher, *A French Genocide* (University of Notre Dame Press). Because this persecution evolved out of the victims' unwillingness to put the state ahead of their faith, Pope John Paul II recently beatified many of the victims (the Martyrs of Avrillé).

36 Michel Riquet, *Chrétiens de France dans l'Europe enchaînée* 98 (SOS: Paris, 1973); Lacouture at 387 (footnote).

37 *See* Lubac at 148.

38 *Id.* at 161-62; Gilbert, *The Holocaust* at 355.

39 Lacouture at 387 (footnote).

40 Lubac at 161-62.

41 Holmes at 164-65. *See also* George Kent, *Shepherds of the Underground*, The Christian Herald, April 1945. Numerous other courageous statements from French bishops are set forth in Susan Zuccotti, *Pope Pius XII and the Holocaust: The Case in Italy*, in *The Italian Refuge* at 257.

42 *Laval Spurns Pope—25,000 Jews in France Arrested for Deportation*, Canadian Jewish Chronicle, September 4, 1942.

43 Goldhagen also quotes a more recent statement of some French bishops (not *the* French bishops as he mistakenly reports) in which they confessed to the failings of French Catholics during the war, but that statement was critical only of those areas and dioceses in France that fell prey to anti-Semitism. As with a 1995 statement from German bishops, there was no criticism of Pope Pius XII or the Holy See.

44 Lubac at 161-62 ("Our bishops were actively supported by the Holy See").

45 Joseph L. Lichten, *A Question of Judgment: Pius XII and the Jews*, in *Pius XII and the Holocaust: A Reader* at 114-15.

46 *Australian Jewish News*, April 16, 1943.

47 English exerpts as quoted by Lapide at 189-190. For exerpts from the original French text of Saliège's pastoral, see Jaques Duquesne, *Les Catholiques Français sous l'occupation* 257 (Paris: 1966). For the general background of Saliège's protests, and those of the other French bishops, *see* Lubac at 157-64.

48 Lubac at 162.

49 *Osservatore della Domenica*, June 28, 1964, p. 28.

50 McCormick at 132 (from a *New York Times* dispatch of December 26, 1945).

51 Holmes at 164.

52 Rychlak, *Hitler, the War, and the Pope* at 362-63.

53 *War News Summarized*, The New York Times, August 6, 1942. This protest has been questioned by some writers, but it is confirmed in a telegram sent from the German ambassador to France. *Ambassador Abetz in Paris to the Office of Foreign Affairs*, dated August 28, 1942, *Akten Zur Deutschen Auswärtigen Politik, 1918-1945*, Series E, Band III, Vandenhoeck & Ruprecht in Göttingen (1974) no. 242 (discussing a

protest from the Nuncio regarding the treatment of the Jews, instructions from the Archbishop of Toulouse telling priests "to protest most vehemently from the pulpit against the deportation of the Jews," and discussing Laval's protest to the Vatican).

54 *The New York Times*, August 27, 1942.

55 British Public Record Office, Reference Number 320/81.

56 British Public Record Office, Reference Number 371 32680.

57 Wyman at 34; *see A Spiritual Ally*, California Jewish Voice, August 28, 1942; *Vichy Seizes Jews; Pope Pius Ignored*, The New York Times, August 27, 1942; and *25,000 Jews Reported Held in South France For Deportation by the Nazis to the East*, The New York Times, August 28, 1942 (noting the Pope's support for appeals made to Vichy leaders by Catholic clergymen).

58 Blet at chapter 11.

59 *Christendom and the Jews*, The Jewish Chronicle (London), Sept. 11, 1942. *See* Lothar Groppe, *The Church and the Jews in the Third Reich*, Fidelity, November 1983, at 25 (quoting parts of the editorial).

60 *Les persécutiens en France contre les Juifs: Une protestation du pape Pio XII*, Geneva Tribune, September 8, 1942.

61 McCormick at 107 (dispatch of September 26, 1942).

62 *La Voix du Vatican #* 28, Vatican Radio broadcast of September 14, 1942.

63 *La Voix du Vatican #* 26, Vatican Radio broadcast of June 30, 1942.

64 Stewart at 9.

65 *See* pp. 117-19.

66 Richard F. Crane, *Maritain's True Humanism*, First Things, Feb. 2005, at 17, 19.

67 Quoted in *id.* at 20.

68 Fogelman at 209. *See also* George Kent, *Shepherds of the Underground*, The Christian Herald, April 1945. For a discussion of how the children were returned to their families, see pp. 106-11.

69 Fogelman at 209; Rychlak, *Hitler, the War, and the Pope* at 145.

70 *The Australian Jewish News*, April 16, 1943.

71 *The New York Times*, June 27, 1943, at 16; *The American Jewish Yearbook, 1943-1944* at 292.

72 Purdy at 256-57.

73 Lubac at 71-102; Rychlak, *Hitler, the War, and the Pope* at 362-64, n. 60; Purdy at 257 (suggesting that there may have been someone at the Vatican who might have made such a statement even though it did not reflect the opinion of the Vatican.)

74 Lubac at 71-102; Rychlak, *Hitler, the War, and the Pope* at 362-64, n. 60.

75 Lubac at 71-102; Rychlak, *Hitler, the War, and the Pope* at 362-64, n. 60.

76 Nevins at 22-23.

77 *Christendom and the Jews*, The Jewish Chronicle (London), Sept. 11, 1942; Wise, *As I See It* (reprinting the 1942 article).

78 *Il Cardinale van Roey e il Cardinale Verdier illustrano la dottrina cattolica di fronte al "razzismo" L'Osservatore Romano*, November 24, 1938, at 2; Kent at 601. *See generally*, The Pius Wars at 245.

79 *Great Untold Stories of World War II* at 88.

80 *Id.*

81 *Id.*

82 *Id.* at 88-89.

83 *Id.* at 89-90 (reporting that the network developed a file of known undercover Gestapo agents, so that everyone along the way would be able to recognize one who might try to infiltrate the system and report back to the Nazis).

84   *La Voix du Vatican* # 23, Vatican Radio broadcast of April 29, 1942.

85   *Great Untold Stories of World War II* at 92.

86   *Id.* at 90.

87   *Id.* at 92.

88   *Divini Redemptoris*, paragraph 58.

89   As late as 1987, Soviet Premier Mikhail Gorbachhev explained: "There must be no letup in the war against religion because as long as religion exists, communism cannot prevail. We must intensify the obliteration of all religions where ever they are being practiced or taught." Mikhail Gorbachhev to a group of Communist Party officials in Uzbekistan, December 15, 1987.

90   During the war, *Time* magazine reported that "if Catholic-Fascist relations have been warm in the case of Spain, tolerable in the case of Italy, bearable in the case of Germany, relations with the democracies have been downright friendly." *Peace & the Papacy*, Time, August 16, 1943, at 55, 59-60.

91   *Controversial Concordats* at 2; Cornwell, *Hitler's Pope* at 263; Cheetham at 284-86.

92   Pope Pius XI had not given up on the hope of establishing better relations with the Soviet Union. In 1929, he sent a letter to all seminarians, "especially our Jesuit sons," asking for men to enter a new Russian center being started in Rome to prepare young clerics for work in the USSR. Walter J. Ciszek, *He Leadeth Me: An Extraordinary Testament of Faith* 13 (Doubleday, 1973). Ciszek entered the seminary and was later arrested in the Soviet Union, charged with being a spy for the Vatican.

93   *The Generals of the Society of Jesus*, available on the Internet at <<http://www.sogang. ac.kr/~gesukr/sj/sjgen15.html>>.

94   Van Hoek at 90.

95   *L'Osservatore Romano*, June 28, 1964, at 68-69.

96   *Inside the Vatican of Pius XII* at 63; *Current Biography, 1941* Maxine Block, ed., the H.W. Wilson Co., 1971 re-issue, at 673; Overy at 284 (noting that some American Catholics had expected him to bless such a "crusade"). Minutes from the British high command, dated September 10, 1941, state: "His Holiness is heart and soul with us in the struggle against Nazism, and his attitude as regards the 'anti-Bolshevist Crusade' leaves nothing to be desired." *Minutes dated September 10, 1941*, British Public Record Office, FO 371/30175 57750. U.S. Representative Harrold Tittmann reported to Washington that "the last thing the Vatican would welcome would be a Hitler victory." *Inside the Vatican of Pius XII* at 42.

97   Gallo at 326, n. 54.

98   German authorities were almost completely uncooperative with Vatican efforts on behalf of prisoners of war— even their own." Purdy at 33.

99   Gallo at 35, 40. When German troops invaded the Soviet Union, Pius even instructed the American bishops to make a statement making clear that the Vatican's opposition to the Soviet government did not reflect opposition to the Soviet people. *Id.* at 37.

100 *Message from the British Embassy in Madrid*, May 10, 1943, British Public Records Office, FO 3711 37538.

101 Office of the United States Chief of Counsel, Supp. B, at 1233.

102 *Inside the Vatican of Pius XII* at 64-65.

103 Some critics have made the charge that Pope Pius XII opposed the Nazis late in the war (once he realized that they would lose), but did not strongly stand against them early in the war. If that were true—which it is not—it would suggest that he moved with the Soviets, as they switched from being unofficial allies with the Germans to joining with the western powers. This is but another inconsistency in the arguments put forth by papal critics.

104 Robert A. Graham, *The Vatican and Communism During World War II* at 156-57 (1996) (citing the archives of the Hungarian Foreign Ministry). *See also Pius XII to Kallay, April 3, 1943*, in the National Archives, Washington, Hungarian Selection/ T973/1/1-201/1153ff; Nicholas de Kallay, *Hungarian Premier: A Personal Account of the Second World War* 169 (1954).

105 Congregation for the Causes of Saints, *Positio*, appendix 25 at 271-72 (reprinting Peter Gumpel, *Cornwell's Cheap Shot at Pius XII*, Crisis, December 1999); Rychlak, *Hitler, the War, and the Pope* at 257. The Auxiliary Bishop of Cleveland, Michael Ready, was assigned to head up the campaign to clarify *Divini Redemptoris* in the United States. Langer & Gleason at 796-97. After the war, in an address to the College of Cardinals and the diplomatic corps, Pius XII said: "We took special care, notwithstanding certain tendentious pressures, not to let fall from our lips or from our pen one single word, one single sign of approval or encouragement of the war against Russia in 1941." Allocution of February 25, 1946, published in the *Acta Apostolica Sedis*, volume 38, p. 154. In his apostolic letter to the Russian people, *Sacro Vergente Anno* (July 7, 1952), Pius was equally explicit: "Never at that time, was heard from our lips a word that could have seemed to any of the belligerents to be unjust or harsh. We certainly reproached, as was our duty, every evil and every violation of rights; but we did this in such a way as to avoid with all care whatever might become, even unjustly, an occasion for greater affliction of the oppressed peoples. Then, when pressure was brought to bear upon us to give our approval in some way, either verbally or in writing, to the war undertaken against Russia in 1941 we never consented to do so."

106 At the time of Pius XII's death, the Communist *Daily Worker* commented: "Progressives throughout the world will remember Pius XII with gratitude for his reiterated appeals on behalf of Ethel and Julius Rosenberg, an intervention unprecedented in Vatican history." *See* The Tablet [London], October 25, 1958. *See also* McGurn at 16 (noting that a significant Communist population was tolerated in Castle Gandolfo); *id.* at 70 (Pius regularly read the Italian Communist newspaper).

107 *See* The International Catholic-Jewish Historical Commission *The Vatican and the Holocaust: A Preliminary Report Submitted*, question 42 ("The case has repeatedly been made that the Vatican's fear of communism prompted it to mute and limit its criticism of Nazi atrocities and occupation policies. We are struck by the paucity of evidence to this effect...."). *See also* Rychlak, *A Response to The Vatican and the Holocaust.*

108 *Chronicle of the 20ᵗʰ Century* at 520-21.

109 Andrew Borowiec, *Croatian-run death site remains dark secret; Unlikely parties kept story of WWII camp suppressed*, The Washington Times, July 5, 1994, at A10. *See generally, The Pius War* at 246.

110 Jere Jareb, *Zlato i Novac Nezavisne Drzave Hrvatske izneseni u Inozemstvo 1944 i 1945* (Hrvatski institut za provijest Dom i svijet: Zagreb, 1997); *see Croatian Catholics and Jewish Gold*, Inside the Vatican, August-September 1998, at 11.

111 Pius quoted this in his Papal Allocution of October 6, 1946. *See* p. 106; Rychlak, *Hitler, the War, and the Pope*, at 414-15, n. 61.

112 *Actes et Documents*, vol. VIII, no. 441. *See also id.* vol. VIII, no. 537 (report on Vatican efforts to "alleviate the sad conditions of the Croatian Jews"); *id.* vol. VIII, no. 473 (efforts to find sanctuary for Croatian Jews in Italy); *id.* vol. VIII, no. 557 (insistence on "a benevolent treatment toward the Jews").

113 *Actes et Documents*, vol. VIII, no. 502.

114 *See Actes et Documents*, vol. VIII, no. 566.

115 *Actes et Documents*, vol. IX, no. 92 (Maglione's notes, dated March 13, 1943).

116 *Id.*

117 *Actes et Documents*, vol. IX, no. 81. On September 24, 1943, Alex Easterman, the British representative of the World Jewish Congress, contacted Msgr. William Godfrey, the apostolic delegate in London and informed him that about 4,000 Jewish refugees from Croatia were safely evacuated to an island in the Adriatic Sea. "I feel sure that efforts of your Grace and of the Holy See have brought about this fortunate result," wrote Easterman. *Id.*, vol. IX, pp. 488-489.

118 *Actes et Documents*, vol. IV, no. 358.

119 An appendix to document 130 in Volume 9 of the *Actes et Documents* lists 34 separate interventions by Stepinac against the persecution of Jews and Serbs in Croatia from 1941-1943. The British Minister to the Holy See during the war years, Sir Francis D'Arcy Osborne, wrote that Stepinac always acted according to the "well-intended dictates of his conscience." *Confidential Letter to Oliver Harvey from D'Arcy Osborne*, February 26, 1947, British Public Record Office, FO 371/67917 60675.

120 Alain Finkielkraut, *Mgr. Stepinac et les deux douleurs de l'Europe*, Le Monde (Paris), October 7, 1998.

121 Rick Hinshaw, *Cardinal's Past*, Chicago Tribune, October 17, 1998, at 26.

122 On March 10, 1999, with a group of eighteen Croatian bishops making their *ad limina* visit to Rome, the Vatican newspaper published a eighty-six-page special supplement in *L'Osservatore Romano* on the life of Alojzije Stepinac. Details about his life can be found in that report.

123 Weigel, *Witness to Hope: The Biography of Pope John Paul II* at 73.

124 *Actes et Documents*, vol. IV, no. 400 ("Pavelic is furious... because... he is treated worse by the Holy See than the Slovaks"). The Vatican never extended diplomatic recognition to Pavelic's government, though it did send Msgr. Joseph Marcone to act as an "apostolic visitor" to the Catholic Church in Croatia. A short time after Marcone assumed his post, Cardinal Maglione instructed him to intervene on behalf of Jews and Serbs who were being persecuted by the regime. Until the end of World War II, Marcone worked tirelessly to alleviate the victims' suffering. The *Actes et Documents* collection shows that he worked closely with Chief Rabbi Miroslav Freiberger of Zagrab. In a dispatch to Cardinal Maglione, Marcone wrote: "In my contacts with Pavelic and the others, I always insisted upon a benevolent treatment for the Jews." *See* Ronald J. Rychlak, *In Defense of Cardinal Aloysius Stepinac of Croatia*, The Catholic Answer, March/April 2004, at 36.

125 *Minutes of August 7, 1941*, British Public Record Office FO 371/30175 57760 (noting that Pavelic was not given an audience with the Secretary of State).

126 *Vatican Book Justifies Cardinal Stepinac: Example of Opposition to Fascism, Nazism and Communism*, Zenit News Agency, March 10, 1999 (quoting Gianpaolo Mattei, author of a book on Stepinac).

127 Rick Hinshaw, *Cardinal's Past*, Chicago Tribune, October 17, 1998, at 26 (quoting Braier); Zenit News Agency, March 10, 1999.

128 Blet, chapter 8; *see* Lapomarda at 210, n.13.

129 Recent testing suggests that he was slowly poisoned by his captors. *See* Bruce Johnston, *Pope to beatify archbishop 'murdered by Tito'*, The Daily Telegraph, May 15, 1998, at 20.

130 Rick Hinshaw, *Cardinal's Past*, Chicago Tribune, October 17, 1998, at 26.

131 *Assembly Condemns Communist Treatment of Cardinal Stepinac and Andrija Hebrang*, BBC Summary of World Broadcasts, February 17, 1992.

132 *Id.*; Peter Hebblethwaite, *John Paul's uphill pilgrimage to Zagreb*, National Catholic Reporter, September 23, 1994, at 7.
133 *Vatican Book Justifies Cardinal Stepinac*, Zenit News Agency, March 10, 1999. *See* Ronald J. Rychlak, *In Defense of Cardinal Aloysius Stepinac of Croatia*, The Catholic Answer, March/April 2004, at 36.
134 "Some Franciscan friars took part in attacks on Serbian villages and one, Fra Filipovic was expelled from the Order in April 1943 for taking part in an attack on a Serbian village in February 1942. From April to October [1943] he was (under the name Filipovic-Majstorovic) commandant of the notorious Jasenovac concentration camp." Stella Alexander, *Croatia: The Catholic Church and Clergy, 1919-1945*, in *Catholics, the State, and the European Radical Right, 1919-1945* 54, 65 n.138-39 (Columbia University Press: New York, 1987).
135 *Id.* at 235 (Biographical Index).
136 All of this is well documented in the archives of the Franciscans, the Croatian archives, and depositions regarding Stepinac's beatification. *See also* Pattee, *The Case of Cardinal Aloysius Stepinac.*
137 *See generally The Pius War* at 270-71.
138 A note from Cardinal Maglione to the Nuncio in Romania [Cassulo], dated January 14, 1943 (*Actes*, vol. IX, at 81), responds to the nuncio's report of December 16, 1942. Maglione wrote that he "read with particular attention... all the steps that you made, behind the instructions of the Holy See, on behalf of Jews in general and the Jews converted to Catholicism especially...." Cardinal Maglione also sent Cassulo a report from a Jewish group in Switzerland that described the miserable conditions of Romanian Jews. The cardinal asked Cassulo to inform him whether the report was accurate, and if so, to act with prudence and a charitable spirit to "modify certain measures that are in contrast with the directives of Christian morality." On February 15, 1943, Cardinal Maglione sent Cassulo a sum of money to help alleviate the conditions of Jews who were imprisoned in Romania's concentration camps (Actes, Vol. IX, pp. 129). *See also* Congregation for the Causes of Saints, *Positio*, appendix 25 at 246 (reprinting the prologue to Levai, *Hungarian Jewry and the Papacy: Pope Pius did not Remain Silent*) (protest by the Romanian nuncio, made at the opportune time, led to partial success of delaying deportation).
139 Morley at 47.
140 *Memoirs: Resisting the Storm, Romania, 1940-1947* (Yad Vashem: Jerusalem, Jean Ancel, ed., 1987); Angelo Martini, *La Santa Sede e gli Ebrei della Romania Durante la Seconda Guerra Mondiale*, La Civiltà Cattolica, 1961, volume 3, at 446-63; Theodore Lavi, *The Vatican's Endeavors on Behalf of Rumanian Jewry During World War II*, 5 Yad Vashem Studies 405 (1963); Lapide at 162-169; David Herstig, *Die Rettung* (Seewald: Stuttgart, 1967); Ion Dumitriu-Snagov, *La Romania Nella Diplomazia Vaticana 1939-1944* (Editrice Pontificia Università Gregoriana: Rome, 1987).
141 *See* David Lampe, *The Danish Resistance* (Ballantine Books: New York, 1957); Leni Yahill. *The Rescue of Danish Jewry* (Jewish Publication Society: Philadelphia, 1969); *The Rescue of the Danish Jews: Moral Courage Under Stress* (New York University Press: New York, Leo Goldberger, ed., 1987).
142 During the war there were also "Catholic bishops, priests and students who wore the 'Jewish star' to declare their fellowship with the persecuted." John M. Oesterreicher, *As We Await "The Deputy"*, America, November 9, 1963, at 570. *See also* Rousmaniere, *A Bridge to Dialogue: The Story of Jewish-Christian Relations* at 121; Marchione, *Yours is a Precious Witness: Memoirs of Jews and Catholics in Wartime Italy* at 178.

143 "All legends to the contrary, King Christian X neither wore nor ever threatened to wear the Jewish star. Nor did he do anything memorable on behalf of the Danish Jews for the simple reason that such a thing was not necessary. No Jew in occupied Denmark was ever obliged to wear the Jewish star. A model satellite, of enormous economic importance to Germany, Denmark was always treated by the Nazis with great consideration." Istvan Deak, *The New York Review of Books*, March 23, 2000. For more information on the treatment of the Danes by the Nazis, *see* Hans Kirchhoff's comments in "Denmark," *The Holocaust Encyclopedia*, edited by Walter Laqueur (Yale University Press: New Haven, 2000), at 145-148.

144 Istvan Deak, *The Pope, the Nazis and the Jews*, The New York Review of Books, March 23, 2000.

145 "The extermination of more than 400,000 Hungarian Jews was the last act of the historical tragedy...." Congregation for the Causes of Saints, *Positio*, appendix 25 at 248 (reprinting the epilogue to Levai, *Hungarian Jewry and the Papacy: Pope Pius did not Remain Silent*). In June 1942, 17 year old Rudolf Vrba was shipped to Auschwitz. Fighting against starvation, typhus, and almost unbelievable brutality, he kept a complete record of Nazi horrors. Finally he managed to escape, and through the intervention of Pope Pius XII, he helped to save the lives of 600,000 Hungarian Jews. *See* Rudolf Vrba & Alan Bestic, *I Cannot Forgive : The Amazing True Story of a 17 Year Old Jewish Boy Who Defied the Germans at Auschwitz and Escaped to Alert the World to the Nazi Horror Camps!* (New York, Bantam Books, 1964).

146 Anti-Semitic laws had been proposed in Hungary prior to the occupation. Cardinal Justinian Séredi, the Primate, openly protested on the Senate floor: "Should your hearts, seized by race-hatred, drive you to vote for this law, hear my words—words which the Lord Himself suggests to me at this fateful moment. In truth I say to you: all the tears, all the victims, all the massacred martyrs will accuse you when your time comes to give an account before the Lord of your infamous act of this day. Remember the warning of Bernard of Clairvaux: 'Do not touch the Jews for they are the apple of God's eye.' In the name of Almighty God I shall vote against this infamous law." Purdy at 263-64.

147 Rychlak, *Hitler, the War, and the Pope* at 221-22.

148 *Id.*

149 Lapide at 151.

150 Pius personally drafted these telegrams. Tardini at 123 (reprinting copies of the original drafts); Holmes at 162. Admiral Horthy took note of the early efforts by the Catholic Church in his memoirs: "A protest made by the Prince-Primate Cardinal Serédi against the anti-Semitic measures was rejected." Admiral Miklós Horthy, *Memoirs* chapter 20 <<http://victorian.fortunecity.com/wooton/34/horthy/20.html>>.

151 Congregation for the Causes of Saints, *Positio*, appendix 25 at 246-47 (reprinting the prologue to Levai, *Hungarian Jewry and the Papacy: Pope Pius did not Remain Silent*); Holmes at 163.

152 *Quoted in* Holmes at 163.

153 Critics attempt to diminish the importance of this telegram by suggesting that it was isolated and late. The facts, however, are against them. Jenö Levai, the great authority on Hungarian Jewry, who had direct access to primary archival evidence, documented the Church's rescue efforts in his appropriately entitled work: *Hungarian Jewry and the Papacy: Pius XII Was Not Silent* (1968). *See* Congregation for the Causes of Saints, *Positio*, appendix 25 at 247.

154 Congregation for the Causes of Saints, *Positio*, appendix 25 at 247 (reprinting the prologue to Levai, *Hungarian Jewry and the Papacy: Pope Pius did not Remain Silent*).

155 *See Memo by Monsignor Tardini*, dated October 18, 1944, *Actes et Documents*, vol. X, p. 446, n.4 (no. 357).

156 *Time*, July 3, 1944.

157 *Memo by Monsignor Tardini*, dated October 18, 1944, *Actes et Documents*, vol. X, p. 446, n.4 (no. 357).

158 Graham, *Pope Pius XII and the Jews of Hungary in 1944* at 5-6 and footnote. *See also*, Roger Butterfield, *Cardinal Spellman*, Life, January 21, 28, 1946 (Spellman "became the Pope's radio expert"). There are several letters from 1964 in Spellman's papers reflecting his conviction that the allegations in *The Deputy* were factually wrong. Some letters refer to an article Spellman wrote on the topic, and one refers to a pamphlet.

159 *See* Blet, chapter 5.

160 *Report of Veesenmayer to Ribbentrop*, 6 July 1944, Nuremberg Trial Documents, NG 6584.

161 Lapide at 153, citing Jenö Levai, *L'Eglise se n'est pas tue* (Editions Du Seuil: Paris, 1966).

162 Graham, *The Vatican and Communism During World War II: What Really Happened?* at 163.

163 *Id.*; Graham, *Pope Pius XII and the Jews of Hungary in 1944* at 19-22.

164 Blet, chapter 9.

165 Lapide at 161. Jenö Levai reports that "in the autumn and winter of 1944, there was practically no Catholic Church institution in Budapest where persecuted Jews did not find refuge." He also affirms that "the Nuncio and Bishops of the Catholic Church intervened again and again on the instructions of the Pope." Levai at 17-54.

166 Blet, chapter 9.

167 *Actes et Documents*, Volume 10, document 227. Rotta commented on this in *Osservatore della Domenica*, June 28, 1964.

168 *Osservatore della Domenica*, June 28, 1964. *See also* Lapide at 152.

169 *See* Rychlak, *Hitler, the War, and the Pope*, at 225.

170 Lapide at 161.

171 Blet, chapter 9 (noting that the Nazis, who later overthrew Horthy, resumed surreptitious deportations). Unfortunately, the Soviets followed the Nazis, and they persecuted the Church and its leaders in Hungary, particularly Cardinal Mindszenty. *See* József Cardinal Mindszenty, *Memoirs* 117 (1974).

172 Blet, chapter 9; Graham, *Pius XII's Defense of Jews and Others: 1944-45*, in *Pius XII and the Holocaust: A Reader* at 61. Rabbi Herzog later wrote to the nuncio, saying: "The people of Israel will never forget what His Holiness and his illustrious delegates, inspired by the eternal principles of religion which form the very foundations of true civilization, are doing for us unfortunate brothers and sisters in the most tragic hour of our history, which is living proof of divine Providence in this world." *Id.*

173 To the entire international Jewish community, on December 3, 1944, Rabbi Safran declared: "My permanent contact with, and spiritual closeness to, His Excellency the Apostolic Nuncio, the Doyen of the Diplomatic Corps of Budapest, were decisive for the fate of my poor community. In the house of this high prelate, before his good heart, I shed my burning tears as the distressed father of my community, which was hovering feverishly between life and death." Graham, *Pope Pius XII and the Jews of Hungary in 1944* at 20. *See also* Congregation for the Causes of Saints, *Positio*,

appendix 25 at 239, 244 (quoting and reprinting the prologue to Levai, *Hungarian Jewry and the Papacy: Pope Pius did not Remain Silent*).

174 *See* Livia Rothkirchen, *The Destruction of Slovak Jewry* (Yad Vashem: Jerusalem, 1961); Livia Rothkirchen, *Vatican Policy and the "Jewish Problem" in "Independent" Slovakia (1939-1945)*, VI Yad Vashem Studies 27-53 (1966); Livia Rothkirchen, *The Churches and the 'Final Solution' in Slovakia*, in *Judaism and Christianity under the Impact of National Socialism 1919-1945*, 413-41 (Otto Dov Kulka and Paul R. Mendes-Flohr, eds. 1987) (mentioning several papal interventions for Jews and contrasting them favorably with the behavior of the local populace.) To the extent that deportations were minimized in Slovakia, Rothkirchen credits the Pope. Commenting on the decision of the Slovak authorities to suspend deportations in the spring of 1943, Rothkirchen says: "The impact of the Holy See at this phase was undoubtedly a decisive factor. This was known and widely commented upon." *Id.* at 419.

175 Rothkirchen, *The Destruction of Slovak Jewry*, at xxxiii; *see also* Lapide at 148; 358, n.28 (citing this passage). In volume XV of *Yad Vashem Studies*, John Conway also states that the archival material "confirms the picture already drawn by such Jewish authors as Livia Rothkirchen and Pinchas Lapide. Where the Nuncios were alert, and the governments susceptible to Papal remonstrances, then the interventions succeeded in delaying or reducing the deportations and other acts of persecution towards the Jews." *See generally The Pius War* at 271-73.

176 This, of course, is the opposite of the argument that Pius always opposed the Soviets, which some other critics advance.

177 Lapide at 138. In the Vatican, the Secretary of the Congregation for Extraordinary Ecclesiastical Affairs (Msgr. Domenico Tardini) recorded in his notes of October 21 and 23, 1941, that if the pro-Nazi statements attributed to Tiso were actually made by him, the Holy Father wanted his name to be removed from a list of prelates designated for special praise. *Actes et Documents*, vol. V, no. 123. Later, Tardini said: "It is a great misfortune that the President of Slovakia is a priest. Everyone knows that the Holy See cannot bring Hitler to heel. But who will understand that we can't even control a priest?" *Notes of Monsignor Tardini*, July 13, 1942, *Actes et Documents*, vol. VIII, no. 426, p. 598.

178 Lapide at 138. *See Actes et Documents*, vol. VIII, no. 305 (Vatican Secretary of State's concern over expulsion of Jews from the Slovak Republic).

179 *Tiso Chosen as First President of Slovakia; Vatican Frowns on Priest as head of State*, The New York Times, October 27, 1939, at 1.

180 *War Criminals and Punishment* (Robert M. McBride and Company: New York, 1944) at 113.

181 While Catholics did not face the same fate as Jews, official post-war documents confirm the Nazi efforts to suppress Catholicism: "At the outbreak of war, 487 Catholic priests were among the thousands of Czech patriots arrested and sent to concentration camps as hostages. Venerable high ecclesiastical dignitaries were dragged to concentration camps as hostages.... Religious orders were dissolved and liquidated, their charitable institutions closed down and their members expelled or else forced to compulsory labor in Germany. All religious instruction in Czech schools was suppressed. Most of the weeklies and monthlies which the Catholics had published in Czechoslovakia, had been suppressed from the very beginning of the occupation.... To a great extent Catholic church property was seized for the benefit of the Reich." Office of United States Chief of Counsel for Prosecution of Axis Criminality, *Nazi Conspiracy and Aggression*, United States Government Printing Office (Washington, D.C., 1947) at 283.

182 Lapide at 141.
183 *See Actes et Documents*, vol. IX, no. 87 (Vatican direction to impede the deportation of 20,000 Jews from Slovakia).
184 *Id.*
185 Jacques Maritain, *Atonement for All*, The Commonweal, Sept. 18, 1942, at 509.
186 O'Carroll at 105-06.
187 Holmes at 159-60; *See Actes et Documents*, vol. VII, no. 346 (Maglione's notes reflecting protests by the Holy See regarding "measures directed against the Jews.")
188 *Actes et Documents*, vol. IX, no. 141.
189 Blet, chapter 9. *See also* Congregation for the Causes of Saints, *Positio*, appendix 25 at 246 (reprinting the prologue to Levai, *Hungarian Jewry and the Papacy: Pope Pius did not Remain Silent*) (protest by the Slovak nuncio, made at the opportune time, led to partial success of delaying deportation). Denis Barton, *Fr. Tiso, Slovakia and Hitler* (Church in History Information Center: Birkenhead, 1990) refutes many accusations about the Catholic hierarchy in wartime Slovakia. Similarly, evidence of the Slovak bishops appeals for Jews is found in *The Tablet*, June 12, 1943, at 283 and July 3, 1943, at 8. Soon after the War, the Tablet re-affirmed that the Slovak Bishops "did in fact, in accordance with the desire of the Holy See, make most emphatic public denunciation of the persecution of the Jews." *The Tablet*, February 15, 1947, at 108.

7 The Hidden Pius XII

1 *The Times* (London), May 20, 1963; *see Confidential Letter to Oliver Harvey from D'Arcy Osborne*, February 26, 1947, British Public Records Office, FO 371/67917 60675. Osborne served as minister to the Holy See from 1936 to 1947.
2 *See* Ronald J. Rychlak, *The Church and the Holocaust*, The Wall Street Journal (European edition), March 28, 2002 (reviewing the motion picture *Amen*, which was based on Rolf Hochhuth's 1963 play, *The Deputy*).
3 "Cardinal Pacelli belongs among the most impressive personalities that I have ever met in my life as man, as intellect, as priest, in short as the prototype of a timeless but at the same time very modern prince of the Church." Kurt von Schuschnigg, *Austrian Requiem* 107 (1946) (as identified on the title page, Schuschnigg was "Chancellor of Austria and Prisoner of Hitler").
4 McCormick at 99.
5 *Id.*
6 Cheetham at 291; Curtis Pepper, *The Pope's Back Yard* 178 (1968); Doyle at 29.
7 *The Story of the Pope* at 33.
8 McCormick at 130 (from a *New York Times* dispatch of December 26, 1945).
9 Hatch & Walshe at 210-11. Critic John Cornwell criticized Pius for appearing in film and suggested that this indicated an egocentric side to his personality. Actually, this was just a matter of technology catching up with the papacy. *See* James W. Demers, *The Last Roman Catholic?* 20 (1991) ("we saw more of [Pope John XXIII] in a short year than we ever saw of Pius XII in the whole of the '50s.")
10 Marchione, *Pope Pius XII* at 83.
11 Joseph F. Dinneen, *Pope of Peace*, Reader's Digest, June 1939, at 83.
12 *Catholic Herald*, May 24, 1963, quoted in Desmond Fisher at 28.
13 Kaiser Wilhelm, who met Pacelli in 1917, gave a "famous" description of him: "Pacelli is an attractive and distinguished man, of high intelligence with very fine manners: he is the perfect model of an eminent prelate of the Catholic Church." *Quoted in*

Purdy at 12. Pius was also a strong advocate for his causes. The cover story in a wartime issue of *Time* magazine identified him as "one of the world's most hardheaded statesmen." *Peace & the Papacy*, Time, August 16, 1943, at 55.

14   Hatch & Walshe at 32.

15   This is in the documents that were gathered for the *Positio*.

16   Doyle at 4.

17   Burton at 17.

18   A version of this story, presented as fact, appears in Lenn & Reardon at 36.

19   Marchione, *Pope Pius XII* at 44.

20   Cal and Rose Samra, *More Holy Humor* (Guideposts, 1977).

21   Marchione, *Shepherd of Souls: A Pictoral Life of Pope Pius XII* at 64.

22   Tardini at 34; *see also* Lenns & Reardon at 130 ("he often smiles").

23   Ann Aubrey Hanson, *San Diego Diplomat Defends Pope Pius XII*, The Southern Cross, January 15, 2004, at 2.

24   Kurt Klinger, *A Pope Laughs* 74 (1964).

25   Lenns & Reardon at 59.

26   *Mr. Kirkpatrick (The Vatican) to Sir R. Vansittart*, August 19, 1933, *Documents on British Foreign Policy*, Series II, vol. V, London, 1956, no. 342, p. 524; Congregation for the Causes of Saints, *Positio*, appendix 25 at 270 (reprinting Peter Gumpel, *Cornwell's Cheap Shot at Pius XII*, Crisis, December 1999).

27   Lapide at 120, quoting Erich Ludendorff, *General and Cardinal-On the Policy of the New Pope Pius XII 1917-1937* at 64. About this same time, Pacelli complained that Germany made more work for him than the rest of the world combined. William M. Harrigan, *Pius XII's Efforts to Effect a Détente in German-Vatican Relations, 1939-1940*, the Catholic Historical Review, July 1963 at 175. As Pope, he caused the German ambassador to complain following an audience: "Why does he insist on talking French [the official diplomatic language] when he speaks German as well as I do?" Purdy at 12.

28   Marchione, *Pope Pius XII* at 57.

29   Lenns & Reardon at 97.

30   Rose Fitzgerald Kennedy, *Times to Remember* 204-05 (Garden City, N.Y.: Doubleday and Co., 1974)

31   Marchione, *Pope Pius XII* at 46.

32   Lenns & Reardon at 98.

33   *Peace & the Papacy*, Time, August 16, 1943, at 55, 56; Hatch & Walshe at 120; *Current Biography, 1941* Maxine Block, ed., the H.W. Wilson Co., 1971 re-issue, at 673, 675.

34   McCormick at 100.

35   Lenns & Reardon at 61.

36   *The Catholic Treasury of Wit and Humor* 136 (Hawthorn Books, Inc., New York: 1960, Paul Bussard, ed.)

37   This story was relayed in *Pope Pius XII*, featuring Sr. Margherita Marchione and Ronald Rychlak, EWTN Home Video (2004).

38   Doyle at 60; Burton at 122; Nazareno Padellaro & Robert L Reynolds, *His Reign*, Wisdom, September 1957, at 25.

39   *See* pp. 5, 182.

40   Marchione, *Pope Pius XII* at 64.

41   Earl Alexander, *The Alexander Memoirs: 1940-1945* 122 (New York: McGraw-Hill, 1962). Shortly after Pius XII's death, Field Marshall Montgomery wrote in the October 12 issue of London's *Sunday Times*: "He was a great and good man, and I loved him."

42 McCormick at 150.

43 Burton at 141.

44 Marchione, *Pope Pius XII* at 63.

45 Korn at 151.

46 O'Carroll at 140. The *sedia gestatoria* is the portable papal throne used in certain pontifical ceremonies. It consists of a richly-adorned, silk-covered armchair, fastened on a platform, which twelve footmen (palafrenieri) in red uniforms typically carry on their shoulders. While Pius sometimes rode in it, "he was embarrassed by the manifestations of filial devotion showered on him.... He was humiliated and mortified when he had to appear with great solemnity and pomp." Marchione, *Pope Pius XII* at 44.

47 Burton, at 142.

48 Jean Guitton, *The Pope Speaks: Dialogues of Paul VI with Jean Guitton* 83 (1968).

49 *Id.*

50 Anton J. Gahlinger, *I Served the Pope* 45 (The Mission Press, Techny, IL: 1952).

51 *Id.*

52 McCormick at 144.

53 James W. Demers, *The Last Roman Catholic?* 26 (1991) ("He raised the papacy to a level of popular recognition never before reached.")

54 *The Story of the Pope* at 35.

55 Marchione, *Pope Pius XII* at 64.

56 In contrast, when the Nazis had attempted to score a diplomatic coup by having former World Heavyweight Champion boxer Max Schmeling meet with the Pope, Pius refused to grant him a private audience. Simpson at 146-47.

57 Marchione, *Pope Pius XII* at 64.

58 *Id.* at 67.

59 *Id.* at 62.

60 Lenns & Reardon at 122.

61 Burton at 143.

62 Doyle at 101.

63 Priests, who were accustomed to kneeling when addressing a Pope, did not know how to act when speaking to Pius on the phone. Some knelt, which led to the ridiculous charge leveled by critic John Cornwell that the Holy Father demanded this of all to whom he spoke on the phone.

64 Lenns & Reardon at 130; *Current Biography, 1941* Maxine Block, ed., the H.W. Wilson Co., 1971 re-issue, at 673, 675.

65 *Current Biography, 1941* Maxine Block, ed., the H.W. Wilson Co., 1971 re-issue, at 673, 675. He replaced the Vatican automotive fleet with new cars that were gifts of manufacturers. *Peace & the Papacy*, Time, August 16, 1943, at 55, 56.

66 *Peace & the Papacy*, Time, August 16, 1943, at 55, 56 (quoting "a Catholic commentator").

67 Tardini at 64.

68 Doyle at 115.

69 Jean Guitton, *The Pope Speaks: Dialogues of Paul VI with Jean Guitton* 83 (1968).

8 *Illogical Arguments and Manufactured Evidence*

1 It was also used to illustrate James Carroll, *The Silence*, The New Yorker, April 7, 1997; James Carroll, *The Holocaust and the Catholic Church*, The Atlantic Monthly, October 1999, at 107; the German version of Peter Godman's book (*Der Vatikan und*

Hitler: Die geheimen Archive (Droemer, 2004); and Matteo L. Napolitano & Andrea Tornielli, *Il Papa Che Salvò Gli Ebrei* (Piemme, 2004) (an Italian book favorable to Pius XII that uses this photo as a response to *Hitler's Pope*).

2   Some reviewers of *Hitler's Pope* did assert that Pius met with Hitler. *See* Linda Massarella, *Book Paints WWII Pope as Hitler Ally—Author: Vatican Files Show Pius Hated Jews*, The New York Post, September 7, 1999, at 12.

3   Congregation for the Causes of Saints, *Positio*, appendix 25 at 268 (reprinting Peter Gumpel, *Cornwell's Cheap Shot at Pius XII*, Crisis, December 1999). The error was corrected in later versions of the dust jacket. "It was only after repeated protests that the publisher provided a new dust jacket for the books not yet sold." Peter Gumpel, *A Journalist Purporting to be a Scholar*, Die Furche, January 6, 2000, at 1.

4   I originally attributed this matter to the publisher, but Cornwell has admitted that he approved the cover. *Vatican Chronicles: A Different Read*, Brill's Content, April 2000, at 60, 120.

5   *Time* magazine received some criticism when it did the same thing to O.J. Simpson during his trial for the murder of Ron Goldman and Nicole Brown Simpson. Les Payne, *An O. J. Portrait Gets Media Sneer*, Newsday July 31, 1994, at 42.

6   The dishonesty was uncovered by Prof. Robert Gorman, who presented a paper on this topic at the October 2001 meeting of the Society of Catholic Social Scientists at Ave Maria Law School in Ann Arbor, Michigan.

7   Thomas Merton, *Dancing in the Water of Life* at 84. This passage was written in anger. The following day, Merton tempered his comments (and his anger) about having been ordered not to publish his essay.

8   The Secretariat of State authorized Cornwell to consult the archive of the section on Relations with States, which he did for some three weeks. The topic of his research was relations with Bavaria (1918-1921); Austria, Serbia, and Belgrade (1913-1915). He had no access to the "closed period," beginning in 1922. Cornwell was neither the first nor the only one to consult the archives of those years. Congregation for the Causes of Saints, *Positio*, appendix 25 at 265.

9   *Una doverosa precisazione in merito ad un libro recente*, L'Osservatore Romano, October 13, 1999 (reprinted in Congregation for the Causes of Saints, *Positio*, appendix 25 at 267.) It was also reported on Vatican Radio. Many of Cornwell's errors are minor to the point of being trivial, or they are discussed in other parts of this book. For a few examples: Cornwell completely misrepresents Pacelli's visit to Budapest to speak at the International Eucharistic Congress in 1938; Pius was not silent during September 1939; Pius intervened early—not late—in France, Hungary, and other occupied nations; FDR's representative Myron C. Taylor had nothing but the highest praise for Pope Pius XII after the war (in fact, he gave his Roman villa to the Church, even though he was not Catholic); radio priest Fr. Charles Coughlin did not stop broadcasting in 1936 (though *at Pacelli's direction* he pulled away from national politics; Pius XII ordered Coughlin off the air after he became Pope); the German ambassador to the Vatican did not plead for a public condemnation of the Nazis, precisely the opposite; Nicholas Horthy was not president but regent of Hungary, and he was a Calvinist not a Catholic, and Pacelli did appeal to him to stop the deportations; and Pius XII's 1942 Christmas address was demonstrably more than "a paltry statement." *See* Ronald J. Rychlak, *The Selling of a Myth*, Inside the Vatican, Oct. 1999, cited in Congregation for the Causes of Saints, *Positio*, appendix 25 at 275; Ronald J. Rychlak, *Historical Dishonesty: The Big Lie of "Hitler's Pope"*, This Rock, January 2001.

10   The "sub-editorial conflation" language was edited out of the Brill's Content piece when it was published.

11   *See* Congregation for the Causes of Saints, *Positio*, appendix 25 at 266.

12   This refers to the transcript of testimony given by 98 witnesses between the years 1967 and 1974. There are two "original" handwritten files containing these documents, but edited versions have been typed, indexed, and printed. They now form the *Positio*'s Summarium.

13   Congregation for the Causes of Saints, *Positio*, appendix 25 at 274 (reprinting Peter Gumpel, *Cornwell's Cheap Shot at Pius xii*, Crisis, December 1999) ("The Acts of the Cause of Beatification and Canonization of Pope Pius xii are not at all secret. Cornwell is not telling the truth...."). *See* Kenneth Woodward, *The Case Against Pius xii*, Newsweek (International), September 27, 1999, at 66 ("I have seen [the files] myself"); Felicity O'Brien, *Looking Back on Pius xii*, Newsweek, October 25, 1999, at 18 ("In the late 1980's I studied the sworn testimonies gathered for the Canonization Cause of Pius xii in Rome"). Deposition transcripts are kept secret while testimony is actively being taken, so that later witnesses are not "tainted" by hearing the testimony of witnesses who came earlier. Once depositions are ended, the files are no longer officially secret. In light of the fabrications set forth by Cornwell, however, the Holy See has been more reluctant than usual to permit access to those particular files.

14   John Cornwell, *Look at the Facts: John Cornwell Replies*, The Tablet (London), September 25, 1999.

15   At least one author has argued that Pius xii's housekeeper, Sister Pascalina Lehnert, dominated the Vatican under Pope Pius xii. *See* Paul Murphy, *La Popessa*. Cornwell largely accepted this depiction, even though it was inconsistent with the picture of Pius that Cornwell presented throughout *Hitler's Pope*. Certainly Sister Pascalina did not present a similar depiction in her testimony. Congregation for the Causes of Saints, *Positio* (*Summarium*). Nor did she suggest anything like that in her memoirs. *See* Sister Pascalina Lehnert, *Ich durfte ihm dienen: Erinnerungen an Papst Pius xii* (Würzburg, 1982); Sister Pascalina Lehnert, *Pio xii* (Rusconi Libri: Milan, 1984) (Italian translation). As one author noted: *La Popessa* "is a world apart from the genuine memoirs of the nun; it is a world of arbitrary invention, carried at times to the wildest extremes." O'Carroll at 244. Those who knew Pius xii's Vatican well did not think that Sister Pascalina dominated the Pope. *See* Sereny at 310, quoting Monsignor Karl Bayer. *See also* Robert A. Graham, *Will the Real Sister Pascalina Please Step Forward*, Columbia Magazine, November 1983, at 9.

16   Congregation for the Causes of Saints, *Positio*, appendix 25 at 265.

17   *Positio, Appendix 25* at 274 (reprinting Peter Gumpel, *Cornwell's Cheap Shot at Pius xii*, Crisis, December 1999).

18   As for Cornwell's publicity campaign, *see* Congregation for the Causes of Saints, *Positio*, appendix 25 at 265.

19   A brief summary of Repgen's work can be found in *Controversial Concordats: The Vatican's Relations with Napoleon, Mussolini, and Hitler*, 236-38 (The Catholic University of America Press, Frank J. Coppa, ed., 1999). His works include: Konrad Repgen, *Das Ende der Zentrumspartei und Entstehung des Reichskonkordats*, Militärseelsorge, 2 (1970), and later reissued in *Historische Klopfsignale für die Gegenwart*, Münster: Verlag Aschendorff, (1974) (concluding that the Center Party was not traded for the concordat); Konrad Repgen, *Dokumentation. Zur Vatikanischen Strategie beim Reichskonkordat, Vierteljahrshefte für Zeitgeschichte* 31 (1983) (the prohibition of clergy from party politics took place after the dissolution of the party); Konrad

Repgen, *Hitlers Machtergreifung und der deutsche Katholizismus. Versuch einer Bilanz,* in *Katholische Kirche im Dritten Reich,* edited by Dieter Albrecht, Mainz: Matth-ias-Grünewald-Verlag (1976) (absolving Ludwig Kaas and the Vatican of initiating concordat negotiations and of making a deal to vote for the enabling act); Konrad Repgen, *Über Umlaut! die Entstehung der Reichskonkordats-Offerte im Frühjahr 1933 und die Bedeutung des Reichskonkordats, Vierteljahrshefte für Zeitgeschichte* 25 (1978) at 499-534 (providing a detailed critique and refutation of Scholder's thesis that concordat negotiations influenced the Center Party's vote for the enabling act). *See also* Konrad Repgen, *Reichskonkordats-Kontroversen und historische Logik,* in *Demokratie und Diktatur.* Geist und Gestalt politischer Herrschaft in Deutschland und Europa. Festschrift für Karl Dietrich Bracher (Düsseldorf, 1987), ed. Manfred Funke et al., pp. 158-77.

20 Congregation for the Causes of Saints, *Positio,* appendix 25 at 269 (reprinting Peter Gumpel, *Cornwell's Cheap Shot at Pius XII,* Crisis, December 1999). *See* Ludwig Volk, *Das Reichskonkordat vom 20. Juli 1933,* Mainz: Matthias-Grünewald-Verlag (1972); *Controversial Concordats* at 241-42 (calling *Das Reichskonkordat* "the most scholarly study of the subject" and briefly summarizing Volk's other work).

21 Alfons Kupper, *Staatliche Akten über die Reichskonkordatsverhandlungen* (Mainz, 1969) (collection of documents showing that the initiative for the concordat came from the Reich government); John Jay Hughes, *The Pope's Pact with Hitler,* 17 Journal of Church and State 63 (1975). *See Controversial Concordats* at 233-34 (synopsis of Kupper). *See also* pp. 23-30, 83-86.

22 *A Requiem for Hitler* xii-xiii (Trinity: Philadelphia, Gerhard Besier, ed., 1989).

23 I have personally seen well marked-up copies of Scholder's work in Gumpel's office.

24 Peter Gumpel, *Cornwell's Pope: A Nasty Caricature of a Noble and Saintly Man,* Zenit News Service, Sept. 16, 1999 (also discussing Cornwell's "blind faith" in the suspect memoirs of Heinrich Brüning).

25 John Cornwell, *Hitler's Pope: The Fight to reveal the secrets that threaten the Vatican,* The Sunday Times (London), Sept. 12, 1999, at l.

26 *Jerusalem Post,* March 23, 2000 (online edition).

27 *Id.* In *The Pontiff in Winter,* Cornwell refers to his own inside-the-Vatican, deep throat: Monsignor Sotto Voce. Taking Cornwell at his word, and accepting his de-scription of Monsignor Sotto Voce, *The Pontiff in Winter* gives an "inside account" from a disgruntled and burned-out Vatican official who trades secrets for a good meal and a couple of bottles of wine. The great advantage for Cornwell, of course, is that this lets him write almost anything, and no one can prove it is false.

28 *See* Ronald J. Rychlak, *Guess Who's Back?,* Catalyst (Jan.-Feb. 2002) (reviewing *Break-ing Faith*); Ronald J. Rychlak, *A Broken Faith: John Cornwell's New Book,* St. Austin Review, July/August 2002.

29 In *Breaking Faith,* Cornwell presented the excommunication of Sri Lankan theologian Fr. Tissa Balasuriya as an example of the harshness of John Paul's "authoritarian rule." Balasuriya was excommunicated for theological aberrations, barely mentioned by Cornwell, that included the assertion that Christianity is on the same level as other religions, the denial of the virgin birth of Christ, and the rejection of the Holy Trinity. *See* Ronald J. Rychlak & Fr. Kevin Slattery, *A Clear-Cut Case For Excom-munication,* New Oxford Review, April 1997. Cornwell used the excommunication to argue that John Paul was insensitive and out-of-touch with the modern world. He did not, however, even mention the extended negotiations between Balasuriya and the Vatican that preceded the excommunication. More incredibly, he failed to

mention that one year after the excommunication was imposed, it was lifted. At that time, Balasuriya signed a statement expressing regret for perceptions of error in his work and agreed to submit future writings to bishops for approval prior to publication. This resolution to the matter, unknown to most readers of *Breaking Faith*, severely undercuts Cornwell's thesis *and* his credibility.

30 Similarly, James Carroll's resolution to this history, as set forth in *Constantine's Sword* (pages 555-58), involves the convening of Vatican III, at which (in addition to rejection of papal infallibility, ordination of women, election of bishops, and relaxation of sexual rules) the Church would acknowledge errors in the Gospels, learn to preach against those errors, and reject the belief that Jesus is the only way to salvation. Similar themes were also advanced by critic Daniel Goldhagen. For a critique of Carroll's work, *see* Gallo at 324, n. 31.

31 On a television appearance he claimed to be completely in agreement with the Church's teaching on abortion, but the book does not read that way. At one point in *Breaking Faith* he refers to it as "a painful choice to be made by individual women."

32 Deal Hudson, *Crisis Interview with John Cornwell*, Crisis, March 2002.

33 In actuality, Pius embraced democratic ideals, particularly in his 1944 Christmas message. *See* McCormick at 125.

34 *Quoted in* G. Thomas Fitzpatrick, *Understanding the Pedophilia Crisis in the Boston Priesthood*, the New Oxford Review (June 2002).

35 Stanley L. Jaki, *Newman: Myths & Facts*, New Oxford Review, November 2001, at 19.

36 Regarding the similar tactics employed by Pius XII and John Paul II, see *Bill O'Reilly Gets in Over His Head*, Catalyst, April 2003 (quoting a press release from the Catholic League for Religious and Civil Rights): "Just last Saturday Fidel Castro presided over the inauguration of a new convent of nuns in Cuba. He did so as a fitting tribute to the fifth anniversary of Pope John Paul II's visit to Cuba.... [T]he pope was able to accomplish this without ever having a position on Fidel Castro. Come to think of it, the pope never had a position on any of the Soviet Union's officials, yet even Gorbachev credited the Holy Father with bringing about the implosion of the U.S.S.R."

37 Alan Cowell, *Demonstrators and Devout Greet the Pope In Germany*, The New York Times, June 24, 1996, section A; page 3.

38 *See* Congregation for the Causes of Saints, *Positio*, appendix 25 at 279. An interesting letter, which confounds Zuccotti's thesis, can be found in *Dietrich Bonhoeffer: Letters and Papers from Prison* (Eberhard Bethge, ed., Collier Books, New York, enlarged ed., 1971). The letter, to Bonhoeffer from a co-conspirator in the resistance, was worded so vaguely that the true message–about meeting with papal assistants who had been "let in on the conspiracy"–is decipherable only because the author of the letter also edited the collection of letters and was able to explain it in a footnote. *Id.* at 214.

39 In addition to the archives, Zuccotti reviewed the Vatican's published documents on the Holy See and the Second World War (*Actes et Documents*). In her introduction, she explained her belief that all of the good evidence about Pope Pius XII appears in these published documents. She wrote that if there were a papal order to help Jews, it "would almost certainly have been preserved by someone clever enough to understand that it might someday help the Pope's reputation." Failing to find a written order from Pius among those documents, she assumed that he did not participate in rescue efforts. She thus rested her case on the absence of documents, not the existence of evidence. *Nowhere* in the book did she cite a single Italian priest, nun, or bishop who criticized Pope Pius XII by name for an alleged failure to assist

Jews. In fact, despite her strained arguments, the actual evidence that Zuccotti has uncovered demonstrates the heroic leadership of the Nazi-era Popes.

40   Eugenio Zolli, *The Nazarene: Studies in New Testament Exegesis* 9 (Cyril Vollert trans. 1999).

41   Kenneth C. Davis, *Don't Know Much About the Bible: Everything You Need to Know About the Good Book but Never Learned* (2001).

42   *See* Alana M. Fuierer, *The Anti-Chlorine Campaign in the Great Lakes: Should Chlorinated Compounds Be Guilty Until Proven Innocent?*, 43 Buffalo L. Rev. 181 (1995) (citing the rule); Ronald Bayer, Lawrence O. Gostin, and Deven C. Mcgraw, *Trades, AIDS, and the Public's Health: The Limits of Economic Analysis*, 83 Geo. L.J. 79 (1994) (same).

43   *See* Ian Buruma, *Depravity Was Contagious*, The New York Times (Books), Dec. 10, 2000 (reviewing Ian Kershaw, *Hitler 1936-45: Nemesis*).

44   *See Dietrich Bonhoeffer: Letters and Papers from Prison* 214 (Eberhard Bethge, ed., Collier Books, New York, enlarged ed., 1971). Bethge, active in the German resistance and a collaborator of Bonhoeffer, noted in a wartime letter that Catholic leaders could express their opposition to the Nazis without words: "How easy it is for Catholics now, as they can largely dispense with words and preach with their dress and gestures." *Id.   See also* McCormick at 118 (from a *New York Times* dispatch of August 24, 1944) ("What the Pope did was to create an attitude in favor of the persecuted and hunted that the city was quick to adapt, so that hiding someone 'on the run' became the thing to do.")

45   Letter of Giovanni Battista Montini to Giovanni Palatucci.

46   Erich Ludendorff had been a leader of the German Army, especially at the end of the First World War. He was an early supporter of the Nazi Party.

47   See p. 14.

48   See p. 14.

49   *New Proofs of Pius XII's Efforts to Assist Jews 1933 Letter Targets "Anti-Semitic Excesses" in Germany*, Zenit News Service, Feb. 17, 2003. "It is significant that the first initiative of the Holy See toward the government in Berlin concerned the Jews. As early as April 4, 1933, 10 days after the Enabling Act, the Apostolic Nuncio in Berlin [Orsenigo] was ordered to intervene with the government of the Reich on behalf of the Jews and point out all the dangers involved in an anti-Semitic policy." Robert Leiber, *Mit brennender Sorge: März 1937-März 1962*, in the March 1962 issue of Stimmen der Zeit, (Volume 169) at 420. *See* Godman at 37-38 ("Orsenigo read the Catholic vice-chancellor, Franz von Papen a lesson on how the legislation represented 'an offense against the divine law.'").

   Similarly, famed Italian bicyclist Gino Bartali helped rescue 800 Jews at the direction of Pope Pius XII, according to other newly-discovered documents. *Pius XII's Directive Helped Save 800 Jews in 3 Cities, Papers Reveal*, Zenit News Service, April 8, 2003. For other new evidence that undercuts Zuccotti's thesis, see the discussion of Adolf Eichmann's memoirs and the events of October 16, 1933, p. 15.

50   Zuccotti, *Under His Very Windows* at 180.

51   *Actes et Documents*, vol. IX, no. 356.

52   Congregation for the Causes of Saints, *Positio*, appendix 25 at 281.

53   In a later article, Zuccotti acknowledged this meaning of these indications. Susan Zuccotti, *Pope Pius XII and the Rescue of the Jews in Italy: Evidence of a Papal Directive?*, 18 Holocaust and Genocide Studies, 255 n.9 (Fall 2004).

54   Lapide at 134 (emphasis added).

55   Richard Owen, *Vatican war hero may have been Nazi 'mole'*, The Times (Europe), July 3, 2000 (noting that German files show that O'Flaherty may have provided inaccurate information to the Germans during the war).

56   "During Rome's occupation by the Nazis, the number of people Monsignor O'Flaherty helped ran well into the thousands. He never asked a person to name his religion. That would not have been like him. Besides, under the Nazi regime if a Jew told the truth about his religion, he would automatically be calling himself a criminal, for to the Nazis, to be a Jew was the biggest crime of all!" Madden at 104-05. *See also* J. P. Gallagher, *Scarlet Pimpernel of the Vatican* (Souvenir Press, 1967).

57   Gallagher, *Scarlet Pimpernel of the Vatican* (emphasis added). Pope Pius xii knew about O'Flaherty's lifesaving activities, and it was a clear breach of neutrality that could endanger the Vatican. Nevertheless, he "continued to turn a Nelsonian blind eye to the figure on St. Peter's steps, a figure he could see from his own study window as well as anyone else." *Id.* at 63. Pius and Cardinal Ottaviano, "the stern disciplinarian of the Holy Office and O'Flaherty's direct superior," kept their eyes "tightly closed" in order to let the "obstreperous Irish Monsignor" carry out his lifesaving operations. *Id.* at 174.

58   Simpson at 78 (emphasis added). Simpson was a Presbyterian from Scotland.

59   *See Under His Very Windows* at 329, n.3 (noting that this was done by Joseph Lichten, the editors of the *Actes et Documents* collection, and Robert Graham—one of the editors of the *Actes* in a different writing).

60   Lapide at 251; Desmond Fisher at 13; personal interview with Peter Gumpel, S.J., December 1999, Vatican City.

61   *Zanichelli's Italian and English Dictionary* (Chicago: NTC Publishing Group, 1993) at 304.

62   See Kenneth D. Whitehead, *The Pope Pius xii Controversy*, 31 The Political Science Reviewer 374 (2002).

63   *Under His Very Windows* at 22.

64   As Desmond Fisher wrote in 1965: "Pope Pius frequently used the word stirpe (race) to identify the Jews and no one could be in any doubt about his attitude." Desmond Fisher at 13.

65   Zuccotti somehow tries to diminish this intervention by reporting that it "should be described not as an official diplomatic protest of the roundup but as a desperate plea for Weizsäcker's intervention to save the victims." *Under His Very Windows* at 160.

66   Italics added for consistency.

67   Compare *Under His Very Windows* at 159 with *Actes et Documents*, vol. IX, no. 368.

68   Even critic James Carroll gave Maglione's entire text in his book, *Constantine's Sword*, at 525-526.

69   Compare *Under His Very Windows* at 103 with *Actes et Documents* vol. VIII, no. 434. *See* Blet at 234-35.

70   Tisserant, *Interview*, Informations Catholiques, April 15, 1964. *See also* O'Carroll at 14, 69.

71   *New York Times*, Feb. 26, 1964, p.41.

72   Tisserant, *Interview*, Informations Catholiques, April 15, 1964; O'Carroll at 14, 69.

73   *See* Stewart at 74. *See also* Robert Leiber, *Pio xii e Gli Ebrei di Roma, 1943-1944*, Civiltà Cattolica, Feb. 1961, vol. 1, at 449 (much aid was provided by Pius to Fr. Marie-Benoît's operations).

74   Stewart at 74.

75 *Actes et Documents*, vol. IX, no. 412.

76 Both Waagenaar and Zuccotti cite an obscure article, attributed to Marie-Benoît, suggesting that he received no real assistance from the Vatican. *Alcune precisazioni di Padre Benedetto*, Israel XLVI, 36, July 6, 1961 at 5. The article does not, however, appear to be credible. Not only does it contradict Benoît's other statements and those of his closest collaborator, Fernande Leboucher, it also is contradicted by Vatican archival records. *See Note of the Secretariat of State, Actes et Documents*, vol. 9, January 9, 1944, at 544-45 (attached to document 412). Perhaps most importantly, it refers to Monsignor Antonio Riberi as the apostolic nuncio to Italy–a post he never held. All rescuers in wartime Italy–and certainly Benoît would have known that this post was held by Franceso Borgongini-Duca.

77 Congregation for the Causes of Saints, *Positio*, appendix 25 at 282; Leboucher, (introduction).

78 Congregation for the Causes of Saints, *Positio*, appendix 25 at 282; Leboucher, at 141, 167-68. *See also* James Rorty, *Father Benoît: Ambassador of the Jews*, Commentary, December 1946 at 507, 513 ("The Nazis were never sure how much support Benoît was getting, or would get, from the Vatican. The record shows that he got a good deal.")

79 Lapide at 187-88, citing Document No. CXLV a-60 in the Archives of the Centre de Documentation Juive in Paris. *See also* Catholic Information Network, *In the Spirit of Christianity: Exhibition Online (History)*, The Holocaust World Resource Center, copyright 1999-2000 <http://www.hwrc.org/inthespirit/vatican.html>.

80 *Under His Very Windows* at 63.

81 *Summi Pontificatus*, para. 48. *See* pp. 91-99.

82 *Under His Very Windows* at 308.

83 The doctrine of subsidiarity teaches that "it is an injustice, a grave evil and a disturbance of right order for a larger and higher organization to arrogate to itself functions which can be performed efficiently by smaller and lower bodies." Pope Pius XI, *Quadragesimo Anno* (1931).

84 Pius wrote specifically about this issue in a letter to Bishop Preysing on April 30, 1943. *Lettres de Pie XII aux Evêques Allmands, 1939-1944*, ADSS, vol. 11, p. 318. *See* Sereny at 297 (noting that Pius also thanked Preysing for a bold sermon on the rights of all men, regardless of race or nationality). *See* ADSS, vol. 11, p. 322. *See also* Congregation for the Causes of Saints, *Positio*, appendix 25 at 246 (reprinting the prologue to Levai, *Hungarian Jewry and the Papacy: Pope Pius did not Remain Silent*) ("A public protest against the persecution of the Jews could only lead to the partial success of gaining time when it was made at a politically and militarily opportune time....")

85 Anne O'Hare McCormick, *Position of Pope in Italy has been Enhanced by War*, New York Times, August 21, 1944. Some critics have tried to argue that Pius was more concerned about buildings and artifacts in Rome than with the people. This absurd argument is rebutted by any of the number of appeals made to spare Rome because "house to house combat in the city would entail tremendous losses to both the attacking and the defending forces, and of course principally to the innocent civilian residents." *Letter to President Roosevelt from Apostolic Delegate, Archbishop Cicognani*, March 13, 1944 (original document posted on the Internet by the FDR Library).

86 Congregation for the Causes of Saints, *Positio* (*Summarium*).

87 Among the witnesses quoted by the Congregation for the Causes of Saints in appendix 25 (which deals with the kind of charges Zuccotti leveled) are: Pascalina Lehnert, Giovanni Stefanori, Maria Conrada Grabmair, Riccardo Lombardi, Giacomo Martegani, Carlo Pacelli, Cesidio Lolli, Enrico Galeazzi, Igino Giordani, Quirino Pa-

ganuzzi, Angelo Martini, P. Paolo Dezza, Cardinale Pietro Palazzini, and, P. Giacomo Martegani. Congregation for the Causes of Saints, *Positio*, appendix 25 at 285-90. There are also discussions of statements made by John Patrick Carroll-Abbing, Michael Tagliacozzo, and Adolf Eichmann. *Id.* at 290-93 (quoting Ronald J. Rychlak, *Comments on Zuccotti's Under His Very Windows*, 7 J. Modern Italian Studies 218 (2002) and *Jewish Historian Praises Pius XII's Wartime Conduct*, Zenit News, October 25, 2000).

88 See pp. 198-202, 216-17.
89 As I understand it, these transcripts are now being maintained in a more private manner than they had been. This is due to the Vatican's conclusion that John Cornwell misrepresented what he found in them. I also have been told, however, that if Zuccotti had sought permission to view these transcripts when she conducted her original research, it would have been granted.
90 According to the *Jerusalem Post* of May 29, 1955, "Conductor Paul Klecki had requested that the Orchestra on its first visit to Italy play for the Pope as a gesture of gratitude for the help his church had given to all those persecuted by Nazi Fascism."
91 Lapide at 137.
92 *Id.* at 181. *See* pp. 271, 263-64.
93 *Inside the Vatican*, June 1997 at 25 (quoting Fr. Peter Gumpel).
94 Pietro Palazzini, *Il clero e l'occupazione tedesca di Roma: Il ruolo del Seminario Romano Maggiore* 19, 29 (Apes: Rome, 1995).
95 *Id.* at 16-17; *see id.* at 35.
96 Ossservatore della Domenica, June 28, 1964, at 68-69.
97 *Interview with Zenit News Agency*, Oct. 26, 2000. *See* pp. 129-33.
98 Personal correspondence with the author. *See* Ronald J. Rychlak, *A "Righteous Gentile" Defends Pius XII*, Zenit News Agency, Oct. 5, 2002; Religious News Service, *Holocaust Hero Defends Papacy*, The Wanderer, Sept. 30, 1983. *See also* Harvey Rosenfeld, *Raul Wallenberg: Angel of Rescue* 72-81 (Prometheus: Buffalo, 1982); Kay Lyons, *Hungarian Catholic Given Highest Honors in Israel*, Western New York Catholic Visitor, March 4, 1979, at 6A-7A.
99 *Interview with Don Aldo Brunacci: The Secret Letter*, Inside the Vatican, January 2004, at 74.
100 Avvenire, June 27, 1996 (direct order from Pius to admit Jews to hospital prior to police sweep); CWN *More Echoes on Pope Pius XII, Nazi Holocaust*, June 27, 1996.
101 Antonio Gaspari, *The Jews Saved by Pius XII* (Gli ebrei salvati da Pio XII) (2001); Zenit News Service, *New Revelations on Jews Saved by Pius XII*, Feb. 16, 2001.
102 Marchione, *Yours is a Precious Witness* at 6.
103 Gaspari, *Gli ebrei salvati da Pio XII.*
104 Zenit News Service, *New Revelations on Jews Saved by Pius XII*, Feb. 16, 2001. *See also Encyclopedia of the Holocaust* (Macmillan, New York, 1990) ("In many monasteries, churches, and ecclesiastical buildings in Italy, Jews were saved during the Nazi occupation, and the simultaneous opening of so many Catholic institutions could have taken place only under clear instructions of Pius XII"). This entry was written by Prof. Israel Gutman, the chief historian at Yad Vashem.
105 Rabbi David Dalin, *Pius XII and the Jews*, The Weekly Standard, February 26, 2001, at 39.
106 Letter of Monty Jacobs of the World Jewish Congress to Edgar Alexander, dated March 24, 1959, enclosing an inter-office memo written by a World Jewish Congress officer "closely involved in these matters."
107 "Zuccotti and [Michael] Phayer; have ignored (not the "big picture"-but that too) clear evidence which refutes their basic contentions." Justus George Lawler, *Review*

Symposium: Proleptic Response, 20 U.S. Catholic Historian 89, 93 (2002).

108 Oppen at 409.

109 Justus George Lawler, author of *Popes and Politics: Reform, Resentment, and the Holocaust*, noted an injustice in Zuccotti's analysis: "It is noteworthy that when *L'Osservatore Romano* publishes an antisemitic sermon, it speaks not just for its editors but for 'Vatican officials, if not for the pope himself,'—the very mention of the pope, of course, unsubtly suggests, 'but yes possibly also for him.' (And the homily is that of [in Zuccotti's words] 'a *mere* bishop in the *prestigious Osservatore Romano*.')When, however, that journal publishes—to take an example from current critics of Pius—two attacks on the antisemitism of Kristallnacht, it is dismissed as 'an unofficial voice,' that does not represent 'the views of the Vatican,' *much less* of the pope." Justus George Lawler, *Review Symposium: Postscriptum Response*, 20 U.S. Catholic Historian 96, 113 (2002).

Lawler goes on explain that against this background, Zuccotti's statements "are at best disingenuous." *Id.* He notes her "cagey gambit of heavily footnoting her flying headers into the conjectural ether"—particularly her derogatory conclusions from *ex silencio* arguments which lead to "reliance on unverifiable" assumptions such as, "but he [Maglione] never denied the report." He elaborates: that is "escalation by insinuation. And when it is a tactic that runs through an entire book, it is called bias. Whether it is virulent depends on whether and how effectively one has been inoculated against falsehood." *Id.* at 117. Lawler provides this example: "Whereas the entire world of Vatican officialdom is depicted as knowledgeable in 1941 of the Nazi concentration camps and, less than a year later, of the beginning of the extermination process, in *The Holocaust, the French, and the Jews* virtually no one seemed to know of the camps. The French are exonerated by succumbing to 'a failure of imagination.' In the summer of 1943, according to Zuccotti, the head of the largest Jewish organization in France when informed of the mass execution of Jews, 'still found it unimaginable.' Whereas in Italy in that same summer, she tells us, 'Vatican officials *were perfectly aware* of the fact [that] millions of European Jews had been murdered in the Soviet Union and in Poland.'" *Id.* at 115.

Lawler goes on to explain that in Zuccotti's earlier book "she cites the opinion of Leon Poliakov and others, that the Vichy government knew of the exterminations by mid-1943. She then adds: 'These statements, however, all address the question of factual knowledge rather than emotional belief. To his own statement, Poliakov adds tellingly, "I did not believe it myself until April 1945."'" *Id.* at 116. In *Under His Very Windows*, as Lawler notes, neither Pius nor anyone else at the Vatican is allowed this distinction between factual knowledge and emotional belief. Lawler openly states that Zuccotti has a virulent bias against the Vatican or the Pope and that she is incapable of objectivity when writing about them. The disconnect between her two books is given as "only one example of such bias." *Id.* at 116.

110 Zuccotti treats her readers to an extended discussion of an order that went out to expel refugees from Church properties. Only after a long, speculative discussion about pressures put on refugees to leave Vatican properties, does she explain that the order was not enforced within the Vatican and had virtually no impact anywhere (those affected by it were referred to other Church properties). It is obvious to anyone giving it a fair reading that the unenforced order was nothing more than a means of appearing to comply with Nazi orders while still protecting the Jews. Congregation for the Causes of Saints, *Positio*, appendix 25 at 283. Such deception was necessary at that time. Considering her focus on original documents, it is worth noting that Zuccotti was unable to find any document linking Pius to the expulsion order. *See*

Ronald J. Rychlak, *Comments on Zuccotti's Under His Very Windows*, 7 J. Modern Italian Studies 218 (2002), cited at the definitive response to Zuccotti in Congregation for the Causes of Saints, *Positio*, appendix 25 at 279.

111 Lewy at 303-04, 400 n.147.

112 *See* Sánchez, *Pius XII and the Holocaust: Understanding the Controversy* at 98-99.

113 Lewy at 336.

114 *Compare* Ernst Troeltsch, *The Social Teachings of the Christian Churches*, trans. by Olive Wyon (New York, 1960).

115 Lewy at 336.

116 Oppen, *Nazis and Christians* at 394-95 (1969). Citing Conway's *The Nazi Persecution of the Churches 1933-45*, Oppen goes on to criticize Saul Friedländer's selective use of documents, which eliminated those that were favorable to the Vatican. *Id.* at 399. "In his discussion of German-Vatican relations, Friedländer has omitted the vast majority of these representations [from the Vatican to the Germans] and has referred only to certain unsuccessful gestures by the Nuncio–an omission which conceals the range and extent of the interventions made by the Vatican throughout the years of Nazi persecution. He has also chosen to overlook the most significant of papal protests, which, despite his contention, are to be found in the sources he used. This arbitrariness in selection is matched by a bias in interpretation which extends even to the various editions of his book." Conway, *The Nazi Persecution of the Churches 1933-45* at 449-50. Oppen further discusses sloppy or intentional mistranslations that magnified Friedländer's argument, to the detriment of the truth. Oppen at 400-402.

117 The claims of Catholic anti-Semitism that surrounded the release of Mel Gibson's movie, *The Passion*, merely brought to public attention a charge that had already been made repeatedly in the Pius XII debate. Critics argue that the Gospels are not historically accurate and that the story of Christ was revised to include anti-Semitic messages in order to advance certain political agendas long after the crucifixion. These critics, including Goldhagen and Carroll, want the Catholic Church (and, presumably, other Christians) either to modify the Gospels or to acknowledge that they contain error and to preach against those portions of scripture. They seem to be urging an ancient heresy called Marcionism, which eliminated politically unwelcome passages from the Bible. *See* Donald Attwater, *A Catholic Dictionary* 305 (1958).

118 *See also* W. Robert Aufill, *A Look at Dave Hunt, Leading Anti-Catholic Fundamentalist*, New Oxford Review (January 1999) at 30.

119 Illustrative of his biased analysis, Goldhagen twists Pacelli's 1933 promise not to interfere "in Germany's internal political affairs" into "the Church's intention to let the Germans have a free hand with the Jews." *See* Ronald J. Rychlak, *Daniel Goldhagen's Assault on Christianity*, 4 Totalitarian Movements & Political Religions 184 (2003); Ronald J. Rychlak, *Goldhagen v. Pius XII*, First Things, June/July 2002, at 37-54.

120 Joseph Cardinal Bernardin delivered a notable lecture at the Hebrew University in Jerusalem on March 23, 1995. It was entitled *Antisemism: the Historical Legacy and the Continuing Challenge for Christians*, and in it the cardinal acknowledged that portions of the Gospels, particularly the Gospel of John, can be misunderstood ("remain open to anti-Judaic interpretation"). Bernardin, however, drew on historical research, modern Catholic teaching, and current Biblical interpretation to show how anti-Semitic arguments come from a misunderstanding of the original texts, not from the Gospels themselves. In the end, Bernardin sided with scholars "who have insisted that 'the Holocaust was the work of a thoroughly modern, neopagan state,' not merely a 'transformed' medieval antisemitism rooted in Christian teachings." *Id.*

121 "Even in John's Gospel, where he refers to these people on occasion simply as 'the Jews,' he makes clear that he is referring to the elite leadership of the second-Temple." David B. Currie, *Are the Gospels Anti-Semitic?*, This Rock, March 2004, at 6, 7 (citing John 7:25-32, 48; 8:13, 22; 11:45; 12:42; 18:3, 14).

122 Luke 19:41-44; 22:2.

123 "Jesus never lost his obvious compassion for and identification with the crowds of Jewish people. In fact, that is what drove his anger with the leaders: They were leading their flock away." David B. Currie, *Are the Gospels Anti-Semitic?*, This Rock, March 2004, at 6, 8.

124 Because of the controversy over this line, it was eliminated from Mel Gibson's movie, *The Passion*.

125 Francis Spirago, *Anecdotes and Examples for the Catechism* (Roman Catholic Books: Fort Collins, CO., 1903). The wording once again makes clear that Catholics saw Jewishness as an issue of faith, not race.

126 *See* paragraph 597 of the Catechism of the Catholic Church.

127 "Pilate holds a preeminent place of moral culpability in this tragic affair. We are reminded of his failure each time we recite the Apostle's Creed." David B. Currie, *Are the Gospels Anti-Semitic?*, This Rock, March 2004, at 6, 8.

128 See pp. 42-43.

129 This is available on the Internet through the Vatican's web page. *See also* Rosalind Moss, *It Was Sin That Killed Our Savior: Reflections on Mel Gibson's The Passion of the Christ*, This Rock, April 2004, at 8.

130 "The long and short of it is that modern anti-Semitism does not find fertile soil in those with a full understanding of the New Testament and its teaching.... According to the New Testament, twenty-first-century Jews are no more nor less responsible for Christ's death than the Catholic sinner writing this article." David B. Currie, *Are the Gospels Anti-Semitic?*, This Rock, March 2004, at 6, 9.

131 This was not true of Jewish leadership during the Nazi era. Jewish leaders recognized a serious difference between Christian and Nazi beliefs. A book published by the Jewish Publication Society of America, Marvin Lowenthal, *The Jews of Germany: A Story of 16 Centuries* 416 (1939), explained why a Jew could never accept the Nazi idea of God: "The new gods of the racial cult are not, like the Christian Deity, his own under another rubric."

132 It is perhaps not surprising that Goldhagen would want to show that the Church has changed its doctrinal teachings over time. In his *Essay on the Development of Christian Doctrine* (1845), Cardinal John Henry Newman gave a lengthy defense of change as a sign of vitality in the Church. But he insisted on what he called "preservation of type," "continuity of principles," and "conservative action on the past." He clearly excluded the possibility of doctrinal reversal. Those who think that Christianity accommodates itself to times and seasons, he said, usually end up abandoning Christianity.

133 After Holy Scripture, the writings of Pope Pius XII are the most cited source in the documents of Vatican II. *See* Congregation for the Causes of Saints, *Positio*, appendix 18: *Documenti del Concilio Vaticano II Nei Quali si fa Riferimento a Testi di Pio XII*, p. 147-72 (reprinted from Paulo Molinari, *Pie XII et la Cité: La pensée et l'action politiques de Pie XII*).

134 Those who are interested in learning more about Catholic teaching regarding relations with Jews (which should include every reader who treated Goldhagen's book with any degree of respect) are advised to read Nostra Aetate, the Second Vatican Council's renewal of the Church's condemnation of anti-Semitism. Other helpful

sources include *The Jewish People and Their Sacred Scriptures in the Christian Bible*, by the Holy See's Pontifical Biblical Commission (available through the Vatican's web page); Eugene J. Fisher, *Faith Without Prejudice: Rebuilding Christian Attitudes Toward Judaism* (The American Interfaith Institute, 1993); *Introduction to Jewish-Christian Relations* (Michael Shermis and Arthur E. Zannoni, eds, 1991); Jacob Neusner, *A Rabbi Talks with Jesus: an Intermillennial, Interfaith Exchange* (Image Books: New York, 1994).

135   See Hugh Barbour, *Has the Church Ever Taught that the Jews Should be Persecuted and Segregated?*, Ad Veritatem, March 2004. "In the early centuries it was the Jews who persecuted the Christians. The Talmud composed back in those days contains slanders against the Christians that easily rival those directed by modern anti-Semites against the Jews. Early Christian writers were well acquainted with such slanders when penning replies to them in kind for which they are today reproached as anti-Semitic." Kenneth D. Whitehead, *Prominent Conservatives Join the Chorus Against "The Passion"*, Catalyst, April 2004, at 8, 9.

136   For a recent expression of different perceptions of Christians and Jews, *see* Meir Y. Soloveichik, *The Virtue of Hate*, First Things, January 2003 (Rabbi Soloveichik is shocked by Christ's last words from the Cross, asking forgiveness for those who crucified him, and suggests an alternative prayer: "Father, forgive them not; they know full well what they are doing.") *Compare* Alice von Hildebrand, *The Wounded Heart Forgives: A Catholic Response to the Claim that Hate is a Virtue*, This Rock, May/June 2003.

137   An Internet search will reveal many alleged quotations from the Talmud that seem very hostile to Christianity. With further effort, one can find more appropriate translations and interpretations of the Talmud. The Talmud certainly contains many references to righteous gentiles whose behavior is held up as a model for all people (*e.g.*, Dama ben Netina). Nevertheless, there has long been concern over some passages in the Talmud. *See* Steinsaltz at 82-85.

138   "...it was the Church, particularly the popes, that were often the protectors of the Jews from popular outbreaks against them. Pope St. Gregory the Great (590-604) strongly condemned violence against them, called for respect for their worship and liberty of conscience, and counseled equity and kindness towards them. Quite a while before Vatican II, the Second Council of Nicaea (787) decreed that the Jews should be allowed to "be Hebrews openly, according to their own religion." Kenneth D. Whitehead, *Prominent Conservatives Join the Chorus Against "The Passion"*, Catalyst, April 2004, at 8, 9.

139   *Id.*

140   A version of the full prayer went like this:
      "Let us pray also for heretics and schismatics: that our Lord and God would be pleased to rescue them from their errors; and recall them to our holy mother the Catholic and Apostolic Christian. Let us pray. Let us kneel. (Arise.) Almighty and eternal God, Who savest all, and wouldest that no one should perish: look on the souls that are led astray by the deceit of the devil: that having set aside all heretical evil, the hearts of those that err may repent and return to the unity of Thy truth. Through our Lord Jesus Christ, Who livest and reignest with God the Father in the unity of the Holy Ghost, through all endless ages. Amen.

      "Let us pray also for the perfidious Jews: that our God and Lord may remove the veil from their hearts; that they also may acknowledge Our Lord Jesus Christ. Let us pray. Let us kneel. (Arise.) Almighty and Eternal God, Who dost not exclude from Thy mercy even the perfidious Jews: hear our prayers, which we offer for the blindness of that people; that acknowledging the light of Thy Truth, which is Christ, they may be delivered from their darkness. Through the same Lord Jesus Christ, Who livest and reignest with God the Father in the unity of the Holy Ghost, through all endless ages. Amen.

"Let us pray also for the pagans: that Almighty God take away iniquity from their hearts: that leaving aside their idols they may be converted to the true and living God, and His only Son, Jesus Christ our God and Lord. Let us pray. Let us kneel. (Arise.) Almighty and Eternal God, Who seekest always, not the death, but the life of sinners: mercifully hear our prayer, and deliver them from the worship of idols: and admit them into Thy holy Church for the praise and glory of Thy Name. Through our Lord Jesus Christ, Who livest and reignest with God the Father in the unity of the Holy Ghost, through all endless ages. Amen."

141 A modern version of the prayer is as follows:
"Let us pray for God's ancient people, the Jews, the first to hear his word: for greater understanding between Christian and Jew; for the removal of our blindness and bitterness of heart; that God will grant us grace to be faithful to his covenant and to grow in the love of his name. (Silent prayer.) Lord, hear us. Lord, graciously hear us. Lord God of Abraham, bless the children of your covenant, both Jew and Christian; take from us all blindness and bitterness of heart, and hasten the coming of your kingdom, when Israel shall be saved, the Gentiles gathered in, and we shall dwell together in mutual love and peace under the one God and Father of our Lord Jesus Christ. Amen."

142 Jacques Maritain, *A Letter on Anti-Semitism*, The Commonweal, Feb. 27, 1948 (referring to "translations of the phrase perfidia Judaica… which are no more than vulgar misreadings, for in the language of the Church this word signifies 'unbelief' and not 'perfidiousness.'"); Alexis Bugnolo, *A Note on the Latin Phrase perfidus Iudaeus*, Seattle Catholic, June 27, 2003.

143 This was the ultimate conclusion of Joseph Cardinal Bernardin when he delivered his lecture, *Antisemism: the Historical Legacy and the Continuing Challenge for Christians*, at the Hebrew University in Jerusalem on March 23, 1995. *See supra* note 120, p. 335. Similarly, *Dabru Emet: A Jewish Statement on Christians and Christianity*, a document signed by nearly 170 Jewish scholars, was published in the *New York Times*, September 10, 2000, at 23, *reprinted in First Things*, November, 2000 at 39-44. The document repudiated the effort to blame the Holocaust on Christianity and explicitly declared: "Nazism was Not a Christian Phenomenon." *See also* Laurie Goodstein, *Leading Jewish Scholars Extend a Hand to Christians*, New York Times, September 8, 2000.

144 Pacelli's view that difficult decisions that could involve the risk of life had to be left to the individuals involved is reflected in an account provided by Dietrich Von Hildebrand, widely regarded as one of the great Catholic philosophers of the 20th Century and a noted opponent of Nazism. He visited Cardinal Pacelli during the Nazi era. According to Hildebrand's widow, Pacelli: "said that there could be no possible reconciliation between Christianity and racism; they were like 'fire and water.' The interview gave von Hildebrand great satisfaction. He was confident that Cardinal Pacelli was fully aware of the gravity of the situation in Germany." Hildebrand at 285-86.

145 *See* p. 153.

146 *The Nazi Master Plan: The Persecution of the Christian Churches.*

147 Hildebrand at 285-86.

148 Reproduced by the Danish press and cited by *Osservatore della Domenica*, June 28, 1964, at 49; *see also* Lapide at 266, 366, n.221; Marilyn Henry, *How pious was Pius*

XII?, The Jerusalem Post, Oct. 15, 1999; Kenneth D. Whitehead, *The Pope Pius XII Controversy*, 31 The Political Science Reviewer 310 (2002).

149 Zolli, *Why I Became a Catholic* at 187.

150 Congregation for the Causes of Saints, *Positio*, appendix 25 at 246 (quoting and reprinting the prologue to Levai, *Hungarian Jewry and the Papacy: Pope Pius did not Remain Silent*).

151 *Id.*

152 Religious News Service, *Holocaust Hero Defends Papacy*, The Wanderer, Sept. 30, 1983; Antonio Gaspari, *The Jews Saved by Pius XII* (Gli ebrei salvati da Pio XII) (2001); Zenit News Service, *New Revelations on Jews Saved by Pius XII*, Feb. 16, 2001. *See also* pp. 11, 149, 218-19.

153 Several sources argue that Pius XII wrote an extraordinary secret letter to the Catholic bishops of Europe entitled *Opere et caritate* (*By Work and by Charity*). Author/rescuer Fernande Leboucher wrote of Pius XII's 1942 "command addressed to all Christians, and particularly to the clergy, to the effect that every means available must be employed to save as many lives as possible." Leboucher at 141. Rabbi Zolli wrote: The Holy Father sent by hand a letter to the bishops instructing them to lift the enclosure from convents and monasteries, so they could become refuges for the Jews." Zolli, *Why I Became a Catholic* at 186. Cardinal Elia Dalla Costa, the archbishop of Florence, reported: "I've been in Rome long enough to understand the Pope's position. Instead of making meaningless declarations that would only antagonize the Germans, perhaps even make them occupy the Vatican itself, he issued orders–to save Jewish lives. We received his message loud and clear. How would Pietro Boetto in Genoa, Nicolini in Assisi, I here [in Florence] and so many other archbishops and bishops all over Italy, provide a sanctuary of Jews, if we did not feel that that is what His Holiness would wish us to do? ...In his own diocese–don't forget that the Pope is also Bishop of Rome–over a hundred convents and over fifty churches and theological seminaries are hiding four thousand Jews, half of the Jews of Rome...." Alexander Ramati, *The Assisi Underground* 50 (Stein and Day: New York, 1978). Similarly, when Monsignor Giuseppe Maria Palatucci, the Bishop of Campagna, and R.P. Alfonso Palatucci, the Provincial of the Franciscan Order in Puglie, were asked what had made them risk their lives for others, both referred to Vatican orders issued in 1942 'to save lives by all possible means.' Lapide at 134-35.

154 *See* Congregation for the Causes of Saints, *Positio*, appendix 25 at 290. *See also* pp. 11, 149, 215, 217.

155 This quotation was translated from a Nazi journal and printed in *The Tablet* (of London), volume 172, at 301 (1938).

156 Lapide at 118.

157 Knight Ridder Newspapers, *Pope's silence during Holocaust debated*, Las Vegas Review-Journal, at March 22, 1998.

158 *Id.*

159 *Id.*

160 The ADSS contains the diplomatic correspondence of the Holy See's Secretariat of State, as well as notes and memoranda from meetings with diplomats and Church leaders from various countries during the period of the Second World War. The documents are published in the languages in which they were originally written (primarily Italian, French, and German, but also some in Latin and English), but the editorial commentary is in French. Volumes I, IV, V, VII, and XI detail the Vatican's diplomatic relations with all the belligerent governments during World War II. Volumes VI, VIII, IX, and X show the Vatican's efforts to alleviate the suffering

of civilians, including the Jews. Volume II is a collection of Pius XII's wartime letters to the German bishops. Volume III, which is published in two parts, discusses the "religious situation" in Poland and the Baltic nations. Unfortunately, too many students and scholars have overlooked these critically important documents.

161 While the group called itself a commission, that term implies a status that this study group did not have. In fact, it was later learned that use of the word commission caused some degree of embarrassment to Cardinal Cassidy within Vatican circles. Catholic coordinator Eugene Fisher expressed regret over this and said that he would not have used the word commission had he known that it was inappropriate.

162 Since the time that the study group disbanded, certain archives that had been sealed were indeed opened, and more will be opened in the future. It has been widely reported in the press that this was due to pressure applied by the study group. The Vatican, however, did not cite that as a reason. In fact, a similar request from the Congregation for the Causes of Saints pre-dated the study group's request.

163 *Jerusalem Report* (Dec. 20, 1999). Later, in reviewing *A Moral Reckoning*, Wistrich noted that Goldhagen's proposals (abandoning papal infallibility, embracing religious pluralism, and re-writing the Bible), while not feasible, would be "highly desirable." *See* Richard John Neuhaus, *The Public Square*, First Things, June/July 2004, at 82.

164 *See* Dimitri Cavalli, *The Commission That Couldn't Shoot Straight*, New Oxford Review, July-Aug. 2002. If there was evidence to be had showing bad faith on the part of Pius XII, it would show up in archives from other nations. Nevertheless, the study group's conviction that hidden documents are in the Vatican archives clearly shaped its work. *See* Ronald J. Rychlak, *This New Commission is a Redundant Exercise*, Inside the Vatican, January 2000; Ronald J. Rychlak, *The Pope Pius XII Study Group: Read the Documents!*, Catalyst, December 2000.

165 I listened to audiotapes of this meeting and helped prepare a transcript of the meeting for the Congregation for the Causes of Saints. *See* Dimitri Cavalli, *The Commission That Couldn't Shoot Straight*, New Oxford Review, July-Aug. 2002.

166 Ronald J. Rychlak, *The Pope Pius XII Study Group: A Wasted Opportunity*, Catalyst, September 2001.

167 The International Catholic-Jewish Historical Commission *The Vatican and the Holocaust: A Preliminary Report. Reprinted in Origins*, November 9, 2000, at 342-351.

168 Dimitri Cavalli, *The Commission That Couldn't Shoot Straight*, New Oxford Review, July-Aug. 2002.

169 John Cornwell also used the opportunity to weigh in with his comments against the Vatican. John Cornwell, *Something to confess?*, Sunday Times (London) July 29, 2001.

170 Cardinal William Keeler said: "Dr. Bernard Suchecky... caused serious damage to the group's credibility by leaking its Preliminary Report during their meeting in Rome." *Statement by Cardinal William H. Keeler on Catholic - Jewish Holocaust Scholars Group*, News in Christian Jewish relations, July 27, 2001.

171 *See* Dimitri Cavalli, *The Commission That Couldn't Shoot Straight*, New Oxford Review, July-Aug. 2002.

172 *See* Ronald J. Rychlak, *The Pope Pius XII Study Group: A Wasted Opportunity*, Catalyst, September 2001.

173 *Catholic and Jewish Holocaust scholars suspend their activities*, News in Christian-Jewish Relations, July 2001.

174 Seth Isenberg, *Holocaust researcher: Vatican uncooperative*, The Jerusalem Post, July 25, 2001.

175 *See The Pius War* at 74 ("Their expectation that the Vatican authorities would yield to this form of pressure from an outside group was surely unrealistic, and could even be considered provocative.")

176 Keith B. Richburg, *Jewish Scholars on Panel Assailed by the Vatican*, The Washington Post, August 8, 2001.

177 Cindy Wooden, Catholic News Service, July 24, 2001; *Catholic and Jewish Holocaust scholars suspend their activities*, News in Christian-Jewish Relations, July 2001.

178 Cindy Wooden, Catholic News Service, July 24, 2001; *Catholic and Jewish Holocaust scholars suspend their activities*, News in Christian-Jewish Relations, July 2001.

179 *See* Rychlak, *A Response to The Vatican and the Holocaust.*

180 Fogarty came to this conclusion. Speaking at St. Joseph's Seminary in Yonkers on March 4, 2004, he was asked by Avery Cardinal Dulles whether there was anything that Pius could have done to save more Jews. Fogarty replied: "No, I don't think so." Gary Stern, *Wartime role of Pope Pius XII defended*, The Journal News, March 5, 2004.

181 *See* Ronald J. Rychlak, *The Pope Pius XII Study Group: A Wasted Opportunity*, Catalyst, September 2001.

182 *See* Gerhart Riegner, *Ne jamais desespérer: soixante années au service du peuple juif et des droits de l'homme* (Cerf: Paris, 1998).

183 Letter from Dr. G. Riegner of the World Jewish Congress to Nuncio Bernadini, datedApril 8, 1942.

184 *The Pius War* at 69.

185 *Judging Pius XII*, Inside the Vatican, February 2000, at 61, 66 (quoting Fr. Blet, who noted that the memorandum had been published in a well-known book prior to the Vatican's collection being published).

186 *Le nonce à Berne Bernardini au Cardinal Maglione*, March 19, 1942, *Actes et Documents*, vol. VIII, no. 314, p. 466.

187 *See* Rychlak *Hitler, the War, and the Pope* at 288; Peter Gumpel, *Cornwell's Pope: A Nasty Caricature of a Noble and Saintly Man*, Zenit News Service, Sept. 16, 1999.

188 With the emphasis that Zuccotti claims to put on original sources, the only explanation for her reliance on Katz is that she likes his conclusions.

189 The abbreviation is sometimes shortened to GAPO. Blet, Chapter 10.

190 Cornwell, *Hitler's Pope* at 320.

191 According to Vatican officials that I spoke with in 1999, Hitler originally ordered a 100-to-one reprisal, but he was talked into the more traditional 10 to one. Some of those executed were people who had already been condemned to death for other offenses.

192 *See* O'Carroll at 242.

193 Blet, Chapter 10.

194 This event was later depicted in an Italian motion picture entitled *La Rappresaglia* (1973).

195 Congregation for the Causes of Saints, *Positio*, appendix 25 at 252.

196 Katz, *The Battle for Rome* at 241.

197 Rychlak, *Hitler, the War, and the Pope* at 215; Blet, chapter 10.

198 Katz, *The Battle for Rome* at 241, 380 n. 7.

199 Gallo at 230 (this information provided nothing of importance to the Vatican).

200 That was why the papal statements following the massacre were appeals for peace rather than condemnations. Gallo at 240-45. Katz criticized Pius for this caution. Katz, *The Battle for Rome* at 73-74.

201 Allessandro Portelli, *L'ordine è già stato eseguito* (Rome, Donselli, 1999); Lutz Klinkhamer, *Stragi naziste in Italia: la guerra contro I civili* (Rome, Donzelli, 1933); Gallo at 230.

202 Congregation for the Causes of Saints, *Positio*, appendix 25 at 254; Robert Graham, *La rappresaglia nazista alle Fosse Ardeatine: P. Pfeiffer, messaggera della carità di Pio XII*, Civiltà Cattolica 1973, vol. 4, at 467-74.

203 *See* Rychlak, *Hitler, the War, and the Pope* at 215.

204 Graham, *Pius XII's Defense of Jews and Others: 1944-45* at 12; Congregation for the Causes of Saints, *Positio*, appendix 25 at 253-54; 256-59; Cornwell, *Hitler's Pope* at 321. Following the war, the German generals who ordered the executions were tried for war crimes, found guilty, and sentenced to death. Katz, *Massacre in Rome* at xii.

205 *Carità Civile, L'Osservatore Romano*, March 25, 1944, at 1.

206 *L'Osservatore Romano* is always released about 2:00 pm on the day before its date.

207 Congregation for the Causes of Saints, *Positio*, appendix 25 at 253.

208 *A Valiant Lady's Struggle on a Matter of Honor*, Columbia, December 1983, at 6. *See* Gallo at 209-27 (Katz's "account has been fabricated").

209 Peter Gumpel, *Cornwell's Pope: A Nasty Caricature of a Noble and Saintly Man*, Zenit News Service, Sept. 16, 1999; *Ponti guilty of defaming Pope Pius XII*, Facts on File World News Digest, (December 27, 1975) at 985 D2 ("Carlo Ponti, the Italian film director, Robert Katz, an American writer, and George Pan Cosmatos, a director, Nov. 27 were found guilty of having defamed Pope Pius XII in a film, "Massacre in Rome," based upon Katz's book, "Death in Rome."). *See* O'Carroll at 242.

210 *Decree of the President of the Republic*, May 22 1970.

211 The Associated Press, *American Writer Convicted of Defaming Pius XII* (July 2, 1981); Associated Press, *Author Says Sentence "Absurd"* (July 2, 1981); Robert A. Graham, *A Valiant Lady's Struggle on a Matter of Honor*, Columbia Magazine, December 1983, at 6. For full details on the lawsuit and final verdict against Katz, as well as his attempt to whitewash the matter, *see a propositio di Katz, in* Matteo L. Napolitano & Andrea Tornielli, *Il Papa che salvò gli Ebrei. Dagli Archivi segreti del Vaticano tutta la verità su Pio XII* 161-66 (Casale Monferrato: Piemme, 2004).

212 Italian attorney Giorgio Angelozzi Gariboldi represented Elena Rossignani in her suit against Katz and the others. In a statement published in Italy, he explained that in two separate decisions on the merits of the charge, Robert Katz was found guilty of having defamed Pius XII. Despite this, Critic John Cornwell says Katz provides "the most authoritative account" of the roundup of Roman Jews in October 1943.

213 According to the authors: "The major powers of the world have repeatedly planned covert operations to bring about the destruction of Israel." During the Six Day War, "The U.S. and British governments, while pretending to be on Israel's side, were giving all of Israel's secrets to the Arabs." Particularly appalling is their discussion of the USS Liberty, which Israel attempted to sink during the Six Day War. *See* James M. Ennes, Jr., Book Review: *The Secret War Against the Jews* by John Loftus and Mark Aarons, St. Martin's Press, 1994 ("In the end, the only thing Loftus and Aarons seem to have gotten right is the fact that the attack was no accident.")

214 Byron York, *Liberal Radio and Its Dark Angel: Meet the amazing Sheldon Drobny*. National Review, Oct 27, 2003.

215 Robert A. Graham, *Another Phony Chapter on 'Pius and the Nazis'*, Columbia Magazine, May 1984, at 4; Sereny at 302 (the Vatican had no money to support such an initiative). In fact, Bishop Hudal had connections with the Red Cross and may have used their assets. *See* Sereny at 306.

216 Godman at 169.

217 *See* Michael Phayer, *The Silent Pope?* Moment, April 2004, at 48.
218 Godman at 169. *See also* Vincent Lapomarda, Catholic Historical Review (October 1992); Sereny at 303.
219 Klich's article and others on similar issues can be accessed on CEANA's web site, at www.ceana.org.ar.
220 It might also be noted that–at least according to one witness who was involved in the relocation project–Hudal "helped Jews before he ever helped SS men; he helped more Jews than SS men." Sereny at 314 (quoting Monsignor Karl Bayer). *See* Lapomarda at 234, n.16 (dismissing allegations that the Vatican was involved in the moving of Nazis).
221 Sanfilippo's article and others on similar issues can be accessed on CEANA's web site, at www.ceana.org.ar.
222 Dr. Josef Mengele, notorious for his genetic experiments at Auschwitz, is thought to have escaped from Germany with papers from the International Red Cross. Like Eichmann, he moved to Argentina where he found employment for a period of time working as an abortionist. Mengele died under an assumed name without ever being brought to justice.
223 Discussing the Vatican and the International Red Cross, German ambassador Weizsäcker said: "It is a matter of course and everybody knows it, that these two agencies of world significance and reputation and world-wide influence would have undertaken any possible step that they considered feasible and useful to save the Jews." O'Connell at 80.
224 One might legitimately wonder why the Vatican or the Red Cross would be involved after the war in moving great numbers of people to nations that clearly were not their homelands. Monsignor Karl Bayer explained that there were four "waves" of help provided to dislocated persons: "The fourth wave—no doubt the largest by far—came after April-May 1945. This one included nationals of many countries who were in Italy, in POW camps and elsewhere, at that time, and didn't want to return to their communist-controlled homelands; German POWs, some of whom would eventually go home, but many of whom didn't wish to at the time; the Polish Army; the Russian Vlasov army (including 15,000 Ukrainians); large numbers of people fleeing from Yugoslavia, Rumania, Hungary, Austria; and then, of course, the comparatively small group of SS personnel who are the people you are particularly referring to." Sereny at 308 (footnotes omitted); *id.* at 303 (the number of Nazis escaping justice "were very few compared with the huge number of other refugees helped by Catholic institutions, and helped with every justification. No one could question in any way the Vatican's motives in giving money towards helping refugees in general–on the contrary.") For a detailed discussion of an earlier wave, *see generally* Simpson, *A Vatican Lifeline*.
225 Sereny at 308 (quoting Monsignor Karl Bayer).
226 Department of State, *Illegal Emigration Movements in and Through Italy*, Office of American Republic Affairs, July 14, 1947 (Top Secret, declassified in 1988; USNA: RG59; FW 800-0128/5-1547).
227 Pius put at the disposal of the prosecution an important collection of documents dealing with the persecution of the Church by the Nazi regime. Louis J. Gallagher, *Edmund A. Walsh, S.J., Founder of the Foreign Service School, Georgetown University*, Benziger Brothers (New York, 1959). *See also* O'Carroll at 138 (suggesting that a memorandum authorized by Pius XII influenced the terms of one charge).
228 Adolf Eichmann is one of the former National Socialist leaders who allegedly escaped Europe with a Vatican passport. As head of the Gestapo's Jewish section from 1939

until 1945, he was responsible for the murder of millions of Jews during the war. After the war, using papers that had been obtained from the Catholic Church, he fled to Argentina where Hitler's friend, President/Dictator Juan Perón (perhaps best known today in the United States as the husband of "Evita"), welcomed the Nazis. Eichmann was captured by the Israeli Secret Service in 1960, deported to Israel, tried, convicted, and executed. Documents from his trial reveal the Vatican's efforts to oppose the Nazis. *See* p. 15.

229 John Cornwell, who presumably looked very hard for such evidence, found nothing to indicate that the Vatican was intentionally involved in helping Nazis escape justice. *Hitler's Pope* at 267. *See Declaration on Nazi Refugees After World War II*, Vatican Information Service, Feb. 14, 1992 (denying any intent to assist war criminals).

230 The Vatican issued a formal denial that it had helped Nazis escape Europe during the war. According to a 1984 news report: "This response is partly to reports about former ss Colonel Walter Rauff, now in Chile. Rauff reportedly told Chilean authorities his escape after the war included 18 months sheltered in Vatican run convents in Italy. Father Antonio Weber who directed the Vatican run refugee protection project during and after the war, told us today some 20,000 Jews and others fleeing from Hitler were housed in Vatican owned property off limits to German troops, like this building which housed 400 people and in many others scattered throughout Rome and Italy. Absolute identification of refugees, he said, was rarely possible in those times, but he insisted no Nazi war criminals were ever knowingly helped by his operation. And in Vienna this morning, Nazi hunter Simon Wiesenthal told ABC News that contrary to *London Sunday Times* reports last week, he has no evidence that Vatican sister Pasqualina, nor the Pope she served, Pius XII, were ever involved in helping Nazis escape. The Vatican rebuttal was also partly in response to the 1947 State Department report, published last week, which speaks of a notorious Mr. Nix, well known smuggler of Nazis who, it says, fled from police after the war into the Vatican. Willi Nix, now 78, a medical doctor who lives in Rome, calls that report slander and yesterday showed reporters here what he said were American army documents which describe him as a valuable anti-Nazi resistance worker." Peter Jennings, *World News Tonight*, January 30, 1984 (Bill Blakemore reporting).

231 *See New York Times*, Jan. 10, 1940 (the Vatican appointed two Jewish scholars to the Vatican Academy of Science). In March, the Vatican appointed another Jewish professor to the Vatican Library to restore ancient maps, twelve hours before the new Italian laws went into effect prohibiting Jews from all professional life. *New York Times*, March 2, 1940.

232 Alois Hudal, *Römische Tagebücher: Lebensbeichte eines alten Bischofs* (Leopold Stocker Verlag: Stuttgart, 1976). The pope, who typically kept Hudal at a distance because of his political views, exploited Hudal's talents here, knowing that the Germans would listen to him. *See* p. 304, note 168.

233 *See* O'Carroll at 96-97 (1980); *Actes et Documents*, vol. IX, p. 506, n.3; *id.* vol. IX, p. 510, n.4.

234 Lapide at 269. At a 1975 Holocaust conference in Hamburg, Germany, Lapide said that his estimate "was based on six months of research in the Yad Vashem, the Holocaust archive in Jerusalem." *The Catholic Historical Review*, April 1999, at 269-270. Yad Vashem recommends Lapide's book in its "Basic Bibliography of the Holocaust," ("Churches and the Holocaust") on its web page: <<*http://www.yad-vashem.org.il*>>.

235 *See* Malachi Martin, *The Keys of This Blood: The Struggle for World Domination Between Pope John Paul II, Mikhail Gorbachev & The Capitalist West* 637 (1990) (Pius XII "personally saved over 1.5 million Jews"); Michael Burleigh, *The Cardinal Basil*

Hume Memorial Lectures: Political Religion and Social Evil, 3 Totalitarian Movements and Political Religions at 38 ("hundreds of thousands"); John S. Conway, *Yad Vashem Studies* XV (1983) at 327-345 (primary archival material "confirms the picture already drawn by such Jewish authors as Livia Rothkirchen and Pinchas Lapide"). Sir Martin Gilbert would place the number of Jews saved at about 500,000. *Historian Sir Martin Gilbert Defends Pius XII; Goebbels Saw in Him an Enemy of Nazism,* Zenit News Service, Feb. 20, 2003 ("the test for Pacelli was when the Gestapo came to Rome to round up Jews. And the Catholic Church, on his direct authority, immediately dispersed as many Jews as they could."); *The Untold Story: Catholic Rescuers of Jews,* Inside the Vatican, August 2003, at 31 (interview with Gilbert, conducted by William Doino). In its 1998 document on the Holocaust, *We Remember: A Reflection on the Shoah,* the Holy See spoke of "what Pope Pius XII did personally or through his representatives to save hundreds of thousands of Jewish lives." *Id.,* section IV; n. 16.

236 Vincent Lapomarda comments: "Susan Zuccotti, in her work *Under His Very Windows* (2000), sought to disprove Lapide but failed to do so. Unwittingly, she lent at least partial support to his view when she showed how helpful were the nuns, monks, priests, bishops and archbishops in saving the Jews in Italy's major cities, especially since these rescuers were, according to her, convinced that they were really doing what the pope wanted." *America,* February 25, 2002, at 38.

237 At a conference held at Millersville University Fr. John T. Pawlikowski referred to a letter written by Fr. Gumpel to the American bishops, and he called it anti-Semitic. Since I was probably the only other person in the room who had read the letter, I challenged him on this point, and he backed down, agreeing that it was not anti-Semitic.

238 *See* Congregation for the Causes of Saints, *Positio,* Statement of the Postulator, p. 6.

239 *Profile of Peter Gumpel, S.J.,* Inside the Vatican, January 2002; personal interview with author.

240 Gallo at 23-24 (Gumpel's teacher, noting his distress, said: "it is better to be excellent in affairs of the heart than in mathematics.")

241 *Profile of Peter Gumpel, S.J.,* Inside the Vatican, January 2002; Nicole Winfield, *Pope Pius XII: Saint or anti-Semite?,* The Commercial Appeal (Memphis, AP), May 24, 2003.

242 *Profile of Peter Gumpel, S.J.,* Inside the Vatican, January 2002.

243 *See* Ronald J. Rychlak, *60 Minutes on Hitler's Pope,* Catalyst, May 2000 (also posted on the Catholic League's web page).

244 "This is one of the foulest things, even worse than some (who) have wanted to accuse me of being a Nazi," said Gumpel about the charge of being an anti-Semite." Nicole Winfield, *German Jesuit nears end of campaign for beatifying Pope Pius XII,* The Associated Press, May 14, 2003. The false claim that Gumpel is insensitive to the Jewish community, or, worse yet, is an outright anti-Semite, stems from an article about him in the National Catholic Reporter, which repeated inaccurate quotes attributed to him; and a grossly inaccurate report about him which aired on CBS Television. The National Catholic Reporter has since reversed itself, publishing a highly favorable article on Fr. Gumpel (July 26, 2002 issue), in which he acknowledges historical anti-Judaism within the Church ("We have apologized for this, as we should.") while simultaneously disproving allegations about Pius XII and the modern Church. For a rebuttal to the CBS report, see *CBS Television Report Seeks to Discredit Church,* Zenit News Service, March 19, 2000, in which Gumpel corrects and clarifies the remarks that CBS took out of context, reaffirms Vatican II's condemnation of anti-Semitism ("This is the position to which I fully and unreservedly adhere."), and concludes by

stating: "This accusation of anti-Semitism that they make not only is absurd, but gravely wounds my honor. Such an accusation is totally out of place, as my family was harshly persecuted by the Nazis and, as a result, I myself had to spend the years of my youth outside my country to avoid being killed." I consulted with Fr. Gumpel regarding his legal options following a misleading news report from Canada, and I worked with him during the satisfactory negotiations that took place with the broadcasters.

9 A Righteous Gentile

1 *The National Jewish Welfare Board to Pope Pius xii*, July 21, 1944, *Actes et Documents*, vol. X, p. 358-59 (no. 272).

2 In fact, in discussing the deportation of baptized Jews from Holland, he does not even mention that it was prompted by a statement of condemnation issued by the Catholic Bishops. *See* pp. 63-64.

3 Righteous Gentile Tibor Baranski, who reports that he was "fantastically near" to Wallenberg, says that if Wallenberg were alive today, he would defend Pope Pius xii. Baranski explains that the Catholic Church collaborated with Wallenberg in his rescue efforts. "Look, there was not [sic] problem or disagreement whatsoever between the Catholic Church and Wallenberg. I personally arranged unofficial, private meetings between Wallenberg and Nuncio Rotta." Baranski reports that Wallenberg "knew Pius was on his side." Ronald J. Rychlak, *A Righteous Gentile Defends Pius xii*, Zenit News Service, October 5, 2002 (quoting personal correspondence from Baranski). *See* Michael Burleigh, *The Cardinal Basil Hume Memorial Lectures: Political Religion and Social Evil*, 3 Totalitarian Movements and Political Religions at 38 ("while Oskar Schindler is celebrated for saving 1,000 people, or Raoul Wallenberg for doing the same for 20,000, no such response is made to a man [Pius xii] leading an institution [the Catholic Church] which across Europe rescued hundreds of thousands of people.")

4 Robert Wistrich, *The Silence of the Popes*, The Times Literary Supplement, March 1, 2002. *See also* Ronald J. Rychlak, *Pius xii and the Holocaust*, The Times Literary Supplement, March 15, 2002.

5 One common argument here is that a papal statement would have let Jewish people of the world know what was happening to the Jews of Germany, while they tended to dismiss statements made by others as propaganda. In 1936, however, The Jewish Publication Society of America published a book which, on the slip cover, made reference to the "National Socialist attempt to exterminate the Jews of Germany." Marvin Lowenthal, *The Jews of Germany: A Story of 16 Centuries* (6th printing, 1939). This suggests that word was out, even from reliable, believable sources. In fact, Lowenthal states: "As the German Jew sinks from the stage of history... no group boasting of numbers and power today may know whether the morrow will not rob it of both, as it has befallen the Protestants and Catholics of Germany." *Id.* at 420.

6 Graham, *Pius xii's Defense of Jews and Others* at 2-3.

7 *See* pp. 91-99 for a more complete discussion of *Summi Pontificatus*. *See also* Rychlak, *Hitler, the War, and the Pope* at 273-77.

8 *See* pp. 119-27.

9 *See* pp. 127-29.

10 *See* pp. 175-76. These telegrams have been compared to "extreme unction to the dying." Charles F. Delzell, *Pius xii, Italy, and the Outbreak of War*, 2 Journal of Contemporary History 137, 156 (1967).

11 *See* Rychlak, *Hitler, the War, and the Pope* at 127.

12 *See* p. 11.

13 McCormick at 118 (from a *New York Times* dispatch of August 24, 1944).

14 Congregation for the Causes of Saints, *Positio*, appendix 25 at 245-46 (reprinting the prologue to Levai, *Hungarian Jewry and the Papacy: Pope Pius did not Remain Silent*).

15 *See* pp. 127, 133-36.

16 William M. Harrigan, *Pius XII's Efforts to Effect a Détente in German-Vatican Relations, 1939-1940*, the Catholic Historical Review, July 1963, at 191 (Pius XII's "prudence" helped to avert an immediate extension of the war"); Gallo at 150 (a protest would not have made things better); Sereny at 283 (by the time the extermination camps were ready for the mass murder of Polish Jews, a protest from the Pope "could have had no practical effect").

17 *Quoted in* Purdy at 258 (noting that the time could come when this conviction could change). The background for the Holy See's concern was the message sent to Poland by Pius that was rejected by Cardinal Sapieha out of fear that it would lead to more persecutions. *Id. See* pp. 153-54.

18 Congregation for the Causes of Saints, *Positio*, appendix 25 at 245 (reprinting Kempner's prologue to Levai, *Hungarian Jewry and the Papacy: Pope Pius did not Remain Silent*).

19 *Id.* at 274 (reprinting Peter Gumpel, *Cornwell's Cheap Shot at Pius XII*, Crisis, December 1999). *See Most of Rome's Jews Were Saved from Hitler's Final Solution*, *L'Osservatore Romano*, weekly edition in English, January 24, 2001 at 11 (German officer reports that a higher profile protest would have backfired).

20 *See generally* Philip Jenkins, *The New Anti-Catholicism: The Last Acceptable Prejudice* (2003).

21 *Letter to Msgr. Walter Brandmueller, president of the Pontifical Committee of Historical Sciences*, April 2004, *quoted in Pope says Ignorance of History Leads to Crisis*, (Vatican Information Service), The Wanderer, April 29, 2004.

22 McGurn at 64.

23 After the fact analysis is, of course, of limited value. *See* Henry Kissinger, *Diplomacy* 27 (1994) ("there is a vast difference between the perspective of an analyst and that of a statesman.... The analyst runs no risk.... The statesman is permitted only one guess.... The statesman must act on assessments that cannot be proved at the time that he is making them....")

24 Fr. Richard McBrien might also be added to this list. *See* Fr. Richard P. McBrien, *The Popes and the Jews*, the 2003 Swig Lecture, Swig Judaic Studies Program at the University of San Francisco, Sept. 11, 2003.

25 Ralph McInerny (*The Defamation of Pius XII*) argues that the root of the attack on Pius is hatred for the Catholic Church—in particular, hatred for Catholic teachings against the "culture of death" as represented, above all, by abortion-on-demand. He argues that the critics are being morally inconsistent by attacking Pius for allegedly not doing enough to oppose the "Final Solution" while they simultaneously support what many consider the "Final Solution" for today's unwanted pregnancies. It is, of course, very difficult to assess the motivation of authors, except in cases where they make it evident. Critics Carroll, Wills, and Cornwell all made their motivations evident, and McInerny seems to have analyzed their motivations correctly.

26 *The Pius War* at 31.

27 Doris L. Bergen, *An Easy Target? The Controversy About Pius XII and the Holocaust*, in *Pope Pius XII and the Holocaust* at 195. Bergen notes the important fact often

overlooked by critics: Pius XII was no more vocal when the victims were Catholic priests than he was when they were Jewish peasants. While she faults Pius for his approach, she does understand that this seriously undercuts any charge of anti-Semitism.

28 *See* pp. 8-9.

29 *See* Pope Paul VI, *Heights of Heroism in the Life of Pope Pius XII*, St. Paul Editions, 1964.

30 David Van Biema, *A Repentance, Sort Of; The Vatican issues a historic statement on the Holocaust but falls short of some Jewish hopes*, Time, March 30, 1998, at 60; *Pope calls Pius XII 'Great'*, Catholic World News, March 23, 1998. John Paul also instructed: "Neither can one forget, together with official pronouncements, the often-hidden action of the Apostolic See, which went out to assist endangered Jews in many ways, as has been recognized, among others, by their authoritative representatives." *John Paul II repeats condemnation of anti-Semitism and praises those who took risks to save Jews*, Zenit News Service, May 24, 2004.

31 McGurn at 106.

32 It is of course possible (though I am told it is unlikely) that despite the merits, the cause would be detained out of concern that people unaware of the truth would resent naming Pius a saint.

33 David G. Dalin, *Pius XII and the Jews: A Defense*, The Weekly Standard, Feb. 26, 2001 ("Pius XII was, genuinely and profoundly, a righteous gentile."). *See* Zenit News Agency, Oct. 5, 2002 (Righteous Gentile Tibor Baranski calls Pius XII a Righteous Gentile); Religious News Service, *Holocaust Hero Defends Papacy*, The Wanderer, Sept. 30, 1983 (similar); Ronald J. Rychlak, *A "Righteous Gentile" Defends Pius XII*, National Catholic Register, Oct. 28, 2002; 32:11 *Briefing* 8 (November 2002) (Catholic Bishops' Conferences of England & Wales and Scotland).

Bibliography

*Actes et Documents du Saint Siège Relatifs à la Seconde Guerre Mondiale,
Volumes I-XI* (Libreria Editrice Vaticana: Citta del Vaticano, 1965-81);
English edition (volume one only; Corpus Books: Washington, D.C.,
Gerard Noel, ed. 1967-77). Volume III is split into two books, thus some
authors refer to 12 volumes instead of 11.

Akten Deutscher Bischöfe über die Lage der Kirche, 1933-1945 (Bernhard Stasiewski and Ludwig Volk, eds.; Matthias-Grünewald-Verlag; six volumes
dated 1968-1985).

Stella Alexander, *Croatia: The Catholic Church and Clergy, 1919-1945*, in *Catholics, the State, and the European Radical Right, 1919-1945* (Columbia University Press: New York, 1987).

David Alvarez & Robert A. Graham, *Nothing Sacred: Nazi Espionage Against
the Vatican 1939-1945* (Frank Cass: London, 1997).

American Intelligence and the German Resistance to Hitler (Westview: Boulder,
Co., J. Heideking and M. Frey, eds., 1996).

The American Jewish Yearbook, 1943-1944 (Jewish Publication Society: Philadelphia, 1944).

Richard Avery, *Why the Allies Won* (W.W. Norton & Co.: New York and London, 1995).

Victoria Barnett, *For the Soul of the People: Protestant Protest Against Hitler*
(Oxford University Press: Oxford, 1992).

A.C.F. Beales, *The Pope and the Jews: The Struggle of the Catholic Church Against* Anti-Semitism *During the War* (Sword of the Spirit: London, 1945).

Jack Bemporad & Michael Shevack, *Our Age: The Historic New Era of Christian-Jewish Understanding* (New City Press: Hyde Park, NY, 1996).

F. Lee Benns, *Europe Since 1914 in its World Setting* (Appleton, Century, Crofts: New York, 1949).

Pierre Blet, *Pius XII and the Second World War* (Paulist Press: New York, Lawrence J. Johnson trans., 1999).

Mark M. Boatner III, *The Biographical Dictionary of World War II* (Presido Press: Novato, CA, 1996).

James Bogle, *The Real Story of Pius XII and the Jews*, The Salisbury Review, Spring 1996.

Emilio Bonomelli, *I Papi in Campagna* (Gherardo Casini Editore: Rome, 1953).

Heinrich Brüning, *Memoiren, 1918-1934* (Deutsche Verlags-Anstalt: Stuttgart, 1970).

Alan Bullock, *Hitler: A Study in Tyranny* (Bantam: Chicago, 1962).

Michael Burleigh, *The Cardinal Basil Hume Memorial Lectures: Political Religion and Social Evil*, 3 Totalitarian Movements and Political Religions 1 (Autumn 2002).

_____, *Death and Deliverance: Euthanasia in Nazi Germany, 1900-1945* (Cambridge University Press: New York, 1994).

_____, *The Third Reich: A New History* (Hill & Wang: New York, 2001).

Timothy A. Byrnes, *Catholic Bishops in American Politics* (Princeton University Press: Princeton, NJ, 1991).

Claudia C. Carlen, *The Papal Encyclicals* (Pierian Press: Ann Arbor, MI, 1990).

William Carr, *A History of Germany* (Edward Arnold: London, 1979).

James Carroll, *Constantine's Sword: The Church and the Jews: A History* (Houghton Mifflin Co.: Boston, 2001).

James Carroll, *The Silence*, The New Yorker, April 7, 1997.

John Patrick Carroll-Abbing, *But for the Grace of God - The Houses are Blind* (Delacorte Press: New York, 1965).

_____, *A Chance to Live: The Story of the Lost Children of the War* (Longman, Green & Co. London, 1952).

Catholics Remember the Holocaust (United States Catholic Conference: Washington, D.C., 1988).

Owen Chadwick, *A History of Christianity* (St. Martin's Press: New York, 1995).

Owen Chadwick, *Britain and the Vatican During the Second World War* 83-85 (Cambridge University Press: Cambridge,1986).

Owen Chadwick, *Weizsäcker, the Vatican, and the Jews of Rome*, 28 Journal of Ecclesiastical History 179 (April 1977).

Nicolas Cheetham, *The Keeper of the Keys: A History of the Popes from St. Peter to John Paul II* (Macdonald: London, 1982).

Chronicle of the 20ᵗʰ Century (Chronicle Publications: Mount Kisco, N.Y., C. Daniel, ed., 1986).

Camille Cianfarra, *The Vatican and the War* (Literary Classics, Inc., distributed by E.P. Dutton & Company: New York, 1944).

The Ciano Diaries (Doubleday & Company, Inc.: New York, Hugh Gibson, ed., 1946).

Lord Clonmore, *Pope Pius XI and World Peace* (Dutton: New York, 1938).

Florence D. Cohalan, *A Popular History of the Archdiocese of New York* (U.S. Catholic Historical Society, New York, 1983).

Naomi W. Cohen, *Not Free to Desist: A History of the American Jewish Committee, 1906-1966* (The Jewish Publication Society of America: Philadelphia, 1972).

Commonweal Confronts the Century: Liberal Convictions, Catholic Traditions (Touchstone Books: New York, P. Jordan & P. Baumann, eds. 1999).

Congregation for the Causes of Saints, *Beatificationis et Canonizationis Servi Dei Pii XII (Eugenii Pacelli) Summi Pontificis (1876-1958): Positio Super Vita, Virtutibus et Fama Sanctitatis* (Rome, 2004) [the *Positio*].

Controversial Concordats: The Vatican's Relations with Napoleon, Mussolini, and Hitler (The Catholic University of America Press: Washington, D.C., Frank J. Coppa, ed., 1999).

John S. Conway, *The Nazi Persecution of the Churches 1933-45* (London: Weidenfeld and Nicolson, 1960; and New York: Basic Books, 1969).

John S. Conway, *The Silence of Pope Pius XII, in The Papacy and Totalitarianism Between the Two World Wars* (Wileys: New York, Charles F. Delzell, ed., 1974).

_____, *The Vatican, Germany and the Holocaust, in Papal Diplomacy in the Modern Age* (Praeger: Westport, CT, Peter C. Kent & John F. Pollard, eds., 1994).

_____, *The Vatican, Great Britain, and Relations with Germany, 1938-1940*, XVI The Historical Journal, 147 (1973).

John Cornwell, *Breaking Faith: The Pope, the People, and the Fate of Catholicism* (New York: Viking Press, 2001).

_____, *Hitler's Pope: The Secret History of Pius XII* (New York: Viking Press, 1999).

_____, *The Pontiff in Winter* (New York: Doubleday, 2004).

David G. Dalin, *History as Bigotry: Daniel Goldhagen slanders the Catholic Church*, The Weekly Standard, February 19, 2003.

_____, *Pius XII and the Jews: A Defense*, The Weekly Standard, Feb. 26, 2001.

James A. Darragh, *The Pope and Fascism* (John S. Burns & Sons: Glasgow, 1944).

Kenneth C. Davis, *Don't Know Much About the Bible: Everything You Need to Know About the Good Book but Never Learned* (Harper Trade: New York, 2001).

Days of Devotion: Daily Meditations From the Good Shepherd Pope John XXIII (Penguin reprint: New York, John P. Donnelly, ed., 1998).

Len Deighton, *Blood, Tears and Folly: An Objective Look at World War II* (Harper Collins: New York, 1993).

Harold C. Deutsch, *The Conspiracy Against Hitler in the Twilight War* (University of Minnesota Press: Minneapolis, 1968).

Die Briefe. an die Deutschen Bischöfe 1939-1944 (Grünewald: Mainz, Burkhart Schneider ed., 1966).

Donald J. Dietrich, *Catholic Citizens in the Third Reich: Psycho-Social Principles and Moral Reasoning* (Transaction: New Brunswick, N.J., 1988).

Stephen M. DiGiovanni, *Pius XII and the Jews: the War Years* (monograph) also published in: 6 Catholic Social Science Review 341 (2000).

Joseph F. Dinneen, *Pius XII: Pope of Peace* (Robert M. McBride and Company: London, 1939).

Charles Hugo Doyle, *A Day with the Pope* (Doubleday: Garden City, 1950).

Eamon Duffy, *Saints & Sinners: A History of the Popes* (Yale University Press: New Haven, CT, 1997).

Jaques Duquesne, *Les Catholiques Français sous l'occupation* (Paris: 1966).

Lawrence Elliott, *I Will Be Called John: A Biography of Pope John XXIII* (Berkley Publishing Corp.: New York, 1973).

Encyclopedia of the Holocaust (Macmillan: New York, 1990).

Andre Fabert, *Pope Paul VI* (Monarch Books: Derby, CT, 1963).

Carlo Falconi, *The Silence of Pius XII* (Little Brown: Boston, B. Wall trans. 1970).

Emma Fattorini, *Germania e Santa Sede: Le nunziature di Pacelli tra la Grande Guerra e la Repubblica di Weimar* (Il Mulino: Bologna, 1992).

Michael F. Feldkamp, *Der Teufelspakt des Anti-semiten. Wer sich bei seinen alten Vorurteilen über Papst Pius XII. bestatigen mochte, wird bei Conwells Buch bestens bedient*, in *Frankfurter Allgemeine Zeitung*, January 10, 2000, at 7.

Desmond Fisher, *Pope Pius XII and the Jews: An Answer to Hochhuth's Play Der Stellvertreter (The Deputy)* (Glen Rock, N.J.: Paulist Press, 1965).

Eugene J. Fisher, *Faith Without Prejudice: Rebuilding Christian Attitudes Toward Judaism* (The American Interfaith Institute: New York, 1993).

Eva Fogelman, *Conscience & Courage: Rescuers of Jews During the Holocaust* (Anchor/Doubleday: New York, 1994).

René Fontenelle, *His Holiness, Pope Pius XI* (Burns, Oates and Washbourne: London, 1923).

Forgotten Survivors: Polish Christians Remember the Nazi Occupation, Richard C. Lukas, ed. (Lawrence: University of Kansas Press, 2004).

Arvid Fredborg, *Behind the Steel Wall*, Reader's Digest, January 1944 at 125.

Saul Friedländer, *Nazi Germany and the Jews, Volume I: The Years of Persecution, 1933-1939* (Harper Collins: New York, 1997).

Saul Friedländer, *Pius XII and the Third Reich: A Documentation* (New York: Knopf, C. Fullman trans., 1966).

From Hitler's Doorstep: The Wartime Intelligence Reports of Allen Dulles, 1942-1945 (Pennsylvania State University Press: University Park, Neal H. Peterson, ed., 1996).

Charles R. Gallagher, *'Personal, Private Views:' A newly discovered report from 1938 reveals Cardinal Pacelli's anti-Nazi stance*, America, September 1, 2003.

Mary Alice Gallin, *German Resistance to Hitler: Ethical and Religious Factors* (The Catholic University of America: Washington, D.C., 1961).

Patrick Gallo, *For Love and Country: The Italian Resistance* (University Press of America: New York, 2003).

Antonio Gaspari, *Gli ebrei salvati da Pio XII* (Edizioni Logos: Rome, 2001).

Martin Gilbert, *Auschwitz and the Allies* (Holt, Rinehart, & Winston: New York, 1981).

_____, *The Holocaust: A History of the Jews of Europe During the Second World War* (Holt, Rinehart, & Winston: New York, 1985).

_____, *The Righteous: The Unsung Heroes of the Holocaust* (Henry Holt & Company, Inc.: New York, 2003).

_____, *The Second World War: A Complete History* (Henry Holt & Company: New York, 1987).

Peter Godman, *Hitler and the Vatican : The Secret Archives that Reveal the New Story of the Nazis and the Vatican* (Free Press: New York, 2004).

The Goebbels Diaries: 1939-1941 (G.P. Putnam's Sons,: New York, Fred Taylor trans., 1983).

The Goebbels Diaries: 1942-1943 (Doubleday & Co.: New York, Louis P. Lochner trans., 1948).

Daniel J. Goldhagen, *Hitler's Willing Executioners: Ordinary Germans and The Holocaust* (Alfred A. Knopf: New York, 1996).

_____, *A Moral Reckoning: The Role of the Catholic Church in the Holocaust and its Unfulfilled Duty of Repair* (Alfred A. Knopf: New York, 2002).

Guido Gonella, *The Papacy and World Peace: A Study of the Christmas Messages of Pope Pius XII* (Hollis and Carter, Ltd.: London, 1945).

Klaus Gotto, *Die Katholiken und das Dritte Reich* (1990).

Robert A. Graham, *Pius XII's Defense of Jews and Others: 1944-45* (Catholic League Publications: Milwaukee, 1987). This is also reprinted in *Pius XII and the Holocaust: A Reader* (Catholic League Publications: Milwaukee, WI,, 1988).

_____, *The Pope and Poland in World War Two* (Veritas: London, 1968).

_____, *Pope Pius XII and the Jews of Hungary in 1944* (United States Catholic Historical Society, undated).

_____, *The 'Right to Kill' in the Third Reich: Prelude to Genocide*, LXII The Catholic Historical Review 56, 65 (January 1976).

_____, *The Vatican and Communism During World War II: What Really Happened?* (Ignatius Press: San Francisco, 1996).

_____, *Vatican Radio Between London and Berlin, 1940-41*, Journal of English Jesuits (April 1976).

Great Untold Stories of World War II (Pyramid: New York, Phil Hirsch ed. 1963).

Beth A. Griech-Polelle, *Bishop von Galen: German Catholicism and National Socialism* (Yale University Press: New Haven, CT, 2002).

Lothar Groppe, *The Church's Struggle with the Third Reich* (IBW Journal, Alan F. Lacy trans.), Fidelity, October 1983, available on the Internet at: <<http://www.cdn-friends-icej.ca/antiholo/struggle.html>>.

Lothar Groppe, *The Church and the Jews in the Third Reich*, Fidelity, November 1983.

Dennis Gwynn, *Pius XI* (Holmes: London, 1932).

Oscar Halecki & James F. Murray, Jr., *Pius XII: Eugenio Pacelli, Pope of Peace* (Farrar, Straus and Young, Inc.: New York, 1954).

Theodore S. Hamerow, *On the Road to the Wolf's Lair: German Resistance to Hitler* (Harvard University Press: Cambridge, MA, 1997).

William M. Harrigan, *Pius XII's Efforts to Effect a Détente in German-Vatican Relations, 1939-1940*, The Catholic Historical Review, July 1963.

Ulrich von Hassell, *The von Hassell Diaries: The Story of the Forces Against Hitler Inside Germany, 1938-1944* (Doubleday: New York, 1947).

Alden Hatch & Seamus Walshe, *Crown of Glory: The Life of Pope Pius XII* (Hawthorn Books: New York, 1957).

Peter Hellman, *When Courage Was Stronger than Fear: Remarkable Stories of Christians and Muslims Who Saved Jews from the Holocaust* (New York: Marlowe & Co., 2004).

Alice Von Hildebrand, *The Soul of a Lion: The Life of Dietrich Von Hildebrand* (Ignatius Press: San Francisco, 2000).

Adolf Hitler, *Mein Kampf* (Houghton Mifflin: Boston, Ralph Manheim trans. 1971).

Hitler's Rise to Power (Church in History Information Center, undated).

Hitler's Secret Conversations 1941-1944 (Octagon Books: New York,1972; Signet edition, 1961).

Rolf Hochhuth, *The Deputy* (Grove Press: New York, Winston trans., 1964).

Kees van Hoek, *Pope Pius XII: Priest and Statesman* (Philosophical Library: New York, 1944).

Peter Hoffmann, *German Resistance to Hitler* (Harvard University Press: Cambridge, MA, 1988).

Peter Hoffmann *Stauffenberg: A Family History, 1905-1944* (Cambridge University Press: Cambridge, 1995).

J. Derek Holmes, *The Papacy in the Modern World 1914-1978* (Crossroad: New York, 1981).

The Holocaust Encyclopedia (Yale University Press: New Haven, CT, Walter Laqueur, ed., 2000).

John Jay Hughes, *Pontiffs: Popes Who Shaped History* (Our Sunday Visitor Books: Ft. Wayne, IN, 1994).

Phillip Hughes, *Pope Pius the Eleventh* (Sheed and Ward: New York, 1937).

Heinz Hürten, *Deutsche Katholiken, 1918-1945* (Ferdinand Schöningh: Paderborn, 1992).

Inside the Vatican of Pius XII: The Memoir of an American Diplomat During World War II (New York: Doubleday, Harold H. Tittmann III, ed., 2004).

The International Catholic-Jewish Historical Commission, *The Vatican and the Holocaust: A Preliminary Report Submitted to The Holy See's Commission for Religious Relations with the Jews and the International Jewish Committee for Interreligious Consultations* (October 2000) posted on the Internet at <<http://www.us-israel.org/jsource/Holocaust/vatrep.html>>.

Introduction to Jewish-Christian Relations (Paulist Press: New Tork, M. Shermis & A. Zannoni, eds., 1991).

The Italian Refuge: Rescue of Jews During the Holocaust (The Catholic University of America Press: Washington, D.C., Ivo Herzer, ed., 1989).

Zygmunt Jakubowski, *Pope Pius and Poland* (New York: America, 1942).

Philip Jenkins, *The New Anti-Catholicism: The Last Acceptable Prejudice* (Oxford University Press: New York, 2003).

The Jewish People and Their Sacred Scriptures in the Christian Bible, by the Holy See's Pontifical Biblical Commission (available through the Vatican's web page).

Robert Katz, *The Battle for Rome: The Germans, the Allies, the Partisans, and the Pope* (Simon and Schuster: New York, 2003).

Robert Katz, *Black Sabbath: A Journey Through a Crime Against Humanity* (Macmillan: New York, 1969).

Robert Katz, *Massacre in Rome* (Ballantine: New York, 1973) (originally released as *Death in Rome*).

Peter C. Kent, *A Tale of Two Popes: Pius XI, Pius XII and the Rome-Berlin Axis*, 23 Journal of Contemporary History 589 (1988).

Ian Kershaw, *Hitler: 1889-1936 Hubris* (W.W. Norton & Company: New York, 1998).

David I. Kertzer, *The Kidnapping of Edgardo Mortara* (Knopf: New York, 1997).

David Kertzer, *The Popes Against the Jews: The Vatican's Role in the Rise of Modern Anti-Semitism* (Knopf: New York, 2001).

Ilse-Lore Konopatzki, *Eugenio Pacelli: Pius XII, Kindheit und Jugend in Dokumenten*, (Universitätsverlag Anton Pustet, Salzburg und München: Salzburg, 1974).

Frank Korn, *From Peter to John Paul II: An Informal Study of the Papacy* (ALBA House: New York, 1980).

Alfons Kupper, *Staatliche Akten über die Reichskonkordatsverhandlungen* (Matthias-Grünewald-Verlag: Mainz, 1969).

La Conciliazione Ufficiosa: Diario del barone Carlo Monti "incaricato d'affari" del governo italiano presso la Santa Sede (1914-1922) (Vatican Press: Vatican City, Antonio Scotta, ed., 1997).

Jean Lacouture, *The Jesuits: A Multibiography* (Counterpoint: Washington, DC, Jeremy Leggatt, trans, 1995).

Langenscheidt's Standard Italian Dictionary (Langenscheidt Publishing Group: New York, 1990).

William L. Langer & S. Everett Gleason, *The World Crisis and American Foreign Policy: The Undeclared War 1940-1941* (Harper Torchbooks: New York, 1953).

Pinchas E. Lapide, *Three Popes and the Jews* (Hawthorn Books: New York, 1967; Sands and Co.: London, 1968).

Vincent A. Lapomarda, *The Jesuits and the Third Reich* (Edwin Mellen Press: Lewiston, N.Y. 1989).

Justus George Lawler, *Popes and Politics: Reform, Resentment, and the Holocaust* (Continuum Pub. Group: New York, 2002).

Justus George Lawler, *Review Symposium: Proleptic Response*, 20 U.S. Catholic Historian 89 (2002).

Fernande Leboucher, *The Incredible Mission of Father Benoît* (William Kimber: London, J. F. Bernard trans., 1970).

Lottie H. Lenn & Mary A. Reardon, *Pope Pius XII: Rock of Peace* (E.P. Dutton & Co.: New York, 1950).

John M. Lenz, *Christ in Dachau or Christ Victorious: Experiences in a Concentration Camp* (Vienna, 1960).

Jenö Levai, *Hungarian Jewry and the Papacy: Pius XII Did Not Remain Silent* (Sands and Co.: London, 1968).

Guenter Lewy, *The Catholic Church and Nazi Germany* (McGraw-Hill: New York, 1964).

Joseph L. Lichten, *A Question of Judgment: Pius XII and the Jews*, in *Pius XII and the Holocaust: A Reader* (Catholic League Publications: Milwaukee, WI, 1988).

Konrad Löw, *Die Schuld: Christen und Juden im Urteil der Nationalsozialisten und der Gegenwart* (Gräfelfing: Resch, 2003).

Marvin Lowenthal, *The Jews of Germany: A Story of 16 Centuries* (Jewish Publication Society of America: Philadelphia, 1939).

Henri de Lubac, *Christian Resistance to Anti-Semitism: Memories from 1940-1944* (Ignatius: San Francisco, 1990).

John Lukas, *The Hitler of History* (Knopf: New York, 1997).

Richard C. Lukas, *Forgotten Holocaust: The Poles under German Occupation 1939-1944* (Hippocrene Books, 2001).

Daniel M. Madden, *Operation Escape: The Adventure of Father O'Flaherty* (Hawthorn Books: New York, NY, 1962).

Avro Manhattan, *The Vatican in World Politics* (Gaer Associates: New York, 1949).

Margherita Marchione, *Man of Peace: Pope Pius XII* (Paulist Press: New York, 2003).

_____, *Pope Pius XII: Architect for Peace* (Paulist Press: New York, 2000).

_____, *Shepherd of Souls: A Pictorial Life of Pope Pius XII* (Paulist Press: New York, 2002).

_____, *Yours is a Precious Witness: Memoirs of Jews and Catholics in Wartime Italy* (Paulist Press: New York, 1997).

Jacques Maritain, *The Pagan Empire and the Power of God,* The Virginia Quarterly Review, Spring 1939.

Malachi Martin, *The Decline and Fall of the Roman Church* (Bantam: New York, 1983).

_____, *The Keys of This Blood: The Struggle for World Domination Between Pope John Paul II, Mikhail Gorbachev & The Capitalist West* (Simon & Schuster: New York, 1990).

Robert Martin, *Spiritual Semites: Catholics and Jews During World War Two* (Catholic League Publications: Milwaukee, WI, 1983).

Peter Matheson, *The Third Reich and the Christian Churches* (T. & T. Clark: Edinburgh, 1994).

Anne O'Hare McCormick, *Vatican Journal 1921-1954* (Farrar, Straus & Cudahy: New York, 1957).

Barrett McGurn, *A Reporter Looks at the Vatican* (Coward-McCann: New York, 1962).

Ralph McInerny, *The Defamation of Pius XII* (St. Augustine's Press: South Bend, IN, 2001).

Memorandum to General Donovan from Fabian von Schlabrendorff, dated October 25, 1945 (Subject: Relationship of the German Churches to Hitler), posted on the Internet by Rutgers Law School and Cornell University at <<*http://camlaw.rutgers.edu/publications/law-religion/nazimasterplan04.pdf*>>. This memorandum is also printed in Leo Stein, *Hitler Came for Niemoeller: The Nazi War Against Religion* 253-57 (Penguin Publishing Co.: New York, 2003 reprint ed.).

Thomas Merton, *Dancing in the Water of Life* (Harper: San Francisco, 1998).

Meir Michaelis, *Mussolini and the Jews: German-Italian Relations and the Jewish Question in Italy 1922-25* (Clarendon: Oxford, 1978).

Anthaniel Micklem, *National Socialism and the Roman Catholic Church: Being an Account of the Conflict between the National Socialist Government of Germany and the Roman Catholic Church 1933-1938* (Oxford University Press: Oxford, 1939).

John F. Morley, *Vatican Diplomacy and the Jews during the Holocaust 1939-1943* (Ktav Pub. House: New York, 1980).

Joseph Müller, *Bis zur letzten Konsequenz* (Süddentscher Verlag: Munich, 1975).

Francis X. Murphy, *The Papacy Today* (Macmillan: New York, 1981).

Paul I. Murphy, *La Popessa* (Warner Books: New York, 1983).

Matteo L. Napolitano & Andrea Tornielli, *Il Papa Che Salvò Gli Ebrei* (Rome: Piemme, 2004).

The Nazi Master Plan: The Persecution of the Christian Churches, documents prepared for the post-war Nuremberg trials, prepared by the Office of Strategic Services (OSS) Research and Analysis Branch, posted on the Internet by The Rutgers Journal of Law & Religion, at <<http://camlaw.rutgers.edu/publications/law-religion/nuremberg.htm>>.

Johann B. Neuhäusler, *Kreuz und Hakenkreuz* (*Katholische Kirche Bayerns*: Munich, 1946).

Albert J. Nevins, *The Story of Pope John xxiii* (Grosset & Dunlap: New York, 1966).

Peter Nichols, *The Pope's Divisions: The Roman Catholic Church Today* (Faber & Faber: New York, 1981).

Peter Novick, *The Holocaust in American Life* (Houghton Mifflin: Boston, 1999).

Michael O'Carroll, *Pius XII: Greatness Dishonored* (Laetare Press: Dublin, 1980).

Beate Ruhm von Oppen, *Nazis and Christians*, 21 World Politics 392 (1969).

Piet Oudendijk, *Pope Pius XII and The Nazi War Against the Catholic Church* (Martin W. Kennedy: Brisbane, 1944).

Nazareno Padellaro, *Pio XII* (Editrice S.A.I.E: Torino, 1956).

_____, *Portrait of Pius XII* (J.M. Dent & Sons: London, 1956).

Pietro Palazzini, *Il clero e l'occupazione tedesca di Roma: Il ruolo del Seminario Romano Maggiore* (Apes: Rome, 1995).

Casimir Papée, *Pius XII e Polska* (Editrice Studium: Rome, 1954).

Georges Passelecq & Bernard Suchecky, *The Hidden Encyclical of Pius XI* (Harcourt Brace & Co.: Boston, 1997).

William L. Patch, Jr., *Heinrich Brüning and the Dissolution of the Weimar Republic* (Cambridge University Press: Cambridge, 1998).

Richard Pattee, *The Case of Cardinal Aloysius Stepinac* (The Bruce Publishing Co.: Milwaukee, WI, 1953).

Robert Payne, *The Life and Death of Adolf Hitler* (Popular Library: New York, 1995).

Curtis Pepper, *An Artist and the Pope* (Giniger Books: New York, 1968).

The Persecution of the Catholic Church in German-Occupied Poland: Reports by H.E. Cardinal Hlond, Primate of Poland, to Pope Pius XII, Vatican Broadcasts and Other Reliable Evidence (Longmans Green & Co.: New York, 1941).

The Persecution of the Catholic Church in the Third Reich: Facts and Documents translated from the German (Burns and Oates: London, 1940; reprinted by Roger A McCaffrey Publishing: Fort Collins, CO, 2002).

Pierre Pfister, *Pius XII: The Life and Work of a Great Pope* (Studio Publications, in association with Thomas Y. Crowell Co., New York, NY, 1955).

Michael Phayer, *The Catholic Church and the Holocaust, 1930-1965* (Indiana University Press: Bloomington, 2001).

Pius xi, *With Burning Concern* (*Mit brennender Sorge*) (1937).

Pius xi und der Nationalsozialismus. Die Enzyklika 'Mit brennender Sorge' vom 14 März 1937, (Ferdinand Schöningh: Paderborn, Heinz-Albert Raem ed., 1979).

Pius xii, *Darkness over the Earth* (*Summi Pontificatus*) (1939).

_____, *On the Mystical Body* (*Mystici Corporis Christi*) (1943).

Pius xii and the Holocaust: A Reader (Catholic League Publications: Milwaukee, WI, 1988).

Pius xii: Selected Encyclicals and Addresses (Roman Catholic Books: Harrison, NY, undated).

The Pius War (Lexington Press: Lanham, MD, D. Dalin & J. Bottum, eds., 2004).

Pope Pius and Poland: A Documentary Outline of Papal Pronouncements and Relief Efforts in Behalf Of Poland, Since March, 1939 (The America Press: New York, 1942).

Pope Pius xii and the Holocaust (Continuum: New York, Carol Rittner & John K Roth, eds., 2002).

Popes of the Twentieth Century (St. Paul Editions: Boston, 1983).

Heinrich Portmann, *Cardinal von Galen* (Jarrolds: London, 1957).

Principles for Peace: Selections from Papal Documents, Leo XIII to Pius XII (National Catholic Welfare Conference: Washington, D.C., Harry C. Koenig, ed., 1943).

W.A. Purdy, *The Church on the Move: The Characters and Policies of Pius XII and John XXIII* (Hollis & Carter: London, 1966).

Records and Documents of the Holy See Relating to the Second World War: The Holy See and the War in Europe March 1939-August 1940 (Corpus Books: Washington, D,C,, Blet, Martini & Schneider, eds., Noel trans., 1965).

Konrad Repgen, *Das Ende der Zentrumspartei und Entstehung des Reichskonkordats*, (*Militärselsorge*, 1970).

_____, *Dokumentation. Zur Vatikanischen Strategie beim Reichskonkordat*, (*Vierteljahrshefte für Zeitgeschichte*, 1983).

_____, *Über Umlaut! die Entstehung der Reichskonkordats-Offerte im Frühjahr 1933 und die Bedeutung des Reichskonkordats* (*Vierteljahrshefte für Zeitgeschichte, 1978*).

Anthony Rhodes, *The Vatican in the Age of the Dictators: 1922-45* (Hodden and Stoughton: London, Sydney, Auckland & Toronto, 1973).

Fr. Martin Rhonheimer, *The Holocaust: What Was Not Said*, First Things, November 2003.

Livia Rothkirchen, *The Churches and the 'Final Solution' in Slovakia*, in *Judaism and Christianity under the Impact of National Socialism 1919-1945* (The Historical Society of Israel and Zalman Zhazar Center for Jewish History: Jerusalem, Otto Dov Kulka & Paul R. Mendes-Flohr, eds., 1987).

_____, *The Destruction of Slovak Jewry* (Yad Vashem: Jerusalem, 1961).

_____, *Vatican Policy and the "Jewish Problem" in "Independent" Slovakia (1939-1945)*, Yad Vashem Studies 6 (1967): 27-53.

John Rousmaniere, *A Bridge to Dialogue: The Story of Jewish-Christian Relations* (Paulist Press: New York, 1991).

Ronald J. Rychlak, Book Review: *The Defamation of Pius XII*, by Ralph McInerny, The Catholic Historical Review, January 2003.

_____, Book Review: *Pius XII und Deutschland*, by Michael F. Feldkamp, The English Historical Review, June 2003, at 840.

_____, *Catholic Answers About Pope Pius XII*, The Catholic Answer, March/April 2001.

_____, *Hitler, the War, and the Pope* (Genesis Press: Columbus, MS, 2000); paperback: (Our Sunday Visitor Press: Ft. Wayne, IN, 2000).

_____, *A Response to The Vatican and the Holocaust: A Preliminary Report By the International Catholic-Jewish Historical Commission*, The Catholic League for Religious and Civil Rights web page, posted Nov. 2000.

_____, *Why Pope Pius XII Was Right: The Holy See v. The Third Reich*, New Oxford Rev., Oct. 1998.

Giovanni Sale, *Hitler, La Santa Sede e Gli Ebrei* (Jaca Book: Rome, 2004).

José M. Sánchez, *Pius XII and the Holocaust: Understanding the Controversy* (Catholic University of American Press: Washington, D.C., 2002).

_____, *The Popes and Nazi Germany: The View from Madrid*, 39 Journal of Church and State 365 (1996).

Marc Saperstein, *Moments of Crisis in Jewish-Christian Relations* (SCM Press/ Trinity Press International: London/Philadelphia, 1989).

María Ruiz Scaperlanda, *Edith Stein: St. Teresa Benedicta of the Cross* (Our Sunday Visitor: Ft. Wayne, IN, 2000).

Fabian von Schlabrendorff, *The Secret War Against Hitler* (Pitman Publishing: New York, Hilda Simon trans., 1965).

Roy H. Schoeman, *Salvation Is From the Jews: The Role of Judaism in Salvation History from Abraham to the Second Coming* (Ignatius Press: San Francisco, 2003).

Klaus Scholder, *The Churches and the Third Reich* (Fortress Press: Philadelphia, 1988).

_____, *A Requiem for Hitler and Other New Perspectives on the German Church Struggle* (Trinity Press International: Philadelphia, 1989).

The Second Vatican Council, *Pastoral Constitution on the Church in the Modern World* (*Gaudium et Spes*) December 7, 1965.

Secretariat for Ecumenical and Interreligious Affairs, National Conference of Bishops, *Catholics Remember the Holocaust* (United States Catholic Conference: Washington, D.C., 1998).

Self-Portrait in Letters 1916-1942 (The Collected Works of Edith Stein, Sister Teresa Benedicta of the Cross, discalced Carmelite, 1891-1942, (ICS Publications: Washington, D.C., J Koeppel trans., 1994).

Gitta Sereny, *Into that Darkness: An Examination of Conscience* (Vintage Books: New York, 1983).

William L. Shirer, *Berlin Diary: The Journal of a Foreign Correspondent 1934-1941* (Alfred A. Knopf: New York, 1941).

_____, *The Rise and Fall of the Third Reich: A History of Nazi Germany* (Fawcett Publications: Greenwich, 1962).

William C. Simpson, *A Vatican Lifeline* (Sarpedon: New York, 1995).

Jan Olav Smit, *Angelic Shepherd: The Life of Pope Pius XII* (Dodd & Mead: New York, J. Vanderveldt trans., 1950).

Robert Speaight, *Voice of the Vatican: The Vatican Radio in Wartime* (Sands and Co.: London, 1942).

Stewart A. Stehlin, *Weimar and the Vatican 1919–1933: German-Vatican Diplomatic Relations in the Interwar Years* (Princeton University Press: Princeton, NJ, 1983).

Richard Steigmann-Gall, *The Holy Reich: Nazi Conceptions of Christianity, 1919-1945* (Cambridge University Press: Cambridge, 2003).

Leo Stein, *Hitler Came for Niemoeller: The Nazi War Against Religion* (Penguin Publishing Co.: New York, 2003 reprint ed.).

Adin Steinsaltz, *The Essential Talmud* (Bantam: New York, 1976).

Ralph Stewart, *Pope Pius XII and the Jews* (St. Martin de Porres Dominican Community & St. Joseph Canonical Foundation: New Hope, KY, 1990).

Alexander Stille, *Benevolence and Betrayal: Five Italian Jewish Families Under Fascism* (Picador: New York, 1991).

The Storm over the Deputy (Grove Press: New York, Eric Bently, ed., 1964).

The Story of the Pope, Peter Alan Meyerson, ed. (Dell Publishing: New York, 1957).

Tad Szulc, *Pope John Paul II: The Biography,* Scribner (Simon & Schuster: New York, 1995).

Domenico Tardini, *Memories of Pius XII* (The Newman Press: Westminster, MD, 1961).

Nechama Tec, *When Light Pierced the Darkness: Christian Rescuers of Jews in Nazi Occupied Poland,* (Oxford University Press: Oxford, 1986).

They Almost Killed Hitler: Based on the Personal Account of Fabian von Schlabrendorff (Macmillan Co.: New York, Gero v. S. Gaevernitz, ed., 1947).

Three Sermons in Defiance of the Nazis Preached During 1941 by Bishop von Galen of Munster (The Church In History Information Center: Birkenhead, United Kingdom, undated).

Ethel Mary Tinnemann, *Attitudes of the German Catholic Hierarchy Toward the Nazi Regime: A Study in German Psycho-Political Culture,* 22 The Western Political Quarterly 333 (1969).

Andrea Tornielli, *Pio XII. Papa degli ebrei* (Piemme: Casale Monferrato, 2001).

Vatican Impressions (Sheed & Ward: New York, Francis Sweeney, ed., 1962).

Voix du Vatican (Vatican Radio broadcasts into France during World War II). The documents that I have are photocopies of what appear to be original pamphlets.

Ludwig Volk, *Das Reichskonkordat vom 20. Juli 1933* (Matthias-Grünewald-Verlag: Mainz: 1972).

_____, *Zwischen Geschichtsschreibung und Hochhuthprosa: Kritisches und Grundsätzliches zu einer Neuerscheinung über Kirche und National-sozialismus*, in *Stimmen der Zeit*, vol. 176 (1965).

Sam Waagenaar, *The Pope's Jews* (Open Court: LaSalle, NY, 1974).

Michael Walsh, *An Illustrated History of the Popes: Saint Peter to John Paul II* (St. Martin's Press: New York, 1980).

Margaret E. Ward, *Rolf Hochhuth* (Twayne Publishers: Boston, 1977).

Wartime Correspondence Between President Roosevelt and Pope Pius XII (Macmillan: New York, Myron C. Taylor, ed. 1947). Reprint edition (Da Capo Press: New York, 1975).

George Weigel, *Witness to Hope: The Biography of Pope John Paul II* (Cliff Street Books: New York, 1999).

Ernst Von Weizsäcker, *Memoirs of Ernst Von Weizsäcker* (H. Regnery Co.: Chicago, J. Andrews trans. 1951).

Kenneth D. Whitehead, *The Pope Pius XII Controversy*, 31 The Political Science Reviewer 283 (2002).

G. Garry Wills, *Papal Sin: Structures of Deceit* (Doubleday: New York, 2000).

Stephen S. Wise, *As I See It* (Jewish Opinion Publishing Corp.: New York, 1944).

_____, *Servant of the People: Selected Letters* (Jewish Publication Society of America: Philadelphia, Carl H. Voss, ed., 1969).

Robert Wistrich, *Hitler and the Holocaust* (Modern Library: New York, 2002).

The World's Great Catholic Literature (Roman Catholic Books: Harrison, NY, George N. Shuster, ed., 1942).

David S. Wyman, *The Abandonment of the Jews: America and the Holocaust 1941-1945* (Pantheon Books: New York, 1984).

Gordon C. Zahn, *German Catholics and Hitler's Wars* (University of Notre Dame Press: Notre Dame, IN, 1962).

Eugenio Zolli, *The Nazarene: Studies in New Testament Exegesis,* Cyril Vollert trans. (New Hope Publications: New Hope, KY, 1999).

_____, *Why I Became a Catholic* (Remnant of Israel: New Hope, KY, 1997), previously released as *Before the Dawn* (Sheed and Ward: New York, 1954).

Susan Zuccotti, *The Holocaust, the French, and the Jews* (Basic Books: New York, 1993).

_____, *The Italians and the Holocaust* (University of Nebraska Press, Lincoln, 1987).

_____, *Pope Pius XII and the Holocaust: The Case in Italy,* in *The Italian Refuge* (Catholic U. of America Press: Washington, D.C., 1990).

_____, *Under His Very Windows: The Vatican and the Holocaust in Italy* (Yale University Press: New Haven, CT, 2001).

Index

1914 Serbian concordat 76-77

1917 Code of Cannon Law 75, 84, 86, 106, 287

1933 concordat with Germany 23-30, 46, 47, 53, 83-86, 87, 103, 114, 203, 270, 275, 291

Aarons, Mark
  The Secret War Against the Jews 244-45
  Unholy Trinity 244-45
Abyssinia [see Ethiopia]
Accioly, Ildebrando 121
Actes et Documents du Saint Siège relatifs à la seconde guerre mondiale 4, 11,. 116, 174, 233, 236, 238, 239, 240, 329, 339-40
Alcazar 116
Alexander, Edgar 264
Allen, John 65

Amen (the motion picture) 5, 182, 189, 281
America (magazine) 90
American Israelite 114
American Jewish Committee 82, 138, 144, 159, 307
American Jewish Congress 233
American Jewish Yearbook 147
American Negro Publishers Association 140
Anti-Semitic Legislation
  Italy 37-41, 119, 273, 275
    Aryan Manifesto 37-38
  Germany 45-46, 53, 280
Antonescu, Ion 173-74
Aquinas, St. Thomas 66,162
Arbeiterzeitung 76
Ardeatine Caves massacre 240-42
Argentina 245-46, 343
Ave Maria 103

Aryan Manifesto 37-38
Associated Press 171, 235
Augustine of Hippo 74
Auschwitz 67-68, 320
Australian Jewish News 161, 216
Austria 150, 151, 287
Austrian clergy 151, 312
Austro-Hungarian Empire 76-77, 278
Aversa, Giuseppe 70

BBC 113
B'nai B'rith 42, 111, 248
Balasuriya, Tissa 328-29
"Baptized Jews" 65, 86, 103, 105-12, 219, 292
  Children 106-111
Baranski, Tibor 11, 16, 218-19, 231, 346
Bartali, Gino 265, 330
Baum, Phil 233
Bayer, Karl 246, 343
Beaulieu, Francois 126-27

Bednarski, Stanislaus 60
Belgium 164-66
Belloc, Hilaire 58
Benedict XV 22, 37, 70, 71, 75, 77-78, 192, 268
Benedict XVI 257
Benoît, Marie 11, 149, 215, 231, 332
Beradinion, Philippe 239
Bérard, Léon 162
Bérard Report 162-64
Bergan, Diego von 126, 277
Bergen, Doris 348
Berlin Lustgarten 50
Bernardin, Joseph 335, 338
Bernardini, Filippo 208
Berning, Cardinal 46
Bertram, Adolph 56-58, 281
  Requiem Mass 58
Bethge, Eberhard 15, 330
Black Nobility 69
Black Sabbath [see Katz, Robert] 240
Blazevic, Jakov 172
Blet, Pierre 4, 235
  Pius XII and the Second World War 116
Blood Libel 268
Boetto, Pietro 339
Bonaparte, Napoleon 133
Bonhoeffer, Dietrich 15, 266, 330
Bonomelli, Emilio 103
Boteach, Shmuley 107, 296
Bourne, Cardinal 268
Braier, Louis 172
Breaking Faith [see Cornwell, John] 10, 204-05, 328-29
Bretton-Granatoor, Gary 55
Brill's Content 197, 202, 327

Brun, Annoinette 110
Brunacci, Don Aldo 18, 219-21, 267
Brüning, Heinrich 291
Burleigh, Michael 282

CBS 345-46
CNN 65
Calamandrei, Piero 39
California Jewish Voice 159
Calixtus II 229
Canadian Jewish Chronicle 159
Capovilla, Loris Francesco 8, 109
Caritas (social agency) 63
Carroll, James 5, 67-68, 225, 325, 329, 331, 335
  Constantine's Sword 8-9, 257-58, 269
  Proposes Vatican III 329
Carroll-Abbing, John Patrick 11, 149, 193, 231, 333
Cassidy, Edward 233, 236, 340
Cassulo, Andrea 173, 319
Castel Gandolfo 72, 89, 102-03, 295
Casti Connubii 28, 281
Castro, Fidel 329
Catechism of the Council of Trent 225
Catholic Action 23, 57, 59, 84
Catholic Center Party 82, 83-85, 290, 291
Catholic-Jewish study group 12, 169, 232-38, 340
Catholic Herald 184
Catholic Historical Review 81

Catholic Youth 298
Chadwick, Owen viii
Chaillet, Pierre 161
Chamberlin, Neville 266
Charles-Roux, Francois 97
Christian X, King 174
Christian Century 266
Christian Resistance to Anti-Semitism [see Lubac, Henri] 162
The Churches and the Third Reich [see Scholder, Klaus] 202
Churchill, Winston 147, 252, 261, 300, 311
Civiltà Cattolica 105-06
Clark, Mark 189
Clement IX 71
Coughlin, Charles 326
College of Cardinals 143
Committee to Save Jews in Europe 307
Commonweal 85
Congregation for the Causes of Saints 54, 129, 184, 249, 340
  Positio, the 19-20, 256, 258, 267, 268, 273
  Deposition transcripts 197-202, 216
Congregation for the Doctrine of Faith 107
Congregation of Ecclesiastical Affairs 70, 75
Constantine's Sword [see Carroll, James] 8-9, 257-58, 269
Conway, John 81, 335, 345
Cornwell, John ix, 6, 9-10, 73-74, 77-81, 82, 83-84, 114, 131, 167, 239,

240, 257, 267, 268, 287, 289, 290, 304, 323, 326, 340, 342, 344
Breaking Faith 10, 204-05, 328-29
Brill's Content 197, 202, 327
Hitler's Pope 4, 10, 18-19, 75, 76, 81, 90, 133, 194-207, 273, 292
Cover photo 194-95
The Pontiff in Winter 18-19, 204-05, 328
Cosmatos, George 243, 342
Costa, Elia Dalla 339
Coughlin, Charles 266, 291
Crisis (magazine) 205
Croatia 150, 169-73, 317, 318
Czechoslovakia 150

Dachau 51, 52, 61, 119, 276, 282
Special barracks for priests 60, 61, 284
Daily Telegraph 98
Dalin, David 5
Das Schwarze Korps 29, 35, 139
Davar 138
Day, Dorothy 291
"Day of Gratitude" 147-48
De Gaulle, Charles 164
Death in Rome [see Katz, Robert] 240
Degrelle, Leon 166
Denmark 150, 174-75, 231
Yellow star 174, 319, 320
The Deputy [see Hoch-huth, Rolf] vii, 3-4, 5, 248
Der Spiegel 236

Desbuquqouis, Gustave 90
Dezza, Paolo 149, 167, 218
d'Herbigny, Michel 167
Die Zeit 76
Divini Redemptoris [see Pius XI] 166, 169, 272, 317
Doino, William 312
Donovan, William J. ("Wild Bill") 15, 53, 46-47, 97-98, 311
Dreyfus, Alfred 268
Dutch clergy 64-65, 125, 301

Easterman, Alex 318
Eastman, A.L 10, 222
Eden, Anthony 159
Eichmann, Adolf 15, 130, 333, 343-44
Einstein, Albert 49
Eisenhower, Dwight 190
Emmanuel, King Victor III 31, 136, 275
Ethiopia 30-32, 87, 292
Euthanasia (Nazi program) 47, 49, 54-55, 281, 281-82, 282

False identification 105-112
Fano, Rabbi da 32
Faulhaber, Michael Cardinal 14, 26-27, 40, 45, 51-53, 57, 209, 266, 280, 281, 293
Feldman, Leon 233-34, 235
Ferdininda, Maria Corsetti 221
Ferramonti, Italy 307
Filopovi -Majstorovi, Miroslav 173, 319
Finaly affair 110-11
Fineschriber, William 266

Fisher, Eugene 237, 340
Flavius Claudius Julianus (Roman Emperor) 40
Fleichner, Eva 233, 237
Forced Labor (in German Churches) 62-63
Fordham University 187
Fogarty, Gerald 233, 237-38, 341
The Forward 296
Four Powers Pact 24
Foxman, Abraham 55, 232, 244-45
France 104, 117-19, 156-64, 213
Vichy France 157-60, 314
France My Country, Through the Disaster [see Maritain, Jacques] 161
Frank, Hans 171. 152-53
Franklin D. Roosevelt Library 122
Freiberger, Miroslav 11, 170, 318
French clergy 117-18, 156-64, 299, 314
French Moroccan troops 139-40, 308
Friedländer, Saul viii, 268, 335
Frost, David 261
Fulman, Bishop 152-53

Gable, Clark 190
Galen, Clemens Count von 46, 51, 53-55, 57, 282, 283
Gallagher, J.P. 211
Gariboldi, Giorgio Ange-lozzi 342
Gaspari, Antonio 221, 310

Gasparri, Pietro   69, 70, 82, 289

Gaudium et Spes [see Vatican II]   290

Geneva Tribune   160

Gerlier, Pierre   111, 158, 161, 216

Germany   77-82, 167-69, 169

German clergy   5, 28, 44-68, 84, 85, 86, 91-92, 252, 276, 291, 291-92, 314

Bertram, Adolph   56-58, 281

Requiem Mass   58

Faulhaber, Michael Cardinal   14, 26-27, 40, 45, 51-53, 57, 209, 266, 280, 281, 293

Forced Labor (in German Churches)   62-63

Galen, Clemens Count von   46, 51, 53-55, 57, 282, 283

Nazi persecution of   58-61

Presysing, Konrad   54, 57, 153-54, 281, 282, 332

Stein, Edith [St. Teresa Benedicta of the Cross]   15, 63-68

German Evangelical Church   62

Gibson, Mel

The Passion   204, 335

Gilbert, Sir. Martin   14-15, 100, 345

The Righteous: The Unsung Heroes of the Holocaust   14

Giovanna, Della   74

Godfrey, William   318

Godman, Peter   27-28, 112, 325

Goebbels, Joseph   26, 36, 98-99, 113, 294, 306

Goering, Hermann   36

Goldhagen, Daniel   5, 37, 44, 48, 51, 52, 54, 80, 97, 107, 115-16, 120, 141, 146-47, 156, 158, 173, 174-75, 225-32, 249, 257, 269, 271, 276, 278, 280, 283, 288, 296, 302, 314, 329, 335, 340

Goldmann, Nahum   10

Goni, Uki   245

Good Friday service   337-38

"Perfidious Jews"   229, 337-38

Gorbachhev, Mikhail   316, 329

Gorman, Robert   326

Grabmair, Maria Conrada   285

Graham, Robert   4, 113-14, 214

Gregoriana   70, 250

Grober, Heinrich   130, 281, 282

Grundlach, Gustav   90, 292

Gruppi di Azione Patriotica   240-43

Gumpel, Peter   12, 203, 234, -34, 236, 237, 249-51, 267, 271, 306, 328, 345

Gumpert, Gerhard   131

Gutman, Israel   333

Gypsies   279

Haggelof, Gunnar   262

Hammerschmidt, Rudolf   62

Harlem Globetrotters   190

Hatch, Alden   211

Hausner, Gideon   130

Havas News Angecy   40

Hentrich, Guglielmo   198, 199, 200

The Heresy of National Socialism   112

Hertz, Joseph   11

Herzog, Isaac   11, 109, 145, 146

Heydrich, Reinhart   26, 98

The Hidden Encyclical of Pius XI [see Suchecky, Bernard and Passelecq, Georges]   90

Hildebrand, Dietrich Von   338

Himmler, Heinrich   51, 53, 59, 125, 131, 134, 135, 154

Hindenburg, Paul von   194

Hinsley, Arthur   266

Hitler, Adolf   14, 15, 24, 25, 26, 29, 30, 36, 45, 48, 57, 58, 59, 71, 83-85, 93, 97, 151, 167, 169, 208, 209, 270, 277, 289, 341

Complains about Catholic leaders   44, 50, 55, 57, 279, 305

Criticized by German clergy   46, 53

Criticized by Pius XI   40, 272, 291

Criticized in L'Osservato Romano   39, 308

Criticized on Vatican Radio   48

Enabling Act 291
Mein Kampf 94, 229-30
Plan to invade the Vatican 127, 133-136, 255, 302, 303
Socialistic promises 85-86
Visits Rome 89, 292
Hitler, the War, and the Pope [see Rychlak, Ronald] vii, 10, 13, 19, 102, 174, 263-64, 267
Hitler and the Holocaust [see Wistrich, Robert] 252
Hitler Youth 52
Hitler's Pope [see Cornwell, John] 4, 10, 18-19, 75, 76, 81, 90, 133, 194-207, 273, 292
Cover photo 194-95
Hlond, August 92, 152
Hochhuth, Rolf viii, 3, 5, 6, 133-34, 136, 268
The Deputy vii, 3-4, 5, 248
Holland 64-65, 230, 346
Holocaust Memorial Museum (Washington, DC) 18
The Holocaust, The French, and the Jews [see Zuccotti, Susan] 334
Homes, Oliver Wendell 6
Horthy, Nicholas 320, 326
Hudal, Aloise 131, 132, 245, 246, 248, 304, 342, 342
Humanae Vitae [see Paul VI] 205, 206
Humanité 144-45

Hungarian Jewry and the Papacy: Pius XII Was Not Silent [see Levai, Jenö] 88
Hungary 88, 130, 143, 168-69, 175-78, 218, 253, 320
Hürten, Heinz 276

Il Corriere della Sera 296
Il Giornale 135
Innitzer, Theodor 46, 151, 266, 312
Irving, David 208
Israel 157, 161, 248, 311
Six Day War 342
Israeli Phiharmonic Orchestra 147-48, 217
An Israeli's Introduction to Christianity [see Lapide, Pinchas] 249
Israelite Central Committee of Uruguay 104
Italy 166, 169
Italian Jewish Community 100

Jareb, Jere 179
Jaromirska, Leokadia 110
Jemolo, A.C. 39
Jerusalem Post 147
Jerusalem Report 236
Jesus Christ 33, 42, 61, 92, 93, 95, 118, 157, 160, 225-26, 229, 258, 299, 336
Jewish Anti-Defamation League 55, 244
Jewish Brigade Group 137
Jewish Chronicle 32, 132, 147, 158, 160, 312, 303, 308, 310

Jewish Law 265
Jewish Ledger 115
The Jewish People and Their Sacred Scriptures in the Christian Bible 227
Jewish Post 150
Jewish Publication Society of America 346
Jewish Social Studies 286
Jewish Welfare Board 137
John, XXIII 8-9, 11, 73, 106-07, 156, 164, 190, 206, 231, 258
Ordered to "save human lives" 217, 263-64, 311
John Paul I 206
John Paul II ix, 72, 173, 203-07, 227, 256-57, 258, 289-90, 296, 314, 329, 348
On Pius XII 207
Johnson, Paul 206
Josef, Franz 76

Kallay, Nicholas de 168-69, 253
Kanayama, Minister 262
Kappler, Colonel 129, 131, 240-41, 242
Kasper, Walter 237-37
Katz, Robert 5, 9, 129, 132, 268, 303, 304, 305, 341, 342
Black Sabbath 240
Death in Rome 240
Lawsuit 240-44
Massacre in Rome 240
Kayser, Ignazia Caterina 199
Keeler, William 340

Kempner, Robert M.W. 11, 231, 256, 282
Kennedy, Joseph P. 17, 151
Kennedy, Rose 186
Kertzer, David 5, 268, 273
Kessel, Albrecht von 133, 134, 262
Kirkpatrick, Ivone 25
Klausener, Erich 59
Kleck, Paul 311
Klich, Igancio 245
Klieforth, Alfred 17, 266
Konen, Georg 63
Kozal, Bishop 284
Kristallnacht 40, 64, 112
Kubovitzky, Leon 109
Kunkel, Nikolaus 131

La Civilta Cattolica 17, 304
La Voix du Vatican 117-19, 161, 298
LaFarge, John 89, 292, 293
Laghi, Pio 236
Lamey, Andy 263
Lamiroy, Bishop 166
Lapide, Pinchas 100, 127, 232, 344, 345
 Estimate of Jewish lives saved by the Catholic Church 248-49
 An Israeli's Introduction to Christianity 249
 A Pilgram's Guide to Israel 249
 The Prophet of San Nicandro 249
 Three Popes and the Jews 232
Lapomarda, Vincent 345
Lateran Treaty 23, 30, 47, 70, 86

Lau Meir 233
Laval, Pierre 159, 160
Lawler, Justus George 334
Lazaron, Morris 308-09
Le Monde 235
League of Nations 24, 30
Leboucher, Fernande 215, 332, 339
Lehmann, Karl 62, 63
Lehnert, Pascalina 198, 200, 201, 285, 327, 344
Leiber, Robert 15, 266, 275
Lemmens, Bishop 66
Leo XIII 56-57, 70, 192, 207
Leo the Great 192
Lettmann, Rienhard 55
Levai, Jenö
 Hungarian Jewry and the Papacy: Pius XII Was Not Silent 88
Levine, Eugen 80-81
Lewy, Günter 223-24, 268, 276, 278
Lichten, Joseph 111, 248
Loftus, John
 The Secret War Against the Jews 244-45
 Unholy Trinity 244-45
Lolli, Cesidio 201
London Tablet 82
Look (magazine) 98
L'Osservatore Romano 28, 37, 38-39, 57, 69, 112, 217, 273, 280, 292, 293, 132, 133, 139, 151, 242-43, 303, 308, 334
 on Kristallnacht 40, 334
L'Osservatore della Domenica 248

Lubac, Henri de 119, 162-63
 Christian Resistance to Anti-Semitism 162
Ludendorff, Erich 14, 45, 209, 265, 276, 330

Madison Square Garden 138
Maglione, Luigi 14, 60-61, 130, 132, 145, 149, 157-58, 159, 163, 170, 209, 212-13, 239, 313, 318, 319, 334
Maher, Fr. 292
Majdanski, Kazimierz 276
Manchester Guardian 114
Marchione, Margherita 221
Marcionism 335
Marcone, Joseph 318
Marconi, Guglielmo 269
Maritain, Jacques 42, 144, 309
 France My Country, Through the Disaster 161
Marrus, Michael 233, 236
Marshall Plan 301
Martegani, Giacomo 17-18, 201
Martini, Angelo 4
Massacre in Rome [see Katz, Robert] 240
McBrien, Richard 347
McCormick, Ann O'Hare 31-32, 190, 216, 271, 286, 309
McGurn, Barrett 258, 301
McInerny, Ralph 349
Medwick, Joe "Ducky" 189
Mein Kampf [see Hitler, Adolf] 94, 229-30

Meir, Golda 10
Mejía, Jorge María 236
Melchior, Marcus 231
Melloni, Alberto 106-08
Mendes, Guido 309
Mengele, Josef 343
Merton, Thomas 195-96, 326
Mindszenty, Jozsef 143
Mistiaen, Emmanuel 117, 118, 298, 299
Mit brennender Sorge [see Pius XI] 15, 26, 32-37, 53, 66-67, 89, 116, 123, 141-42, 212, 230, 273
Molinari, Paul 267
Mollhöusen, Eitel 129
Montgomery, Bernard 324
Montgomery, Hugh 184
Monti, Carlo 77-78
Montini, Giovanni Battista [see Paul VI] 14, 113, 114, 144, 148, 149, 156, 209, 210, 217, 245, 246
Morley, John 174, 233
Müller, Heinrich 98, 135
Müller, Joseph 15, 16, 265, 266, 305
Mundelein, Cardinal 36, 273
Murphy, Robert 190-91
Mussolini, Benito viii, 22-23, 26, 30-31, 37, 40, 43, 70, 113, 136, 137, 148, 167, 269, 275, 295
Mystici Corporis Christi [see Pius XII] 127-129, 254-55, 302

Napolitano, Matteo 108, 326

National Catholic Reporter 292, 345
National Jewish Monthly 42
National Jewish Welfare Board 252
The National Monthly 42
National Socialist Congress 116
Natural Law 94, 119
Netherlands 123, 301
Neuhäusler, Johann 51, 279-80, 282
The New Testament 5, 45, 225-27, 335, 336
New York Times 29, 31, 42, 48-49, 82, 87, 98, 99, 101, 107, 114, 119, 123, 125, 129, 143, 146-47, 156, 159, 160, 183, 190, 214, 216, 235, 245, 255, 271, 298, 310
New Yorker 67
Newman, John Henry 207, 336
Newsweek 34-35, 283-84
Nicolini, Giuseppe 220
Niemoeller, Martin 28, 52, 57, 266, 281, 284
Non Abbiamo Bisogno [see Pius XI] 23
Norwegian Catholic Church 263
Notre Dame Cathedral 87-88, 292
Notre Dame University 187
Novak, Michael vii, 144
Nowowiejski, Juliusz 284
Nuremberg 46, 111, 116, 231
Prosecution report 35-36, 49-50, 55, 97-98, 230

Racial laws 45-46
Vatican assistance to the prosecution 247, 343
Office of Strategic Services (OSS)
files 51, 139, 262
O'Flaherty, Hugh 210-11, 331
Old Testament 228-29
Opere et Caritate [see Pius XII] 153
Oppen, Beate Ruhm von 224, 335
Ormesson, Wladimir d' 262
Orsenigo, Cesare 14, 48, 52, 209, 265, 277-78, 282, 283, 330
Osborne, Francis D'Arcy 84, 121, 130, 138-39, 151, 159, 182, 262, 300, 318
Ossicini, Adriano 148, 221, 275, 294
Ottaviani, Alfredo 105-06, 331

Pacelli, Carlo 198, 201, 242, 248
Pacelli, Elisabetha 197, 198, 202
Pacelli, Eugenio, [see Pius XII] 14, 17, 24, 25, 28, 33, 36, 42, 45, 51, 53, 57, 66, 70-71, 208, 265, 270, 276, 277-78
Budapest Trip (International Eucharistic Congress) 88-89
Cardinal Secretary of State 82-89, 91, 151, 167, 186, 209-10

Pacelli, Eugenio (cont.)
  Childhood 73-74, 184-
    85, 188
  Early Career 75-77
  Forced conversions 106
  France 87
  Lourdes trip 87
  Nuncio to Germany
    77-82, 186, 235
  Relationship with Pius
    XI 84-85, 87, 141, 167,
    287, 290
  Serbian concordat
    76-77
  Visit to United States
    82, 186-88
Pacelli, Filippo 69
Pacelli, Francesco 69
Pacelli, Marcantonio 69
Pacelli, Teresa 100
Padellaro, Nazareno
  Portrait of Pius XII 74
Paganuzzi, Quirino 153,
  200, 201
Palatucci, Giovanni 13-
  14, 209
Palatucci, Giuseppe Maria
  13-14, 209, 339
Palazzini, Pietro 11, 149,
  217, 231
Palestine 311
Palastine Post 109
Papal States 22
Papée, Casimir 124, 156, 313
Papen, Franz von 265,
  270, 330
Passelecq, Georges
  *The Hidden Encyclical
    of Pius XI* 90
The Passion [see Gibson,
  Mel] 204, 335

Paul VI 2, 11, 14, 73, 148,
  156, 217, 222, 231, 258
  Humanae Vitae 205,
    206
Pavelic, Ante 169, 170,
  171. 318
Pawlikowski, John 345
Pax Christi 63
"Perfidious Jews" [see
  Good Friday service]
  337-38
Perón, Jaun 344
*The Persecution of the
  Catholic Church in the
  Third Reich* 59
Pètain, Henri Philippi
  157-58, 159, 160, 162, 313
Pfeiffer, Pancratius 131,
  132, 149, 242, 248
Phayer, Michael 5, 88,
  141, 245, 333
Pignatelli, Enza 130
Pilate, Pontius 226, 227, 336
A Pilgram's Guide to Israel
  [see Lapide, Pinchas]
  249
Piscator, Erwin 261
Pius IV 228-29
Pius VI 273
Pius VII 133
Pius IX 226
Pius X 70, 75, 83, 289
Pius XI [see Ratti, Am-
  brose Damian Achille]
  5, 16, 21-43, 57, 65, 71, 83-
  85, 87, 90-91, 164, 206,
  245, 266, 281, 286, 292
  The concordat (with
    Germany) 23-30
  Condemnations of anti-
    Semitic laws 37-41

Divini Redemptoris
  166, 169, 272, 317
  Italy's invastion of
    Ethiopia 30-32
  Mit brennender Sorge
    15, 26, 32-37, 53, 66-67,
    89, 116, 123, 141-42,
    212, 230, 273
  Non Abbiamo Bisogno 23
  Quadragesimo Anno
    269, 290
  "Spiritually We are all
    Semites" 41-43, 89,
    227, 232, 273
    repeated by Pacelli 42
Pius XII [see Pacelli,
  Eugenio] vii, viii, ix,
  3, 4, 5, 6, 7, 8, 9, 11, 12,
  13, 14, 21, 19-20, 37, 54,
  59, 61, 65, 66, 69-99, 112,
  122-23, 150, 164, 165, 166,
  170, 172, 174, 206, 209,
  210, 214, 218-19, 249,
  252-54, 258, 265, 270,
  275, 281
  1942 Christmas State-
    ment 53, 119-27, 254,
    282
  1943 Roman roundup
    129-133, 302
  1944 Christmas State-
    ment 247, 302, 329
  Cardinal Secretary of
    State 82-89
  Childhood 73-75
  "Coloured Troops"
    138-40
  Communist campaign
    against 310
  Contact with the Ger-
    man resistance 15

Early career 75-77

Election commentary
286

France (comments on)
157, 158, 159, 160

"Hidden Encyclical"
89-91

Mystici Corporis Christi
127-129, 254-55, 302

Neutrality 124-25, 301

Nuncio in Germany
77-82

Occupation of Rome by
the Germans 100-05,
129-38, 242-43, 248,
304

Offer to pay ransom
129, 302, 303

Opere et Caritate 153

Opinion of Nazis 17,
61, 87-88, 92-94, 98,
127-129, 141-42, 168-
69, 316

Personality 182-92

Plot to kidnap the pope
133-36

Plot to overthrow Hitler
148-49

Poland (comments on)
96, 121, 152-54, 256, 313

Post-war statements
141-45

"Rat Line" to South
America 244-47, 344

Righteous Gentile
259-60

Roundup of French
Jews 117-119

Summi Pontificatus 52,
90, 91-99, 116, 123, 140,
216, 254, 280, 293

Testimony concerning
198-202, 216-17, 231,
332-33

Tributes to 16, 18, 69,
100, 145-49, 150, 156,
182, 193, 217-21, 232,
252, 323

Vatican Radio (author
of broadcasts) 113-
14, 119, 126, 142, 152,
158, 158, 159

Virgin Mary 73

*Pius XII and the Second
World War* [see Blet,
Pierre] 116

Poland 96, 113, 114-116,
121, 124, 150, 152-56,
213-14, 230, 256, 297,
298, 300

Warsaw ghetto 119-20,
154-55

Poliakov, Leon 334

Polish clergy 22, 113,
114-15, 152-56, 276, 298,

Ponti, Carlo 243, 342

The Pontiff in Winter [see
Cornwell, John] 18-19,
204-05, 328

Pontifical Aid Commis-
sion 71

Pontifical Biblical Com-
mission

*The Jewish People and
Their Sacred Scrip-
tures in the Christian
Bible* 227

Pontifical Commission
for Religious Relations
232

Pontifical Committee of
Historical Sciences 256

Pontifical Relief Commis-
sion 255

Pope Pius XII study group
[see Catholic-Jewish
study group]

Pope Pius and Poland 297

Porta, Paolo 135

Portrait of Pius XII [see
Padellaro, Nazareno] 74

Positio [see Congrega-
tion for the Causes of
Saints] 19-20, 256, 258,
267, 268, 273

Deposition transcripts
197-202, 216

Positive Christianity 56

Presysing, Konrad 54, 57,
153-54, 281, 282, 332

*The Prophet of San
Nicandro* [see Lapide,
Pinchas] 249

Proskauer, Joseph 82, 138

Quadragesimo Anno [see
Pius XI] 269, 290

Radonski, Karol 313

Rahn, Rudolf 134

Rarkowski, Franz-Justus 48

"Rat Line" to South
America 244-47, 344

Ratti, Ambrose Damian
Achille, [see Pius XI]
21-43

Rauff, Walter 344

Reader's Digest 3, 58, 183

Ready, Michael 317

The Real Odessa [see
Goni, Uki] 245

Red Cross 104, 246, 247,
342, 343

Reich, Seymour 233, 235, 236, 237

Repgen, Konrad 202-03, 283, 327

A Requiem for Hitler and Other New Perspectives on the German Church Struggle [see Scholder, Klaus] 58

Restituta, Maria 312

Rhonheimer, Martin 284

Ribbentrop, Joachim 29, 46, 60-61, 111, 125-26, 135, 168, 271, 306

Riberi, Antonio 332

Riegner, Gerhard 238-40

The Riegner Memo 238-40

The Righteous: The Unsung Heroes of the Holocaust [see Gilbert, Martin] 14

Riquet, Michel 119, 160

Rocca, Nasalli 134, 242

Roman Question 22, 69, 70

Romania 173-74

Rome (occupation by Nazis) 100-05, 331

Ardeatine Caves massacre 240-42

Plot to kidnap the pope 133-36

Liberation 136-38, 141

Roundup of Jews 129-33, 248, 304

Roncalli, Angelo [see John XXIII] 106, 108, 156, 164, 190, 217, 311

Roosevelt, Franklin D. 17, 18, 98, 119-20, 121, 122, 168, 169, 187, 252, 300, 306

Rosa, Luca De 8

Rosenberg, Ethel and Julius 169, 317

Rossignani, Elena Pacelli 243, 342

Rothkirchen, Livia 345

Rotondi, Virginio 201

Rotta, Angelo 218, 219

Ruffini, Ernesto 41

Rutgers Journal of Law & Religion 97-98

Rychlak, Ronald *Hitler, the War, and the Pope* vii, 10, 13, 19, 102, 174, 263-64, 267

Sacred Congregation for Seminaries and Universities 41

Sacro Vergente Anno 317

Safran, Alexander 11, 174

St. Bonaventure University 18

St. Magdalen's Convent 66

St. Paul 116, 141

St. Teresa Benedicta of the Cross [see Stein, Edith]

Sacred Congregation for Bishops 138

Saliège, Jules Gèrard 143, 156-57, 158-59

Sanfilippo, Matteo 246

Sapieha, Adam 143, 153-54, 230

Schindler, Oskar ix, 285, 346

Schioppa, Lorenzo 80-81

Schlabrendorff, Fabian von 15, 46, 52, 311

Schmeling, Max 325

Schneider, Rev. Burkhart 4

Scholder, Klaus 202-03, 283 *A Requiem for Hitler and Other New Perspectives on the German Church Struggle* 58 *The Churches and the Third Reich* 202

Schönhöffer, Johannes 15

Schuster, Ildefonso 40

The Secret War Against the Jews [see Aarons, Mark and Loftus, John] 244-45

Selvaggiani, Marchetti 189

Senatra, Eduardo 224

Serbia 169

Seredi, Justinian 320

Sermon on the Mount 142

Sertum Laetitiae 140

Sharett, Moshe 146

Sheen, Fulton 11

Shirer, William 29

Sikorski, Wladyslaw 261

Six Day War 342

Slovakia 119, 179-81, 239

Social Justice 85, 290, 291

Sodano, Angelo 268

Solages, Bruno de 118, 160

South America 5

Soviet Union 24, 72, 93, 166-69, 269, 310, 316, 329

Spain 103, 298

Spellman, Francis 11, 16, 121, 299-300

"Spiritually We are all Semites" [see Pius XI] 42-43, 89, 227, 232, 273 repeated by Pacelli 42

Stahel, Rainer 131, 132, 248

Steigmann-Gall, Richard 49

Stein, Edith [St. Teresa Benedicta of the Cross] 15, 63-68

Stepinac, Alojzij 170-73, 252, 299, 318

Sterilization Laws 28

Stirpe (use and definition) 126, 211-12, 302

Strauss, Lewis 82

Streicher, Julius 231-32

Stroop, Juergen 154

Struth, Hans 199

Subsidiarity 332

Suchecky, Bernard 233, 236, 340

The Hidden Encyclical of Pius XI 90

Suhard, Emanuel 214

Summi Pontificatus [see Pius XII] 52, 90, 91-99, 116, 123, 140, 216, 254, 280, 293

Swiss Guard 104, 190, 295

Switzerland 103

The Tablet 42, 52, 117, 118-19, 158, 293, 308

Tafari, Ras 271

Tagliacozzo, Michael 132, 218, 333

The Talmud 337

Tardini, Demenico 108, 149, 185

Taylor, Myron 18, 121, 122-23, 124-25, 168, 300, 301, 326

Ten Commandments 46, 92

Theresienstadt 175

Three Popes and the Jews [see Lapide, Pinchas] 232

Time (magazine) 99, 110-11, 146, 316, 324, 326

The Times 125, 147

Times Literary Supplement 253-54

Tisserant, Eugene 214

Tito, Josip Broz 171

Tittman, Harold 16, 18, 114, 121, 133, 168, 256, 270, 305, 309, 311, 316

Toaff, Elio 11, 147

Tojo, Hideki 247

Tornielli, Andrea 108, 326

Trier, Bornewasser von 282

Troeltsch, Eenst 224

Truman, Harry 190

Unholy Trinity [see Aarons, Mark and Loftus, John] 244-45

Union of Orthodox Rabbis 104

United Jewish Appeal 115, 309

U.S. Bishops 16, 41, 120, 301, 316

U.S. Congress Honors Pius XI 43

U.S. Constitution 6

USS Liberty 342

Under His Very Windows [see Zuccotti, Susan] 208, 334

Ustashi 169, 171

Valeri, Valerio 157, 159, 163-64, 213, 313

Van Roey, Joseph-Ernst 40, 117, 164-66

Vanity Fair 197

Vatican II 73, 86, 226, 228, 287, 337

Gaudium et Spes 290

Nostra Aetate 336

Pius XII frequently cited by 336

Vatican Information Office 255, 297

Vatican Library 22

Vatican Radio 48, 61, 112-19, 128-29, 139-40, 151, 153, 157, 160-62, 165, 281, 284

Information Office 297

La Voix du Vatican 117-19, 161, 298

Pius XII as author of broadcasts 113-14, 119, 126, 142, 152, 158, 158, 159

Verdier, Pierre 40

Vichy France 157-60, 314

Vitucci, Monsignor 149

Volk, Ludwig 203

Völkischer Beobachter 35, 59

Vrba, Rudolf 320

Waagenaar, Sam 332

Wallenberg, Raoul ix, 16, 219, 253, 346

Walshe, Seamus 211

We Remember: A Reflection on the Shoah 232-33, 345

Weber, Antonio 344

Weimar Republic 25, 27, 29, 195

Weizsäckerp, Ernst 129, 130, 132, 133, 134, 136, 212-13, 277, 303, 306, 343

Weltmann, Meir Touval 172
Wetmanski, Leon 284.
Wiesenthal, Simon 245, 344
Wilhelm, Kaiser 323
Wilken, Robert Louis 257
Wills, Garry 5, 257
Wisdom (magazine) 147
Wise, Steven 15, 53, 164
Wistrich, Robert 5, 233,
 234, 236, 237, 252-57, 340
 Hitler and the Holocaust
 252
Wolff, Karl Otto 127, 131,
 134-35, 200, 302, 306
Wolsey, Louis 266
World Council of
 Churches 73

World Jewish Congress
 109, 145, 146, 264, 333
World War I 70, 76, 82,
 91, 94, 257, 265, 269,
 278
World War II vii, 3, 15,
 18, 30, 58, 71, 92, 97, 106,
 140, 173, 245, 249, 250,
 260, 275, 312, 318
Wurm, Alois 280

Yad Vashem 13, 100,
 209, 217-18, 248, 259,
 333, 344
Yugoslavia 146, 169, 171-
 72, 307

Zolli, Rabbi Israel (Eu-
 genio) 10, 11, 39-40,
 101, 138, 231, 302, 339
Zuccotti, Susan 5, 93,
 102, 103, 113, 130-33, 141,
 144-45, 146-47, 148-49,
 207-23, 240, 248, 268,
 273, 274, 303, 304, 310,
 329-30, 332, 333, 334-35,
 341, 345
 *The Holocaust, The
 French, and the Jews*
 334
 Stirpe (use and definition) 126, 211-12, 302
 *Under His Very Win-
 dows* 208, 334

A NOTE ON THE AUTHOR

Ronald J. Rychlak, is Mississippi Defense Lawyers Association Professor of Law and associate dean for academic affairs at the University of Mississippi School of Law. A member of the committee appointed by the Mississippi Supreme Court to revise that state's criminal code, he is also an academic fellow at the Foundation for the Defense of Democracies. He is an advisor to the Vatican's delegation to the United Nations and has received three papal medals for his diplomatic service to the Holy See.

He is the author of the acclaimed *Hitler, the War, and the Pope*, as well as the author or co-author of three legal textbooks. He has written for the *Washington Post*, the *Wall Street Journal*, and the *Times Literary Supplement*, among other legal, political, and historical journals. He lives in Oxford, Mississippi, with his wife and six children.

This book was designed and set into type
by Mitchell S. Muncy,
with cover design by Stephen J. Ott,
and printed and bound
by Thomson-Shore, Inc.,
Dexter, Michigan.

℮

The text face is Minion Multiple Master,
designed by Robert Slimbach
and issued in digital form by Adobe Systems,
Mountain View, California, in 1991.

℮

The paper is acid-free and is of archival quality.

43